AQA AS PE

NESTA WIGGINS-JAMES
ROB JAMES
GRAHAM THOMPSON

www.heinemann.co.uk

✓ Free online support
✓ Useful weblinks
✓ 24 hour online ordering

01865 888118

Heinemann is an imprint of Pearson Education Limited, a company incorporated in England and Wales, having its registered office at Edinburgh Gate, Harlow, Essex, CM20 2JE. Registered company number: 872828

www.heinemann.co.uk

Heinemann is a registered trademark of Pearson Education Limited

First published 2009

12
10 9 8 7 6 5

British Library Cataloguing in Publication Data
A catalogue record for this book is available from the British Library

ISBN 978 0 435499 50 1

Designed by Wooden Ark Studios
Typeset by HL Studios
Original illustrations © Pearson Education Limited 2009
Cover design by Wooden Ark Studios
Cover photo © Polka Dot Images/Jupiter Images
Printed in China (GCC/05)

Websites
The websites used in this book were correct and up-to-date at the time of publication. It is essential for tutors to preview each website before using it in class so as to ensure that the URL is still accurate, relevant and appropriate. We suggest that tutors bookmark useful websites and consider enabling students to access them through the school/college intranet.

Contents

Introduction vi

Unit 3 Optimising performance and evaluating contemporary issues within sport 1

Section A Applied physiology to optimise performance

Chapter 1: Energy systems – the sources, supply and recovery of energy in the body 2
Chapter 2: The physiology of skeletal muscle 32
Chapter 3: Preparation and training for successful performance 46
Chapter 4: The nature of injury in sport 72
Chapter 5: The mechanics of movement 80

Unit 3 Optimising performance and evaluating contemporary issues within sport 108

Section B Psychological aspects that optimise performance

Chapter 6: Aspects of personality 110
Chapter 7: Arousal 128
Chapter 8: Controlling anxiety 140
Chapter 9: Attitudes 156
Chapter 10: Aggression 166
Chapter 11: Confidence 174
Chapter 12: Attribution theory 186
Chapter 13: Group success 194
Chapter 14: Leadership 204

Unit 3 Optimising performance and evaluating contemporary issues within sport 215

Section C Evaluating contemporary influences

Chapter 15: Factors affecting the nature and development of elite performance 216
Chapter 16: The legacy of 'rational recreation' and its relevance in the modern-day sports world 240
Chapter 17: Sport, ethics, deviancy and the law 268
Chapter 18: Factors that have influenced the commercialisation of modern-day sport 284

Unit 4 Optimising practical performance in a competitive situation 311

Chapter 19: Practical coursework 312

Index 326
Acknowledgements 332

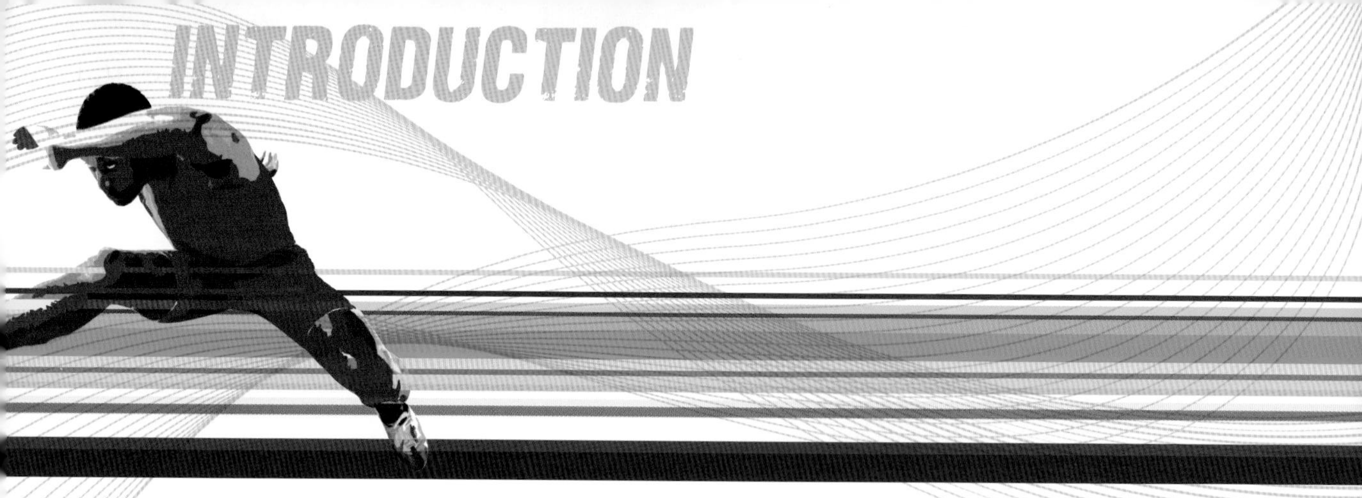

INTRODUCTION

This book has been specifically written for those students following the AQA A2 Physical Education course. This text will support and reinforce the teaching that you receive in your centre and will help you apply your understanding of theory to practical performance. The content of this book is presented in a form that is identical to the AQA specification and is arranged under the same sections and sub-headings.

Specification at a glance

There are two units you must complete in order to gain your A2 Physical Education. Unit 3 is assessed by written examination, while Unit 4 is the more practically based unit, assessed by your teachers in the first instance, and then subject to an external moderation by the examination board.

Unit 3 – Optimising performance and evaluating contemporary issues within sport		
2 hour written examination	84 marks available	30% of A Level
Section A How exercise physiology can optimise performance	**Section B** How application of psychological knowledge can optimise performance	**Section C** Contemporary influences in sport and their impact on the performer

Unit 4 – Optimising practical performance in a competitive situation *Candidates are assessed on their ability to perform, analyse and evaluate their own performance.*		
Internal assessment with external moderation	120 marks available	20% of A Level
Section A Optimising practical performance in a competitive situation	**Section B** Observation, analysis and critical evaluation of performance	**Section C** Application of knowledge and understanding to optimise performance
A performer assesses their own performance; a coach/leader assesses another performer; an official/referee assesses their own performance		
AS + A2 = A level		

There are four sections to this book, three for Unit 3 and one for Unit 4. The sections are divided into a number of chapters which, as well as giving you the exact information you need to be successful, provide a number of different features that will help you achieve your potential. These are outlined below:

Learning outcomes – these help to ensure you understand fully the content of the chapter. When you have completed a particular topic area, make sure you can achieve each learning objective stated. These will also prove invaluable when preparing for your examination – you should collate all the learning objectives stated and tick them off as you prepare

Tasks – these are designed to help you understand and apply your knowledge in a way similar to the requirements of your final examination

Athlete profiles – these profiles will help you understand how world class performers have put theory you have studied into practice

Key terms – definitions and explanations of important terminology that you should be using in your written answers

Exam tips – essential bits of exam technique and advice that should help you beat the examiner

Apply it – this feature will help you place theory work into a practical context

Stretch and challenge – this feature should help strengthen your knowledge and understanding by exercising your brain and challenging you a little more

Remember – some helpful ways that help you retain important bits of information

Hotlinks – these give you some ideas where you can find out more information on particular topics and so should encourage independence of learning. Be aware however that sometimes hotlinks are associated with an activity.

The ExamCafé

In addition to these features that occur throughout each chapter, this book is unique in that it contains an Exam**Café**. The Exam**Café** includes a number of **Revise as you go** questions and a **Summary checklist** of the key points of information from the chapter. In addition, at the end of each section there will be some general revision guidelines for that particular topic as well as some marked past paper questions which have the added benefit of an examiner commentary.

The Exam**Café** has been specifically written to help you improve your examination performance so do pay particular attention to the advice offered here!

We hope you enjoy this book and that it increases your appetite to learn more about physical education and sport.

NW-J, RJ, GT

ExamCafé

Relax, refresh, result!

Maximising learning capacity

The human brain is a complex organ that allows us to think, move, feel, see, hear, taste, and smell. It controls our body and receives, analyses and stores information (our memories).

Your brain is made up of approximately 15 billion brain cells joined together by interconnecting pathways. We actually access very little of our brain power and we must train the brain if we are to maximise our potential. The brain is divided into two halves known as hemispheres. The right side is your creative brain that deals with shapes and patterns, pictures and visual awareness. The left side of the brain is more logical dealing with numbers, words and language. If we can engage both sides of the brain at once when studying we can increase our brain power and memory capacity.

Use your whole brain!

There are essentially three ways or avenues that information can reach the brain:

- through sight (visually)
- through sound (auditory)
- through physical movement (kinaesthetic).

Many of us might favour learning through one method but we should aim to use all three avenues.

If we can use all three we will be able to learn more effectively retaining up to 90 per cent of information presented. Compare that to 60 per cent if doing (physically moving) alone, 50 per cent using solely visual stimuli or 20 per cent using solely auditory cues.

So when learning or revising make sure you try to present the information in the following ways:

- **Draw it!** (visual) – use mind maps and posters
- **Describe it!** out loud if necessary (auditory) – use audio tapes, podcasts and mnemonics
- **Do it!** (kinaesthetic) – make models, jigsaws or even move around while learning.

Building learning capacity

Some studies have shown that successful learners have similar characteristics and these are outlined below. You are encouraged to develop some or all of these when studying for your AS qualification.

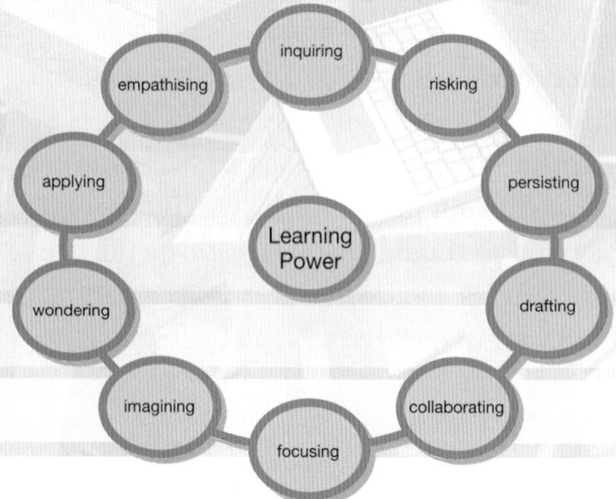

Fig. Generalised characteristics of learners based on G Claxton's Positive Learning Dispositions (2006)

Getting started...

TASK

Match each of the characteristics of learners to each of the statements below:

- I love learning new things
- I'm willing to have a go at something new
- If something is hard, I keep at it until I've got it
- I can blot out distractions when concentrating
- I like to think how things could be different
- My head is full of questions
- I think about how I can improve what I have done
- I think how I can apply new things I've learned
- I like exploring things with other people
- I wonder how things seem to other people.

Ask yourself the questions in the context of each of the characteristics; if it sounds like you then you are on your way to being a successful learner. If it doesn't sound anything like you at all, then you can work on these particular characteristics to try to improve them and in the process improve your learning capacity.

What is different about A2?

During the **AS** course you studied the nature of skilled performance, methods to optimise the learning of skills and how a performer processes the information available to him or her in order to produce an efficient performance. The psychological and physiological aspects of the course for **A2** build on that knowledge but focus on the factors which influence an elite performer during competition.

Get the result!

Examiner's tips

1. Read the questions thoroughly so that you understand what they are asking you and what you have to do.
2. Relate your answer to the number of marks available for that question.
   Remember that you usually have to make one point in your answer for each mark that is available.
3. Wherever possible, apply theory to a practical activity and make sure that you name that activity.
4. Make sure that in your anatomy and physiology, and skill answers you use the appropriate technical terms.
5. Make sure that you plan the use of your time properly.
6. In the exam you will write your answers on the question paper. The number of lines available gives you an indication of the length of answer required.
7. Make sure that you revise all aspects of each area. Do not think that just because a topic was in a previous exam it will not be in yours.
8. When you are happy that you know what the question is asking underline or highlight all the question cues and key words; only then should you put pen to paper and attempt an answer. The table opposite lists some common question cues, or doing words, together with an idea of the requirements from the candidate in their answer.

Get the result!

Question cues/ doing words	What you need to do ...
Account for	Explain, clarify, give reasons
Analyse	Resolve into its component parts, examine critically
Assess	Determine the value of, weigh up
Compare	Look for similarities and differences between examples, perhaps reach conclusion about which is preferable and justify this clearly
Contrast	Set in opposition in order to bring out the differences sharply
Compare and contrast	Find some points of common ground between *x* and *y* and show where or how they differ
Criticise	Make a judgement backed by a discussion of the evidence of reasoning involved about the merit of theories or opinions or about the truth assertions
Define	State the exact meaning of a word or phrase, in some cases it may be necessary or desirable to examine different possible or often-used definitions
Describe	Give a detailed account of
Discuss	Explain, then give two sides of the issue and any implications

Question cues/ doing words	What you need to do ...
Distinguish/ Differentiate between	Look for differences between
Evaluate	Make an appraisal of the worth/validity/ effectiveness of something in the light of its truth or usefulness
Explain	Give details about how and why something is so
To what extent	Usually involves looking at evidence/ arguments for and against and weighing them up
Illustrate	Make clear and explicit, usually requires the use of carefully chosen examples
Justify	Show adequate grounds for decisions or conclusions and answer the main objections likely to be made about them
Outline	Give the main features or general principles of a subject omitting minor details and emphasising structure and arrangement
State	Present in a brief, clear form
Summarise	Give a concise, clear explanation or account of the topic, presenting the chief factors and omitting minor details and examples
What arguments can be made for and against this view	Look at both sides of this argument

Get the result!

Finally, why not try to apply the ten 'habits of success' to your study of Physical Education?

What's the habit	Apply the habit	Top tip
Take responsibility for yourself	Be proactive, take responsibility for your life. Only you can change your studying behaviour	If it's to be, it's up to me
Be resilient and persistent	Never give up, always keep trying even if things are hard. Learn from your mistakes	If at first you don't succeed try, try and try again. There's no such thing as failure only feedback!
Be optimistic	Look for the positive outcomes from all actions	Always look on the bright side of life!
Have confidence and self-belief	Believe in yourself and your talents.	Say to yourself, 'I'm brilliant!'
Have self-discipline	Learn to wait for things you want (delayed gratification)	No pain, no gain!
Take some risks	Stretch yourself. It's good to venture outside your comfort zone	Challenge yourself
Set yourself some learning goals	Write down your goals and keep a note of your progress towards them	Don't forget your goals need to be SMARTER (specific, measurable, agreed, realistic, time-bound, exciting and recorded)
Make a plan and prioritise tasks	Be organised and make a list of what you need to get done	Never put off what can be done today
Work with others	Take notice of what successful students do and copy them!	Listen and learn
Be good to yourself	Get enough sleep and don't party too hard! Exercise	A healthy body makes for a healthy mind

UNIT 3

Optimising performance and evaluating contemporary issues within sport

Section A: Applied physiology to optimise performance

Energy systems

–the sources, supply and recovery of energy in the body

LEARNING OBJECTIVES:

By the end of this chapter you should be able to:

- *define energy*
- *identify the sources and locations of energy within the body*
- *explain the role of ATP in providing energy for movement*
- *identify the predominant energy system used related to the type, duration and intensity of exercise for a given activity*
- *compare the effectiveness of the ATP-PC, lactic acid and aerobic systems*
- *identify the chemical/food fuel used, the site of the reaction, the controlling enzymes, the energy yield and any by-products produced for each of the energy pathways*
- *explain the term 'energy continuum' in context of a range of physical activities*
- *explain how the body recovers from exercise with reference to the excess post-exercise oxygen consumption (EPOC)*
- *explain the fast and slow components of the recovery process*
- *define VO_2 max and its role in limiting performance*
- *define and explain the relationship between VO_2 max and OBLA (onset of blood lactate accumulation).*

Introduction

Central to our study of exercise physiology is **energy**. As exercise physiologists we are interested in where we get the energy to exercise from, how we can optimise our energy usage during exercise and how we can recover our energy stores following exercise. In this chapter we will look at how the body converts energy from food into energy for muscular contractions which enable us to run, jump, throw or indeed perform any number of movements used in sporting activity. We will examine the energy requirements of a number of activities ranging from a gymnastic vault to marathon running and determine how the intensity or duration of a particular activity can impact upon how the body supplies energy. Perhaps most importantly we will discover how a knowledge of energy supply can help both coach and athlete maximise performance.

Defining energy

Energy exists in a number of different forms. Electrical, heat and light energy are just some of the forms that we all use on a daily basis. Energy is never lost, it is constantly recycled, often being transferred from one form to another. When boiling a kettle, for example, electrical energy is transformed into heat energy.

KEY TERMS

Energy:
the capacity of the body to perform work

Adenosine triphosphate (ATP):
the energy currency of cells. ATP is the only direct source of energy for all energy requiring processes in the body

EXAM TIP:

Make sure you can give the correct units of measurement of energy. Energy can be measured in calories (kcal) or joules (J); 1 calorie = 4.184 joules

Similarly, energy found in the chemical bonds of food fuels that we eat is transformed into mechanical energy enabling us to move and participate in sporting activity. It is this conversion of chemical energy into mechanical and heat energy that is of particular interest to the sports physiologist and forms the basis of discussion for the rest of this chapter.

Sources of energy in the body

You will recall from your AS studies that for movement to occur chemical energy must be transferred into mechanical energy. Chemical energy in the body is stored in an easy access, energy-rich compound called **adenosine triphosphate** (ATP). ATP exists in all cells and consists of a number of atoms held together by high energy bonds. It is through breaking down these bonds that energy is released for those processes in the body that require energy.

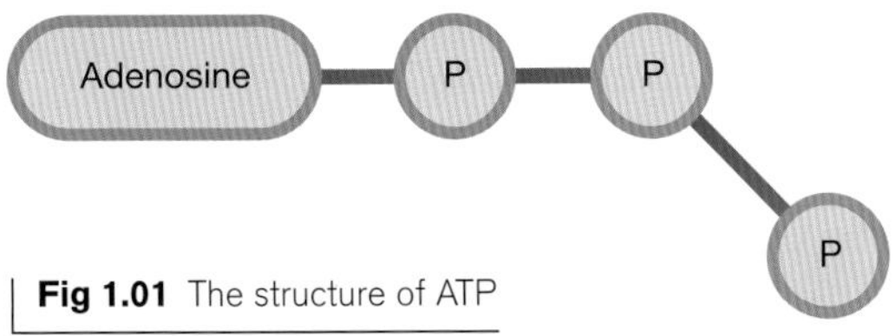

Fig 1.01 The structure of ATP

When energy is required, the enzyme ATPase is released which initiates the breakdown of ATP. It is the outermost bond of ATP that most interests ATPase as it is this bond that stores most energy. Through the breakdown of ATP energy is released leaving Adenosine Diphosphate (ADP) and an inorganic phosphate (Pi), which is illustrated in Fig.1.02.

This reaction can be summarised as follows:

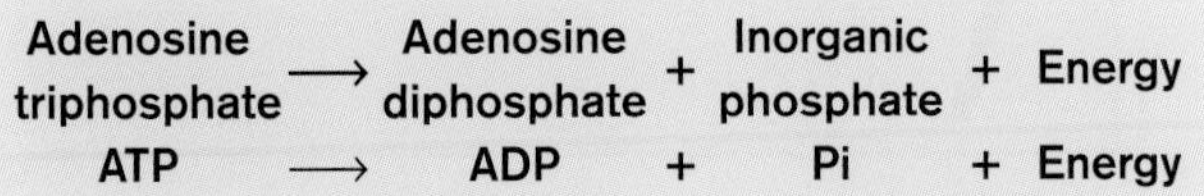

Adenosine triphosphate	⟶	Adenosine diphosphate	+	Inorganic phosphate	+	Energy
ATP	⟶	ADP	+	Pi	+	Energy

Because some of the energy is given off as heat this reaction is termed **exothermic**.

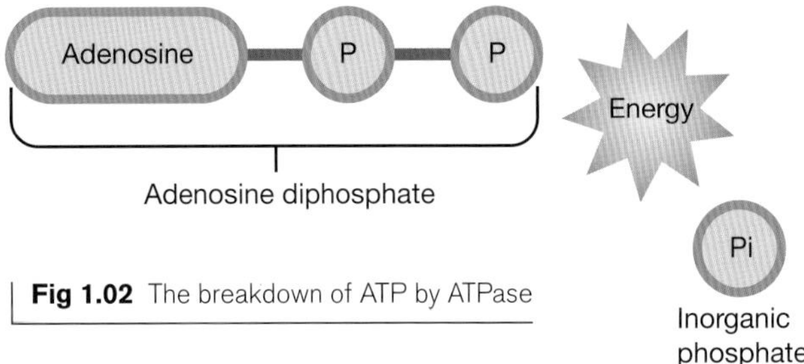

Fig 1.02 The breakdown of ATP by ATPase

REMEMBER!

Through the breakdown of ATP, energy is released to enable the muscles to contract, the heart to beat, and the brain to fire electrical impulses.

There is only a limited supply of ATP within the muscle cell, probably only enough to perform, for example, a maximal weight lift in the weights gym or a sprint start for 2 or 3 seconds. This is because if we were to have an unlimited supply of ATP we would have to carry around a supply equivalent to our own body weight in order to meet the body's daily energy requirements! This is obviously not very practical, so the body has adapted to become a green recycling machine. ATP is constantly recycled to ensure a continuous supply of energy. However recycling or resynthesising of ATP itself requires energy and this energy is acquired from the food that we eat.

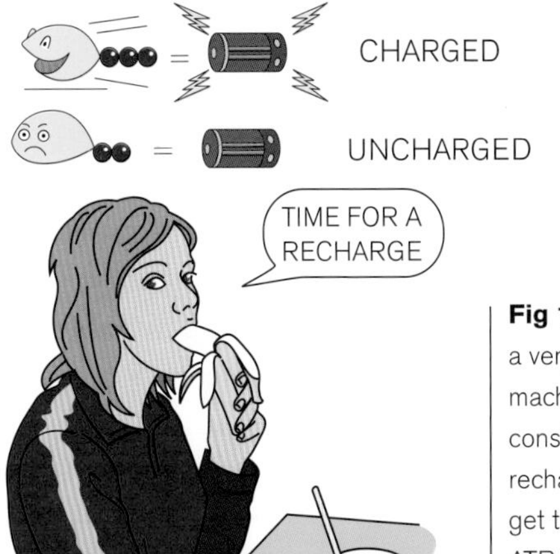

Fig 1.03 The body is a very effective green machine, as ATP needs constant recycling or recharging. We typically get the energy to recycle ATP from the foods that we eat.

KEY TERMS

Exothermic reaction:
a chemical reaction that releases energy

Phosphocreatine:
a high energy compound which exists in the muscle cells alongside ATP and provides the energy for ATP resynthesis when the intensity of exercise is very high

Anaerobic metabolism:
the release of energy through the breakdown of food fuels in the absence of oxygen

Aerobic metabolism:
the release of energy through the breakdown of food fuels in the presence of oxygen

REMEMBER!

There is only sufficient ATP stored within the muscle cell to perform high intensity activity for 2 or 3 seconds.

The fuels for ATP resynthesis are derived from the following sources:

- **Phosphocreatine:** Phosphocreatine (PCr) is used to resynthesise ATP in the first 10 seconds of intense exercise. To help facilitate this immediate resynthesis of ATP, PCr is stored within the muscle cell itself alongside ATP. However, stores of PCr are limited. Good dietary sources of creatine include red meat and fish.
- **Glycogen** (stored carbohydrate)**:** Glycogen is stored in the muscles (350g) and liver (100g). It is first converted to glucose before being broken down to release the energy for ATP resynthesis. During high intensity exercise glycogen can be used without the presence of oxygen (**anaerobic metabolism**). However much more energy can be released from glycogen during **aerobic metabolism** when oxygen is available. Stores of glycogen are maintained through eating complex carbohydrates such as pasta and porridge oats.
- **Triglycerides** (muscular stores of fat)**:** At rest up to two-thirds of our energy requirement is met through the breakdown of **fatty acids**. This is because fat can provide more energy per gram than glycogen (1g of fat provides 9.1kcal of energy compared to 4.1kcal of energy for every 1g of glycogen). In spite of the fact that fat requires about 15% more oxygen than glycogen to metabolise it remains the favoured fuel source at rest and during endurance-based activity.

Fats can only be used as an energy source when there is a plentiful supply of oxygen and must be used in conjunction with glycogen. This is because the transport of fatty acids in the blood is poor (and slow!) due to their low solubility. Consequently fatty acids do not arrive at the muscle cell in sufficient quantities to sustain muscle contraction on their own. Glycogen must therefore provide the supplementary energy.

- **Proteins:** Protein is the least favoured source of energy, only contributing 5–10% of the total energy yield. In the presence of oxygen, protein is used as an energy provider, usually when stores of glycogen are low. Good dietary sources of protein include meat, fish and dairy products. You will recall that protein's primary function is to facilitate the growth and repair of the body's cells, including muscle tissue.

KEY TERMS

Fatty acids:
the component of fat used for energy provision

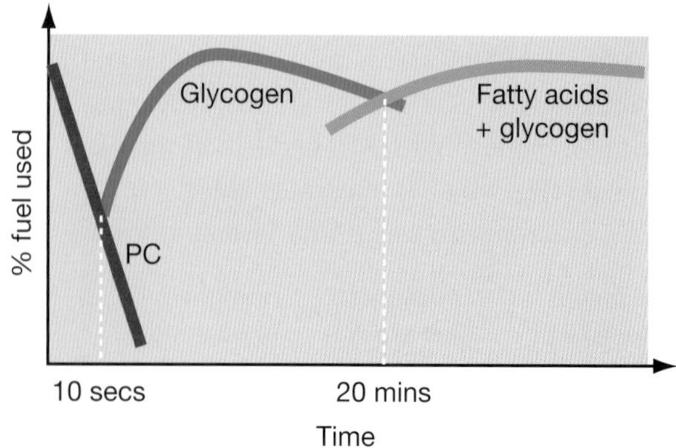

Fig 1.04 Sources of energy for ATP resynthesis against time

REMEMBER!

When exercising at higher intensities, the body will rely more upon glycogen as a source of fuel.

TASK 1.01

Keep a diary of all the food and drink that you consume in one day.

From the packaging calculate how much energy you have consumed in both calories (kcal) and Joules (j).

TIP – You may need to measure out quantities of foodstuffs to give an accurate picture of your energy intake.

The conversion of these fuels into energy which can then be used to resynthesise ATP occurs through one of three pathways or **energy systems**. It is the intensity and duration of the exercise that dictates whether oxygen is present and ultimately which energy system predominates.

The three energy systems are:

1. the aerobic (oxidative) system
2. the lactic acid or lactate anaerobic system
3. the ATP-PC or alactic system.

The more intense the activity (e.g. the harder the athlete is working, signalled perhaps by a higher heart rate) the more the performer will rely on the production of energy from anaerobic pathways such as the ATP-PC system or lactic acid system. As exercise intensity decreases and endurance increases the more the athlete will rely on the aerobic system for providing the energy to resynthesise ATP.

As most of our daily energy requirements are supplied by the aerobic system, it is this system we will visit first.

REMEMBER!

The source of energy for ATP resynthesis is dependent largely upon the intensity and duration of the sporting activity.

The aerobic (oxidative) energy system

During resting conditions or during exercise where the demand for energy is low, oxygen is readily available (hence the name aerobic system) to release stored energy from muscle glycogen, fats and proteins. The aerobic system is the body's preferred energy pathway as it is by far the most efficient in terms of ATP resynthesis. In fact the energy yield from aerobic metabolism is 18 times greater than that gained from anaerobic processes.

During times where there is a plentiful supply of oxygen (i.e. oxygen supply exceeds oxygen demand) glycogen is first converted to glucose-6-phosphate before it is broken down into pyruvate (pyruvic acid). This all takes place in the sarcoplasm of the muscle cell and results from the actions of the enzyme phosphofructokinase (PFK) and is illustrated as the first few stages in Figure 1.07.

Under anaerobic conditions pyruvic acid (pyruvate) is converted into fatigue-inducing lactic acid by the enzyme **lactate dehydrogenase** (LDH). However when oxygen is in rich supply, pyruvic acid is instead converted into **acetyl-coenzyme-A** by combining with the enzyme **pyruvate dehydrogenase**. The site for energy release now moves to specialised parts of the cell known as **mitochondria**. These industrious units are in abundance within the muscle and manufacture energy for ATP resynthesis by facilitating the many chemical reactions required to completely break down our stores of glycogen and fats to ensure a continuous supply of energy. Because of their ability to supply lots of energy mitochondria are particularly found in large numbers in slow twitch muscle fibres.

Fig 1.05 illustrates a mitochondrion. You can see from this diagram that there are two key stages of the aerobic system that take place within the mitochondria: the **Krebs cycle** and the **electron transport system**.

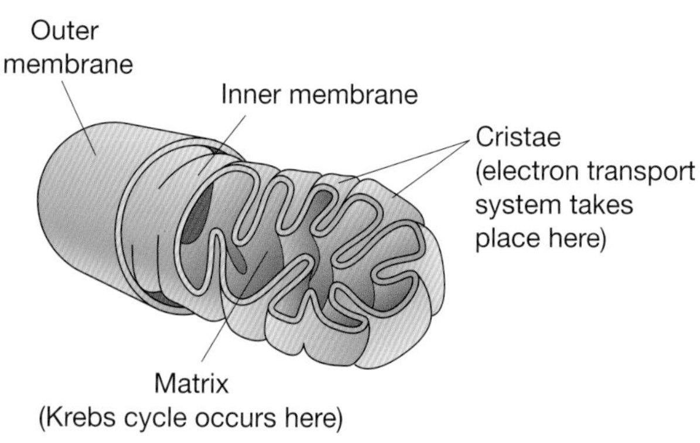

Fig 1.05 A mitochondrion

REMEMBER!

The aerobic system is of particular use to athletes who need to perform relatively low intensity exercise for a long period of time. A triathlete or marathon runner are obvious examples.

Fig 1.06 A race walker will utilise the aerobic system to provide energy for muscular contractions

KEY TERMS

Mitochondrion:
the powerhouse of the cell. Mitochondria are specialised structures within all cells that are the site of ATP production under aerobic conditions

Krebs cycle:
a series of chemical reactions that occur in the matrix of the mitochondria yielding sufficient energy to resynthesise 2 ATP molecules and carbon dioxide. It forms part of the aerobic system

Electron transport system:
a series of reactions in the cristae of the mitochondria where the majority of energy is yielded for ATP resynthesis. 34 moles of ATP can be resynthesised from just 1 mole of glycogen at this stage of the aerobic system

Mole:
an amount of a substance that contains a standardised number of atoms (6.0225×10^{23} known as Avogadro's number)

REMEMBER!

Slow twitch muscle fibres house many more mitochondria than fast twitch fibres and hence are more suited to aerobic activity such as marathon running.

The Krebs cycle

The **Krebs cycle** takes place in the fluid-filled matrix of the mitochondria which has a rich supply of enzymes that are ready to perform the necessary chemical reactions to help release the remaining energy stored within the molecule.

Three significant events occur at this stage.

1. **Oxidation of citric acid.** This involves the removal of hydrogen atoms from the compound which enter the final stage of the aerobic system; the electron transport system.
2. **Production of carbon dioxide.** The removal of hydrogen means that only carbon and oxygen remain. These combine to form carbon dioxide which is carried around to the lungs where it is breathed out.

3. **Resynthesis of ATP.** Sufficient energy is released at this stage to resynthesise 2 **moles** of ATP

The electron transport system

This final stage of glycogen breakdown occurs in the **cristae** of the mitochondria. Hydrogen given off at the Krebs cycle stage is carried to the electron transport system.

There are two important features of this stage of the aerobic pathway:

1. **Water (H_2O)** is formed when the hydrogen ions (H+) and electrons (e-) combine with oxygen through a series of enzyme reactions.
2. **Resynthesis of ATP:** By far the majority of energy is released here for the resynthesis of ATP. In fact 34 moles of ATP can be resynthesised, making this by far the most efficient source of energy in the body.

Other fuels used in aerobic energy production

So far we have only focused our attention on the aerobic breakdown of glycogen. However fat and protein can also be metabolised under aerobic conditions to form CO_2, H_2O and energy for ATP resynthesis. Fats stored in the muscle as triglycerides must first be broken down into glycerol and free fatty acids (FFAs) before they go through the process of **beta(ß)-oxidation** (the fat equivalent of glycolysis). Following beta-oxidation fatty acids can enter the Krebs cycle where they can then follow the same path of metabolism as glycogen. The main difference between fat and glycogen metabolism, however, is that substantially more energy (for ATP resynthesis) can be elicited from one mole of fatty acids than from one mole of glycogen. Consequently, fatty acids become the preferred fuel as the duration of exercise increases. Typically this occurs after 20 minutes of sub-maximal activity. This has important consequences for endurance performers as it enables them to spare their glycogen for later in the event or competition, when intensity of the exercise might increase.

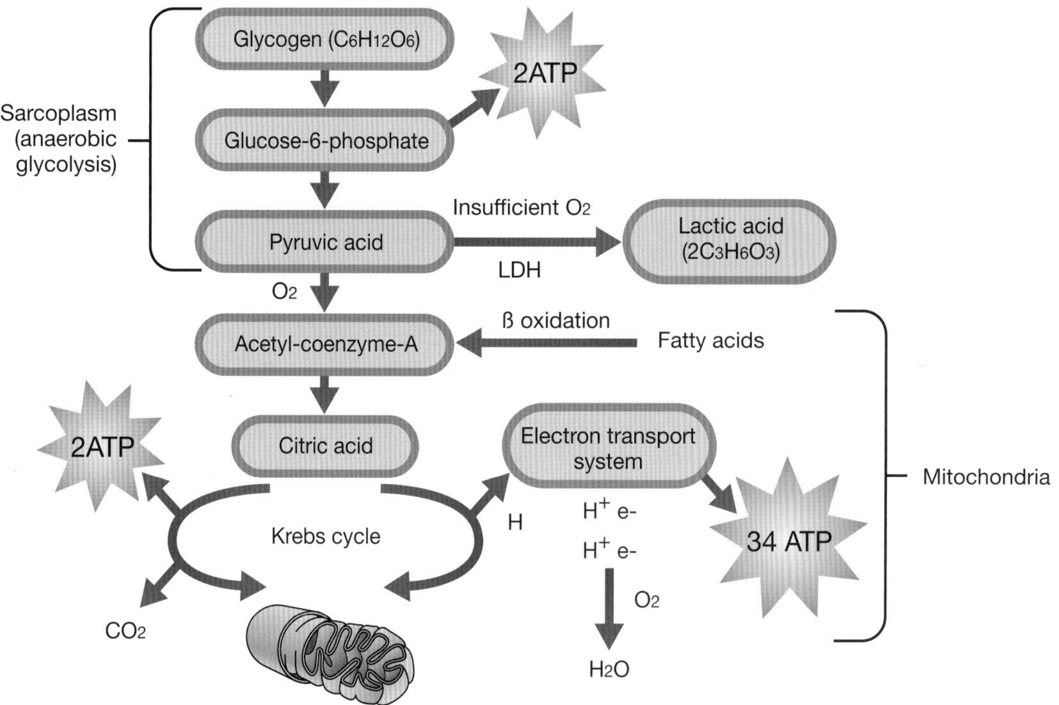

Fig.1.07 ATP resynthesis via the aerobic system

Advantages to the athlete of using the aerobic system

- Significantly more ATP can be resynthesised under aerobic conditions than anaerobic (36 ATP aerobically compared to 2 ATP anaerobically – from one mole of glycogen).
- The body has substantial stores of muscle glycogen and triglycerides to enable exercise to last for several hours.
- Oxidation of glycogen and fatty acids do not produce any fatiguing by-products.

Drawbacks of this system to the athlete

- When we go from a resting state to exercise it takes a while for sufficient oxygen to become available to meet the new demands of the activity and enable the complete breakdown of glycogen and fatty acids. Consequently this system cannot provide energy to resysnthesise ATP in the immediate short term (unless the activity is of particularly low intensity) or during higher intensity activity
- Although fatty acids are the preferred fuel during endurance events such as a marathon, the transport of fatty acids to the muscle is slow and requires about 15% more oxygen than that required to break down the equivalent amount of glycogen.
- Due to the low solubility of fatty acids the endurance athlete will usually use a mixture of both glycogen and fatty acids to provide the energy for ATP resynthesis. When glycogen becomes depleted and the body attempts to metabolise fatty acids as a sole source of fuel, muscle spasms may result. This is commonly known as hitting the wall.

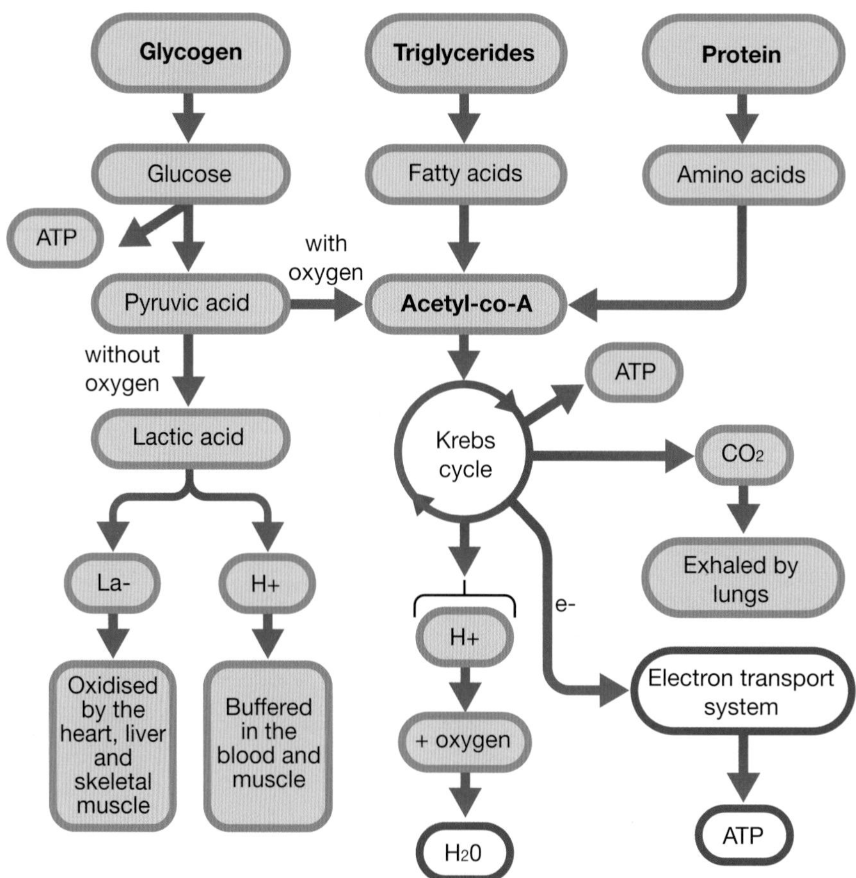

Fig 1.08 A summary of ATP resynthesis from the three main energy providing nutrients

The complete breakdown of one mole of glycogen can be summarised as follows:

$$C_6H_{12}O_6 + 6O_2 \longrightarrow 6CO_2 + 6H_2O + \text{ENERGY}$$
$$\text{Energy} + 38\text{ADP} + 38\text{Pi} \longrightarrow 38\text{ATP}$$

TASK 1.02

During a 10,000m race the aerobic system will be used for the majority of the event to resysnthesise ATP. Complete the table below with the required information.

	Site of reaction	Fuels used	Active enzymes	Molecules of ATP produced
Aerobic system (oxidative)				

The aerobic system and recovery

The **recovery** process is concerned with returning the body to its pre-exercise state so that heart rate, oxygen consumption, blood lactate levels and glycogen stores are at exactly the same levels as they were **before** the exercise commenced!

You will know from your own experience that whatever the exercise you may have performed, whether it be a maximal lift in the weights room or a 5km run, the recovery period involves a period where breathing and heart rates are elevated. This occurs because all recovery is dependent upon the consumption of oxygen, and the elevated respiratory and heart rates ensure that adequate amounts of oxygen are taken into the body and delivered to the muscles to enable a swift recovery. The oxygen delivered to the muscles will help rebuild stores of PC and ATP as well as remove any lactic acid that may have accumulated during the activity.

KEY TERMS

Recovery:
the return of the body to its pre-exercise state

REMEMBER!

As recovery can only occur when there is sufficient oxygen available then it is often associated with the aerobic energy system.

TASK 1.03

An investigation to examine recovery heart rate response to varying intensities of exercise.

Equipment: heart rate monitor, stop watch, gymnastics bench, metronome. (If you do not have access to a heart rate monitor then record your heart rate at the carotid artery for a 10 second count and multiply by 6 to convert to beats per minute.)

1. Record resting heart rate at the beginning of the class.
2. Record heart rate just prior to exercise.
3. Commence exercising by stepping onto and off the bench in time with the metronome that has been set at a low intensity.
4. Record your heart rate after one, two and three minutes of exercise. After the third minute of exercise stop the test. Continue to record your pulse each minute during recovery.

Time	Exercise intensity		
	Low	Medium	High
Resting HR			
HR prior to exercise			
Exercise 1 min			
Exercise 2 min			
Exercise 3 min			
Recovery 1 min			
Recovery 2 min			
Recovery 3 min			
Recovery 4 min			
Recovery 5 min			
Recovery 6 min			
Recovery 7 min			

Table 1.01 Example table: copy out a similar one for this task

TASK 1.03 CONTINUED

5. Once your heart rate has returned to its resting value (or within a few beats) repeat the test at a medium intensity. Record your results as before.
6. Repeat the exercise for a third time but at very high intensity. Once again record your results.
7. Now use your results to plot a graph for each of the three workloads. Plot each graph using the same axes placing heart rate along the *y* axis and time along the bottom *x* axis. Don't forget to show your resting heart rate values on the graph.
8. For each of your graphs explain the pattern of recovery heart rate.

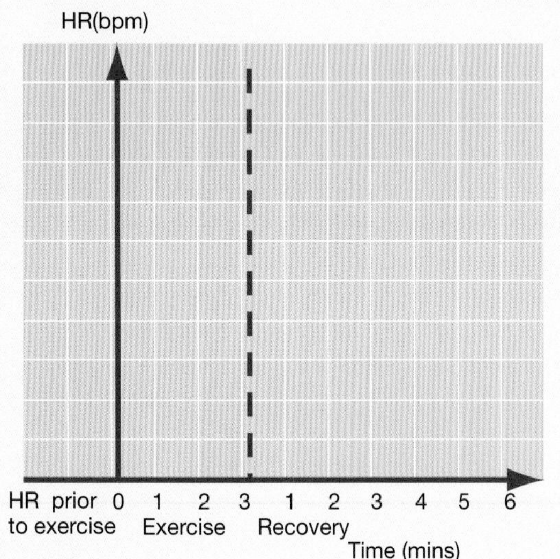

NB: The length of the recovery period depends upon the intensity and to a lesser degree the duration of the previous exercise.

Fig. 1.09 Example graph: copy out a similar one on graph paper

Excess post-exercise oxygen consumption (EPOC)

Excess post-exercise oxygen consumption represents the extra volume of oxygen consumed following exercise that enables the body to fully recover and return to its pre-exercise state.

At the very beginning of exercise (even at low intensities) or when exercise is of high intensity it is likely that the body will need to work anaerobically for a period of time as there may be insufficient oxygen available to use the aerobic energy system exclusively to provide the energy for muscular work, i.e. a **deficit** occurs in the oxygen supply. The oxygen deficit thus represents the amount of extra oxygen required to enable the entire activity to be completed using the aerobic energy system. Since it takes a while for the aerobic system to 'kick in' and provide the muscles with energy at the beginning of activity, a deficit will always develop.

Researchers have identified two stages of recovery:

- **Stage 1:** The **fast replenishment stage** (formerly referred to as the alactacid debt)
- **Stage 2:** The **slow replenishment stage** (formerly known as the lactacid debt).

REMEMBER!

The term oxygen debt was often used to explain the restoration of ATP and PC and removal of lactic acid during recovery. But this failed to explain the extra oxygen needed during recovery to restore muscle oxymyoglobin and to keep respiratory and heart rates elevated. EPOC is therefore the preferred term now and the oxygen debt viewed as one part of this process.

TASK 1.04

Examine the graphs you drew in Task 1.03.
Can you identify a fast and slow stage of oxygen consumption during the recovery phase? If so shade these stages on the graph and label them 'fast stage' and 'slow stage'.

KEY TERMS

Excess post-exercise oxygen consumption (EPOC):
the volume of oxygen consumed during recovery above that which normally would have been consumed at rest during the same period of time

Oxygen deficit:
the volume of extra oxygen required to complete the entire activity aerobically

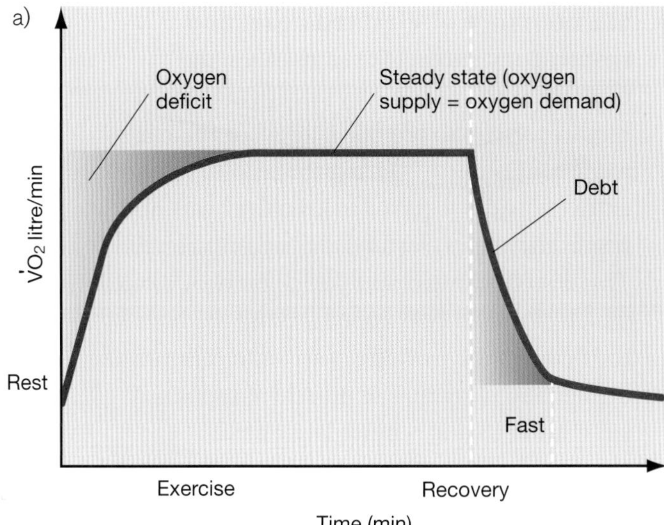

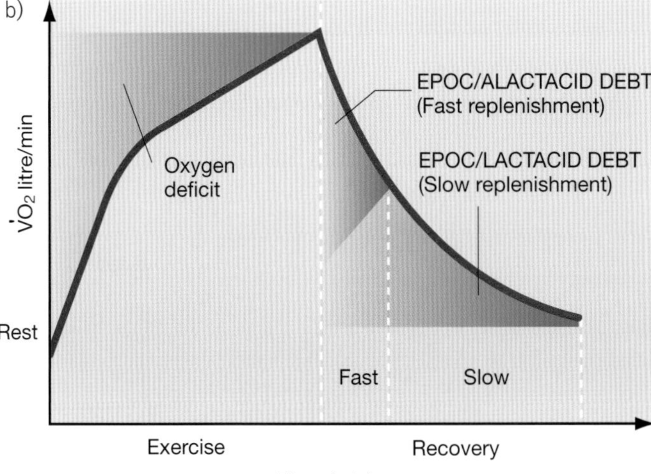

Fig 1.10 Oxygen consumption during and following (a) a sub-maximal task and (b) maximal task

REMEMBER!

1. You will notice from Figure 1.10a that the volume of EPOC is greater than the volume of oxygen deficit. This is because the 'muscles' of recovery such as the heart and respiratory muscles require oxygen to keep breathing and heart rates elevated.
2. You will note from Figure 1.10b that the 2 stages of recovery are clearly visible following maximal or high intensity exercise. However following sub-maximal or low intensity exercise only the fast stage may be evident. This is because the majority of the work has been completed aerobically and little lactic acid has accumulated during the exercise.

Excess
Post – exercise
Oxygen
Consumption

Fast component
- Restoration of muscle ATP + PC
- Re-saturation of myoglobin with oxygen

Slow component
- Removal of lactic acid
- Maintenance of elevated heart and respiratory rates
- Replenishment of glycogen stores
- Elevated body temperature

Fig. 1.11 The components of excess post-exercise oxygen consumption (EPOC)

KEY TERMS

Fast replenishment:
the first component of EPOC. Oxygen consumed is used to resaturate myoglobin and resynthesise ATP and PC. It takes approximately 2–3 minutes

Slow replenishment:
the second component of EPOC. Oxygen consumed during this stage is largely used to remove lactic acid which takes about 1 hour. In addition oxygen is also used to maintain cardiac and respiratory rates and normalise body temperature

The fast replenishment stage

This is the first stage of the recovery process and relates to the immediate consumption of oxygen following exercise. Its primary function is to re-saturate myoglobin with oxygen and provide aerobic energy to resynthesise adenosine triphosphate (ATP) and phosphocreatine (PC).The fast stage of recovery is usually completed within 2–3 minutes and utilises up to 4 litres of oxygen.

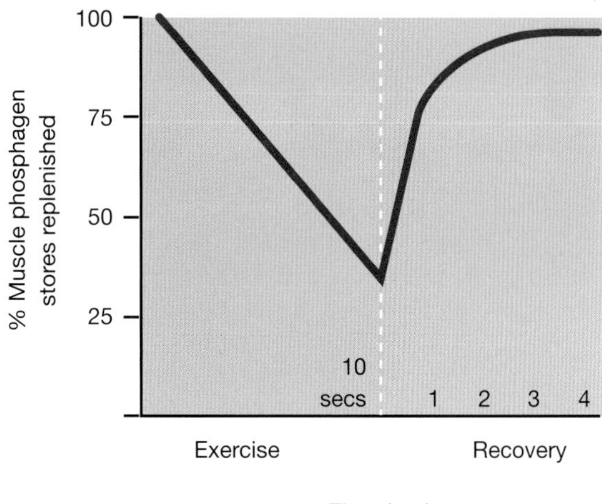

Fig 1.12 The replenishment of muscle phosphagens following maximal exercise

REMEMBER!

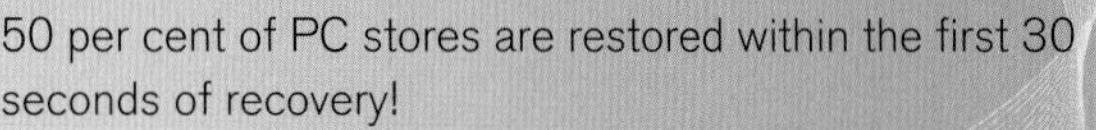

50 per cent of PC stores are restored within the first 30 seconds of recovery!

The slow replenishment stage

The slow replenishment stage of EPOC can take up to 2 hours and utilises between 5 and 10 litres of extra oxygen depending upon the intensity of the preceding exercise.

The oxygen consumed during the slow stage of recovery has several functions:

- **Removal of lactic acid:** Lactic acid accumulated during exercise must be removed if the body is to recover fully. You will recall that most lactic acid is converted back into pyruvate and then into CO_2 and water, the remainder being converted into muscle glycogen, blood glucose and protein. Much of the oxygen consumed during this stage is therefore used to provide the energy to enable this removal of lactic acid to take place. Typically the oxidation and removal of lactic acid takes about an hour, but this can be accelerated by performing a cool down. The cool down or **active recovery** helps keep the metabolic activity of the muscles high and the capillaries dilated so that oxygen can be flushed through the muscle tissue oxidising and removing any lactic acid accumulated.
- **Maintenance of elevated heart and respiratory rates:** Like all muscles, the muscles of the respiratory system and the heart require oxygen to provide energy for them to work continuously. During the recovery period extra energy is required to keep the heart and respiratory rates elevated above resting levels. This is so the lungs can take in plenty of oxygen which can then be pumped around the body by the heart to the working muscles to re-saturate myoglobin, resynthesise muscle phosphagens (ATP and PC) and remove lactic acid.
- **Replenishment of muscle glycogen stores:** During all types of exercise it is likely that some muscle glycogen stores will become depleted. It is in the interests of the performer to replenish these stores as soon after exercise as possible. The replenishment of these muscular stores of glycogen is largely dependent upon two key factors:

  1. The type of exercise that has been performed
  2. The amount and timing of carbohydrate consumption following exercise.

REMEMBER!

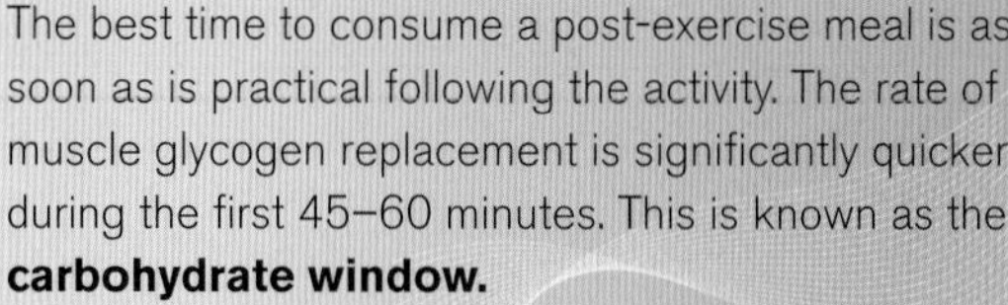

The best time to consume a post-exercise meal is as soon as is practical following the activity. The rate of muscle glycogen replacement is significantly quicker during the first 45–60 minutes. This is known as the **carbohydrate window.**

First of all let us consider the type of exercise performed. Studies have suggested that following **continuous, endurance-based activity** little glycogen is restored in the period immediately following activity. Complete muscle glycogen repletion can take up to 48 hours in this instance. During **high intensity, short duration activity**, however, a significant amount of muscle glycogen can be resynthesised within 30 minutes to one hour immediately following exercise (probably due to conversion of lactic acid back into glycogen via the **cori cycle**) and complete resynthesis requires a 24-hour recovery period.

The second key factor concerns the amount of carbohydrate consumed following exercise. Muscle glycogen repletion occurs more rapidly when a high carbohydrate meal is consumed within the first 45–60 minutes following exercise: this is commonly known as the **carbohydrate window**. A high carbohydrate meal should consist of 200–300g of carbohydrate.

- An **elevated body temperature**: You have probably all experienced the increase in body temperature that accompanies all exercise whether it is a maximal all-out effort on the bench press or a 5Km run. This increase in body temperature generally results from the increased metabolic activity of the body which provides the energy to perform work. However with every 10° increase in body temperature the metabolic activity of the cells doubles. Oxygen is needed to feed this increase even during the recovery period and continues to do so until the body has cooled right back down to normal resting temperatures. The oxygen for this comes through the slow replenishment stage of EPOC.

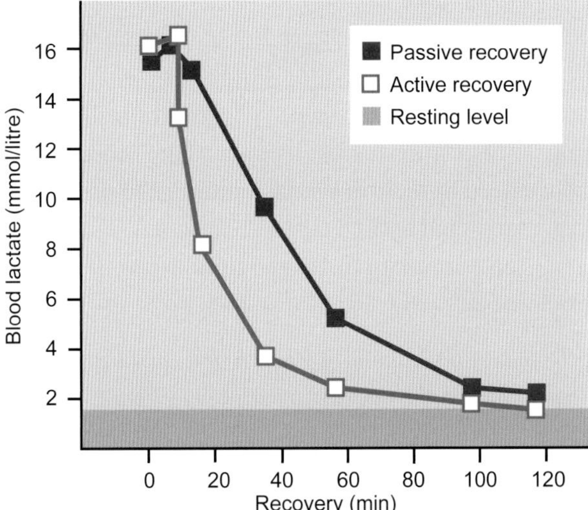

Note that blood lactate levels return towards normal resting levels much quicker when a period of active recovery has taken place.

Fig 1.13 The effect of cool down or active recovery on recovery time following a bout of high intensity work

REMEMBER!

A 400m runner will consume a large volume of oxygen during the slow replenishment stage as a large amount of lactic acid will have accumulated in their muscles.

KEY TERMS

Active recovery:
a recovery period during which time light exercise is performed

Rest recovery:
a recovery period during which time the performer has rested passively

Cori cycle:
the process where lactic acid is taken to the liver for conversion into glucose and glycogen

REMEMBER!

The exercise intensity during a cool down that best removes lactic acid is between 30–45% VO_2max for untrained subjects and 50–65% VO_2max for trained performers.

TASK 1.05

Figure 1.14 is often used to illustrate EPOC.

1. From the graph state what each of the letters A–E represents.
2. For what is the oxygen consumed during part 'D' used?
3. Which letters can be used to determine EPOC?

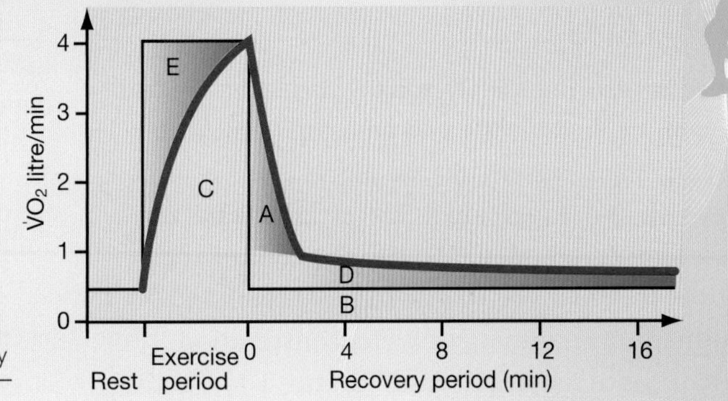

Fig 1.14 Oxygen consumption during exercise and recovery

TASK 1.06

The data in table 1.03 relates to the rate of lactate removal during recovery from exhaustive exercise following (i) **rest recovery** and (ii) active recovery.

1. Draw a graph of % lactate removed against time using the data in the table. Briefly explain what the graph shows.
2. On your graph mark off the times for each type of recovery when 50 per cent of blood lactate had been removed. What does this suggest?
3. What type of activity would you suggest a performer undertake during a period of active recovery?
4. What intensity of exercise (measured as a percentage of VO_2max) would you suggest the active recovery period is completed for a) an untrained subject b) a trained performer?

% lactate removed	Recovery time (mins) (Rest recovery)	Recovery time (mins) (Active recovery)
20	8	4
40	20	8
60	35	15
80	55	25
100	180	70

TASK 1.07

Copy out the following table and complete the approximate recovery times for each factor

Recovery process	Recovery time
Re-saturation of myoglobin with oxygen	
Resynthesis of muscular stores of ATP and PC	
Repayment of fast component of EPOC	
Removal of lactic acid: • with active recovery • with rest recovery	
Repayment of slow component of EPOC	
Restoration of muscle glycogen stores	

Maximal oxygen consumption (VO_2max)

Lance Armstrong's is **VO_2max** reported as 83.8ml/kg/min, Paula Radcliffe's an amazing 80ml/kg/min and Matt Pinsent has the highest ever recorded in the UK at a staggering 8.5 litres/min! What do these figures represent? Well it's their VO_2max of course! Indeed if you go into the chat rooms of any marathon running web sites conversation soon turns to the size of your VO_2max. For effective endurance performance we need a big and efficient pump to deliver oxygen-rich blood to the muscles and we need mitochondria-rich muscles to use the oxygen and enable high rates of exercise.

VO_2max or maximal oxygen uptake can therefore be defined as:

'...the maximum volume of oxygen that can be utilised or consumed by the working muscles per minute...'

A high VO_2max, or maximal oxygen uptake, is indeed one of the hallmark characteristics of great endurance performance in activities such as swimming, cycling, rowing and running. However, it is elite cross country skiers that are considered the most powerful in oxygen uptake capacity. This is probably because cross country skiing engages just about all of the major muscle groups of the body. This is not, however, the only determining factor of VO_2 max.

The ability of the muscles to consume the greatest amount of oxygen as possible the body is dependent upon two further key factors:

1. An effective oxygen delivery system that brings oxygen from the atmosphere into the working muscles
2. An aerobic-friendly muscle structure which possesses a large volume of myoglobin and a high density of mitochondria which can be used to produce ATP via the aerobic energy system.

Measuring maximal oxygen consumption (VO_2max)

You will recall from your AS studies that there are several tests of maximal oxygen consumption (VO_2max). These tests are listed below:

- The multi-stage fitness test
- Harvard step test
- PWC170 test
- Cooper 12-minute run test.

Whilst the multi-stage fitness test gives a reasonable prediction of VO_2max it cannot give a truly objective measure of the volume of oxygen actually consumed by the working muscles. The only way we can possibly do this is in a sports science laboratory where **direct gas analysis** can take place. In order to determine an athlete's true maximal aerobic capacity, exercise conditions must be created that maximally stress the blood delivery capacity of the heart.

Fig.1.15 Cross-country skiers reportedly have the highest VO_2max of all sports performers

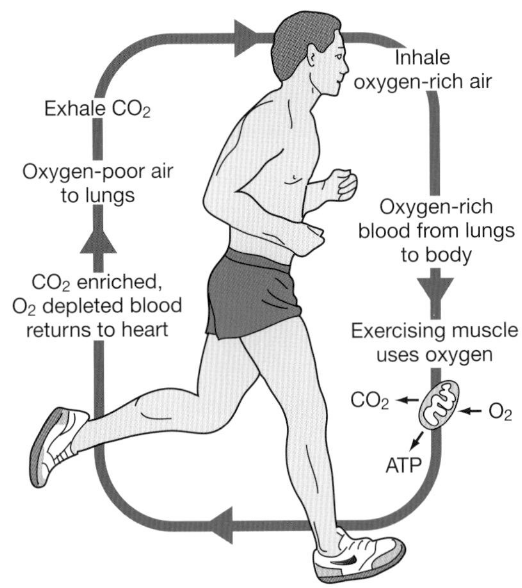

Fig 1.16 Oxygen transport and consumption during exercise

Here is an example of a VO_2 max treadmill test using Johnny, a typical A level student as a subject:

1. Firstly Johnny is weighed. This is so his VO_2 max can be given relative to his body weight. A simple reading of ml/min would ignore the fact that larger people have larger lungs and are capable of taking in more oxygen into their bodies.
2. Following a warm-up, Johnny places a mask over his mouth which is attached to the computer by a hose tubing. Johnny begins the treadmill test at a speed of 10km/h. Whilst running he breathes through a two-way valve system. The computer analyses the relative concentrations of oxygen and carbon dioxide inspired and expired respectively. From this it is possible to calculate the amount of oxygen extracted and consumed by the muscles and the amount of carbon dioxide produced over time. In order to reach an exhaustion point and get a maximum reading the treadmill speed is increased by 1km/h every minute.
3. After 2 minutes the speed of running has increased to 12km/h, the graph below shows an increase in the level of oxygen breathed in and carbon dioxide breathed out. The distance between the two values shows that Johnny is

working aerobically with a good supply of oxygen to the muscles. He is in steady state where oxygen demand is being met by oxygen supply.

4. After 7 minutes the speed has increased to 17 km/h and Johnny's heart rate has increased significantly to 192 bpm. His breathing rate has become faster as the levels of carbon dioxide increase further. Now the level of oxygen begins to level out. Johnny will have to call on more and more anaerobic energy to meet any further extra energy demands as his body struggles to get oxygen to his muscles.
5. After 10 minutes Johnny is racing along at 20 km/h, his heart is doing overtime at over 200 bpm and his lungs are working at their maximum to get oxygen into the body. This is the point where the VO_2 max is taken. His reading is 57.6 ml/kg/min. After nearly 10.5 minutes Johnny is completely exhausted. He can no longer exercise and the test is stopped.
6. Johnny's reading of 57.6 ml/kg/min is good and shows that he has some capacity to perform endurance based activity.

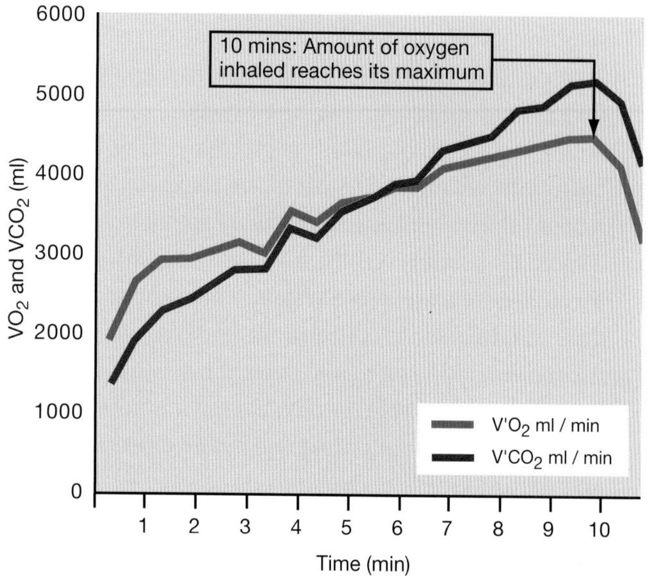

Fig 1.17 VO_2max timeline: Johnny's results

KEY TERMS

Direct gas analysis:
the most valid and reliable method of measuring VO_2max. During the test, subjects are measured at progressively increasing intensities on a treadmill, cycle ergometer or rowing machine. Concentrations of oxygen and carbon dioxide inspired and expired are monitored

Maximal oxygen consumption (VO_2max):
the maximum volume of oxygen that can be utilised or consumed by the working muscles per minute. It is usually measured in ml/kg/min

REMEMBER!

VO_2max is expressed as a rate, either millilitres per kg of bodyweight per minute for weight bearing activities such as running or litres per minute for partial weight bearing activities such as rowing or cycling.

TASK 1.08

Use the following data to plot a bar graph illustrating the expected VO_2max scores for the activities shown.

Activity	Male (ml/kg/min)	Female (ml/kg/min)
Triathlete	80	72
Marathon runner	78	68
Distance swimmer	72	64
Middle distance runner (800–1500)	72	63
Games player	66	56
Gymnast	56	47
Weightlifter	52	43

KEY TERMS

Absolute VO_2max:
a VO_2max value given in litres/min

Relative VO_2max:
a VO_2max value that takes account of bodyweight and measured in millilitres of oxygen per kg of bodyweight per minute (ml/kg/min)

REMEMBER!

1. The average VO_2max score for an average 'A' level student should be around 45–55 ml/kg/min for males and 35–44ml/kg/min for females.
2. Surprisingly, endurance training such as following a continuous training regime can only improve VO_2max by between 10 and 20%.
3. When we consider **absolute VO_2max** the typical untrained male has a value of 3.5 litres/min whilst that of a female is approximately 2 litres/min – a 43% difference! When we consider bodyweight to give a **relative** value this difference is reduced to 15–20%.
4. As a rule of thumb when VO_2max is measured in relative terms (taking bodyweight into consideration) female athletes have a score of approximately 10ml lower than comparable males of the same activity group

Factors affecting maximal oxygen consumption (VO_2max)

Fig 1.18 summarises the main factors that affect an individual's maximal oxygen consumption.

Physiology
The physiological make up of the body will almost certainly affect VO_2 max. Below are just a few physiological factors that contribute to a higher VO_2max score:
* a high percentage of slow twitch (type 1) muscle fibres
* high capillary density
* high mitochondrial density and myoglobin content
* high blood volume and haemoglobin content.

Lifestyle
Smoking, leading a sedentary lifestyle and having a poor diet can greatly reduce VO_2max values.

Age
Typically VO_2max will decrease with age. After the age of 25 years, VO_2max is thought to decrease by about 1 per cent per year. Regular physical activity can slow down the rate of this decline.

Genetics
Studies on identical and fraternal twins have suggested that genetics accounts for 25 to 50 per cent of VO_2max scores.
It appears that Olympic champions are born with a unique potential that is transformed into athletic performance through years of hard training.

Body composition
Research shows that VO_2max scores decrease as the percentage of body fat increases. This is because fat is non-functional weight that must be carried around. Typically males should aim for a body fat per cent of between 14–17 per cent whilst females should aim for a value between 24–29 per cent.

Gender
When we consider absolute VO_2max, the typical untrained male has a value of 3.5 litres/min whilst that of a female is approximately 2l/min – a 43 per cent difference! When we consider bodyweight to give a relative value this difference is reduced to 15 to 20 per cent.

Training
VO_2max can only be improved by 10 to 20 per cent following training. This is somewhat surprising given the vast improvement in the delivery and transport of oxygen resulting from long-term endurance training. The best methods of training to improve VO_2max include continuous training, Fartlek and aerobic interval training.

Fig 1.18 Factors affecting maximal oxygen consumption (VO_2max)

TASK 1.09

If your absolute VO_2max was measured at 4.0 litres/min and you weighed 75kg, calculate your relative VO_2max.

TASK 1.10

Design a training programme aimed at improving the VO_2max of a performer. Make sure you prescribe appropriate methods of training and clearly state the expected intensity of training.

EXAM TIP:

Make sure you are able to describe a test of VO_2max. You must be able to critically evaluate the test commenting on its validity and reliability.

The respiratory exchange ratio (RER)

The **respiratory exchange ratio** is the ratio of the volume of carbon dioxide expired per minute to the volume of oxygen consumed per minute and is used by the coach and athlete as a measure of the intensity at which the athlete is training.

The respiratory ratio can be assessed as follows:

$$\text{Respiratory exchange ratio} = \frac{\text{Carbon dioxide expired per minute } (VCO_2)}{\text{Oxygen consumed per minute } (VO_2)}$$

However, the amount of energy released through the consumption of every litre of oxygen is dependent upon the type of food fuel that is metabolised.

You will recall from page 9 that the following formula can be used to summarise the aerobic breakdown of glucose (our usable form of carbohydrate):

$$C_6H_{12}O_6 \text{ (glucose)} + 6O_2 \longrightarrow 6CO_2 + 6H_2O + \text{energy}$$

From this equation we can see that to break down one mole of glucose, 6 moles of oxygen are required which elicits energy plus 6 moles of carbon dioxide and 6 moles of water. Notice that all the oxygen inspired here is used to form carbon dioxide.

$$RER = \frac{VCO_2}{VO_2} = \frac{6CO_2}{6O_2} = 1.0$$

However, when fat is oxidised the oxygen inspired does not only combine with carbon to form carbon dioxide but some is also required to combine with hydrogen to produce water:

$$C_{16}H_{32}O_2 \text{ (fat)} + 23O_2 \longrightarrow 16CO_2 + 16H_2O$$

So this formula tells us that in order to break down one mole of fat 23 moles of oxygen is required: 16 moles of which combine with carbon to form carbon dioxide, the remaining 7 moles combine with hydrogen to form water.

$$RER = \frac{VCO_2}{VO_2} = \frac{16\ CO_2}{23\ O_2} = 0.17$$

So the metabolism of fat only elicits 70% of the energy per litre of oxygen consumed than when compared to carbohydrate. So although fat contains twice the chemical energy of carbohydrate per gram, it requires more oxygen to release the energy stored within it.

KEY TERMS

Respiratory exchange ratio: a method of determining which metabolic fuel is predominantly in use during exercise. It is calculated by analysing oxygen consumption and carbon dioxide production

EXAM TIP:

It is usual to refer to VCO_2/VO_2 at cellular level as the respiratory quotient (RQ) and at lung level as the respiratory exchange ratio (RER).

The respiratory exchange ratio is important for the coach and athlete when planning training, as it can be used to assess the intensity at which a performer is working. If the RER is closer to 1 this suggests that the athlete is working hard and training at a higher intensity as more carbohydrate is being used as a metabolic fuel. Conversely, if the RER is closer to 0.7 then the body is relying more heavily on fat as a metabolic fuel and the intensity of the training will be comparatively lighter.

REMEMBER!

The respiratory exchange ratio can only be assessed under laboratory conditions where the consumption of oxygen and the production of carbon dioxide can be analysed through direct gas analysis.

The anaerobic energy systems

The ATP-PC (alactic) system

We have established that muscular stores of ATP will have depleted after about 3 seconds of maximal activity. For high intensity activity to continue the immediate recycling of ATP is necessary. However the rapid increase in activity results in insufficient oxygen being available (an oxygen deficit) to sustain this ATP resysnthesis. The body therefore relies upon a second energy-rich compound found alongside ATP in the muscle cells. This compound is **phosphocreatine (PCr)**.

Like ATP the breakdown of phosphocreatine takes place in the **sarcoplasm** of a muscle cell and is facilitated by the enzyme **creatine kinase**. The release of creatine kinase is stimulated by the increase in ADP and inorganic phosphates (both products of ATP breakdown)

$$\text{PCr} \longrightarrow \text{Creatine} + \text{Pi} + \text{energy}$$

Unlike ATP, the energy released from the breakdown of phosphocreatine is not used for muscle contraction but is instead used to recycle ATP, so that it can once again be broken down to maintain a constant energy supply.

$$\begin{matrix}\text{Energy} \\ \text{(from PCr breakdown)}\end{matrix} + \text{ADP} + \text{Pi} \longrightarrow \text{ATP}$$

As energy is required for this reaction to take place it is known as an **endothermic reaction**.

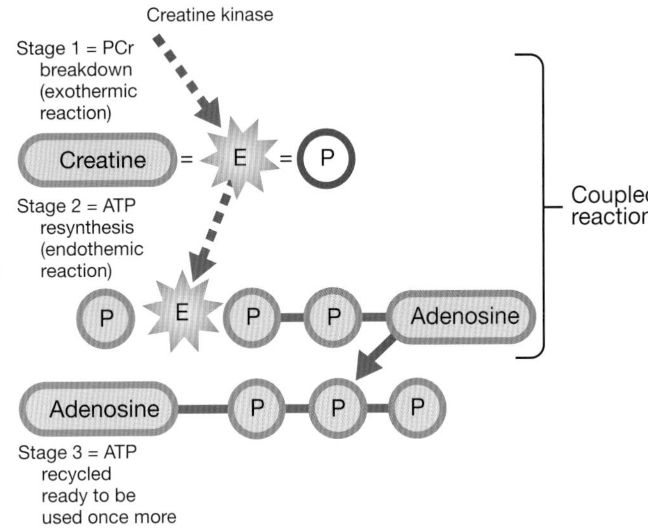

Fig 1.19 The ATP-PC system as a coupled reaction

The coupled reaction

Because PCr exists alongside ATP in the sarcoplasm of the muscle cell, as rapidly as energy is released from ATP during exercise it is restored through the breakdown of PCr. This linked reaction more or less occurs simultaneously and It takes one molecule of PCr to recycle one molecule of ATP.

Advantages of this system to the athlete

- The most important feature of this system is that ATP can be resynthesised very rapidly (almost immediately) by PCr.
- PCr stores are recovered very quickly, within 2–3 minutes of exercise stopping. This means that high intensity exercise can once again be undertaken.
- It is an anaerobic process and so does not need to wait for the 3 minutes or so for sufficient oxygen to be present.
- There are no fatiguing by-products which could delay recovery.
- Some athletes may seek to extend the time that they can use this system through **creatine supplementation**.

REMEMBER!

1. The ATP-PC system is of particular use to athletes who compete at high intensity for about 10 seconds such as a 100m sprinter or a gymnast performing a vault
2. **Creatine supplementation:** Some athletes seek to extend the threshold of the ATP-PC system by ingesting creatine monohydrate. Side effects such as abdominal cramps, bloating and dehydration have been recorded.

Drawbacks of this system to the athlete

- The main drawback is that there is only a limited supply of PCr stored in the muscle cell, sufficient only to resynthesise ATP for approximately 10 second or so. Fatigue occurs when concentrations of PCr fall significantly and can no longer sustain ATP resynthesis.
- Resynthesis of PCr can only take place when there is sufficient oxygen available – this is usually during resting conditions once exercise has ceased.
- Only 1 mole of ATP can be recycled through 1 mole of PCr.

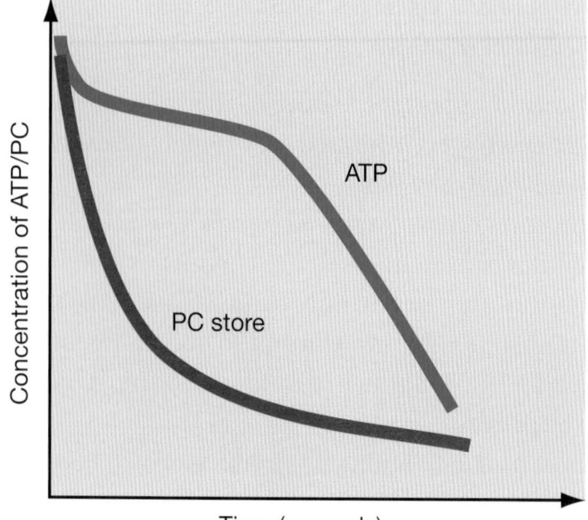

Fig.1.20 Muscle phosphagen depletion during a 100m sprint

Note that ATP levels remain high at the start of the race due to the action of PCr providing energy to maintain levels. However, after pproximately ten seconds, stores of phosphocreatine have become depleted and ATP levels fall rapidly.

REMEMBER!

Don't forget that for very high intense activities lasting less than 3 seconds, such as a maximum weight lift, energy will be provided solely through the breakdown of ATP.

KEY TERMS

Sarcoplasm:
fluid that surrounds the nucleus of a muscle cell, that is the site for both anaerobic energy pathways

Creatine kinase:
the enzyme used to release energy from phosphocreatine

Endothermic reaction:
a chemical reaction that consumes energy

Coupled reaction:
a reaction where the product of one reaction is used in a linked (second) reaction. the ATP-PC system is an example of a coupled reaction

The lactic acid (lactate anaerobic) system

Most activities last longer than the 10 second threshold of the ATP-PC system. If strenuous exercise is required to continue, ATP must be resynthesised from another fuel source. In fact, the body switches to **glycogen** (our stored form of carbohydrate) to fuel the working muscles once phosphocreatine stores have been depleted. The glycogen which is stored in the liver and muscles must first be converted into glucose-6-phosphate before it is broken down to **pyruvate** by the enzyme **phosphofructokinase (PFK)** in a process known as **glycolysis**. It is during glycolysis (which takes place in the sarcoplasm of the muscle cell) that energy is released to facilitate ATP resynthesis. In fact a net gain of 2 moles of ATP are gained for every mole of glycogen broken down. In the absence of oxygen, pyruvate is converted into lactate (lactic acid) by the enzyme **lactate dehydrogenase (LDH)**.

TASK 1.11

During a 100m sprint ATP will initially split to enable the athlete to drive away from the starting blocks. PCr is then broken down to maintain a constant supply of energy for the remainder of the race. Complete the table below with the required information.

	Site of reaction	Fuel used	Active enzyme	Molecules of ATP produced
ATP splitting				
ATP-PC system				

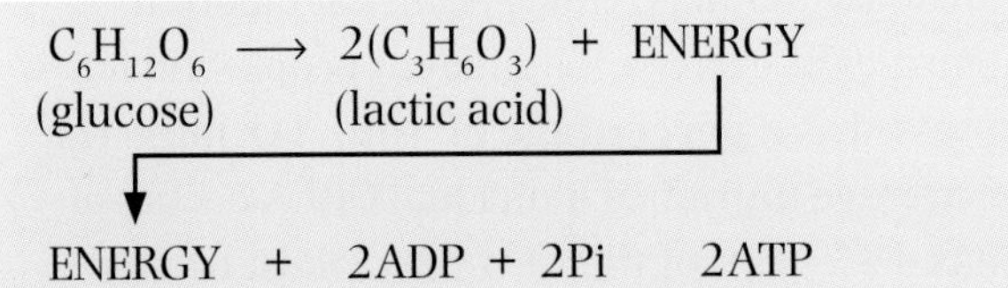

- During aerobic activities such as a 10,000m run the lactic acid system can be called upon to produce an extra burst of energy during the race or indeed at the end of the race during a sprint finish.

Advantages of this system to the athlete

- Because there are few chemical reactions, ATP can be resynthesised relatively quickly for activities or bouts of exercise that last between 10 seconds and 3 minutes.
- It is an anaerobic process and so does not need to wait for the 3 minutes or so for sufficient oxygen to be present.
- Any lactic acid that has accumulated can be converted back into liver glycogen or indeed be used as a metabolic fuel by reconversion into pyruvate and entry into the aerobic system.

Drawbacks of this system to the athlete

- The most obvious drawback of this system is the accumulation of lactic acid which can make glycolytic enzymes acidic. This causes them to lose their catalytic ability, inhibiting energy production through glycolysis. The intensity of the exercise must be reduced or in the worst case scenario stopped so that the body can remove the lactic acid that has accumulated.
- Only a small amount of energy (approximately 5%) locked inside our glycogen molecule can be released in the absence of oxygen. The remaining 95% can only be released in the presence of oxygen.

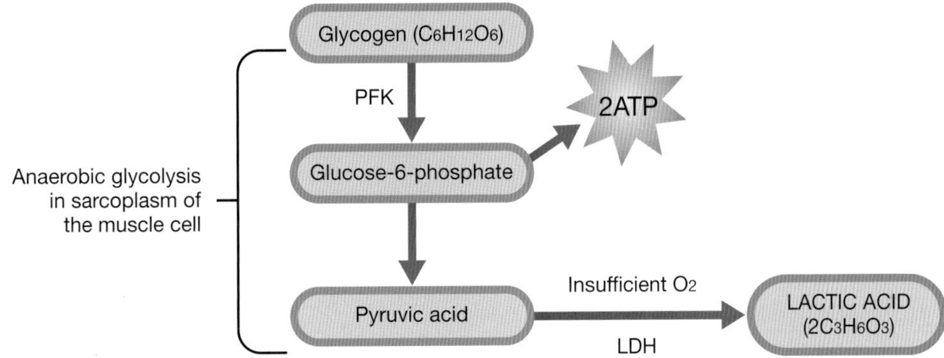

Fig.1.21 A summary of the lactic acid system

TASK 1.12

During a 400m hurdles race the ATP-PCr system will be used during the first 10 seconds or so and then the lactic acid system will provide the energy for ATP resysnthesis for the remainder of the race. Complete the table below with the required information.

	Site of reaction	Fuel used	Active enzyme	Molecules of ATP produced
Lactate anaerobic system				

KEY TERMS

Threshold:
the point where one energy system is exhausted and another takes over as the predominant system, e.g. the LA-O_2 threshold represents the point where sufficient oxygen becomes available to enable the aerobic system to take over as the major energy provider

Glycogen:
the form of carbohydrate stored in the muscles and liver

Glycolysis:
the breakdown of glucose to pyruvic acid

REMEMBER!

The lactic acid system is of particular use to athletes who need to perform high intensity exercise for a period of 1–2 minutes. A 400m runner is an obvious example, as is a squash player during a lengthy rally.

Onset of blood lactate accumulation (OBLA)

A large VO_2max sets the ceiling for endurance performance and is an indication of the size of our aerobic performance engine. However it is the onset of blood lactate accumulation **(OBLA)** that determines the actual percentage of that engine power that can be utilised.

The onset of blood lactate accumulation describes the point at which lactic acid starts to accumulate in the muscles. During normal resting conditions the amount of lactic acid circulating in the blood is between 1 to 2 **millimoles**/litre. This rises dramatically during intense exercise. Quite simply, the more intense the exercise the greater the extent of lactic acid production. The OBLA is said to occur when concentrations of lactic acid in the blood reach 4millimoles/litre.

Just like VO_2max, OBLA occurs at different intensities of exercise for different people and it is expressed as **a percentage of your VO_2max**. For the average untrained individual OBLA occurs at around 55–60% of their VO_2max whilst trained endurance performers can delay OBLA until they have utilised 85–90% of their VO_2max.

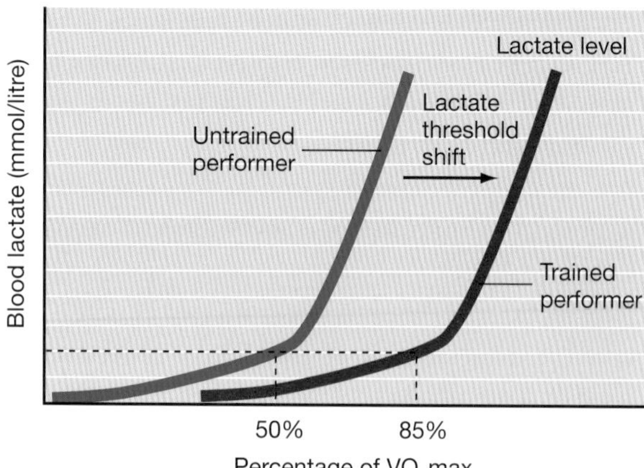

Fig 1.22 A comparison of the point of OBLA between trained and untrained athletes when measured as a percentage of their VO_2max

REMEMBER!

You may have heard of the lactate **threshold** and anaerobic threshold. Together with OBLA these describe the same phenomenon.

KEY TERMS

Onset of blood lactate accumulation (OBLA):
the point at which lactic acid begins to accumulate in the blood. Usually taken when concentrations of lactic acid reach 4mmole/litre of blood

Millimole (mmole):
a unit used to measure the amount of a chemical substance. It is equal to 1/1000 of a mole

APPLY IT!

Lance Armstrong can tap into an exceptionally high percentage of his VO_2max. His OBLA reportedly occurs at 88.6% of his VO_2max.

Lactate sampling and measuring OBLA

OBLA can only truly be measured in a sports science laboratory. The test should be conducted using a mode of exercise most suited to the performer, usually a treadmill, bicycle ergometer, rowing ergometer or swimming bench. Typically the test is conducted in 4–6 stages. During the first stage the exercise intensity is set at about 50% of VO_2max and increases in intensity at the start of each of the subsequent stages. Each stage generally lasts about 5 minutes. At the end of each stage heart rate recorded, oxygen consumption measured and blood samples are taken by a small prick on the finger or earlobe and the concentration of blood lactate is analysed. The point at which blood lactate levels rise to 4mmol/litre of blood usually signals OBLA. The exercise intensity, oxygen consumption and heart rate at this point is now recorded and used to monitor progress and assess exercise intensity during training.

OBLA and training

Improvements in endurance capacity can be observed where lower lactate levels are recorded for any given exercise intensity. This shows that the body has adapted to cope with higher levels of blood lactate and increased the rate of its removal through effective **buffering**. You will recall that untrained individuals usually reach OBLA at about 55–60% of VO_2max. With training this figure can increase to 70% or even higher. Elite endurance athletes such as Lance Armstrong have values approaching 90%. Whist OBLA is a much greater product of training than VO_2max it is still influenced by genetics.

A word on lactic acid

You will recall that lactic acid is produced when there is insufficient oxygen available to sustain a given exercise intensity. The pyruvic acid produced during glycolysis is converted to lactic acid by the enzyme lactate dehydrogenase. Once formed lactic acid quickly dissociates into lactate and hydrogen ions (H+). It is the presence of hydrogen ions that make the muscle acidic and ultimately causes muscle fatigue. The acidic environment slows down enzyme activity and ceases the breakdown of further glycogen. High levels of acidity can also irritate nerve endings which can cause some degree of pain – the 'heavy legs' often associated with lactic acid can thus be blamed on the hydrogen ions.

However lactic acid is not always the bad guy it is made out to be. The heart, the liver, the kidneys and inactive muscles are all locations where lactic acid can be taken up from the blood and either converted back into pyruvate and metabolised in the mitochondria producing energy or converted back to glycogen and glucose in the liver. The table below summarises what happens to the lactic acid once it has been removed from the muscle.

Lactic acid from blood	
Conversion into CO_2 and H_2O	Up to 65%
Conversion into glycogen	Up to 20%
Conversion into protein	Up to 10%
Conversion into glucose	Up to 5%
Conversion into sweat and urine	Up to 5%

Table 1.02 The fate of lactic acid

TASK 1.13

Using the information from table 1.04 plot a graph of blood lactate accumulation (mmol/litre on *y* axis) against running speed (ms^{-1} on *x* axis).

1. On your graph show the point of OBLA. Give a brief explanation as to why you have chosen this point on the graph.
2. At what running speed did OBLA occur?

Blood lactate (mmol/litre)	2.9	3.7	5.7	9.1
Running speed ms^{-1}	3.5	4.00	4.5	4.9

Factors influencing the rate of lactic acid accumulation

- **Exercise intensity:** the higher the exercise intensity the greater the ATP demand which can only be sustained using glycogen as a fuel. As fast twitch fibres possess greater stores of glycogen (and therefore lactate dehydrogenase) pyruvate is soon converted to lactic acid.
- **The respiratory exchange ratio (RER):**

$$\frac{VCO_2 \text{ expired/min}}{VO_2 \text{ uptake/min}}$$

The closer the value is to 1.0 the more likely the body is using glycogen as a fuel and the greater the chance of lactic acid accumultation. If the value is nearer 0.7 then fatty acids is the likely fuel. This is also known as the respiratory quotient.

- **Muscle fibre type:** Slow twitch fibres produce less lactate at a given workload than fast twitch fibres. As slow twitch muscle fibres possess greater amounts of mitochondria, pyruvate will tend to converted into Acetyl Co A and move into the mitochondria with little lactate production.
- **Rate of blood lactate removal:** If the rate of lactate removal equals the rate of production then blood lactate concentrations should remain constant. When the rate of lactate production exceeds the rate of removal then blood lactate will accumulate as we reach OBLA.
- **The trained status of the working muscles:** If muscles are trained then they benefit from the associated **adaptive responses**. These include improved capacity for aerobic respiration due to higher mitochondrial and capillary density, improved use of fatty acids as a fuel (which do not produce lactic acid!) and increased stores of myoglobin.

TASK 1.14

The graph below provides data gained from an OBLA test on a middle distance runner.

1. Use the graph to calculate OBLA of the runner given she has a VO_2max of 61ml/kg/min.
2. If her HRmax is 182bpm at what percentage of HRmax does OBLA occur?

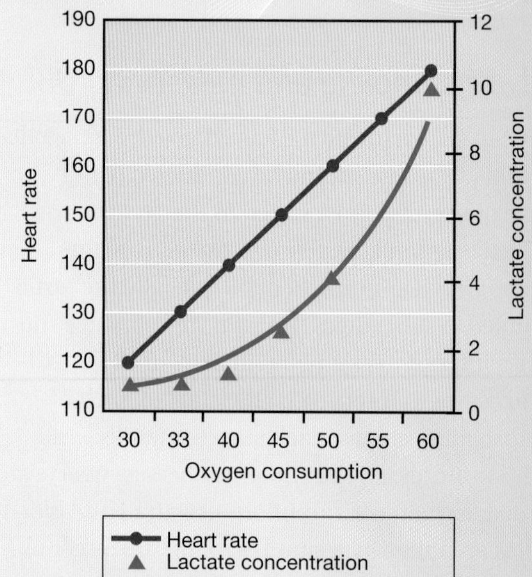

Fig 1.23 The relationship of oxygen consumption to heart rate and lactate concentration of a middle-distance runner during a maximal test to exhaustion

APPLY IT!

A cyclist during a time trial can use data from the OBLA test to determine her racing heart rate by calculating the percentage of HRmax that leads to OBLA. If she had a HRmax of 182bpm and OBLA occurred at a HR of 158bpm this equates to about 87 per cent of HRmax. Her racing heart rate should be somewhere just below this point.

KEY TERMS

Buffering:
a process which helps in the removal of lactic acid and maintains blood and muscle pH (acidity)

Adaptive responses:
the anatomical and physiological changes that occur to the body as a consequence of training

EXAM TIPS:

1. Although lactic acid and lactate are often used interchangeably, they are not in fact the same thing.
2. The following equation can be used to calculate the percentage of VO_2max used by a performer:

$$\frac{VO_2 \text{ (amount of } O_2 \text{ used)}}{VO_2max \text{ (max potential)}}$$

ATHLETE PROFILE

Becky Wing is currently studying AS PE at Sixth Form College in Farnborough, Hampshire. At the age of 16, Becky is already an Olympian. She was a member of the Great Britain Gymnastics team in the Beijing Olympics finishing in 9th place in the team event. She is currently preparing for the 2012 London Olympics.

Becky has access to three personal coaches at her Heathrow Gymnastics Club and two National gymnastic coaches. She trains between 4 to 6 hours, 6 days per week. Each session will consist of a half-hour warm up and up to 1 hour of conditioning work. The conditioning work mainly focuses on the development of explosive strength and muscular endurance, the two key components of fitness required by gymnasts. Her explosive strength training which consists of plyometrics type activity will help develop and improve the efficiency of her ATP-PC system whilst the muscular endurance training will seek to enhance the removal of lactic acid extending the time that she can use the lactate anaerobic system before fatigue sets in. This will of course be essential during a floor routine which consists of approximately 90 seconds of very high intensity activity.

ExamCafé

Relax, refresh, result!

Refresh your memory

Revision checklist

Make sure you know the following:

- Energy is the capacity to perform work.
- Energy is measured in calories (kcal) or joules (J). 1 calorie = 4.184 joules.
- The food fuels: fats, carbohydrates and proteins are the major energy sources in the body.
- Food fuels however are only a secondary source of energy – the energy stored within them must first be converted and stored as adenosine triphosphate (ATP) before it can be accessed.
- ATP is the energy currency of all cells and is the only direct source of energy in the body.
- When energy is required ATP is broken down by the enzyme ATPase to release energy plus ADP (adenosine diphosphate) and an inorganic phosphate (Pi) ATP ⟶ ADP + Pi + Energy.
- This reaction is exothermic which means that energy is released in the form of heat.
- There is only sufficient ATP stored within the muscles to perform high intensity exercise for 2 or 3 seconds.
- Once ATP has been broken down to release energy it must be constantly recycled.
- There are three energy systems that provide the energy for ATP resynthesis.
- The source of energy for ATP resynthesis is dependent upon primarily the intensity and then the duration of the activity.
- During low intensity exercise of longer duration the aerobic (oxidative) energy system is used for ATP resynthesis.
- During medium–high intensity exercise the lactic acid system is used for ATP resynthesis.
- During short periods of maximum exercise intensity the ATP-PC (alactic) energy system is used for ATP resynthesis.

Aerobic energy systems

- The aerobic system uses a combination of fats and carbohydrates to provide the energy for ATP resynthesis.
- The aerobic system is the most efficient energy system yielding 18 times more energy than anaerobic processes.
- The site for aerobic respiration are the mitochondria which are the powerhouses of the muscle cells.
- The Krebs cycle takes place in the matrix of the mitochondria and produces carbon dioxide and sufficient energy to recycle 2 moles of ATP.
- The electron transport system is the final stage of the aerobic system which produces water and enough energy to resynthesise 34 moles of ATP.
- Enzymes used in the aerobic system include phosphofructokinase (PFK), glycogen phophorylase (GP) and lipase.
- As the duration of the exercise period increases fatty acids become the preferred fuel as more energy can be elicited from one mole of fatty acids than from one mole of glycogen.
- The complete breakdown of one mole of glycogen can be summarised as follows:

  $C_6H_{12}O_6 + 6O_2 \longrightarrow 6CO_2 + 6H_2O + \text{Energy}$

  $\text{Energy} + 38\text{ADP} + 38\text{Pi} \longrightarrow 38\text{ATP}$
- Recovery is concerned with returning the body to its pre-exercise state.
- Recovery can only occur via the aerobic system and only then when there is sufficient oxygen available.
- The oxygen deficit is the volume of oxygen required to complete an activity entirely aerobically.
- Excess post-exercise oxygen consumption (EPOC) is the volume of oxygen consumed during recovery above that which normally would have been consumed at rest during the same period of time.
- There are two stages to EPOC: the fast and slow stages.
- The fast stage of EPOC occurs rapidly, taking just 2–3 minutes. The oxygen consumed during this stage is used to replenish ATP and PC stores and to re-saturate myoglobin.
- The slow stage of EPOC takes up to 1 hour. The oxygen consumed during this stage is used to remove lactic acid and provide the energy to maintain elevated heart and respiratory rates.
- A low VO_2max score can limit performance in endurance activities.
- Factors that can limit VO_2max include: genetics, physiological make-up, lifestyle choices, age, sex, and the volume of training undertaken.

Anaerobic energy systems

- The ATP-PC system is the first of the anaerobic energy systems and used in those activities that are of the highest intensity but short in duration, lasting between 3 and 10 seconds – such as a 100m sprint.
- The fuel for resynthesis in the ATP-PC system is phosphocreatine, a high energy compound found in all muscle cells.
- Enzymes used in the ATP-PC system include creatine kinase which breaks down PC.
- The ATP-PC system involves a coupled reaction which occurs when the product of one reaction is used in a second reaction.
- The ATP-PC system can be summarised as follows:

  $PC \longrightarrow Pi + C + \text{Energy}; \text{Energy} + ADP + Pi \longrightarrow ATP$

- The main drawback of the ATP-PC system is that there is only a limited supply of PC in the muscle cell which is exhausted after approximately 10 seconds.
- The lactate anaerobic or lactic acid system is predominant in activities of moderate to high intensity that are of 1–3 minutes' duration – such as a 400m run.
- The lactate anaerobic system involves the process of glycolysis, which relates to the breakdown of glycogen and glucose.
- Under the lactate anaerobic system, energy resulting from the breakdown of glycogen into pyruvate is sufficient to recycle 2 moles of ATP.
- Enzymes involved in glycolysis include phosphofructokinase (PFK) and glycogen phosphorylase (GP).
- In the absence of oxygen pyruvate is converted into lactic acid by the enzyme lactate dehydrogenase.
- Any lactic acid produced during exercise can be converted back into liver glycogen or used as a metabolic fuel by reconversion into pyruvate and entry into the aerobic system.
- The lactate anaerobic system can be summarised as follows:

  $C_6H_{12}O_6 \longrightarrow 2C_3H_6O_3 + \text{Energy}; \text{Energy} + 2ADP + 2Pi \longrightarrow 2ATP$

- Drawbacks of the lactate anaerobic system include the fatiguing effect of lactic acid on the muscles, and the fact that only a tiny amount (5%) of the energy stored within the glucose molecule can be accessed to provide energy for ATP resynthesis.
- The onset of blood lactate accumulation (OBLA) is the point at which lactic acid begins to accumulate in the blood.
- OBLA is usually said to have occurred when concentrations of lactic acid reach 4mmol/litre of blood.
- OBLA can be expressed as a percentage of VO_2max. Trained performers can achieve a higher percentage of their VO_2max than the untrained. Training therefore delays OBLA.
- The rate of lactate accumulation is dependent upon exercise intensity, muscle fibre type, the trained status of the working muscles and the rate of blood lactate removal.
- Buffering is a process which helps in the removal of lactic acid and maintains blood and muscle pH at acceptable levels.
- The removal of lactic acid occurs in a number of different ways: up to 65% is converted into carbon dioxide and water; up to 20% is converted back into muscle and liver glycogen; up to 10% is converted into protein, up to 5% is converted into blood glucose; up to 5% is removed as sweat and urine.

Revise as you go

1. Write out an equation which summarises each of the three energy systems.
2. Explain the specialist role of the mitochondria in the production of energy.
3. Draw a diagrammatic representation of each of the three energy systems.
4. Compare the three energy pathways with regard to their relative efficiency.
5. Explain the energy continuum in relation to a games player of your choice. Use specific examples from the game when each energy system is likely to be in use.
6. Explain what happens when a marathon runner 'hits the wall'.
7. What nutritional advice would you give a marathon runner preparing for a major competition in the coming week?
8. Construct a food fuel graph which illustrates the predominant food fuel against time during a triathlon.
9. Why might performers take creatine supplements? What type of performer is likely to benefit from creatine supplementation?
10. Outline some methods of training you would use to develop and improve your ATP-PC system. For one of these methods give an example of a training session.
11. Define VO_2max.
12. Suggest typical VO_2max values for the following:
    a) a healthy male 'A' level PE student
    b) a centre in netball
    c) an Olympic rower.
13. The multi-stage fitness test or 'bleep test is often used to determine the VO_2max of an athlete. Briefly outline this test and give reasons why this may not be the most accurate test to use.
14. Identify and explain the procedures of a more valid test that may be used.
15. Outline the factors that could limit VO_2max.
16. Suggest a method to improve VO_2max.
17. Explain why the VO_2max of women is typically 15–20 per cent lower than that of men from the same activity group.
18. Define the following terms:
    - recovery
    - oxygen deficit
    - EPOC
19. How long does it take the fast component of EPOC to recover?
20. How is lactic acid removed from the muscle following a 400m run? What organs and tissues are involved in the removal of lactate?
21. Explain the terms 'active recovery' and 'rest recovery'. How do these different types of recovery influence the speed of lactate removal?

22. Explain the replenishment of muscle glycogen stores with reference to:
    - the type of exercise performed
    - the post-event meal.
23. Outline the recovery patterns for the following performers:
    - a gymnast performing a vault
    - an 'iron-man' triathlete
    - a 200m butterfly swimmer.
24. Swimmers are often required to compete in several events during a swimming gala. What advice would you give a swimmer concerning recovery between events?
25. Briefly explain why EPOC is often larger than the oxygen deficit.
26. How can knowledge of the recovery process be of use to the coach and athlete when designing training programmes?
27. Explain what you understand by the term 'OBLA'.
28. OBLA and lactate threshold are often used interchangeably. How is the lactate threshold related to VO_2max?
29. At what point does OBLA typically occur? What might cause an athlete to reach OBLA?
30. Andrew Johns represents Great Britain in Triathlon. Explain how knowledge of blood lactate levels during a triathlon might assist his performance.
31. Briefly outline the factors that affect the rate of lactate accumulation.
32. Explain what you understand by the term 'buffering'. How does the body buffer lactic acid?
33. What happens to lactic acid once it has been produced in the body?

CHAPTER 2

The physiology of skeletal muscle

LEARNING OBJECTIVES:

By the end of this chapter you should be able to:

- *explain the basic structure of skeletal muscle*
- *distinguish between the different muscle fibre types in the body and explain how each can be of benefit to specific performers*
- *give a definition of a motor unit and explain its role in muscle contraction*
- *explain the term 'spatial summation' in relation to muscle contraction and apply it to sports performance*
- *explain the contraction of skeletal muscle using the sliding filament hypothesis*
- *state the adaptive responses expected of the muscle following a period of resistance training.*

Introduction

The coach and athlete must have a sound understanding of the muscular system in order to devise training programmes which lead to improved performance. From your study of AS PE you will recall that you considered the role of the muscles when performing a range of sporting movements.

The purpose of this chapter, however, is to discuss both the structure and function of skeletal muscle, detailing how knowledge at this microscopic level can be applied in order to enhance the effectiveness of training.

The structure of skeletal muscle

When viewed at molecular level you will see that a muscle is composed of many different structures. The **muscle belly** is wrapped in a thick connective tissue that allows for movement of the muscles and carries nerves and blood vessels, called the **epimysium**. Another connective tissue, the **perimysium**, surrounds bundles of muscle fibres named **fasciculi**. Finally the **endomysium** surrounds each individual muscle fibre. Together the epimysium, perimysium and endomysium extend to form **tendons** which attach the muscle to the bones of the body.

KEY TERMS

Fasciculi:
bundles of muscle fibres that make up the muscle belly

Muscle belly:
the whole muscle composed of many individual muscle fibres

Epimysium, perimysium, endomysium:
connective tissue that surrounds the muscle belly, fasciculi and muscle fibres respectively

Actin:
the thin protein filament found in muscle cells that together with myosin form sarcomeres, the contractile units of skeletal muscle

Myosin:
the thick protein filament that together with actin form sarcomeres, the contractile units of skeletal muscle

Sarcomere:
the contractile units of skeletal muscle. They are composed of two myofilaments, actin and myosin

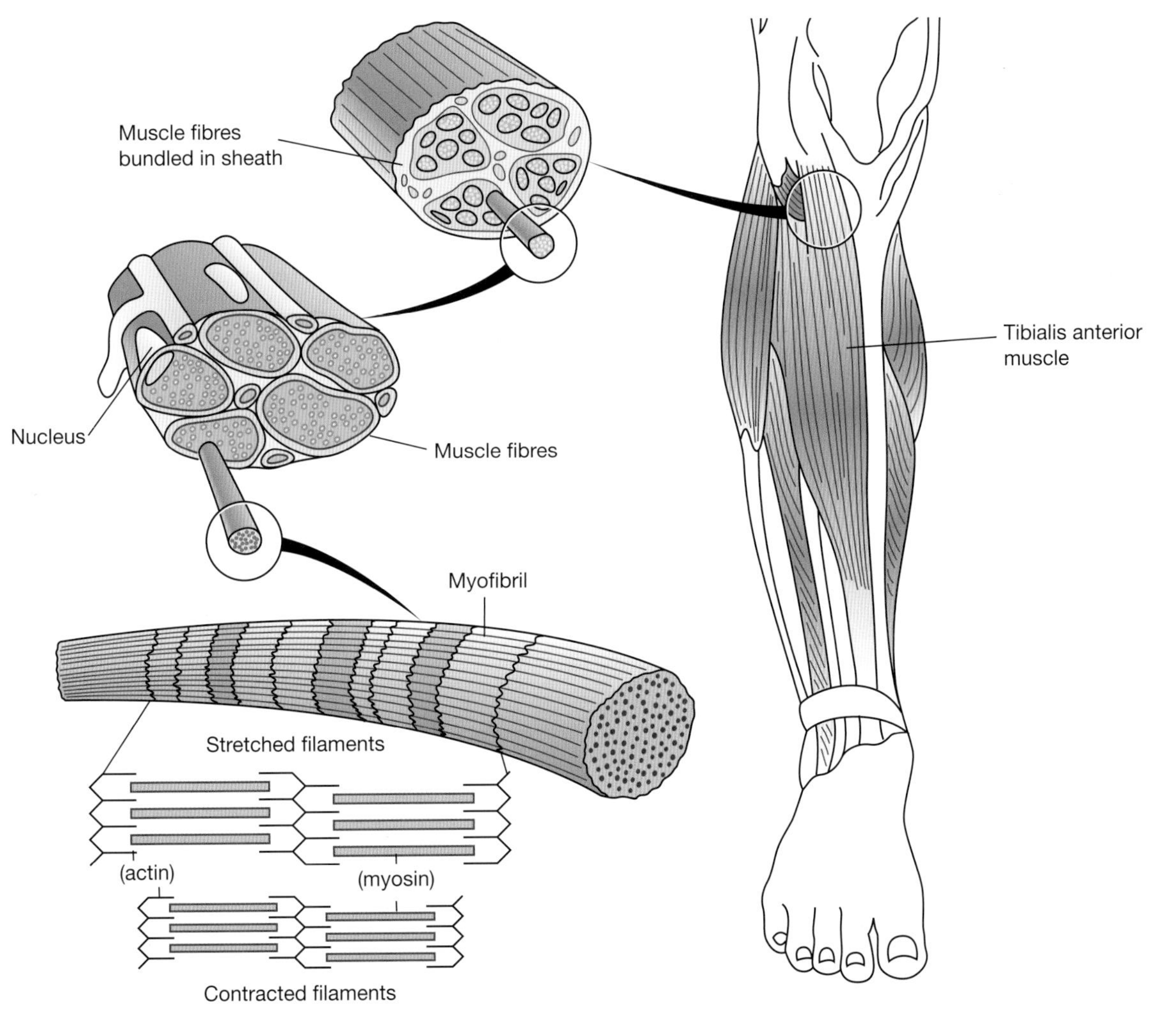

Fig 2.01 The structure of skeletal muscle

Upon closer inspection it can be seen that individual muscle fibres are made up of hundreds of smaller elements called **myofibrils**. These myofibrils contain the proteins responsible for muscle contraction, **actin** and **myosin**, together with the components necessary for energy production and the control of movement: mitochondria, glycogen and fat deposits and muscle spindles.

The sliding filament theory of muscle contraction

The sliding filament theory explains the sequence of events leading up to skeletal muscle contraction. This process can be explained by the complex co-operation of the two proteins that make up all skeletal muscle cells. These two proteins are called actin and myosin. Actin and myosin together form **sarcomeres**, which are the contractile units of the myofibril and are joined end to end along the length of the myofibril. During muscle contraction the thin actin filaments slide inwards over the thicker myosin filaments causing a shortening of each sarcomere along the entire length of the myofibril. This causes shortening of each muscle fibre and therefore the characteristic shortening of the entire muscle during muscle contraction.

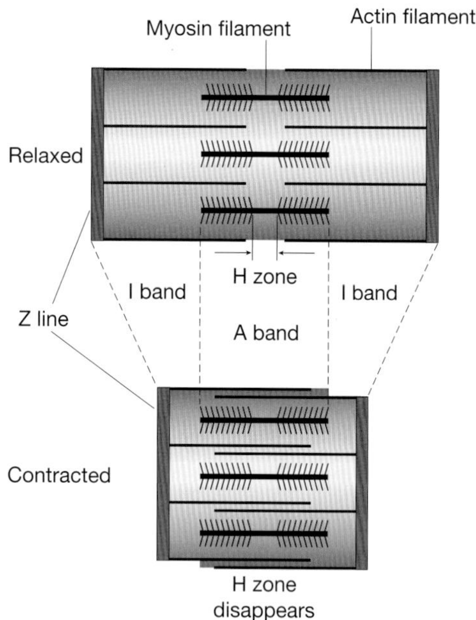

Fig 2.02 A sarcomere during relaxed and contracted states

Figure 2.02 illustrates a sarcomere during a relaxed and a contracted state. Note that the Z lines mark the boundary of each sarcomere; the dark A band identifies where both actin and myosin exist; the light I band identifies that part of the sarcomere where only actin exists; the H zone consists of myosin only – note that the H zone disappears in the sarcomere's contracted state .

The sequence of events of the sliding filament theory

It is important to note that at rest the protein **tropomyosin** on the thin filament blocks access to the myosin binding site.

- **Step 1 Preparing the binding site**
  Upon receiving an action potential (the signal to contract) the sarcoplasmic reticulum (a specialist layer of cells that surround each myofibril) releases calcium ions (Ca^{++}).

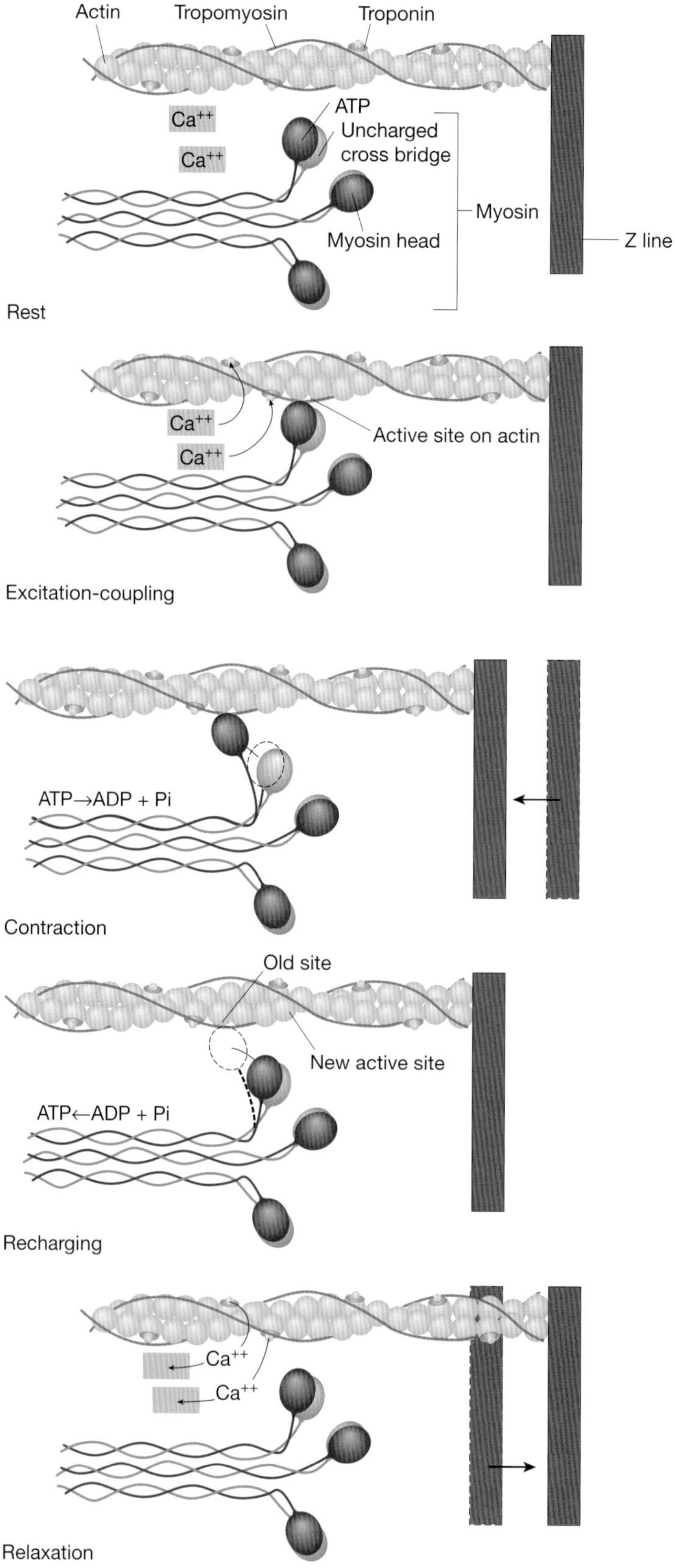

Fig 2.03 The coupling of actin and myosin and the power stroke

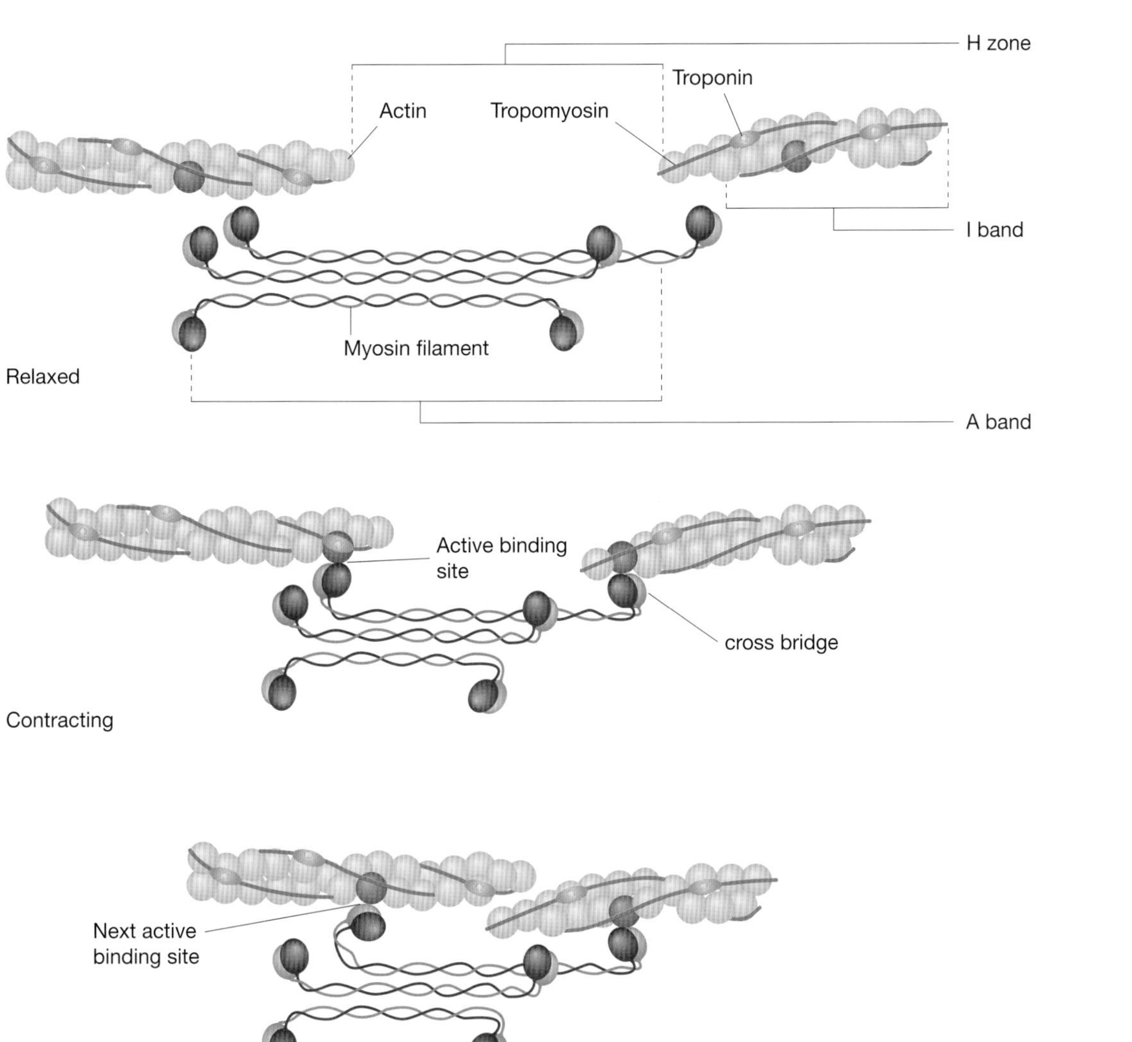

Fig 2.04 Stages of the sliding filament mechanism of muscular contraction

The influx of calcium binds to a second protein on the actin filament called **troponin** which pulls tropomyosin out of the way exposing the myosin binding sites on the actin filament.

- **Step 2 The power stroke**
  The myosin filament extends a golf-club shaped 'cross-bridge' which attaches to the binding site of the thin actin filament. When it binds the myosin head is in an energised state and pulls on the actin filament pulling it inwards towards the centre of the sarcomere. This is referred to as the **power stroke**.
- **Step 3 The binding of ATP**
  In chapter 1 you learned that ATP provides the energy for all processes in the body. In order to re-energise the myosin head ATP is required. Therefore to expose the ATP binding site the myosin filament uncouples from the actin filament allowing ATP to bind on to it causing the myosin head to return to its high-energy state.

- **Step 4 The ratchet mechanism**
  Assuming sufficient calcium is available Step 2 can now be repeated. In fact, the power stroke pulling actin filaments past the myosin filaments will continue in a ratchet-like manner (which involves the sequential coupling and uncoupling of myosin and actin) until each sarcomere shortens and the H zone disappears.
- **Step 5 The return of calcium ions back into the sarcoplasmic reticulum**
  Once the action potential has diminished, all the calcium ions responsible for revealing the myosin binding site on the actin filament will be returned into the sarcoplasmic reticulum. The shape of troponin will once again be changed allowing tropomyosin to return to its protective position of covering the **myosin cross bridge** binding site. Tropomyosin will remain in this position as long as the muscle is relaxed.

KEY TERMS

Tropomyosin:
threadlike spirals that wrap around the actin filament which covers the myosin binding site which prevents myosin attachment during the relaxed state

Troponin:
a calcium receptor that sits on top of troponin. In the presence of calcium it pulls tropomyosin away from the myosin binding site and allows myosin to bind to the actin filament and the sliding filament mechanism to commence

Myosin cross bridge:
the arm and head of the myosin filament which extends to bind on to the actin filament

Sarcoplasmic reticulum:
a system of membranous sacs that surround the myofibrils. The sarcoplasmic reticulum stores calcium and regulates its release during muscular contraction

TASK 2.01

Copy out and complete the table below stating the functions of each of the named elements during the sliding filament theory.

Element	Function during the sliding filament theory
Tropomyosin	
Troponin	
Myosin cross bridge	
Calcium ions	
ATP	
Sarcoplasmic reticulum	

Types of muscle fibre

Skeletal muscle fibres are not all uniform, in fact they can differ in both structure and function. A single muscle such as the bicep brachi will be composed of two principal types of muscle fibres: **slow twitch (type 1)** and **fast twitch (type 2)**. Slow twitch fibres contract more slowly but are highly resistant to fatigue and are therefore favoured by endurance athletes, whilst fast twitch fibres can contract more rapidly, generating greater forces but are more liable to fatigue. These fibres are more prevalent in sprinters and power athletes. Fast twitch fibres have been further classified into **type a** and **type b**. Type 2a fibres, also known as **fast oxidative glycolytic fibres (FOG)** are more resistant to fatigue than type 2b fibres which have a greater anaerobic capacity and are termed **fast twitch glycolytic fibres (FTG)**.

Table 2.01 summarises the main structural and functional characteristics of each of the three types of muscle fibres.

KEY TERMS

Slow twitch muscle fibre:
a type of muscle fibre that uses oxygen to produce energy (high oxidative capacity). They are associated with endurance-based activities

Fast twitch muscle fibre:
a type of muscle fibre that has a high glycolytic capacity (anaerobic). They are associated with speed and power-based activities

REMEMBER!

An average muscle will typically be composed of approximately 50% slow twitch fibres 25% fast twitch (a) fibres with the remaining 25% fast twitch (b) fibres.

	Slow twitch (type 1)	Fast oxidative glycolytic (FOG) (type 2a)	Fast twitch glycolytic (FTG) (type 2b)
Functional characteristic			
Speed of contraction (ms)	Slow (110)	Fast (50)	Fast (50)
Force of contraction	Low	High	Highest
Resistance to fatigue	Very high	Moderate	Low
Aerobic capacity	Very high	Moderate	Low
Anaerobic capacity	Low	High	High
Structural characteristic			
Fibre size	Small	Large	Large
Mitochondrial density	High	Moderate	Low
Capillary density	High	Moderate	Low
Myoglobin content	High	Moderate	Low
PC store	Low	High	High
Glycogen store	Low	High	High
Triglyceride store	High	Moderate	Low
Motor neuron size	Small	Large	Large
Activity suited	Marathon	1500m	Shot put

Table 2.01 Structural and functional characteristics of slow and fast twitch muscle fibres

Fig 2.05 A weightlifter will possess a high percentage of fast twitch glycolytic fibres

Fig. 2.06 An endurance athlete will possess a high number of slow twitch muscle fibres

TASK 2.02

Draw up a continuum like the one shown below. Now collect as many sporting pictures from magazines, newspapers or downloaded from the internet as you can and place them along the continuum according to the fibre type predominantly used by the selected performer.

Type 1 —————— Type 2a —————— Type 2b

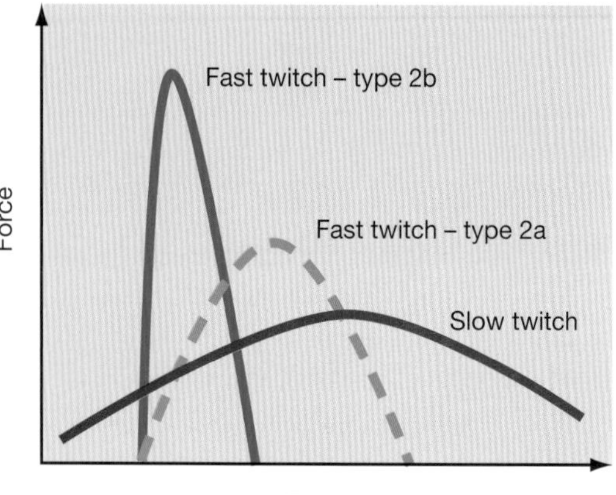

Note that although fast twitch fibres can generate much greater forces than slow twitch fibres, they have a higher fatigue index meaning contraction time is shorter.

Fig 2.07 Muscle fibre contractile response

TASK 2.03

Use Figure 2.08 to help explain the relationship between VO_2max and per cent distribution of slow twitch muscle fibres in both athletes and non-athletes.

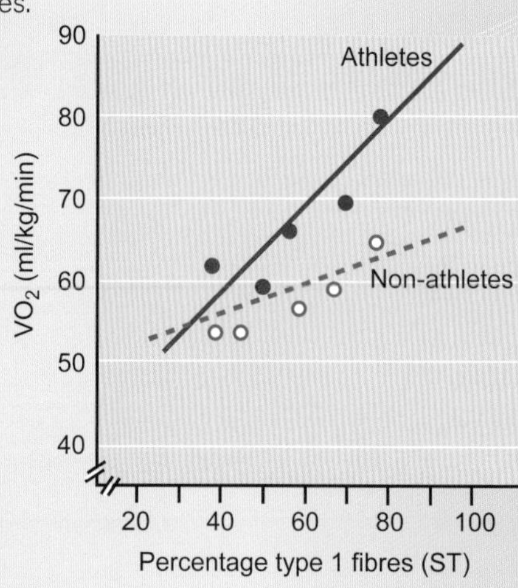

Fig 2.08 The relationship between aerobic capacity and per cent distribution of slow twitch fibres of trained athletes and non-athletes

REMEMBER!

There are many differences between the distribution of fibres between different muscles of the same person and between different people. In humans virtually all muscles are a mixture of all three fibre types.

TASK 2.04

Using Figure 2.09 explain the distributions of fibre types for each of the 'populations' identified.

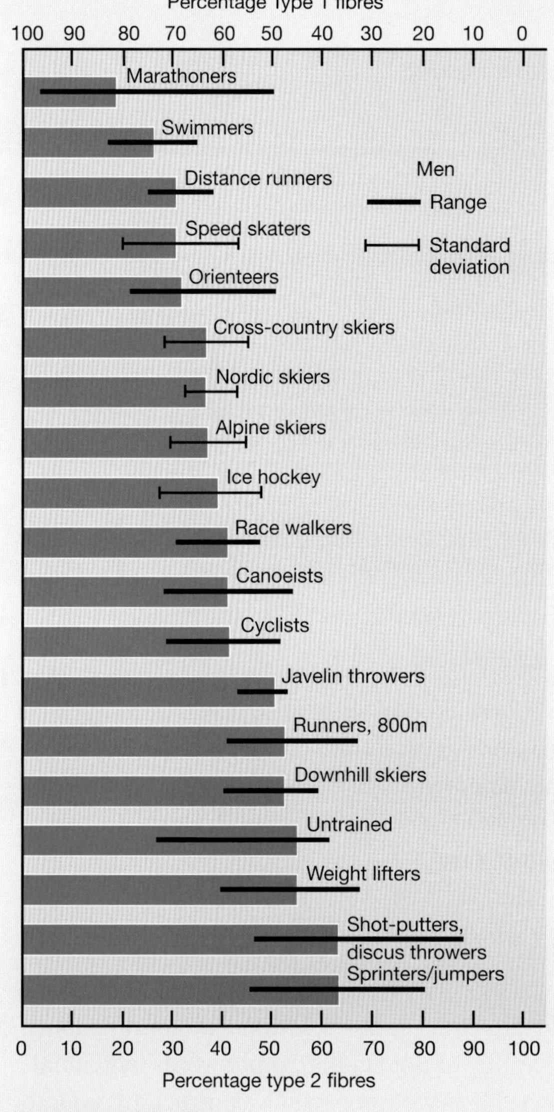

Table A Men (fibre types)

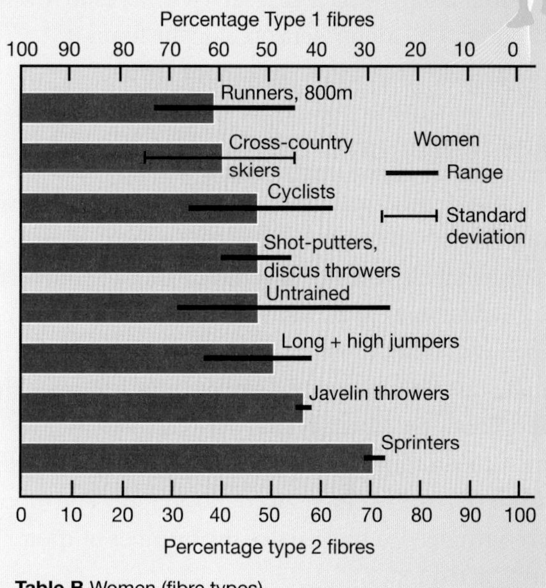

Table B Women (fibre types)

Fig 2.09 Distribution of muscle fibre types expressed as a percentage of total muscle for different human 'populations'.

STRETCH AND CHALLENGE

In your group discuss the role of genetics in the determination of muscle fibre distribution. Can muscle fibre distribution predict success in certain sporting activities?

Muscle fibre recruitment

The primary function of skeletal muscle is to contract and facilitate movement of the body. Muscle contraction involves the interaction of the muscles with the nervous system. Individual muscles such as the anterior deltoid are connected to the nervous system via a group of motor neurons. Each muscle fibre within the muscle belly is supplied by only one motor neuron, however this neuron can innervate (stimulate) anything from just a few fibres to several hundred. The motor neuron plus the fibres it innervates is known as the **motor unit**.

The motor unit

The motor unit is the basic functional unit of skeletal muscle. Stimulation of one motor neuron causes all the muscle fibres in that motor unit to contract simultaneously. Each individual muscle will be made up of a number of motor units (just like a school is made up of a number of form or tutor groups). The number of motor units that are recruited at any one time in the muscle varies with the amount of strength required for a given movement. The more strength needed the greater the number of motor units activated.

The number of fibres within a particular motor unit is dependent upon the control of movement required in that muscle. A small muscle that is required to perform fine motor control such as those that enable the eye to focus may only have one fibre per motor neuron; whereas large muscles responsible for gross movements such as the quadriceps group when kicking a ball may be innervated by a motor neuron supplying 500 or more fibres.

Motor units are usually made up of the same type of muscle fibre. Consequently we see both fast and slow twitch motor units in a muscle. Fast twitch motor units are generally recruited during high intensity activity such as sprinting or throwing the javelin whilst slow twitch motor units are used during lower intensity exercise such as running a half marathon or cross country skiing.

REMEMBER!

More motor units will be recruited when performing a bicep curl against a load of 10kg than of 5kg.

KEY TERMS

Motor unit:
the motor nerve and the group of muscle fibres that it controls

All or none law:
if a motor impulse is of sufficient intensity, the motor unit is stimulated and all the muscle fibres within it will contract to their maximum possible extent

REMEMBER!

Motor units are usually made up of the same type of muscle fibre. Consequently we see both fast and slow twitch motor units in the body. Fast twitch motor units are generally recruited during high intensity activity such as sprinting or throwing the javelin while slow twitch motor units are used during lower intensity exercise such as running a half marathon or cross country skiing.

Innervation

The innervation of skeletal muscle is accomplished by a motor neuron transmitting a nerve impulse or action potential to the muscle fibre. Just how the muscle fibre responds is governed by the **'all or none law'**.

The all or none law

The all or none principle essentially states that individual muscle fibres within a motor unit contract either fully or not at all. In other words individual muscle fibres cannot partially contract! In order to activate these muscle fibres however a minimum amount of stimulation is needed (termed the threshold). If the stimulation equals or exceeds the threshold all the fibres within the motor unit will contract at the same time and to their maximum possible extent. If the stimulus falls short of the threshold, however, the muscle fibres do not respond and muscular contraction fails to occur.

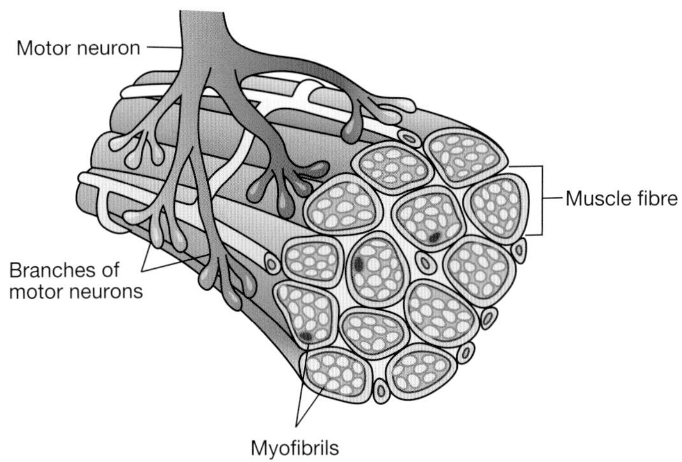

Fig 2.10 A motor unit of skeletal muscle

REMEMBER!

When kicking a conversion in rugby, the quadriceps muscle group will need to recruit more motor units depending on the kicker's distance from the posts.

Spatial summation

For a muscle to contract the excitatory postsynaptic potential (EPSP) must be of a certain level of intensity to initiate the sliding filament mechanism of muscle contraction.

Spatial summation describes the progressive increase in size of the **excitatory postsynaptic potential (EPSP)** as a result of the arrival of a number of impulses at the synaptic cleft of individual muscle fibres.

KEY TERMS

Spatial summation:
an increase in responsiveness of a nerve resulting from the additive effect of numerous stimuli. A certain level of intensity is needed before a muscle fibre responds by contracting

Acetylcholine (ACh):
a chemical substance that allows the transmission of an impulse across the synaptic cleft and enables a muscle fibre to contract

Excitatory postsynaptic potential (EPSP):
an increase in the electrical potential of a motor neuron that allows a muscle fibre to contact

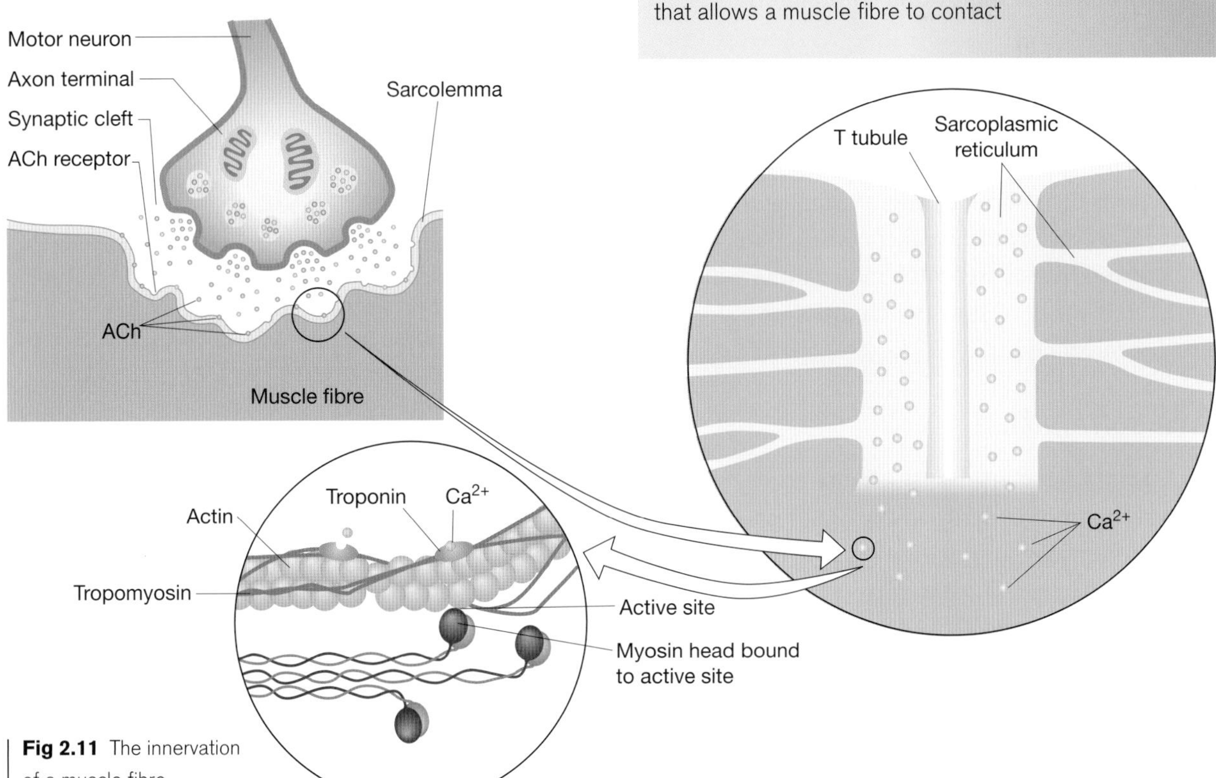

Fig 2.11 The innervation of a muscle fibre

On arrival at the neuromuscular junction the transmitter substance **acetylcholine** is released which enables the impulse to cross the synaptic cleft and create electrical potentials (EPSPs) in the muscle fibre (the potential to contract). However, if the EPSP is not of sufficient intensity the muscle fibre will not contract, consequently the additive effect of a number of stimuli arriving can be used which ensures that the excitatory threshold is reached and the muscle fibres contract – all or nothing!

Variations in the strength of the muscle response

Sporting performance requires variations in strength or muscular force from very weak efforts such as a short putt in golf to all out maximal efforts such as a shot put. How then does the body cope with these different requirements?

The strength of a muscle can be graded in several ways:

- multiple unit summation
- wave summation
- synchronicity of motor unit stimulation.

Multiple unit summation

The strength of a muscle contraction can be increased by recruiting more motor units. Maximal contractions will recruit all motor units within a particular muscle whilst weaker contractions will recruit fewer units. Fast twitch motor units will be recruited ahead of slow twitch units for more powerful contractions.

Wave summation

Wave summation considers the **frequency** with which impulses arrive at the motor unit. Typically the motor unit will respond to an impulse (innervation) by giving a **twitch** – a very short period of contraction followed by relaxation. If a second impulse arrives at the motor unit before it has had time to completely relax from the first twitch the motor unit responds with a stronger contractions since the effect of the second stimulus is added to the first. They summate creating greater tension within the motor unit. When a motor unit is stimulated many times in quick succession there is little or no time for relaxation. This produces the highest level of sustained tension referred to as **tetanus** or **tetanic contraction** and will continue until fatigue ensues. This is illustrated in Figure 2.12.

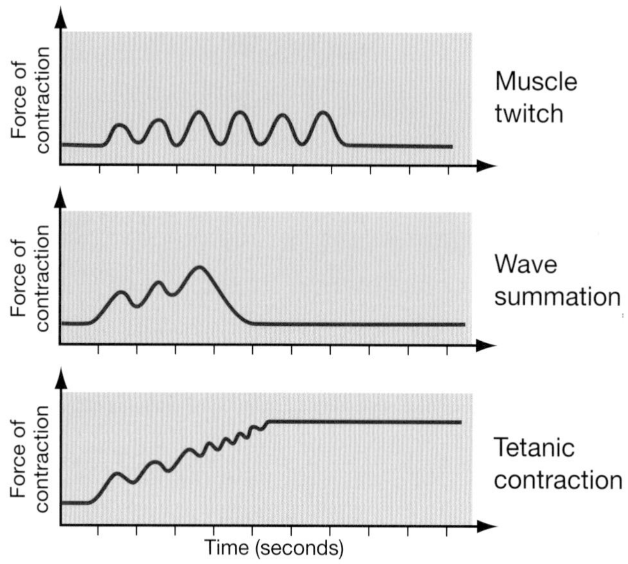

Fig 2.12 Varying the strength of muscular contraction by wave summation

TASK 2.05

1. Draw a diagram to illustrate the following passage. You should not use any words in the diagram.
   'The motor unit will respond to a stimulus by giving a 'twitch'*: a brief period of contraction followed by relaxation. When a second impulse is applied to the motor unit before it completely relaxes from the previous stimulus, the sum of both stimuli occurs, increasing the total contraction. Sometimes rapid firing of stimuli occurs giving motor units little or no time for relaxation this increases total contraction further …'*
2. Now, without looking at the passage, explain your diagram to a friend. How closely did your explanation match the passage? If it was fairly close, this is a good indication that you understand this topic! Well done!

Neuromuscular adaptations to resistance training

It is of course possible to optimise the efficiency and effectiveness of muscle contraction through participation in a well-planned strength training programme.

Resistance training will signal some long term physiological responses to the **neuromuscular system**.

- **Recruitment of more motor units** – More motor units may be trained to act synchronously (together) so that greater forces can be generated therefore resulting in greater strength gains.
- **Muscle hypertrophy** – The size of the muscle belly will increase due to an increase in the size of individual muscle fibres (hypertrophy) and the possible splitting of fibres (hyperplasia).
- **Hypertrophy of fast twitch muscle fibres** – As fast twitch fibres are predominantly recruited during resistance training, these fibres in particular will enlarge.
- **Hyperplasia of fast twitch muscle fibres** – There is some evidence to suggest that muscle fibres split, particularly with heavy resistance training. This splitting will contribute to the general hypertrophy of the muscle.
- **Conversion of type 2b fibres to type 2a fibres** – Some studies have shown that the percentage of type 2b fibres within a trained muscle actually decrease in favour of type 2a fibres. This could account for the delay in muscular fatigue associated with prolonged training.

KEY TERMS

Neuromuscular system:
the interaction of the nervous system with the muscular system

Muscle hypertrophy:
a term used to describe the enlargement of individual muscle fibres or the whole muscle belly associated with resistance training

Hyperplasia:
the splitting of individual muscle fibres to create new fibres

ATHLETE PROFILE

Amy Woods competes at senior level for Great Britain in aerobic gymnastics, competing out of Heathrow Aerobic Gymnastic Club. She is currently studying AS PE at Sixth Form College in Farnborough, Hampshire. Amy's fitness training and conditioning largely consists of circuit training, weight training and plyometrics training although some continuous training is undertaken at various times throughout the year. The key components of fitness required by an aerobic gymnast are elastic strength, power and muscular endurance. Amy's training is therefore designed to maximise the physiological adaptations of the muscles. Including particularly, the recruitment and hypertrophy of fast twitch muscle fibres – type 2a (fast oxidative glycolytic) through circuit and weight training and type 2b (fast twitch glycolytic) through plyometric and weight training.

Exam**Café**

Relax, refresh, result!

Refresh your memory

Revision checklist

Make sure you know the following:

- Skeletal muscle has a complex structure. Each muscle is made up of thousands of muscle fibres. Each fibre is composed of hundreds of myofibrils. Each myofibril is made up of contractile elements known as sarcomeres, which are joined end to end along its length. Each sarcomere is made up of contractile proteins known as actin and myosin.
- It is the interaction of actin and myosin that enables a muscle to contract.
- The sliding filament theory explains the stages of muscle contraction.
- A motor neuron together with the fibres it innervates is known as the motor unit.
- The motor unit is the basic functional unit of skeletal muscle.
- When a motor unit is called upon to contract all the muscle fibres under its control will contract simultaneously.
- The all or none law is the principle that explains that individual muscle fibres within a motor unit will either contract fully or not at all.
- In order to cause the muscle fibres within the motor unit to contract fully the level of stimulation must reach a certain 'critical' threshold.
- A muscle can vary the strength of its contractile response through multiple unit summation and wave summation.
- There are two principal types of muscle fibre, each having a different structure and function.
- Slow twitch fibres (type 1) contract more slowly and are highly resistant to fatigue, so are favoured more by endurance athletes who use the aerobic system to supply the majority of their energy during the exercise period.
- Fast twitch fibres (Type 2) can contract more rapidly and generate greater forces so occur more widely in sprinters and power athletes.

- Fast twitch fibres can be further sub-divided into Type 2a (fast oxidative glycolytic) and type 2b (fast twitch glycolytic).
- Type 2a fibres have a slightly better resistance to fatigue than type 2b fibres and so are prominent in athletes who use the lactic acid pathway to supply energy such as a 400m hurdler.
- Type 2b fibres have the highest anaerobic capacity. Although they produce the greatest forces they fatigue the most rapidly. Type 2b fibres are most widely found in athletes who predominantly use the ATP-PC system during the exercise period.
- There are a number of neuro-muscular adaptations to resistance training which include: Muscle hypertrophy, hypertrophy of fast twitch muscle fibres, hyperplasia of fast twitch muscle fibres, recruitment of more motor units and possible conversion of type 2b fibres to type 2a fibres.

Revise as you go

1. Name the three types of muscle fibre and give a sporting example where each of these fibres prevail.
2. Give two structural and two functional characteristics of each.
3. Explain the role of motor units in controlling the strength of muscular contractions in sporting activity.
4. Name a muscle of the body that will contain motor units composed of several hundred fibres and a muscle which will contain motor units of relatively few fibres.
5. What types of training would cause hypertrophy (enlargement) of a) slow twitch fibres b) fast twitch (type 2b) fibres?
6. Outline the stages of the sliding filament process of muscle contraction.
7. Explain how the strength of muscle contraction can be varied in relation to a high jumper and a distance runner.
8. Give three neuromuscular adaptations to training.

CHAPTER 3

Preparation and training for successful performance

LEARNING OBJECTIVES:

By the end of this chapter you should be able to:

- *outline the range and function of sport supplements available to the performer to include: creatine, protein and herbal supplements, bicarbonate of soda and caffeine*
- *explain the ergogenic effects and associated health implications of the following substances: EPO, anabolic steroids, Human Growth Hormone and beta-blockers*
- *suggest a glycogen loading regime for an endurance performer*
- *explain the relationship between water intake and electrolyte balance*
- *briefly outline the different methods of training at the dispense of coach and athlete*
- *apply the most appropriate methods of training to particular sporting performers*
- *give a detailed explanation of plyometrics as a method of training*
- *give a detailed explanation of PNF (Proprioceptive neuromuscular facilitation) as a method of training*
- *give a detailed explanation of altitude training as a method of training*
- *explain the term 'periodisation' in the context of designing training programmes.*
- *outline a typical periodised year for a 100m sprinter and a games player*
- *explain the process and physiological reasons behind altitude training*
- *explain the mechanism of thermoregulation to maintain body temperature when exercising in different climatic environments.*

Introduction

Kelly Holmes was obviously at the peak of condition during the Athens Olympics in 2004. Her training and preparation for the championships was wholly effective and she was rewarded with two gold medals and a place in the record books for a British female athlete. This chapter will examine how coaches and athletes apply training theory when designing training programmes for elite performers. Designing effective training programmes is a science and we will see the specialised training regimes that coaches can use and how they structure the training year so that the performer can peak at the right time. In addition, athletes will often compliment their training by consuming and using a range of supplements and ergogenic aids to optimise their performance and gain the winning edge. We will therefore begin this chapter by investigating the range of sports supplements and ergogenic aids available to performers so that we might understand why this has become such a lucrative business in the sporting industry.

Sports supplements and ergogenic aids

The sports supplement business is huge, and is reportedly worth a staggering £121 million pounds in the UK alone. Performers are drawn to using sports supplements as many are marketed as having performance enhancing benefits. Indeed any substance, method or object used by performers in training or competition that has the sole intention of enhancing athletic performance is known as an ergogenic aid and these therefore include sports supplements. Ergogenic aids range from the legal supplementation of essential nutrients such as protein (e.g. drinking protein shakes) through to the illegal use of drugs such as anabolic steroids (such as THG) which are all designed to give the athlete the winning edge. In an attempt to optimise performance, athletes will often succumb to the temptation of engaging in the use of a whole range of supplements and ergogenic aids. The supplements and aids you are required to know for your examination are outlined below. For each you will be required to state the intended purpose, the athlete most likely to use them, the perceived benefits and the associated risks.

Fig 3.01 Kelly Holmes was at the peak of physical conditioning during the Athens Olympics in 2004

KEY TERMS

Ergogenic aid:
an ergogenic aid is any substance, method or object used by performers in training or competition that has the sole intention of enhancing athletic performance

Creatine supplementation:
the consumption of creatine monohydrate in powder, capsule or liquid form which can increase the levels of phosphocreatine stored in the muscle cell

Caffeine:
a mild stimulant that occurs naturally and found in coffee, tea and colas

EXAM TIP:

In your examination you will be required to state the intended purpose , the athletes most likely to use them, the perceived benefits and the associated risks for each sport supplement and ergogenic aid.

Creatine supplementation

Some athletes seek to extend the threshold of the ATP-PC system by ingesting creatine monohydrate powder or liquid which ensures a readily available source of phosphocreatine in the muscle. Some studies have shown that creatine supplements boost maximal strength and lean muscle mass and as such are used by a variety of athletes from sprinters to weight lifters. As with most supplements and ergogenic aids creatine supplementation does come with associated side effects. Some of the side effects recorded by athletes include abdominal cramps, water retention and bloating, diarrhoea and weight gain.

Protein supplements

In the main, assuming a well balanced diet, protein supplementation should not be necessary for any athlete. However they may be taken to make up a protein shortfall in the diets of those athletes in heavy training or who are vegetarian. Protein or meal replacement shakes may also be useful for those who have trouble fitting regular meals into busy schedules.

Herbal remedies

Herbal preparations have been used for centuries, today however, the massive demand for supplements has meant that companies offer a wide range of herbal supplements – from products that claim to reduce body fat, increase levels of hormones and increase muscle mass to those that enhance energy and improve stamina. The effectiveness of these supplements (such as ginseng and echinacea) is largely untested, so that although some traditional herbal remedies might have some mild benefits for health and performance, it is generally agreed that there is no substitute for the benefits of a well-planned training programme.

Athletes should be alerted to the potential risks of using herbal supplements, as some herbal supplements may have side effects that are unknown or not described on the packaging, such as reacting adversely with prescription drugs or even testing positive to banned substances!

Bicarbonate of soda – soda loading

By drinking a solution of bicarbonate of soda (something found in everybody's kitchen cupboard!) the pH of the blood increases, making it more alkaline. This enhances the buffering capacity of the blood improving its ability to neutralise the negative effects of lactic acid. Consequently the threshold of the lactic acid system can be extended enabling performers to work at higher intensities for longer. Before you raid your kitchen cupboards, however, take a moment to consider the side effects. Bloating, diarrhoea, stomach cramps and nausea are just a few that have been reported!

Caffeine

Caffeine is a mild stimulant that occurs naturally and is predominantly found in coffee, tea and colas. It is probably the most widely available and accessible pharmacological aid. Until 2004, caffeine was listed as a banned substance by WADA, the World Anti-doping Agency, as its consumption was deemed to give performers an unfair advantage. Some studies cite that caffeine reduces the athlete's perception of muscle fatigue and results in an increased ability of the muscle to mobilise and utilise fat as a fuel. Consequently, caffeine is deemed to be of particular benefit to endurance performers such as runners and cyclists. However, as with other supplements, there are some side effects which include dehydration, sleep deprivation and muscle and abdominal cramping.

Water and electrolyte balance

Water is another essential nutrient of an athlete's diet. Endurance performers especially should drink a lot more than the 2–3 litres suggested for the typical adult. It is recommended that performers drink between 400–500ml 15 minutes before training or competition, whilst during exercise it is recommended that 150–200ml be taken on board every 15–20 minutes. Fluid replacement should obviously continue during the recovery period. Sports drinks are often used by endurance performers during training and recovery to maintain blood glucose levels, replace lost fluids and electrolytes. Sodium, potassium, and chlorine form **electrolytes** which help to maintain the correct rate of exchange of nutrients and waste products into and out of the muscle cell. This ensures optimum performance during the activity and facilitates recovery.

Failure to remain sufficiently hydrated can reduce the effectiveness of the circulatory system, the blood effectively becomes 'thicker' or more viscous which slows down the flow to the working muscles. To try and compensate, the heart beats faster putting the body under greater stress. The loss of electrolytes through sweating can cause fatigue and cramps so it is essential that performers remain hydrated. Conversely drinking too much water can lead to **hyponatremia**: a condition which causes the concentration of sodium in the blood to fall below normal levels. This condition essentially weakens the water-electrolyte balance, and can cause swelling of the brain leading to seizures and even death.

Health implications of using illegal substances

Rh EPO (recombinant erythropoietin)

Recombinant erythropoietin is a synthetic product that mimics the body's naturally occurring hormone EPO which is produced by the kidneys and stimulates the body to manufacture red blood cells in the bone marrow. This illegal ergogenic aid is used widely in endurance-based sports and activities such as cycling and distance running. This is because the increase in EPO stimulates the bone marrow to produce more red blood cells and therefore enhance the oxygen carrying capacity of the blood. Although EPO has proven benefits such as increased haemoglobin content and increased VO_2max, it can have fatal consequences. The increase in the red blood volume of the blood dramatically increases the viscosity of the blood which can lead to clotting and heart failure. Furthermore the production of the body's natural form of EPO is adversely affected when the synthetic version is used.

KEY TERMS

Recombinant erythropoietin (Rh EPO):
a synthetic product that mimics the body's naturally occurring hormone EPO which is produced by the kidneys and manufactures red blood cells in the body

Viscosity:
a measure of the resistance to the flow of blood. An increase in the viscosity of the blood suggests that the blood becomes excessively thick, impeding its flow

Anabolic steroids

Anabolic steroids are a group of synthetic hormones that are related to the male hormone testosterone. They are often used illegally in sport and are most widely used by strength and power-based performers such as track and field athletes and weight lifters. Anabolic steroids are typically taken orally or injected and facilitate the storage of protein and the growth of lean muscle mass. Athletes also report that they are able to train harder and recover quicker from high intensity work-outs enabling them to get the most out of their training.

KEY TERMS

Anabolic steroids:
a group of synthetic hormones that promote the storage of protein and the growth of tissue, sometimes used by athletes to increase muscle size and strength

Human growth hormone:
a synthetic product that mimics the body's natural growth hormone. When injected it can stimulate protein synthesis and bone growth

Beta blockers:
beta blockers are a group of hormones that are used by sports performers to lower metabolic activity, reduce heart rate and blood pressure and therefore help to steady nerves and stop trembling

However, anabolic steroids are used at the athlete's peril! It is clear that the associated health risks of injecting are great. These risks include liver damage; heart failure; increased aggression and mood swings commonly referred to as 'roid rage'; development of masculine effects in females such as deepening of the voice and growth of facial hair; and testicular atrophy, reduced sperm count, baldness and breast development in males.

Fortunately there are now many tests available to detect the use of a wide range of different anabolic steroids.

Examples of anabolic steroids known to have been taken by sports performers include THG (tetrahydrogestrinone) and Stanozolol.

Human growth hormone (HGH)

Human growth hormone is a synthetic hormone that mimics the body's naturally occurring growth hormone that facilitates protein synthesis and increases lean muscle mass. An increase in muscle mass is directly linked to increases in muscle strength and HGH is therefore illegally used in a wide range of sporting activities from weightlifting to rugby. Other benefits include increased bone density and decreases in body fat that result from the increased metabolic activity that accompanies increases in muscle mass. There are a number of health risks associated with the use of HGH which includes the enlargement of internal organs such as the heart which can lead to heart failure and high blood pressure, the abnormal development of bone tissue that causes the broadening of facial features, hands and feet (known as acromegaly) as well as an increased risk of some cancers.

Beta blockers

Beta blockers are a group of hormones that are used by sports performers to lower metabolic activity, reduce heart rate and blood pressure and therefore help to steady nerves and stop trembling. Consequently beta blockers are illegally used in activities such as archery, shooting and snooker that consist predominantly of fine skills. Associated side effects of beta blockers are low blood pressure and chronic fatigue.

TASK 3.01

Copy out and complete the table below which investigates the use of supplements and ergogenic aids in sport and physical activity.

Supplement or ergogenic aid	What does it do?	Benefits	Drawbacks and associated health risks	Which athletes do they benefit particularly?
Creatine monohydrate				
Protein shakes				
Bicarbonate of soda				
Caffeine				
Rh EPO				
Anabolic steroids				
Human growth hormone				
Beta blockers				
Water and electrolytes				

TASK 3.02

Some senior athletic coaches believe that there can no longer ever be a clean and fair playing field in the sport of track and field athletics. Some even go as far as saying that the only way to create a level playing field again is by accepting the use of illegal performance enhancing drugs.

Organise a debate in your class with the motion: *Illegal performance enhancing drugs should be accepted in all competitive sports.*

Specialised training regimes

You will recall from your study at AS the range of training methods available to the coach and athlete. This section of the chapter focuses on more specialised training methods.

Table 3.01 The benefits of the different types of training

Type of training	Brief description	Major components of fitness stressed	Example of a session and of a performer	Advantages	Disadvantages
Continuous training	Low intensity rhythmic exercise that uses large muscle groups. The intensity of the training should be between 60–85% HRmax and the duration of the session between 30 mins and 2 hours. Distance running, swimming and cycling are good examples of this	• Cardio-respiratory endurance • Muscular endurance	5–10k steady runs at 65% HRmax e.g. Paula Radcliffe (marathon)	• Time-efficient • Routine programmes are easy to follow • Less chance of injury due to lower intensities	• Can be monotonous • Athletes may need to train at higher intensities • May not be specific to some activities such as team sports
Fartlek training	A form of continuous training where the intensity or speed of the activity is varied throughout the session-from sprinting to walking. The beauty of this type of training is that it develops both aerobic and anaerobic fitness. It is ideal for games players	• Cardio-respiratory endurance • Muscular endurance • Speed	Jog at 60% HRmax 15 mins Sprint × 50m : jog × 150m Repeat 10 times Walk for 90 seconds Jog at 70% HRmax 5 mins Sprint × 200m Jog gently to finish e.g. Wayne Rooney (football)	• Adds variety of pace • Higher intensities can be achieved than in continuous training	• Not specific to all sports • Higher intensities may increase the risk of injury
Sprint interval training	An intermittent training regime that involves periods of alternating exercise and rest. Widely used in athletics and swimming the main benefit of this training method is its versatility, since there are many variables that can be altered in order to stress the required components of fitness. These variables include: • Distance of work period • Intensity of work period • The number of sets • The number of reps • Duration of rest period	• Speed • Power	3 sets x 10 reps × 30m sprints (wbr) 5 mins rest between sets e.g. Craig Pickering (100m sprint)	• Adds variety of pace and duration of work periods • Can be sport-specific, e.g. sprinting • Training at higher intensities leads to significant adaptation	• Requires a measured work distance (e.g. an athletics track) or timed duration • Resting periods need to be timed • More recovery time may be needed when compared to continuous training
Anaerobic interval training		• Speed • Power • Muscular endurance	2 sets x 4 reps x 300m runs (90 secs rest, work relief) e.g. Chris Hoy (1km cycle time trial)		
Aerobic interval training		• Cardio-respiratory endurance • Muscular endurance	3 × 1000m runs (125% personal best time) work: relief ratio = $1:\frac{1}{2}$ e.g. Mo Farah (5k/cross-country)		

Table 3.01 continued

Type of training	Brief description	Major components of fitness stressed	Example of a session	Advantages	Disadvantages
Weight training	An intermittent training method that uses free weights or resistance machines to overload the body. The resistance is determined by working as a percentage of your 1 rep max. and the session is divided into sets ad repetitions which can be manipulated to stress the required aspect of strength	• Maximum strength • Power • Muscular endurance	Maximum strength Heavy weights, low reps 5 sets × 6 reps x 85% 1RM e.g. Naim Suleymanoglu (weightlifting) Elastic strength (must be rapid contractions) 3 sets x 12 reps x 75% 1RM e.g. Delon Armitage (rugby) Strength endurance Light weights, high reps 3 sets × 20 reps x 50% 1RM e.g. Kirsty Balfour (swimming)	• The best method to improve all types of strength and power • Some actions can replicate sporting movements	• Greater risk of injury due to higher intensities • Specialised equipment is needed • Requires some knowledge of appropriate technique to ensure maximum development of the target muscle • More recovery time may be needed when compared to continuous training
Circuit training	A general conditioning activity in which a series of exercises are used to work different muscle groups. Exercises can be made activity or game-specific	• Muscular endurance • Cardio-respiratory endurance	Circuit A = 8 exercises x 30 secs Circuit B = 8 exercises x 30 secs Circuit C = Run for 4 mins Total = 12 mins Repeat 2 or 3 times e.g. Kelly Sotherton (heptathlon)	• Large numbers can perform at once • Can be tailored to meet the needs of particular sports • Can develop a number of components of fitness, e.g. muscular endurance and CV endurance	• Need access to equipment and large facility • Does not produce maximal improvements in strength or CV fitness • General circuits may not meet the needs of some activities

Table 3.01 continued

Type of training	Brief description	Major components of fitness stressed	Example of a session	Advantages	Disadvantages
Plyometrics	A type of training that involves an eccentric muscle contraction followed immediately by a concentric contraction. When the quadriceps lengthen, for example when jumping down from a box top, it pre-loads the muscle and initiates the stretch reflex which causes a rapid and forceful concentric contraction	• Power • Strength • Speed	A plyometrics circuit to include depth jumping, hopping, skipping, press-ups with claps, throwing and catching a medicine ball e.g. Phillips Idowu (triple jump)	• Excellent method of developing power and elastic strength • Can develop power in both upper and lower body • Activities can be made to replicate actions from sport	• The high intensity activities can increase the risk of injury • Appropriate technique is essential to the prevention of injury • More recovery time may be needed when compared to continuous training
PNF (proprioceptive neuromuscular facilitation)	A stretching technique that seeks to inhibit the stretch reflex that occurs when a muscle is stretched to its limit. By isometrically contracting the muscle that is being stretched (usually with the aid of a partner), the stretch reflex is diminished and a greater stretch can occur.	• Flexibility	With the aid of a partner stretch the muscle to it's limit Isometrically contract the muscle for a minimum of 6 seconds (this can be achieved through pushing against your partner) Relax the muscle When the stretch is performed a second time the range of movement should have increased e.g. Beth Tweddle (gymnastics)	• The best method of improving flexibility and therefore increasing the range of movement possible about a joint • Can also help improve speed and elastic strength of a performer	• Must be done with the assistance of a partner • Can only be performed under the watchful eye of a trained coach • Extreme flexibility can lead to joint instability and increase the risk of injury
SAQ (speed, agility and quickness)	A type of training designed to improve the speed, agility and quickness of performers, particularly games players	• Speed • Agility • Power	Training activities include: Ladder drills Resistance drills eg: parachute runs, bungee rope runs Plyometric drills e.g. James Willstrop (squash)	• A wide variety of activities can be used • Can be sport-specific • Activities can develop speed, agility and power simultaneously	• Requires specialist equipment

Plyometrics

Plyometrics is a type of training designed to improve power, strength and speed in the trained muscles. It typically takes the form of bounding, hopping and jumping, although medicine ball activities can be used to train muscles of the upper body. The action of plyometric exercises is crucial to their success. The aim is to preload the muscle by taking it through an eccentric contraction which is then immediately followed by a rapid concentric contraction. When performing a depth jump for example (an exercise where a performer drops down from one platform and immediately jumps up onto a second platform) the quadriceps group perform an eccentric contraction upon landing. This stores elastic energy which is released almost immediately when the quadriceps group perform a rapid forceful contraction to drive the performer up on to the second platform. Furthermore the quicker the transition from eccentric to concentric contraction the more effective the plyometric exercise. Regular plyometric sessions can improve both the elasticity and contractility of muscle fibres which are prerequisite characteristics in the development of speed and power.

Fig 3.02 An athlete performing depth jumps

Plyometrics can therefore help athletes to move more quickly, accelerate faster, jump higher, throw further or even hit a ball harder. So whether you are a rugby or squash player, a triple jumper or hammer thrower – everybody can benefit from plyometrics.

How plyometrics work

Muscle spindles are very sensitive proprioceptors that lie between skeletal muscle fibres. When a muscle is stretched during the eccentric contraction phase of the plyometric exercise, the spindle stretches along with it and sends an impulse back to the central nervous system (CNS) informing it of the extent and speed of muscle lengthening. If the CNS believes that the muscle is lengthening too much or too quickly then it will control the movement by initiating a stretch reflex. When performing the triple jump for example the quadriceps muscle group lengthens rapidly upon landing from the 'hop' stage. The muscle spindles detect the rapid lengthening and send sensory (afferent) impulses to the CNS which then reciprocates by sending an efferent (motor) neuron to the quadricep muscles initiating a stretch reflex causing a powerful concentric contraction. This drives the jumper into the next 'step' phase of the jump.

In doing so the muscle spindles have prevented the quadricep muscles from over-stretching and causing injury.

KEY TERMS

Plyometrics:
is a type of training designed to improve power, strength and speed in the trained muscles. Plyometrics take the form of bounding, hopping and jumping

TASK 3.03

Design and take part in a plyometric circuit. Justify the exercises you include.

In sporting activity, **eccentric contractions** occur when a muscle lengthens under tension and are used as a braking system to decelerate the body. In doing so, **elastic energy** is stored, ready to be used during powerful concentric contractions.

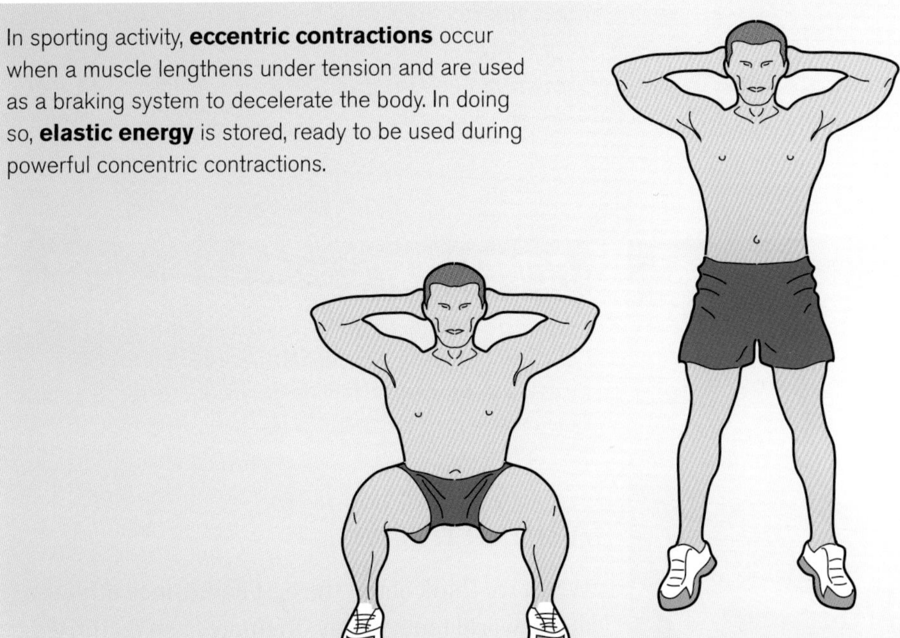

In many sporting skills, eccentric contractions are often followed by concentric contractions. When performing a squat jump, elastic energy is stored in the quadricep muscle group during the down phase. In this instance the quadricep group is lengthening, undergoing an eccentric contraction. Muscle spindles detect the lengthening of the muscle group and may initiate a stretch reflex, causing the quadricep muscle to contract concentrically enabling the performer to jump vertically upwards. It's like an elastic band!

Fig 3.03 The stretch reflex at work during a squat jump

Proprioceptive neuromuscular facilitation (PNF)

PNF is an advanced stretching technique used to improve the flexibility and mobility of elite performers. PNF training is the most effective form of stretching activity as it takes the full advantage of the muscles' safety mechanisms. You will recall that a muscle contains stretch receptors known as muscle spindles (that lie adjacent to muscle fibres) which detect changes in the length and rate of change of length of muscle fibres. When a muscle is stretched so is the muscle spindle. Sensory information is sent to the central nervous system which triggers a **stretch reflex** if the muscle has been stretched too far. Other receptors are sensitive to tension developed within a muscle when it contracts. These are called **Golgi tendon organs** (GTOs). If the critical tension threshold is exceeded within the muscle, Golgi tendon organs initiate muscle relaxation something known as autogenic inhibition. Because the GTOs override the stretch reflex the window of relaxation is extended, allowing a greater stretch, enabling PNF to be very effective.

Undertaking a PNF	
Method	• With the aid of a partner a peformer moves a body part to the limit of its range of movement (ROM) and stays in position for several seconds. • The performer should now isometrically contract the target muscle for between 6 and 10 seconds. This can be done by pushing against a resistance offered by the partner. • The muscle is then relaxed. • The target muscle is moved once again to the limit of its ROM by the partner (which should be further).
How it works!	• When the target muscle is contracted isometrically inhibitory signals from the Golgi tendon organ (GTO) override excitory signals from the muscle spindles which delay the stretch reflex. This causes further relaxation of the target muscle allowing it to be stretched further.
Adaptation	• With regular practice of PNF, the range of movement (ROM) is increased due to increased length of muscle and connective tissues such as tendons and ligaments.

Table 3.02 A full description of a PNF

Fig 3.04 PNF in action

KEY TERMS

Proprioceptive neuromuscular facilitation (PNF):
a stretching technique that overrides the stretch reflex to enable a performer to achieve a greater range of movement at a joint

Golgi tendon organ (GTO):
proprioceptors found at the attachment of muscle and tendon fibres that are sensitive to changes in muscle tension

Stretch reflex:
the stretch reflex is initiated when a muscle is stretched too far. It acts to prevent damage to the muscle fibres

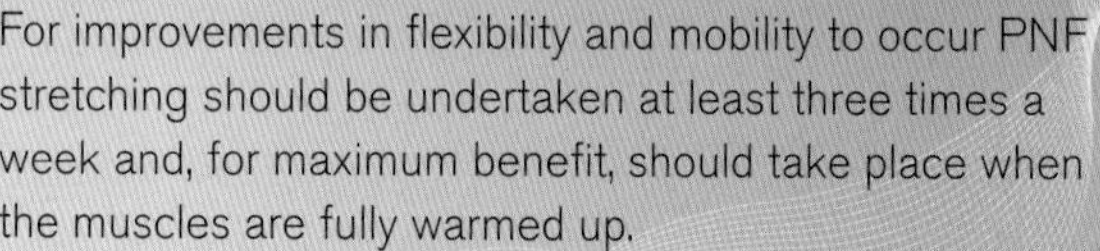

REMEMBER!

For improvements in flexibility and mobility to occur PNF stretching should be undertaken at least three times a week and, for maximum benefit, should take place when the muscles are fully warmed up.

Altitude training

When we think about the best endurance athletes in the world today many originate from countries that have an altitude of 1,000m or more – Morocco, Ethiopia and Kenya for example. No wonder then that training at high altitude has been favoured by elite endurance performers when preparing for major competitions. So why does training at altitude work? ... or does it?

The reasoning behind training at altitude is based around the fact that the concentration of oxygen in a given volume is reduced at altitude. In fact the partial pressure of oxygen decreases by about 50% at an altitude of 5,000m so the body compensates by breathing more quickly and deeply in an attempt to increase blood–oxygen concentrations to normal levels. Heart rate also increases in order to deliver more oxygen to the tissues. These responses occur immediately whereas others may take up to 30 days to complete. These other adaptations include an increased production of red blood cells resulting in an increase in the haemoglobin concentration of the blood.

Upon returning to sea level these increased concentrations of red blood cells and haemoglobin remain for a period of 6–8 weeks and greatly enhance the oxygen carrying capacity of the blood.

The major problem with **training at altitude** is that, because of the decreased availability of oxygen, training becomes very hard and it becomes very difficult to train at the same intensity as you would do at sea level. Additionally lactate levels at a set speed increase and VO_2max is reduced. Together these factors may lead to a **detraining** effect.

Because the beneficial effects of living at altitude can be offset by the negative effects of training (exercise performance impairment) it is now argued that the best solution is for athletes to live at altitude and train at sea level. In fact athletes have simulated low oxygen environments (hypoxic) at sea level through the use of altitude tents and hypoxic apartments.

Fig 3.05 Paula Radcliffe regularly undertakes a period of altitude training as part of her preparation for competition

Altitude training	
Perceived benefits	**Likely drawbacks**
• Increased haematocrit (concentration of red blood cells) • Increased concentration of haemoglobin • Enhanced oxygen transport	• Expensive • Altitude sickness • Due to the lack of oxygen training at higher intensities is difficult • Detraining • Any benefits are soon lost on return to sea level

Table 3.03 Benefits and drawbacks of altitude training

KEY TERMS

Altitude training:
a type of training usually above 2,500m above sea level. The reduced pO_2 of oxygen causes the body to compensate by producing more red blood cells. Hypobaric chambers can now be used at sea level to mimic the effects of altitude

Detraining:
the reversal of positive training effects

Glycogen loading:
manipulating the consumption of carbohydrate in the week prior to a competition can increase muscle glycogen storage capacity

APPLY IT!

High altitude gives more red blood cells
Paula Radcliffe spends 4 months in Albuquerque (1600m, 5250ft above sea level) in the USA when preparing for her marathon events and 3–4 weeks in Font Romeu, France, (1980m, 6500ft above sea level) where she undertakes higher intensity training runs ready for her 5000m and 10,000m events on the track.

Glycogen loading

Glycogen loading is the manipulation of the dietary intake of carbohydrate prior to competition so that muscle glycogen stores are maximised. This process is favoured by endurance athletes as it seeks to elevate muscle glycogen stores above their normal resting levels which facilitates the effective resynthesis of ATP via the aerobic pathway. Typically, this practice involves depleting the glycogen levels seven days prior to the event through endurance-based training. This is then followed by three days of a low carbohydrate diet whilst performing some kind of tapering exercise. On the remaining days leading up to the competition the athlete consumes a diet rich in carbohydrates whilst performing little or no exercise.

Studies have shown that following a carbohydrate regime like this can almost double muscular stores of glycogen.

Recent research indicates that the initial depletion stage of the glycogen loading process may not be necessary for trained athletes. Simply resting for the three days prior to competition and eating carbohydrate-rich meals may be sufficient to maximise glycogen stores.

Whichever glycogen loading method you follow, it is important to increase the consumption of water as it helps to facilitate glycogen synthesis and storage. This will have the added bonus of preventing dehydration during the endurance race.

Pre-competition programme		
Day 1	Long bout of exercise	
Day 2	Tapering exercise	Low carbohydrate (200–300g)
Day 3	Tapering exercise	Low carbohydrate (200–300g)
Day 4	Tapering exercise	Low carbohydrate (200–300g)
Day 5	Tapering exercise	High carbohydrate (500–600g)
Day 6	Rest / Little exercise	High carbohydrate (500–600g)
Day 7	Rest / Little exercise	High carbohydrate (500–600g)
Day 8	COMPETITION	Pre-competition meal Moderate carbohydrate intake

Table 3.04 A suggested glycogen loading method

Benefits of glycogen loading to the athlete	Drawbacks of glycogen loading
• Increased glycogen synthesis	• Water retention and bloating
• Increased muscle glycogen	• Possible weight increase
• Increased endurance capacity	• Fatigue and muscle soreness
• Delays fatigue/reduces risk of 'hitting the wall'	• Irritability during the depletion phase

Table 3.05 The advantages and disadvantages of glycogen loading

Planning training programmes

You will recall from your study at AS the key factors to consider when designing a training programme.

Table 3.06 revisits the principles of training, something that should always be at the forefront of a coach's thinking when planning his or her athletes' training.

Principle of training	Explanation	Application
Specificity	All training must be relevant to the activity or sport. For example a cyclist must perform most of their training on a bike. There is of course some value in other forms of training, but the majority must be performed on the bicycle. Actions from the activity should also be replicated during training.	Be sure to train the: • relevant muscles • energy systems • relevant fibre types • fitness components • use appropriate technique
Progression	As the body becomes better at coping with the training over time, greater demands must be made if improvement is to continue. This is often linked to overload and known as 'progressive overload'.	Increase: • % HRmax • %1RM • duration • frequency of training

Table 3.06 Applying the principles of training

continued

Principle of training	Explanation	Application
Overload	If training is to have the required effect then the performer must find the training taxing. The level of training must be pitched at a level greater than the demands regularly encountered by the player. The old adage 'no pain, no gain' can be applied here!	• Use heart rate to gauge how hard you are working • Work at an appropriate % of max heart rate or 1RM • Increase the duration of the activity if needed
Reversibility	Use it or lose it! If the training load decreases or if training stops altogether then the benefits of the prior training can be lost.	Unless injured, training should continue.
Tedium (Variety)	Variety is the spice of life so make sure training sessions are varied using a range of different methods and intensities. Try to incorporate an element of fun into some sessions. This will hopefully prevent staleness and boredom and your athletes will keep coming back!	A swimmer will follow a programme that includes pool-based work and land-based training including weights work. Some pools even have the facility to play music underwater to keep boredom at bay!
FITT	F (Frequency) = How often we train I (Intensity) = How hard we train T (Time) = How long we train for T (Type) = What type of training we use	• Train 3–6 days/week • %HRmax or %1RM • 30mins–2hrs/session • Use the principle of specificity
Warm-up/ cool-down	Start as you mean to go on. A thorough warm-up and cool-down is an essential ingredient to every training session. This ensures you get the most out of the session and recover quickly for subsequent sessions.	A warm-up will typically include 3 different stages: • Stage 1 pulse raiser • Stage 2 stretching activity • Stage 3 skill-related practices A cool-down will typically include only Stages 1 and 2 of the warm-up.
Individuality	Training programmes need to be tailor-made to meet the needs of individual performers. Athletes respond differently to the same training; what may help one athlete to improve may not help another. The coach must therefore be sympathetic to the individual performer – particularly if they are part of a training group.	Swimmers and athletes often train in small groups. Everybody will respond and adapt to the same training differently. It is essential, therefore, that the coach respects the particular needs of each person in the group so that they can focus on particular strengths or weaknesses, such as the start for a 100m sprinter.
Moderation (Prevention of over-training and adequate recovery)	Sufficient recovery time must be built into the training programme to prevent over-training. Rest allows the body to overcompensate and adapt to the training, leading to improved performance. Over-training is characterised by muscular fatigue, illness and injury.	Heavy training sessions should be followed by lighter sessions or even rest days. The ratio of 3:1 is often used to express the ratio of hard sessions to easy sessions within a week's training cycle.
Periodisation	This is the organisation of the training programme into blocks. Each block may have a particular focus, such as the development of stamina or strength endurance. By following a periodised programme the performer is more likely to peak and avoid the scourge of many an athlete – over-training.	A sprinter: • Preparation period (usually subdivided into 2 phases): development of aerobic and muscular endurance, max strength, followed by development of elastic strength, power and speed • Competition period (sometimes subdivided into 3 phases): development and maintenance of speed and power; technique work; tapering and peaking for competitions • Transition or recovery period (1 phase) active rest

Table 3.06 continued

ATHLETE PROFILE

Andrew Willis is a competitive swimmer who currently attends Sixth Form College, Farnborough. He is the British record holder for the 17 Age Group – 200m Breast Stroke with a long course PB of 2mins 15.86secs.

Figure 3.06 shows just a section of his periodised year. Interestingly you will note that his training year is broken down into 3 macrocycles since his competitive season is very long. The first macrocycle lasts between September and December with his competitive season commencing in October. His training during this time focuses on a mixture of aerobic, anaerobic and technique development culminating in his Club Championships. The second macrocycle extends between January and March culminating in the British Championships. The number of competitions during this time is significantly reduced and there is a 3–4 week taper ahead of the big event. This taper reduces the volume of training by about one-third yet maintains the intensity and allows Andrew to peak ahead of the championships.

The third macrocycle is the longest, beginning in April and ending in August. The training here is a mixture of the previous 2 macrocycles focusing first on aerobic endurance and then more specific endurance training. Towards the end of this macrocycle there is further taper, ahead of the National Age Group and National Youth Championships. This is the end of Andrew's training year and he can now afford himself a transition period of 3–4 weeks where he can have a training holiday!

Periodisation

Effective planning is crucial when designing a training programme. Periodisation is simply the organisation of training into blocks or 'cycles' which each have a particular focus and enable optimal physiological and psychological peak to be reached during major competition. Essentially periodisation involves the manipulation of specificity (type), intensity and volume of training and whilst the general principles of periodisation are common to all sports they must be adjusted to suit the needs of different sports and individual performers.

Periodising the training programme is based around three distinct periods more commonly referred to as cycles:

- **Macrocycles:** the long term performance goal. In games such as football the macrocycle will usually correspond to the year-long season. For other athletes, who perhaps have the ambition of competing in the Olympics, it could be as long as 4 years.
- **Mesocycles:** typically mesocycles are sub-divisions of a macrocycle that may last between 2 and 8 weeks. A mesocycle will usually have a particular focus, e.g. the development of speed during the pre-season phase of training.
- **Microcycles:** are sub-divisions of a mesocycle which are usually a week in duration. They provide more detailed information regarding the specific intensity and volume of training.

A further important component of the periodised year is of course the individual training session which in this case is referred to as the **training unit**.

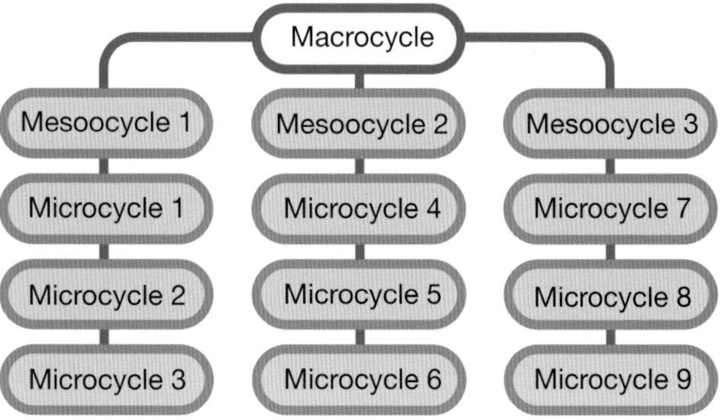

Fig 3.06 The sub-division of the training year

A macrocycle – the long term training goal!

The planning of the macrocycle should be focused around peaking for major competitions or important games on the fixture card. The basic structure of a macrocycle will be the same whatever the sport or activity, whether it be a four-year Olympic cycle, a two-year world championship cycle, or an annual or seasonal cycle. In its simplest form the macrocycle will be made up of three distinct periods:

- Preparation period (subdivided into 2 phases)
- Competition period (sometimes subdivided into 3 phases).
- Transition or recovery period (1 phase).

The preparation period (Phases 1 and 2)

The preparation period is perhaps more commonly referred to as pre-season training and is typically divided into two parts:

- General conditioning training (Phase 1)
- Competition specific training (Phase 2).

The **general conditioning stage** of the preparation period is characterised by high volume, low intensity work. The key theme or focus should be on the development of a solid endurance base upon which to build future training. A good general conditioning programme should aim to develop aerobic and muscular endurance, general strength and mobility.

REMEMBER!

Even those athletes using anaerobic sources of energy such as 100m sprinters or 400m hurdlers need to develop a sound aerobic endurance base during the general conditioning stage of the preparation period.

The **competition specific training** sees an increase in the intensity of training. This is the time when much of the strength and speed work should be undertaken. The performer should therefore be working at higher speeds or working against greater resistances (e.g. by lifting heavier weights). In addition to competition specific fitness requirements, technique and tactical appreciation should also be developed now so that the performer is fully prepared and finely tuned for the first day of the competitive season.

The competition period (Phases 3, 4 and 5)

The main goal of the competition period is to develop optimal competition performance. Maintaining levels of fitness and conditioning is essential during this stage as is the continued development of competition-specific aspects of training. During this stage the overall extent or volume of training is decreased but the intensity of the training is increased. During a long season or where an athlete may need to peak on more than one occasion, the competition period may be subdivided into the following phases:

- **Phase 3 (6–8 weeks):** the typical competition period. There should be a reduction in the volume of general training but an increase in intensity of competition specific training. Trials and qualifying competitions should fall within this phase.
- **Phase 4 (4–6 weeks):** during a long competitive season it is recommended that a period where competitions are eliminated altogether is introduced and the level of competition specific training is reduced. It can be likened to a mini transition period where the body can recover and prepare for phase 5 in which major competitions or cup finals occur.
- **Phase 5 (3–4 weeks):** effectively this is the culmination of the training year! The major events of the performer's calendar will fall during this phase, e.g. Olympic finals, Cup finals etc. Competition-specific training is maintained and **tapering** for peak performance should take place. Tapering involves the manipulation of training volume and intensity to promote peak performance.

The coach's task is to manage training so that peak performance can occur in a window between the removal of training-induced fatigue and the reversal of the training effect. A typical taper will last between 10 and 21 days but will vary between sports and different performers, see Table 3.07. The application box suggests how a swimmer might taper ahead of a major competition. The two key ingredients to a successful taper are:

1. Increase training to or maintain training at competition intensities.
2. Decrease the volume of training by approximately one-third.

Fig 3.07 Swimmers will often taper their training prior to competition

KEY TERMS

Peaking:
the planning and organisation of training so that a performer can be at the height of physical and psychological conditioning during major competitions

Tapering:
a reduction in the volume of training prior to major competition. It enables an athlete to reach peak performance

The transition period (Phase 6)

The transition period is the final stage of the periodised year yet perhaps the most important phase of all! Crucially it helps the performer recover from the previous year of training and competition and prepare for the next! Following a hard season of training and competition a period of 3–6 weeks of active recovery is needed to allow the performer to fully recharge their physical and psychological batteries so that they are injury free and highly motivated for the forthcoming season. This active recovery should take the form of general exercise where performers engage in a variety of fun activities.

REMEMBER!

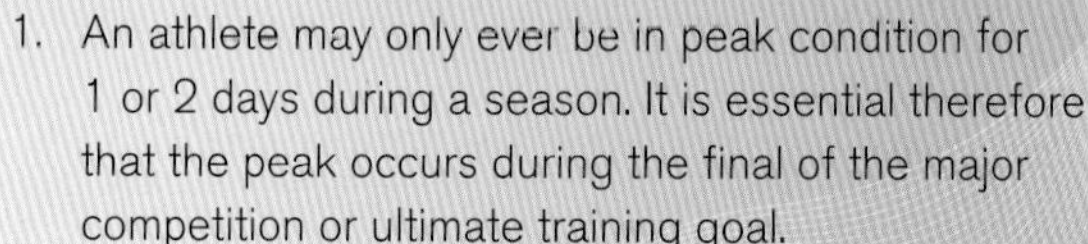

1. An athlete may only ever be in peak condition for 1 or 2 days during a season. It is essential therefore that the peak occurs during the final of the major competition or ultimate training goal.
2. Two to three weeks prior to competition a swimmer may gradually taper from 4000m to 2500m a day whilst maintaining the same intensity. Many male swimmers will also shave their body hair at the end of their taper period to reduce drag and give them a psychological boost during the competitive swim.

Month	1	2	3	4	5	6	7	8	9	10	11	12
Periodisation phase	Preparatory 1				Preparatory 2			Competition				Trans
	General preparation				Specific preparation PC			Competition Maintenance			Taper	Light recreative activity

Key: Trans – transition phase: 4–5 weeks long
PC – pre-competitive, or exhibition competitions/games/matches
Taper – unloading/tapering for the major competition of the year

Table 3.07 An example of a single periodised year

TASK 3.04

Consider the following stages of a swimmer's training programme and place them in the correct order as they would appear in the periodised year:

- Swim 6000–7000m. High intensity sprints. Speed training.
- Swim less than 5000m. Tapering.
- Swim 7000m. Introduce anaerobic training. High distance, high intensity. Technique and skill work.
- Swim 7000–8000m. Low intensity, long distance. Aerobic training.

STRETCH AND CHALLENGE

1. Make a copy of the training pyramid. For a games player of your choice, write down the focus of training in each of the 4 periods of the macrocycle. Be sure to give examples of specific components of fitness trained together with the intensity and volume of training in each stage. Write your training guidelines actually in the relevant section of the training pyramid.
2. Study Table 3.07 . For each of the mesocycles 1–8 give examples of a specific training unit or session that we might expect to see.

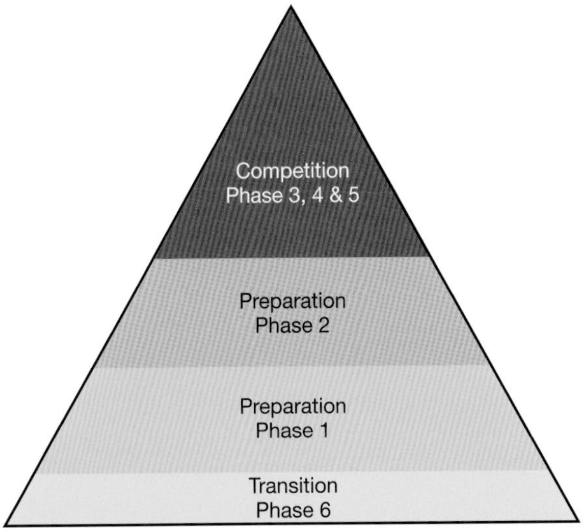

Fig 3.08 Training pyramid

	Jun	Jul	Aug	Sept	Oct	Nov	Dec	Jan	Feb	Mar	Apr	May
Mesocycle		Prep 1	Prep 2				Competition					Tran
	8	1 2	3	4	5			6		7		8

↑ Pre-season starts here (Jun/Jul)

The season finishes here ↑ (May)

Table 3.08 An example of a macrocycle or periodised year for an elite netball player

A mesocycle – The short term training goal!

The macrocycle is sub-divided into blocks of training known as mesocycles. The mesocycles are typically 2–8 weeks in duration and are usually closely related to the performance goals of the particular cycle and have as the focus a particular component of fitness, e.g. aerobic endurance, strength, power, or active rest etc.

A microcycle – the training week!

The weekly training plan is referred to as a microcycle. Microcycles are planned around the objectives of the mesocycle but should contain more detail concerning the intensity, volume and sequence of training programmes. It is especially important to plan the appropriate ratio of training to recovery sessions to enable effective **adaptation** of the body. A balance between training and recovery must be struck so that the performer is not faced with several successive sessions that are of very high intensity. A coach will often apply a 3:1 ratio where a rest unit is given following 3 training units within a particular microcycle.

APPLY IT!

In many team games the microcycle is based around a weekly competitive fixture. A small taper or rest day will therefore be needed immediately prior to the competition.

KEY TERMS

Adaptation:
the long term structural and physiological responses of the body to training that explain the improvements in performance

REMEMBER!

In order to prevent over-training the coach may adopt a 3:1 ratio. During a microcycle the performer may have three hard sessions followed by one easier session or in a mesocycle the athlete may undergo three hard weeks of training followed by one easier one!

The training unit – the training session!

The training unit is a single training session. The main section of the session should have as a focus the key training objective. For example if the coach and swimmer seek to improve lactate tolerance then the training unit may look something like this:

- 5 × 100m on 4 minutes, maximum effort, aim for a PB on all
- 3 × 200m on 5 minutes, maximum effort, aim for a PB on all
- 8 × 75m on 3 minutes, maximum effort on all.

If, however, the training unit forms part of a mesocycle in phase 1 of the preparation stage then it is likely that aerobic endurance may be the main training objective and the session may look something like this:

- 3 × 800m Alternate FC/Choice + 30 secs [Even pace, target pulse = HR max – 50]
- 8 × 400m IM + 30 secs Alternate drill/swim, even effort 1600, 800, 400, 200, 100, 50 FC + 30 secs [Increase pace, target pulse = HR max – 50]

Where FC = front crawl, IM = individual medley.

Double periodisation

Some sports require a performer to peak on more than one occasion throughout the year. Consider the athlete who needs to peak for cross-country competitions in the winter and track championships in the summer or the tennis player wishing to peak for each of the four Grand Slam competitions which are spread throughout the year. In this instance the coach and performer must follow a double (or even multi!) periodised year. Table 3.08 illustrates the double periodised year for a swimmer wishing to peak for both short course and long course championships.

Fig 3.09 Track and field athletes will often follow a double periodised year so that they can peak for both indoor and outdoor competitions

TASK 3.05

Using Table 3.09 as a guide construct a chart that illustrates a double periodised year for a sprinter wishing to compete in both indoor and outdoor championships.

Month	1	2	3	4	5	6	7	8	9	10	11	12
Periodisation (phase)	Preparatory 1			Competition 1			T1	Preparatory 2		Competition 2		T2
	General prep.			PC	Specific preparation	Taper	M	General prep.	Comp-etition	PC	Taper	

Key: T – transition phase: the first one of only 2 weeks, while the second one should consist of 4 weeks rest, allowing the body to recover between last season's competitions and next year's training.
M – maintenance

Table 3.09 An example of a double periodised year

TASK 3.06

Copy out Table 3.10 – a blank periodisation template.
For an activity of your choice attempt to design a year-long training programme.
On your periodisation chart you will need to identify the following:

- the major competitions for peaking
- an example of a microcycle and training unit for each mesocycle
- a taper.

Training phases	Preparatory phase	Competitive phase	Transition
Mesocycles			
Microcycles			

Table 3.10 The periodisation of an annual plan

Thermoregulation during exercise

The human body regulates temperature by maintaining a fine balance between heat production and heat loss. At the heart of temperature regulation is the preservation of the body's **core temperature** which at rest ranges between 36.5°C and 37.5°C. The core temperature of the body is regulated by the **hypothalamus** in the brain, which can be likened to an in-built thermostat, which reacts to changes in body temperature caused by both internal and environmental factors. Located around the body are a number of **thermoreceptors** (temperature receptors), which feed information to the hypothalamus to help in the maintenance of a constant core temperature.

KEY TERMS

Core temperature:
the internal temperature of the human body, which is maintained at 37°C

Hypothalamus:
the area of the brain responsible for homeostasis (the maintenance of status quo). One aspect of this is the maintenance of the body's core temperature

Thermoreceptors:
sensory receptors sensitive to changes in body temperature

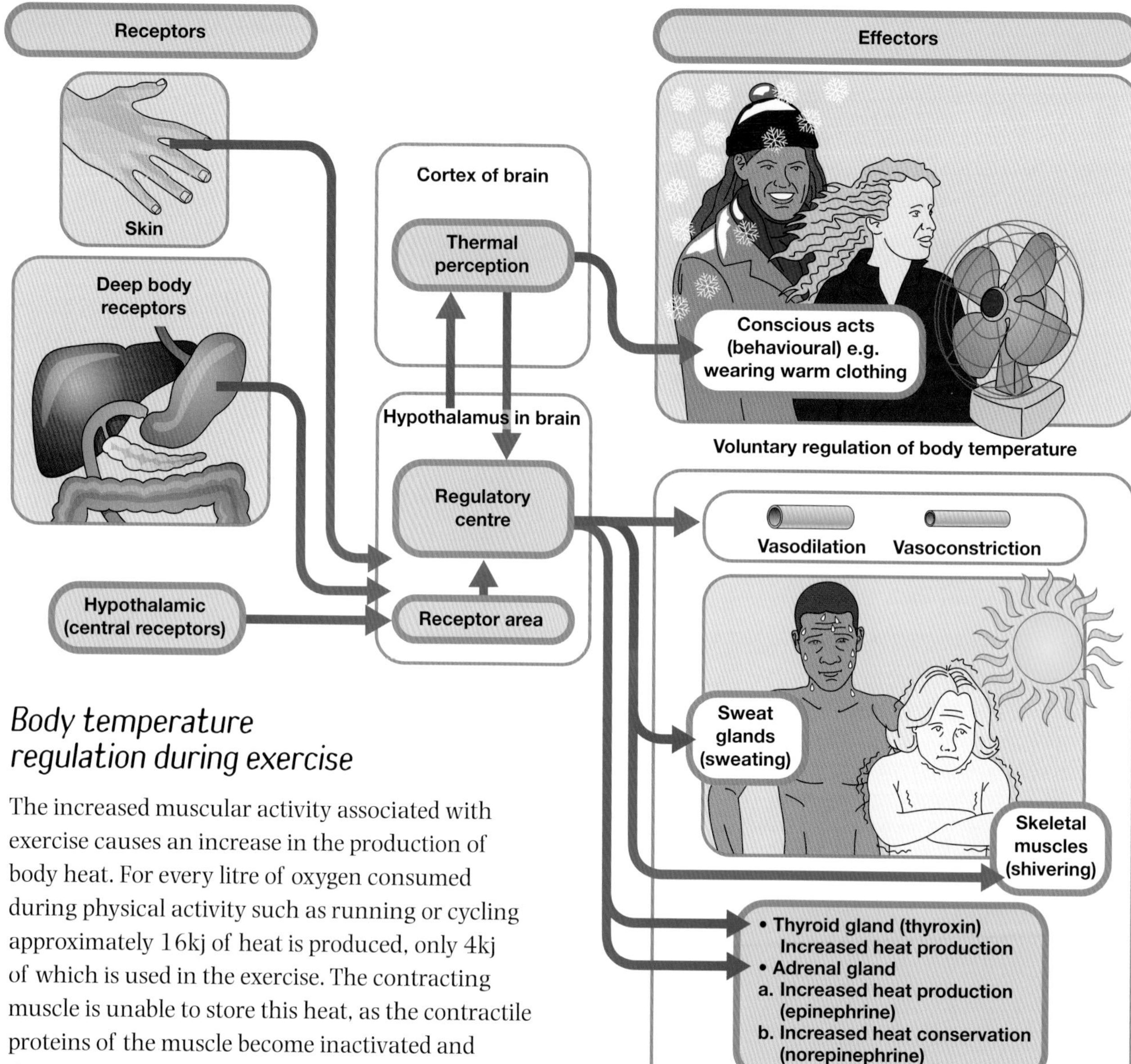

Fig 3.10 The thermoregulatory system

Body temperature regulation during exercise

The increased muscular activity associated with exercise causes an increase in the production of body heat. For every litre of oxygen consumed during physical activity such as running or cycling approximately 16kj of heat is produced, only 4kj of which is used in the exercise. The contracting muscle is unable to store this heat, as the contractile proteins of the muscle become inactivated and the enzymes that facilitate energy release become de-natured in a hot environment. Accordingly, most of the heat produced by the muscle is transferred to the body's core, increasing the core temperature of the body. Consequently, the body's core temperature can be raised to above 40°C!

Heat loss

The body disperses heat through a number of different processes:

- conduction
- convection
- radiation
- evaporation

- **Conduction** is the process whereby heat is lost through physical contact between one object and another. The direction of heat flow is always from the warmer to the cooler object. For example if an athlete sits on a cold metal chair heat will be transferred from his body to the chair.
- **Convection** is the process of losing heat through contact between the skin and moving air or water molecules. Standing in front of a fan blowing out cold air to cool the body down is one example of convection.
- **Radiation** is a method of losing heat via infrared rays, where heat is transferred to the environment without physical contact with another object. We lose heat through radiation when our body temperature is warmer than the surrounding environment.

- **Evaporation** is the process by which the body loses heat through the conversion of liquid to a vapour. This is the form of heat loss that we are perhaps most familiar, and is the major portion of heat loss during exercise as it involves the loss of body heat through sweating.

Fig 3.11 Whereas a runner may lose most of their body heat through sweating a swimmer will maintain their core body temperature through convection

Heat loss through sweating

When the hypothalamus detects an increase in core body temperature it reacts by increasing the blood flow to the skin, which stimulates the 2.5 million sweat glands. The sweat glands secrete sweat, which is composed of water and electrolytes such as potassium, sodium and chloride, and as we learned earlier the body cools down through evaporation of the sweat from the surface of the skin.

During moderate to high-intensity exercise a performer can lose between 1 and 2 litres of sweat per hour, the precise amount depends on a number of factors including the temperature of the local environment, humidity, exercise intensity and fitness level of the individual. Of these, relative humidity (the water vapour concentration of the air close to the body's surface) deserves a little further discussion, since a high humidity can severely compromise the body's ability to lose heat through sweating. In order to achieve a cooling effect, sweat must evaporate from the surface of the skin, but high humidity has a limiting effect on the evaporative loss of sweat and can lead to further rises in core temperature and possible complications such as dehydration and heat stroke.

Cardiovascular drift: you may recall from your AS studies that exercising in a warm environment can cause an increase in heart rate when compared to exercising at the same intensity in a cooler environment. The explanation for this is two-fold.

1. Firstly, stroke volume decreases when exercising in a warmer environment. This is because there is an increase in blood flow to the skin in an attempt to lose heat through conduction, convection and evaporation. However this does mean that less blood is returning to the heart, causing a drop in stroke volume. To maintain cardiac output heart rate must therefore increase.
2. Secondly, blood plasma volume decreases, as some fluid seeps into surrounding tissues and cells and some fluid is lost through sweating. If the athlete fails to re-hydrate sufficiently this can further reduce the volume of blood returning to the heart, causing a fall in stroke volume.

EXAM TIP:

Training improves the thermoregulatory process of the body by enhancing the sweating ability of the body. Training increases the total blood volume and maximal cardiac output which improves the flow of blood to the skin, allowing an earlier onset of sweat secretion. Furthermore, training appears to induce hypertrophy of the sweat glands increasing the total amount of sweat that can be produced.

APPLY IT!

Acclimatisation to heat: Acclimatisation relates to the physiological changes occurring within an individual that allows him or her to better adjust to the local environmental conditions.

Exercising in cold climates: does not present too serious a problem as performers are usually well prepared and are expectant used to the climatic conditions. It is rare for example that we hear of downhill skiers or triathletes (during the swim) suffering from hypothermia. This is because exposure to the cold is usually limited, appropriate clothing is worn and the physical activity utilises large muscle groups generating large quantities of heat.

ExamCafé

Relax, refresh, result!

Refresh your memory

Revision checklist

Make sure you know the following:

- ▷ There are many sports supplements and performance enhancing aids available to the elite performer.
- ▷ An ergogenic aid is any substance, method or object used by performers in training or competition that has the sole intention of enhancing athletic performance.
- ▷ Creatine supplementation is the consumption of creatine monohydrate in powder, capsule or liquid form which can increase the levels of phosphocreatine stored in the muscle cell.
- ▷ Athletes such as 100m sprinters use creatine to increase their stores of phosphocreatine and increase the duration of the ATP-PC system.
- ▷ Reported side effects of creatine supplementation include, water retention, stomach cramps and diarrhoea.
- ▷ Protein supplements are often taken by athletes in the form of protein shakes. A well balanced diet however should include sufficient protein for all the athletes' needs.
- ▷ The body will only use the protein it needs as any excess cannot be stored. Over-supplementation of protein can cause kidney problems.
- ▷ Soda loading involves the consumption of a solution of bicarbonate of soda. Bicarbonate of soda enhances the buffering capacity of the blood and aids in the removal of lactic acid thus delaying OBLA.
- ▷ Soda loading is favoured amongst athletes working at medium to high intensity.
- ▷ Side effects of soda loading include nausea, stomach cramps and diarrhoea.
- ▷ Caffeine is a mild stimulant that occurs naturally and found in coffee, tea and colas.
- ▷ Caffeine can increase mental alertness, enhances reaction time and reduces the effects of fatigue allowing performers to continue working at higher intensity for a longer duration.
- ▷ Side effects of caffeine use include dehydration, sleep deprivation and muscle and abdominal cramping.

- Glycogen is the manipulation of dietary intake of carbohydrates prior to an endurance event in which performers try to maximise stores of glycogen.
- Depletion of glycogen stores is followed by restricted dietary intake for three days. In the three days prior to the competition a much higher quantity of carbohydrate is included in the athlete's diet.
- Benefits of glycogen loading include increased muscle glycogen stores, increased endurance capacity and delayed fatigue.
- Side effects of glycogen loading include water retention, weight increase, irritability and fatigue during the depletion phase.
- Maintaining the correct water and electrolyte balance is essential to avoid the negative effects of dehydration.
- Dehydration can increase blood viscosity, increase heart rate and reduce cardiac output leading to premature fatigue and decreased performance.
- Recombinant erythropoietin (Rh EPO) is a synthetic product that mimics the body's naturally occurring hormone EPO which is produced by the kidneys and manufactures red blood cells in the body.
- Rh EPO has some performance benefits including increased haemoglobin content and increased VO_2max.
- There are many health risks associated with using Rh EPO including increased blood viscosity which can lead to clotting and heart failure. The production of the body's natural form of EPO is also adversely affected when the synthetic version is used.
- Anabolic steroids are a group of synthetic hormones that promote the storage of protein and the growth of tissue. They are sometimes used by athletes to increase muscle size and strength.
- Risks associated with anabolic steroid abuse include liver damage, heart failure, increased aggression, and mood swings.
- Human growth hormone is a synthetic product that mimics the body's natural growth hormone. When injected it can stimulate protein synthesis and bone growth.
- Health risks associated with the use of HGH include the enlargement of internal organs such as the heart which can lead to heart failure and high blood pressure, the abnormal development of bone tissue known as acromegaly.
- Beta blockers are a group of hormones that are used by sports performers to lower metabolic activity, reduce heart rate and blood pressure and therefore help to steady nerves and stop trembling.
- Side effects of beta blocker use include low blood pressure and chronic fatigue.
- Proprioceptive neuromuscular facilitation is an advanced stretching technique that overrides the stretch reflex to enable a performer to achieve a greater range of movement at a joint.

- ▷ The stretch reflex is initiated when a muscle is stretched too far. It acts to prevent damage to the muscle fibres.
- ▷ With regular practice of PNF, the range of movement (ROM) is increased due to increased length of muscle and connective tissues such as tendons and ligaments.
- ▷ Altitude training is a type of training that usually takes place above 2500m above sea level. The reduced pO_2 of oxygen causes the body to compensate by producing more red blood cells allowing significant improvements in the aerobic capacity of a performer .
- ▷ The drawbacks of altitude training include the possibility of developing altitude sickness which diminishes the effectiveness of training and any benefits of the training do not stay with the athlete for long!
- ▷ Hypobaric chambers can now be used at sea level to mimic the effects of altitude. This allows the athlete to live at altitude yet train at sea level. The best combination according to exercise physiologists.
- ▷ Periodisation is the organisation of training into blocks, which each have a particular physiological focus.
- ▷ Periodisation involves the manipulation of specificity, intensity and volume of training.
- ▷ A macrocycle is the long term performance goal, usually lasting between 1 and 4 years.
- ▷ A mesocycle is a block of training lasting between 2 and 8 weeks which has a particular physiological focus.
- ▷ A microcycle is typically a week's worth of training.
- ▷ The training unit is an individual training session.
- ▷ There are three distinct period of the training year: preparation, competition and transition periods.
- ▷ The preparation period is subdivided into two phases: Phase 1 – general endurance based conditioning and Phase 2 – competition specific training.
- ▷ The competition period is subdivided into three phases: Phase 3 – early competition, Phase 4 – a reduction in competition and training ahead of the major competition, Phase 5 – tapering and peaking for competition.
- ▷ The transition period is phase 6, which is the recovery and rest period between competitive seasons. It is a time for the performer to recover and recuperate at the end of a tiring season.
- ▷ A double periodised year is followed when an athlete requires to peak twice in a season.
- ▷ Thermoregulation is controlled by the hypothalamus in the brain.

- It is the job of the thermoregulatory centre to maintain the core temperature of the body.
- In warm environments maintenance of the core body temperature becomes increasingly difficult.
- The body cools itself by diverting blood (and heat) away from the core, towards the skin where the processes of evaporation, radiation, conduction and convection can take place.

Revise as you go

1. Outline the arguments for and against the use of the following sports supplements:
   - creatine monohydrate
   - bicarbonate of soda
   - protein shakes.
2. Outline the arguments for and against the use of the following illegal ergogenic aids:
   - anabolic steroids
   - human growth hormone
   - recombinant erythropoietin.
3. Justify the inclusion of a plyometrics session into an athletes training programmes. Give at least six different exercises you would include in the session.
4. Describe the method commonly used in proprioceptive neuromuscular facilitation (PNF).
5. With reference to Golgi tendon organs and muscle spindles explain why PNF stretching can produce better results in terms of increased flexibility than other forms of stretching.
6. What are the arguments for and against altitude training?
7. Why do some athletes follow a programme of dietary manipulation (glycogen loading)? Outline how a performer may carry out a glycogen loading regime.
8. Explain how the coach of a triple jumper may sub-divide the training year.
9. Give a definition and a practical example for each of the following:
   - macrocycle
   - mesocycle
   - microcycle
   - training unit.
10. Using the example of a swimmer, explain what you understand by the term 'tapering'.
11. Describe the process of thermoregulation when exercising in a warm environment.

CHAPTER 4

The nature of injury in sport

LEARNING OBJECTIVES:

By the end of this chapter you should be able to:

- *describe the nature of injury in sport*
- *explain the steps that can be taken to avoid injury in sport*
- *outline methods to promote recovery and rehabilitation including hyperbaric chambers, oxygen tents and ice baths*
- *explain the concept of DOMS and how it can be avoided following exercise.*

Introduction

Injuries in sport occur for a variety of reasons from a clumsy tackle in football to a stress fracture through over-use and although some injuries can be prevented, for the elite athlete who trains and competes regularly the occasional injury is unfortunately inevitable. The exact nature of the injuries we see in the competitive sporting arena arise from two main sources:

1. **Intrinsic factors**, which relate to the physiological make-up of the individual concerned, and
2. **Extrinsic factors**, which relate to those injuries derived from external sources.

Fig 4.01 Injury in sport occurs for a number of different reasons

Intrinsic factors	Extrinsic factors
• Age • Sex • Body weight and composition • Muscle weakness (particularly the imbalance between agonist and antagonist) • Joint hyperlaxity • Poor flexibility • Malalignment of body parts (e.g. leg length discrepancies)	• Training methods (e.g. poor training techniques) • Training volume: particularly over-training • Inappropriate or unfamiliar playing surfaces • Inappropriate equipment • Inappropriate clothing such as footwear • Environmental conditions (e.g. an inadequate warm-up when exercising in cold conditions)

Table 4.01 Intrinsic and extrinsic causes of injury in sport

Injury prevention

Perhaps the key factor in contributing to sporting injury (both to intrinsic and extrinsic factors) is the lack of preparation on behalf of both coach and athlete. Failing to prepare appropriate training sessions or an athlete trying to do too much too soon or not paying the necessary attention to detail in acquiring appropriate kit or equipment can all result in serious injury and the need to spend a number of weeks or even months rehabilitating. So, effective preparation is key to the avoidance of injury in sport.

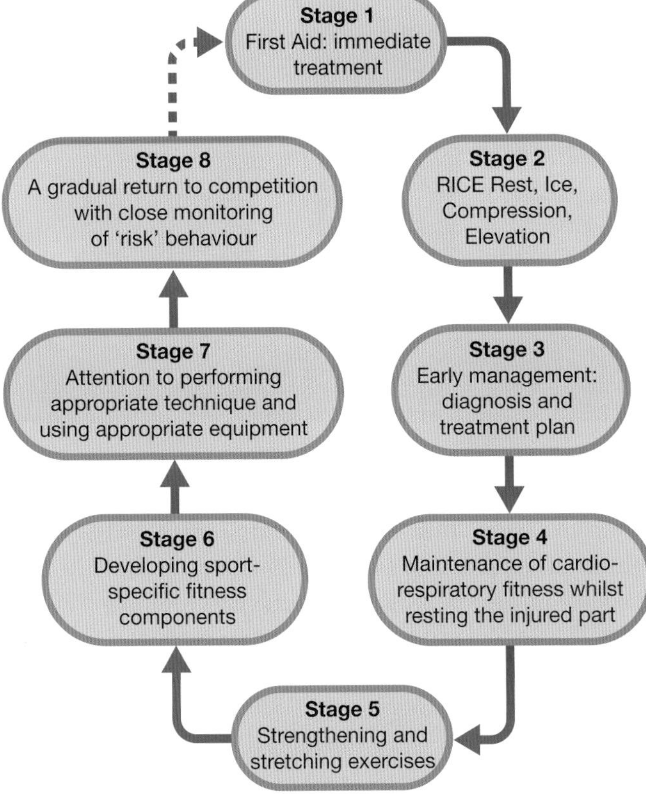

Fig 4.02 Stages in the management of a sporting injury

Intrinsic considerations	Extrinsic considerations
• Ensure the athlete performs an appropriate warm-up prior to training and competition • Ensure the athlete has the necessary fitness levels to perform the tasks required of him/her • Ensure the athlete is not suffering from fatigue so allow sufficient recovery between exercise sessions • Encourage the athlete to perform strengthening exercises appropriately to avoid the imbalance of muscle strength and power • Ensure the athlete has a sound nutritional programme	• Avoid abrupt changes to the athlete's training schedule, in terms of methods used and the intensity of training • Ensure the correct and appropriate use of training equipment • Ensure that appropriate clothing, including footwear is worn by the athlete • Pay the necessary attention to environmental factors and conditions • Ensure the rules of the activity are adhered to

Table 4.02 The intrinsic and extrinsic considerations necessary to avoid and prevent injury in sport

Injury management

Management of a sporting injury initially requires an assessment of why the injury occurred, followed by treatment of the actual injury itself. Maintaining and minimising losses in fitness and establishing an appropriate structured rehabilitation programme that allows a gradual return to competition should also be carefully planned. A suggested strategy in sports injury management is outlined in Fig 4.02.

REMEMBER!

You may have used RICE in the treatment of soft tissue injuries but perhaps PRICE is more appropriate where:

- P = protection of the injured part by the use of slings or crutches
- R = rest the injured part not the whole body!
- I = ice
- C = compression to reduce swelling
- E = elevation to restrict blood flow to the injured part

Sports rehabilitation

Athletes, coaches and physiotherapists all have one aim: to successfully rehabilitate the injured performer, so that they can return to training as quickly as possible and minimise fitness losses. In striving to achieve this the coach and athlete can turn to a variety of rehabilitative methods all designed to reduce recovery time. For your examination you need to know a little about the following methods:

- **hyperbaric chambers**
- **oxygen tents**
- **ice baths.**

For each one you are required to **state what is involved**, **the physiological reasons for its use**, **those performers likely to benefit**, and **a comment on whether it achieves the desired effect**.

EXAM TIP:

For each rehabilitative method you will need to know what is involved, the physiological reasons for its use, those performers likely to benefit, and give your opinion on whether you think it is appropriate or not.

The use of hyperbaric chambers in the treatment of sports injuries

Hyperbaric chambers were originally developed to treat decompression sickness developed by scuba divers. Essentially the chamber delivers oxygen to the injured athlete at very high pressure (approximately 2½ times greater than normal atmospheric pressure). In normal environmental conditions the air that we breathe is composed of approximately 20% oxygen and 80% nitrogen. A hyperbaric chamber delivers 100% pure oxygen to the body.

As pressure increases within the chamber the amount of oxygen inspired by the injured performer increases. Haemoglobin within the red blood cells quickly becomes fully saturated with oxygen and because the oxygen is delivered at high pressure any excess oxygen is dissolved into the plasma component of the blood. The very high pressure allows oxygen to reach parts of the body at higher concentration levels that it wouldn't normally reach. Consequences of this include improved blood supply and the formation of new blood cells, and a faster rate of cell turnover enhancing the growth and repair of tissue cells.

Fig 4.03 A performer undergoing hyperbaric therapy

Hyperbaric chambers can be used to treat the full range of injuries and conditions to allow athletes to recover more quickly from athletic performance:

- soft tissue (muscular) injuries and oedema (swelling)
- tendon and ligament damage (including tendonitis)
- tissue infections
- compromised immune systems that may have arisen from overtraining.

Some studies have suggested that recovery time is cut by half if a hyperbaric chamber is used in the rehabilitation process!

KEY TERMS

Hyperbaric chamber:
a chamber that delivers 100% pure oxygen at very high pressure to promote recovery of injured athletes

Oxygen (hypoxic) tent:
a chamber designed to mimic conditions at altitude and are used by performers to maintain fitness levels while injured

Ice bath:
immersion of a performer's body (usually legs) in ice cold water which is believed to reduce muscle soreness and tissue swelling that accompanies hard training or competition

The use of oxygen tents in the treatment of sports injuries

Oxygen tents (or hypoxic tents as they are sometimes called) have famously been used by soccer stars such as David Beckham and Wayne Rooney in the run-up to the World Cup in 2002 and 2006 respectively. They are more widely used however by endurance athletes who wish to mimic the environmental conditions of altitude. Oxygen tents are essentially specialised chambers that regulate the amount of oxygen available to the injured performer while they sleep. By replicating the low-oxygen conditions of altitude the body responds by increasing its production of red blood cells which then allows the fitness of the performer to be maintained even though training has ceased because of the injury. Oxygen tents are therefore used to preserve the fitness of the injured athlete rather than to treat the injury itself and are most commonly used when an athlete's training is hampered because of injuries to the legs or feet.

APPLY IT!

Several studies confirm the benefits of sleeping in low-oxygen tents. A five-year study by the US Olympic Committee confirmed that performers who live at high altitude (or sleep in low-oxygen tents) and train at sea level perform better. A further study by exercise physiologists at Staffordshire University found that the aerobic capacity of elite athletes improved as much as 30% following several months of sleeping in a low-oxygen tent.

Fig 4.04 Oxygen masks can be used to maintain fitness levels if an athlete is injured

The use of ice baths to promote recovery

From marathon runners to rugby players the use of ice baths is ubiquitous in the world of elite sport. The sight of athletes standing in wheelie bins filled with cold water is not uncommon at the side of many a training ground. So why do athletes put themselves through this muscle-numbing procedure?

Ice baths can treat both tissue swelling and soreness that occurs following hard exercise and is believed to speed up the recovery process. Essentially immersion in cold water allows even and controlled constriction of blood vessels surrounding all the muscles, effectively squeezing and draining blood and waste products away from the leg. Exiting the ice bath (after about 6 minutes or so) then invokes a blood rush, which flushes the muscles with fresh oxygenated blood carrying the nutrients and components necessary to revitalise the damaged and sore tissue. Just like an oil change allows the engine of a car to run smoothly, so a rush of fresh blood can revitalise the muscles and allow the athlete to recover from the training session or competition more quickly.

TASK 4.01

Copy out and complete the table below summarising key aspects of different methods used to promote recovery in athletes.

Method	What is involved?	Physiological reasons for its use	Who benefits?	Does it work?
Hyperbaric chambers				
Oxygen tents				
Ice baths				

Fig 4.05 Ice baths are often used to promote recovery from training sessions and competition

APPLY IT!

It is reported that some England rugby players, including Lawrence Dallaglio and Joe Worsley, have taken their obsession with ice baths one step further by actually visiting a cryotherapy clinic at an Olympic training centre in Poland. Cryotherapy chambers are essentially human deep freezes into which an athlete steps and shivers at temperatures of between minus 120°C–160°C for a period of approximately 4 minutes!

A word about DOMS

DOMS or **delayed onset of muscle soreness** is a term used to explain the feelings of muscle stiffness and tenderness often experienced in the days (usually 48 hours) following exercise. It is perhaps more common in those embarking upon a new exercise regime or when performing **eccentric muscle contractions** such as those experienced when lowering weights or running downhill.

It is thought that DOMS occurs as a result of microscopic tears to the muscle fibres and surrounding connective tissue along with the associated swelling. Although DOMS is an annoying hindrance, symptoms are usually temporary and go within a couple or days or so once the muscle fibres have repaired themselves. There are a few tips that can be followed to prevent and avoid DOMS:

- Warm up thoroughly before exercising and cool down completely following the activity.
- During the training session, progress from lower intensity bouts of work through to higher intensity periods.
- When beginning a new activity start gradually and build up intensity slowly.
- Limit the amount of eccentric contractions performed early in the training session.

REMEMBER!

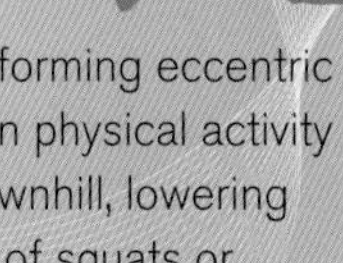

DOMS are most likely to occur when performing eccentric muscle contractions. These might occur in physical activity when performing plyometrics, running downhill, lowering weights and during the downward phase of squats or press-ups.

KEY TERMS

Delayed onset of muscle soreness (DOMS): the painful and tender muscles often experienced 48 hours following exercise

Eccentric muscle contraction: the lengthening of a muscle whilst contracting, such as happens in the quadriceps muscle group when landing during the hop phase of a triple jump

ATHLETE PROFILE

Paula Radcliffe is perhaps our most experienced female athlete, yet her career has been blighted by injury. In March 2009 she sustained a fracture to the second toe on her right foot while altitude training in Alberquerque, New Mexico which caused her to pull out of the 2009 Flora London Marathon. This was not the first time injury has caused Paula to miss out on competing on the world stage. In fact Paula's athletic career has been characterised by injury. A fracture of her femur prevented her from being a competitive force at the Beijing Olympics in 2008. She failed to finish the marathon in the 2004 Olympics in Athens due to a prior hamstring injury which also caused her to pull out of the World Cross-Country Championships, and a leg strain forced her to withdraw from the 2003 World Championships. No doubt Paula has access to a fantastic medical team who will ensure she receives the best rehabilitative care. There is a very fine line, however, between being at the peak of your physical performance and training the body too hard causing it to physically break down. Paula's determination and motivation to succeed is without question. However, we must pose the question at what cost to her body?

ExamCafé

Relax, refresh, result!

Refresh your memory

Revision checklist

Make sure you know the following:

- ▷ Injury in sport is almost inevitable and occurs for a variety of reasons.
- ▷ The locus of causality of an injury can be either intrinsic or extrinsic.
- ▷ Intrinsic factors include age, body weight and composition, muscle weakness and poor flexibility.
- ▷ Extrinsic factors include poor training methods, inappropriate use of equipment and clothing, and environmental conditions.
- ▷ Preparation is the key to injury prevention and avoidance.
- ▷ If the intrinsic and extrinsic factors that cause injuries are addressed then injury can possibly be avoided.
- ▷ There are many rehabilitative methods to treat the injured performer.
- ▷ For your examination you are required to know about the use of hyperbaric chambers, oxygen tents and ice baths.
- ▷ For each of these you are required to state what is involved, the physiological reasons for its use, those performers likely to benefit and a comment on whether it achieves the desired effect.
- ▷ Hyperbaric chambers are used by injured performers to speed up recovery by delivering oxygen to the injured part at very high pressure.
- ▷ Hyperbaric chambers can be used to treat the full range of injuries and conditions.
- ▷ Oxygen tents (or hypoxic tents) replicate the low oxygen conditions of altitude.
- ▷ Oxygen tents are not used specifically to treat a particular sports injury but rather to maintain fitness levels while the performer is rehabilitating.

- Ice baths are used to treat both injury and the soreness that occurs following hard exercise, speeding up the recovery process.
- Ice baths create a rush of fresh oxygenated blood carrying the nutrients and components necessary to revitalise the damaged and sore tissue.
- Delayed onset of muscle s oreness (DOMS) is a term used to explain the feelings of muscle stiffness and tenderness often experienced in the days (usually 48 hours) following exercise.
- DOMS typically occurs following eccentric muscle contractions.
- DOMS can be reduced by warming up thoroughly before exercise and cooling down completely following the activity.

Revise as you go

1. Outline the intrinsic and extrinsic factors that can contribute to sports injury.
2. Outline the intrinsic and extrinsic factors that can be addressed to avoid and prevent injuries from occurring.
3. How do hyperbaric chambers promote the recovery of injured performers?
4. What are hypoxic tents and how do they help in the rehabilitation of injured athletes?
5. Why do some performers feel it necessary to torture themselves by taking an ice bath following training and competition?
6. What is DOMS and how can it be avoided?

CHAPTER 5

The mechanics of movement

LEARNING OBJECTIVES:

By the end of this chapter you should be able to:

- define and give units of measurement for quantities of linear motion
- apply each of Newton's three laws of motion to sporting activity
- describe the application of forces in sporting activities
- explain the concept of impulse in sprinting
- explain the relevance of momentum to sporting techniques.
- use high jump to demonstrate the concept of net forces
- identify the nature of forces acting on a sports performer
- sketch free body diagrams identifying the type, size and application of forces acting on a sports performer or object at a particular moment in time
- explain the factors that govern the flight of projectiles, using shot put as a reference
- apply each of Newton's three laws to angular motion
- define and give units of measurement for quantities of angular motion
- identify the three major axes of rotation and give examples of sporting movements that take place around them
- explain the concept of angular momentum and its conservation during flight
- explain the relationship between moment of inertia and angular velocity when somersaulting and spinning.

Introduction

Aspects of biomechanics touch all sports performers, from the club sprinter wishing to improve technique to the Olympic ski jumper aiming to stay in flight for longer. At the heart of our study will be Newton's Laws of Motion and we will establish how these can be applied to sporting activity to help develop and enhance performance.

Fig 5.01 A hammer thrower uses biomechanics to maximise efficiency of technique

Linear motion

Linear motion occurs when a body moves in a straight or curved line with all parts of the body moving the same distance in the same direction at the same speed.

The following are quantities of linear motion that are useful in your study of the mechanics of motion:

- vector quantity
- scalar quantity
- inertia
- acceleration
- mass
- speed
- displacement
- momentum
- weight
- velocity
- distance

Vector v scalar quantities

Some quantities of linear motion are only considered in terms of their size or magnitude. These are known as **scalar quantities**. Other quantities are described in terms of both a magnitude and a direction. These are termed **vector quantities**.

To help explain this further consider the following scenario: a car is travelling at 30 mph. From this statement we have information regarding the magnitude or speed of the car but no information regarding its direction. In this instance a scalar quantity has been described. Now consider this same car travelling at 30 mph in a north-easterly direction. We now have information with respect to both magnitude and direction: a vector quantity (velocity) has just been described.

Mass v weight

Mass is the quantity of matter a body possesses. The greater the density and volume of the body, the greater the matter and the bigger the mass. A shot put therefore has a greater mass than a table tennis ball as it is greater in both density and volume. Students often confuse mass and weight of an object.

Mass of an object always remains the same at any place. **Weight** on the other hand is the force which a given mass feels due to gravity. If you go to the moon your mass remains same, e.g. 60 kgs, but your weight becomes less by one-sixth, since the moon's gravity is one-sixth that of earth.

Weight is a force and as such is measured in Newtons (the units of force). As weight always acts downwards from the centre of mass it has a direction as well as a magnitude. Weight is therefore a **vector quantity** with its direction signified by an arrowhead and its magnitude by the length of the arrow. Mass on the other hand only has size (no direction) and so is a **scalar quantity**.

Calculating your weight force

If your mass is 60 kgs then your weight is:

$60 \times 10 = 600$ newtons

This is because:

Force = mass × acceleration
(From Newton's Second Law)

Thus weight = mass × acceleration due to gravity

TASK 5.01

Find your mass using a pair of bathroom scales. Use your mass to calculate your weight force.

KEY TERMS

Scalar quantity:
a quantity which is fully described by magnitude alone

Vector quantity:
a quantity which is fully described by both a magnitude and a direction

Mass:
the quantity of matter a body possesses

Weight:
the force exerted on the mass of a body by gravity

Inertia

Inertia is the reluctance of a body to move or change its state of motion. The bigger the mass of an object the harder it is to move or change its motion and therefore the larger its quantity of inertia. A sumo wrestler has a large amount of inertia and is therefore difficult to move. Moving objects or bodies that have high inertia will need a large force to change the state of motion. Consider two rugby league players running with the ball at the same speed. The larger, heavier player will have greater inertia and will therefore be more difficult to stop than the smaller, lighter player.

KEY TERMS

Inertia:
the reluctance of a body to move or change its state of motion

Distance:
a measure of the path a body takes in moving from one position to another, measured in metres (m)

Displacement:
the shortest possible route between the starting and finishing point of a body that has moved. This will normally be in a straight line 'as the crow flies', measured in metres (m)

REMEMBER!

If equal force is applied to a cricket ball and a shot put, the acceleration of the cricket ball will be greater as it has lower inertia.

Distance v displacement

The quantity of **distance** refers to the amount of ground an object covers during its motion. **Displacement** on the other hand considers how far the position of the object has changed as a result of the motion, and is usually measured 'as the crow flies' from the starting to the finishing position. For example, consider a 400m runner who has just completed a race. She has just covered a distance of 400m but because the start and finish line are in the same place her displacement is in fact zero.

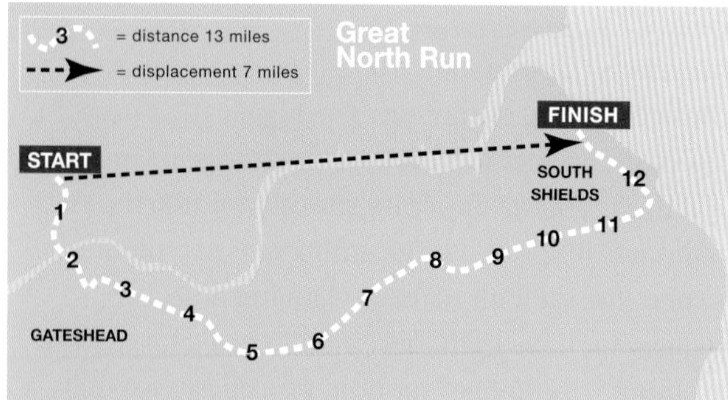

Fig 5.02 Distance covered and displacement during the Great North Run

Since distance is the length of the path taken by a body in moving from one place to another it is a scalar quantity. Displacement, however, is a vector quantity as it has a direction as well as size. The Great North Run is an annual half marathon event. The route is shown in Figure 5.02 and the displacement by the vector arrow. The distance covered is 13.1 miles yet the displacement is approximately 7 miles.

Speed v velocity

Speed and **velocity** are terms that are often used interchangeably. They are however very different with regard to biomechanical analysis.

Speed is the rate of change of distance or a body's movement per unit of time and has no consideration for direction. Speed is therefore a scalar quantity.

$$\text{Speed (ms}^{-1}\text{)} = \frac{\text{Distance (m)}}{\text{Time (secs)}}$$

Velocity is the rate of change of displacement and is a **vector quantity** and as such is 'direction-aware'. When evaluating the velocity of an object we must therefore keep track of direction. It would not be enough to simply say that an object has a velocity of 30 mph, we must include directional information in order to fully describe the velocity of the object. We should therefore say that the car was travelling at 30 mph in an easterly direction.

$$\text{Velocity (ms}^{-1}\text{)} = \frac{\text{Displacement (m)}}{\text{Time (secs)}}$$

Fig 5.03 Velocity is speed with a direction

TASK 5.02

Kelly Holmes won the 800m gold medal at the 2004 Athens Olympics in a time of 1 minute 56.38 seconds.

1. Calculate Kelly's average speed during the race.
2. Calculate Kelly's average velocity during the race.

KEY TERMS

Speed:
a body's movement per unit of time with no consideration for direction, measured in metres/second (ms^{-1})

Velocity:
the rate of change of displacement. The speed of a body in a given direction, measured in metres/second (ms^{-1})

Acceleration:
the rate of change of velocity measured in metres/second/second (ms^{-2})

TASK 5.04

Draw up a two-column chart. Decide whether the following are vector or scalar quantities and write them in the appropriate columns:
mass, distance, velocity, inertia, acceleration, weight, displacement, force, air resistance, speed, deceleration.

Quantities of linear motion	
Vector	Scalar

Acceleration and deceleration

Acceleration or deceleration is the rate of change of velocity of an object. Just like velocity they are 'direction-aware' and are therefore vector quantities. Acceleration is the rate of increase in velocity and deceleration the rate of decrease in velocity.

$$\text{Acceleration } (ms^{-2}) = \frac{\text{Change in velocity } (ms^{-1})}{\text{Time (secs)}} = \frac{Vf - Vi}{t}$$

Where: Vf = final velocity; Vi = initial velocity; t = time taken

REMEMBER!

A high jumper accelerates in an upwards direction at take-off!

TASK 5.03

The table below shows 100m split times of Maurice Greene in an Athens Grand Prix event in 1997.

10m	20m	30m	40m	50m	60m	70m	80m	90m	100m
1.71s	2.75s	3.67s	4.55s	5.42s	6.27s	7.12s	7.98s	8.85s	9.73s

Table 5.01 Split times for 100m race

Distance	Time	Time for 10m section	Average speed ms^{-1}	Average acceleration ms^{-2}
10m				

1. Under the headings in the above table give the required information for each 10m section of the race.
2. Plot a graph of average speed (ms^{-1}) against time (sec).
3. Using your graph highlight the point where Greene reaches maximum velocity.
4. Calculate Greene's average acceleration between 0.5 and 1.5 seconds.

Momentum

Momentum is the amount of motion a body possesses and is the product of mass and velocity:

- **Momentum = Mass (kg) × Velocity (ms^{-1})**
- The standard unit of measurement of momentum is kilogram metres per second ($kgms^{-1}$)

The momentum of a 90kg prop forward travelling at a velocity of $10ms^{-1}$ is therefore $900kgms^{-1}$. Interestingly because the mass of an object or performer tends to remain constant during sporting activity any changes in momentum must be as a result of a change in velocity (i.e. acceleration or deceleration).

When we consider an object or performer in flight, such as a long jumper, neither mass nor velocity can be altered so momentum is said to be conserved. The long jumper therefore tries to maximise his/her velocity during the run-up and at take-off since it cannot be changed once in the air!

This relates to Newton's First Law of Motion and is known as the law of conservation of momentum.

TASK 5.05

Complete the table below that considers the momentum of a variety of projectiles used in sport.

Ball	Mass	Velocity ms^{-1}	Momentum $kgms^{-1}$
Hockey	0.16kg	$20ms^{-0}$	
Table tennis	0.0024kg	$20ms^{-1}$	
Tennis	0.067kg		0.3
Tennis		$50ms^{-1}$	3.0
Squash	600g	$35ms^{-1}$	

Table 5.02 Momentum of a variety of projectiles used in sport

Impulse

Another way of thinking about force is in terms of **impulse**. Impulse is concerned with the length of time a force is applied to an object or body and relates to a change in momentum that occurs as a consequence.

Impulse = force × time

A change in momentum is synonymous with a change in acceleration therefore:

$$F = ma \longrightarrow a = \frac{Vf - Vi}{t}$$

$$\downarrow$$

$$Ft = mVf - mVi \longleftarrow F = \frac{m(Vf - Vi)}{t}$$

Impulse (Ft) is therefore equal to a change in momentum.

Impulse is used in sporting activity to:

- add speed to a body or object
- slow down moving bodies slowly on impact.

For example, the O'Brien technique whereby a shot putter performs a 1¾ turn before release does so to maximise the time over which a force is applied to the shot, increasing outgoing acceleration. Similarly a follow-through is used in racket and stick sports to increase the time the racket or stick is in contact with the ball which will also increase the outgoing momentum of the ball (as well as giving direction!).

Fig 5.04 A good slip fielder follows the ball through. Marcus Trescothick takes a slip catch successfully.

A fielder in cricket will cradle a fast moving cricket ball by meeting the ball early and moving his hands backwards in the direction of the ball's motion. This increases the time during which his hands are in contact with the ball, cushioning the impact and preventing the ball from bouncing off uncontrollably.

Similarly, a gymnast landing from a vault or dismount will flex at the hip and knee to extend the time over which the impact force is imparted to the body. In doing so they can reduce the likelihood of impact injuries.

Impulse and sprinting

Figure 5.06 illustrates the impulse experienced by a 100m sprinter during a race. As the sprinter drives out of the blocks (d) a large positive impulse is produced which allows the sprinter to accelerate.

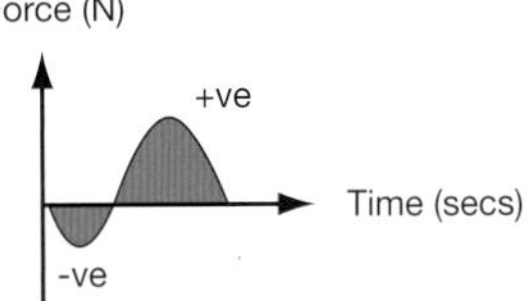

a) An accelerating body (+ve > –ve)

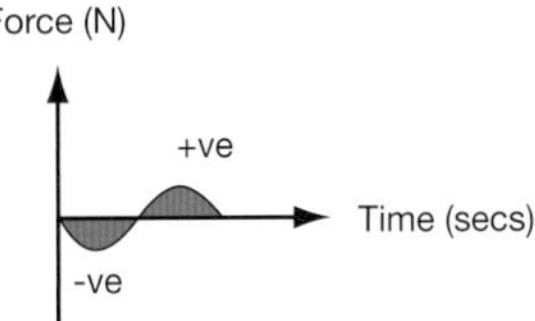

b) A body moving at constant velocity (+ve = –ve)

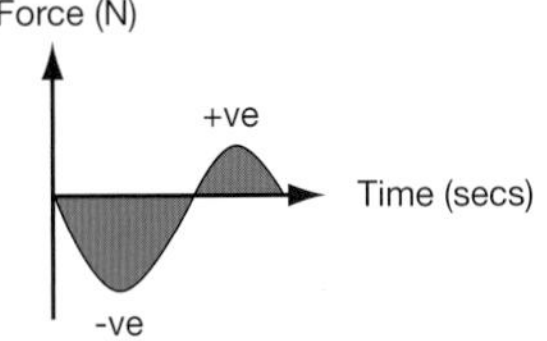

c) A decelerating body (+ve < –ve)

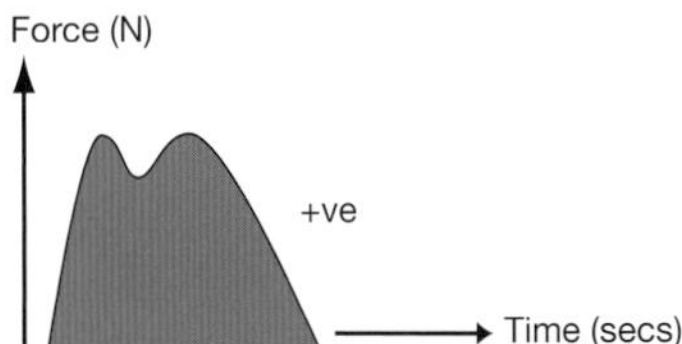

d) A large +ve impulse is generated by a sprinter as he or she drives away from the blocks.

Fig 5.05 Graphs showing the effects of +ve and –ve impulses on a sprinter

As long as the positive impulse exceeds the negative impulse created when landing on the track, acceleration will occur (a). The sprinter moves with constant velocity when positive and negative aspects of impulse are equal (b). Towards the end of the race, fatigue sets in and the sprinter cannot generate as strong a reaction force as earlier in the race. Consequently the negative impulse becomes greater than any positive impulse generated causing the sprinter to decelerate (c). The shaded area below the graph (–ve impulse) represents a body landing on the ground. The +ve impulse above the graph represents the impulse of a body due to the ground reaction force.

Newton's Laws of Motion

Newton's Laws go some way in helping to explain the principles of movement within the sporting arena.

Newton's First Law – the law of inertia

Earlier in this chapter you learned that inertia is the reluctance of a body to move or change its state of motion. Newton's First Law relates to this notion:

'Every body at rest, or moving with constant velocity in a straight line, will continue in that state unless compelled to change by an external force exerted upon it.'

In pursuit of an explanation to Newton's First Law, consider a golf ball at rest on a tee. There are two forces acting upon the golf ball:

- One force is the Earth's gravitational pull which exerts a downward force through the centre of mass of the ball, (i.e. a weight force).
- The other force is the reaction force from the tee which pushes back onto the ball.

Since these two forces are of equal magnitude and pull in opposite directions (see Newton's Third Law), they balance each other out. The golf ball is said to be at equilibrium and therefore remains at rest on the tee. The golf ball will remain on the tee motionless, until it is struck by the golf club which transfers an 'action force' causing it to overcome inertia and change its state of motion.

Similarly once the golf ball has been struck it will continue to travel with constant velocity in a straight line as long as forces remain balanced.

Newton's Second Law – the law of acceleration

Newton's Second Law of Motion states that the acceleration of an object or body is directly proportional to the force acting upon it. It is formally stated as:

'The rate of change of momentum of a body (or the acceleration for a body of constant mass) is proportional to the force causing it and takes place in the direction in which the force acts.'

This therefore implies that, in order to produce a greater acceleration, an athlete must generate proportionally greater forces. Using golf as an example once more, when teeing off, the golf ball receives a greater change in velocity (i.e. acceleration) than during a putt. In both instances the golf ball will accelerate in the direction of the force. This law also tells us that the greater the mass the greater the force required to give the same acceleration.

EXAM TIP:

Sometimes Newton's Second Law is stated as $F = ma$. This suggests that if mass of the body or object remains constant then acceleration is equal to the size of the force causing it. It also tells us that assuming the action force remains constant, acceleration will be greater for lighter bodies or objects.

Newton's Third Law – the law of action and reaction

'For every force that is exerted by one body on another, there is an equal and opposite force exerted by the second body on the first' or more simply ... *'For every action, there is an equal and opposite reaction.'*

TASK 5.06

Apply Newton's three Laws of Motion to the following sporting situations:

- a high jumper at take-off
- a high diver performing a dive
- a gymnast performing a vault
- a football player taking a penalty.

Fig 5.06 Newton's Laws of Motion in action

The statement means that in every interaction, there is a pair of forces acting. The size of the force on the first object is equal to the size of the force on the second object and the direction of the force on the first object is opposite to the direction of the force on the second object. To help explain this law further, think of what happens when you step off a boat that is on the water onto dry land. As you step onto the land, the boat tends to move in the opposite direction (leaving you face down in the water, if you aren't careful!). If we go back to golf this implies that the golf club receives an equal and opposite force from the golf ball to that imparted by the golf club onto the ball.

May the force be with you! – The role of force in sporting activity

One key factor in any kind of sporting performance is force. Without force we would not be able to jump, kick, throw or even move. Force can be a push or pull; more force is needed to move a larger object than a smaller one. When a force is applied to an object, the velocity of that object changes. This change in velocity constitutes an acceleration. So, forces are tied to accelerations.

Forces can therefore:

- cause a body at rest to move
- cause a moving body to accelerate
- cause a moving body to decelerate
- cause a moving body to change direction
- cause a body to change shape.

Understanding net force – balanced v unbalanced

Balanced forces occur where two or more forces are in operation that are of equal size but opposite in direction. All the forces cancel each other out so that there is zero net force. In this instance an object or body will either remain stationary or if moving will continue to do so at constant velocity. A sprinter running at constant velocity does so because there is zero net force acting.

Unbalanced forces on the other hand occur where a force acting in one direction is larger than that acting in the opposite direction so that the object or body will start to move or accelerate/decelerate in the direction of the bigger force. If we consider the high jumper in Figure 5.07 he is able to accelerate upwards because the reaction force is greater than the weight force (i.e. reaction force = weight force + applied muscular force).

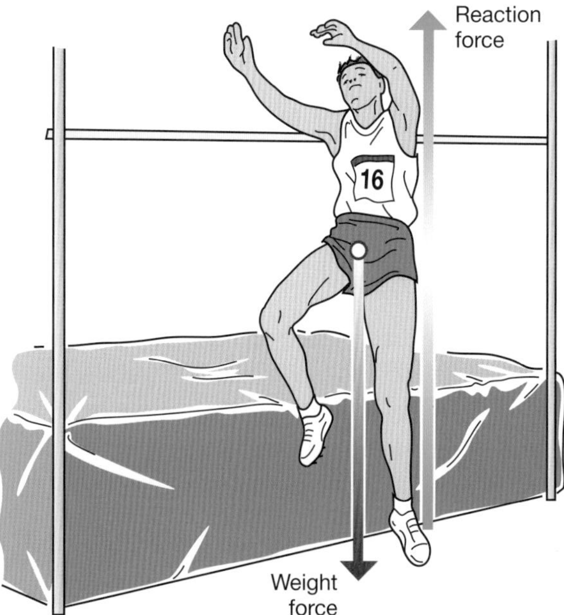

Fig 5.07 The high jumper accelerates upwards as the reaction force is greater than the weight force

KEY TERMS

Net force:
the resultant force acting on a body having considered all other forces acting. If all forces cancel each other out then there is zero net force

REMEMBER!

Force is measured in newtons (N). A Newton is the force required to give a 1kg mass an acceleration of $1 ms^{-2}$.

Types of force

By understanding the role of force in sport the coach and athlete can manipulate technique to use force to best effect. Although there are many different forces at play the following are those that you are required to know for your examination:

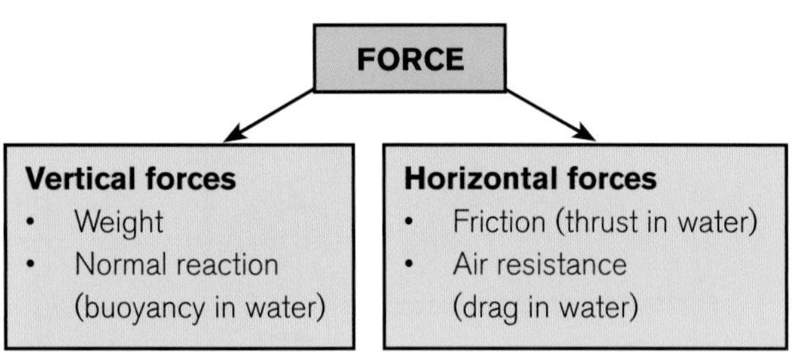

Fig 5.08 Types of force

Vertical forces

- **Weight:** We discovered earlier that mass and weight are not the same. A weight force is equal to the product of the mass of an object or body and the acceleration due to gravity.

  Weight = mass × acceleration due to gravity ($10ms^2$)

  Weight always acts downwards (from the centre of mass of an object or body) towards the centre of the earth.
- **Reaction force:** You will remember from Newton's third law that every action has an equal and opposite reaction. Reaction forces will therefore always occur whenever two bodies are in contact with one another. Reaction forces will always act at right angles (90°) to the contacted surface. (This is an important rule when drawing free body diagrams.) Figure 5.09 illustrates the reaction forces that might occur on a tennis player playing a forehand drive.

REMEMBER!

When describing a force make sure you state or show:

- a point of application
- a direction shown by the arrowhead
- a magnitude or size shown by the length of the arrow.

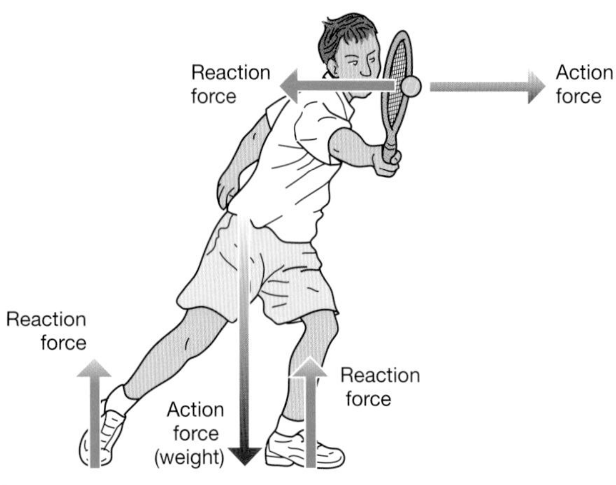

Fig 5.09 Reaction forces occur whenever two bodies are in contact with each other

Horizontal forces

- **Friction:** Some see friction as the 'evil' of all motion. It seems as if nature has given us friction to stop us from moving anything. Regardless of which direction something moves in, friction always seems to pull it the other way. In simple terms **friction opposes motion**.

  But friction is not all bad. In fact, it has a lot to do with our sporting lives. Without it, we wouldn't be able to walk, run or play the majority of sports as we know them. Everything would just keep slipping and falling all over the place.

  Friction is actually a force that appears whenever two things rub against each other or slide over one another. Although two objects might look smooth, microscopically they're very rough and jagged. As they slide against each other, their contact is anything BUT smooth. They both grind and drag against each other and this is where friction comes from.

  Factors affecting friction include:
  - **The roughness of the surfaces in contact** – the rougher the surfaces the greater the friction, e.g. football studs or spikes worn by athletes are designed to increase friction. Hard courts with a rough surface will also increase friction.
  - **The greater the down force or mass of an object the greater the friction.** A mountain biker will sit back over the driving wheel when riding up a muddy slope in order to gain a better grip of the tyre on the surface.

   - **Warmth of surfaces** – dependent upon the surface this will either increase or decrease friction. Consider the metal blade of an ice skate moving over the ice, for example. This will heat up and create a thin film of water which decreases the friction between the two surfaces.
- **Air resistance:** Air resistance is a form of fluid friction and therefore opposes motion. The degree of air resistance (often referred to as drag) experienced by sports performers such as swimmers, cyclists, motor racers and skiers very much depends upon the following:
   - **The velocity of the moving body** – the faster an object is moving the more it is subject to the effects of air resistance.
   - **The frontal cross-sectional area of the moving body** – the larger the frontal cross sectional the greater the effects of air resistance.
   - **The shape and surface characteristics of the moving body** – the less streamlined and rougher the surface of the moving body the more it will be affected by air resistance and drag.

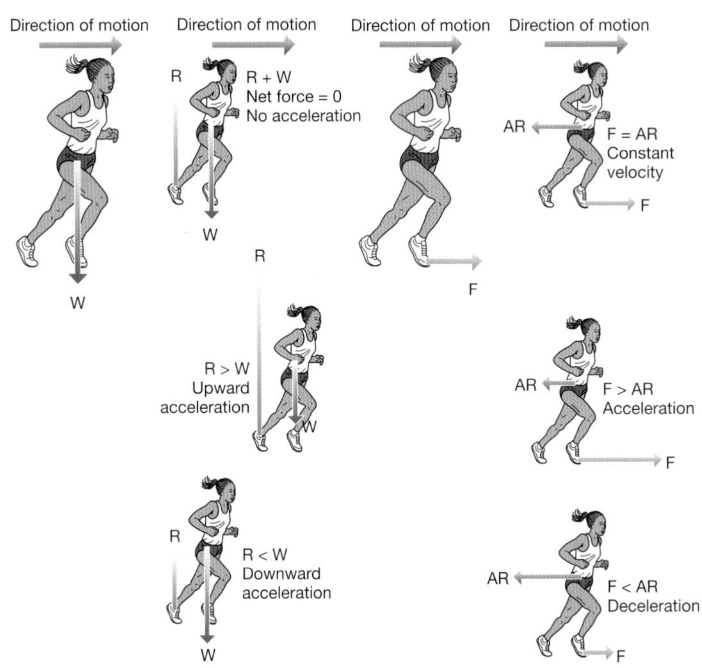

Fig 5.10 Key points to remember when drawing free body diagrams

TASK 5.07

Discuss with your classmates how sports performers such as swimmers, cyclists, motor racers and skiers try to reduce the effects of air resistance and drag.

KEY TERMS

Friction:
a resistive force encountered when two or more bodies in contact move past one another

Air resistance:
the force of air pushing against a moving object. It is a form of fluid friction that acts on something moving through the air

Free body diagrams

In your examination you may be required to draw or interpret free body diagrams. Free body diagrams are diagrams used to show the relative magnitude and direction of all the forces that are acting upon an object or body in a given situation. The length of the arrow in a free body diagram reflects the magnitude of the force and the position of the arrow head reveals the direction in which the force is acting.

The diagrams in Figure 5.10 summarise the main guidelines to follow when constructing or interpreting free body diagrams.

EXAM TIP:

When drawing or labelling free body diagrams always:

1. Draw on a direction of motion arrow.
2. Add your vertical forces: weight and reaction.
   Remember: if W = R the object/body will remain at the same height.
   If R>W then the object or body will accelerate upwards.
3. Add your horizontal forces: friction and air resistance.
   Remember: if F = AR the object/body will be travelling at constant velocity.
   If F>AR then the object/body is accelerating.
   If F<AR the object/body is decelerating.

Projectile motion

Projectile motion is central to the performance of many sporting activities. Objects and implements are used as projectiles in basketball, tennis and athletics whereas it is the human body that acts as a projectile in high jump, ski jumping and gymnastic events. Once in the air projectiles are only usually subject to the forces of gravity and air resistance although in some activities it is possible to produce a 'lift' force. As gravity always remains constant (approx. $10ms^{-2}$) any changes to the velocity of the projectile can be explained by the effects of air resistance. For some projectiles such as a shot or the human body the effects of air resistance are minimal and the flight path will be symmetrical or **parabolic**, for others such as a shuttlecock or table tennis ball the effects of air resistance are great which causes the projectile to veer away from the normal parabolic path to form an asymmetrical or **distorted parabola**.

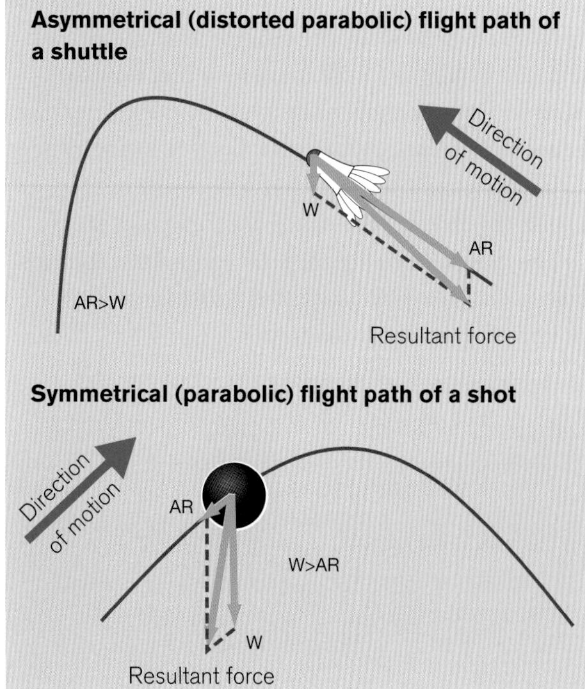

Fig 5.11 A comparison of the flight paths of a shot and a shuttlecock

Three factors determine the horizontal displacement of a projectile such as a shot:

- velocity of release
- height of release
- angle of release.

Generally, an increase in the velocity of the shot at release and an increase in the height of release will increase the horizontal displacement of the shot. However, for any given velocity and height of release there is an optimal release angle which maximises the horizontal displacement.

The velocity of release

An increase in the release velocity will increase the horizontal displacement of the projectile. Throwing events in athletics are very technical. The shift or rotation of a shot putter is designed to ensure that the shot leaves the performers hand at maximum velocity.

The height of release

An increase in the release height will increase the horizontal displacement of the projectile. We can conclude therefore that taller shot putters have an advantage over shorter ones! That is not to say that shorter shot putters can never win, they simply need to manipulate the angle of release that suits them best!

The angle of release

The optimum angle of release of a projectile is dependent upon the relative heights of release and landing. Where release height and landing height are the same such as when performing the long jump the optimum angle for take-off is 45°. Where release height is greater than landing height, for example, when putting the shot, the optimum angle is less than 45°. Where release height is below the landing height, such as when performing a free throw in basketball (the landing height in this instance is the hoop and not the floor!) the optimum angle of release is greater than 45°.

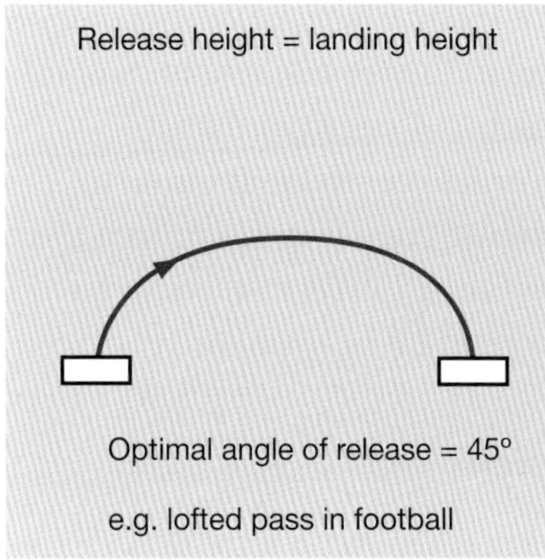

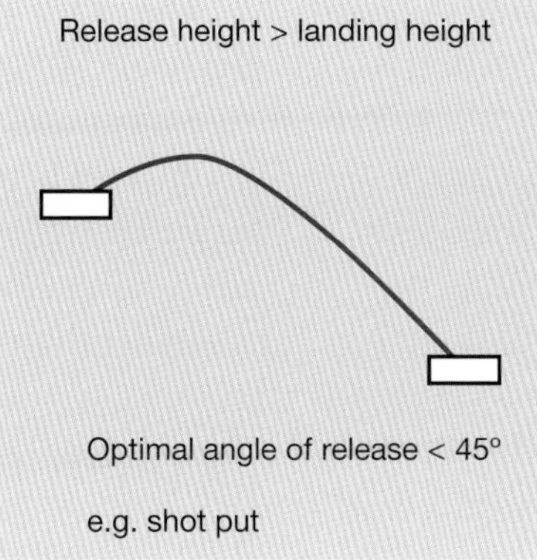

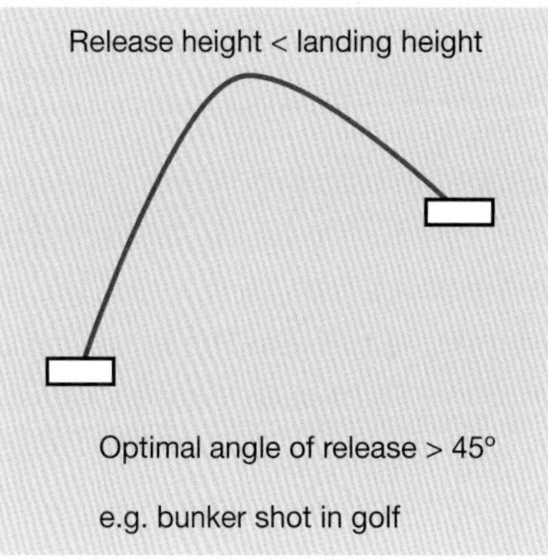

Fig 5.12 Optimal angles of release relative to release and landing heights of projectiles

TASK 5.08

Video another member of your class performing several of the following skills. (Make sure you are at right angles or side on to the performer.)

- Free throw in basket ball
- Drop kick in rugby
- Shot put
- Penalty flick in hockey
- Shooting in netball
- A tennis serve

In each situation study the angle of release and sketch the flight path of the projectile. Share your findings with others in your class and between you come up with the optimum angle of release for each situation. (NB: You may need to consider the horizontal displacement of each projectile as well as the accuracy of the sill performed!)

Vector components of parabolic flight

Air resistance on a shot is negligible therefore there are no additional horizontal forces acting on the shot other than the action force that was applied by the shot putter. Consequently the shot maintains its initial horizontal vector quantity throughout the duration of the flight. Note from Fig 5.13 that the length of the horizontal arrow is the same throughout each stage of the flight.

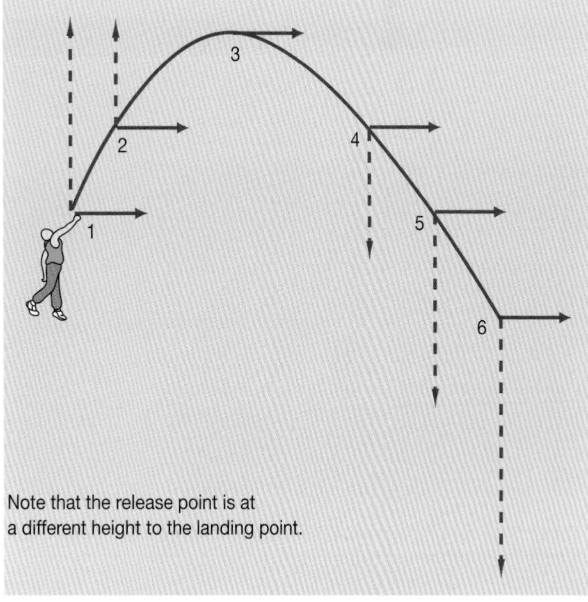

Fig 5.13 The flight path of a shot showing the changes in vertical and horizontal vector components

Other than the initial vertical vector quantity applied by the shot putter, the only vertical force acting is gravity; consequently the vertical vector component changes at a rate of $9.8ms^{-1}$ for every second the shot remains in the air. As the vertical component changes at a regular rate and the horizontal component remains the same throughout the resulting flight path is parabolic.

Note from Figure 5.13 the length of the vertical component of the vector is the same at stage 1 and 5 and at stage 2 and 4.

Table 5.03 shows the changes in the vertical and horizontal vector components of the flight path of a ball.

Time from release (secs)	Velocity (ms^{-1})	Acceleration (ms^{-2})
0.0	14.7	-9.8
1.0	4.9	-4.9
1.5	0.0	
2.0	−4.9	-4.9
3.0	−14.7	-9.8

Table 5.03 the changes in vertical velocity of a ball thrown in the air (Adapted from source: Walder, 1994)

The exact shape of the parabola will depend upon the relationship between the vertical and horizontal components of the vector. A steep parabola is produced when the vertical component is much larger than the horizontal component. Whilst a less steep parabola occurs when the vertical component is smaller than the horizontal component.

Angular motion

Angular motion occurs whenever a force acts outside the centre of mass of a body or object. This off-centre force is called an **eccentric force** and is necessary if rotation is to occur. Applying to sport we see that a gymnast performing a back flip will lean backwards just before take off so that the internal force generated by her leg muscles passes outside her centre of mass and initiates rotation. Likewise a footballer taking a free kick may kick the ball slightly off-centre so that the ball spins and follows a curved flight path around the defensive wall.

Relationship between vector components	Shape of parabola
Vertical component > Horizontal component	
Vertical component < Horizontal component	

Table 5.04 The influence of horizontal and vertical components of vectors in determining the flight path of projectiles.

	Position	Angular movements possible at joints	Sporting examples
Longitudinal axis	Runs through the body or joint from top to bottom	Rotation, Pronation and Supination	Spinning ice skater
Horizontal or transverse axis	Runs through the body or joint from side to side	Flexion and extension	Front/backward somersaulting high diver
Frontal axis	Runs through the body or joint from front to back	Abduction and adduction	A gymnast performing a cartwheel or side somersault

Table 5.05 Summary of the actions that occur about each axis

KEY TERMS

Eccentric force:
a force applied outside the centre of mass of an object or body. Eccentric forces cause angular motion

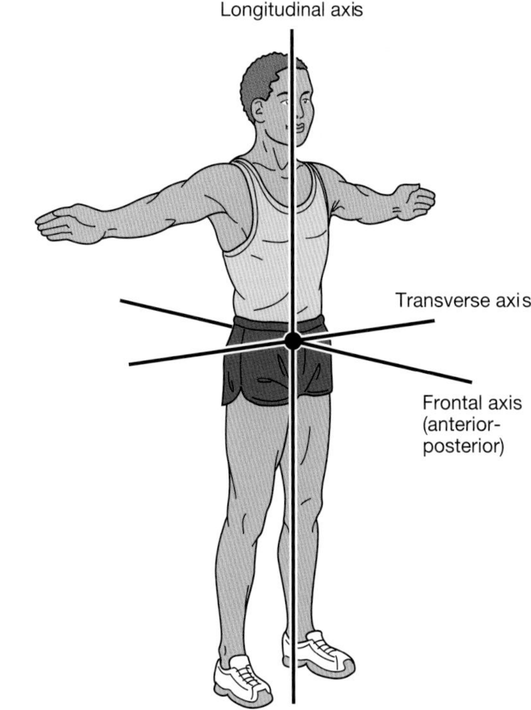

Fig 5.14 Principal axes of the body

Rotational movements

Axes of rotation: You will recall from your AS studies that the body has three imaginary poles running through the body that are the axes of rotation. Table 5.05 summarises the actions that occur about each axis.

REMEMBER!

The axis of rotation is always at right angles to the plane in which the movement occurs.

Torques or moments of force

Torques are the turning effects or rotational consequences of a force. The torque caused by a force depends upon the size of the force and the distance that the force acts from the axis of rotation (referred to as the moment arm):

Torque = Size of force (F) × Moment arm (d) (perpendicular distance from the fulcrum)

The standard unit of measurement of a torque is Newton metres (Nm).

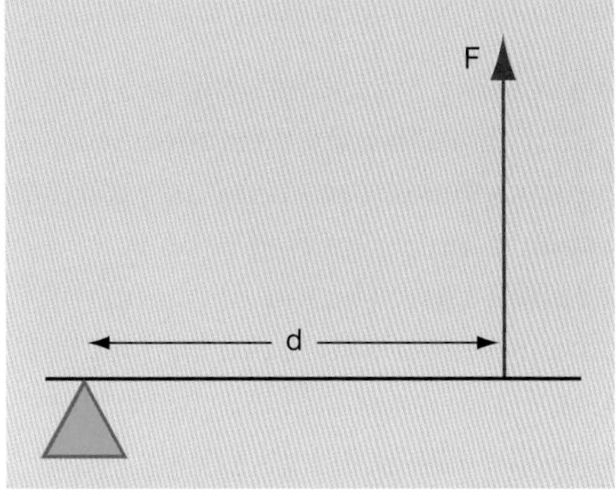

Fig 5.15 A torque in the body is the product of force x distance the force acts from the joint

Quantities of angular motion

All the quantities of linear motion have angular counterparts! The following measurements should aid your understanding of angular motion:

- angular distance
- angular displacement
- angular speed
- angular velocity
- angular acceleration.

TASK 5.09

It will be useful for you to know a definition, an equation and unit of measurement for each of the quantities of angular motion. Revise the definitions used in linear motion and see if you can work out these angular equivalents.

NB: If you get stuck have a look at the key terms.

REMEMBER!

Angular distance and angular displacement are usually measured in radians. A radian is a measurement of angle. 1 radian = 57.3 degrees

KEY TERMS

Angular distance:
the angle turned about an axis, measured in degrees (°) or radians (rads)

Angular displacement:
the smallest angle between starting and finishing positions, measured in degrees (°) or radians (rads)

Angular speed:
the angular distance travelled in a specified time. Angular speed is measured in rads/sec

$$\frac{\text{Angular distance (rads)}}{\text{time taken (secs)}}$$

Angular velocity (AV):
the angular displacement travelled in a specified time. Angular velocity is measured in rads/sec

$$\frac{\text{Angular displacement (rads)}}{\text{time taken (secs)}}$$

Angular acceleration:
the rate of change of angular velocity, measured in rads/sec^2

$$\frac{\text{Angular velocity (rads/secs)}}{\text{time taken (secs)}}$$

Angular analogues of Newton's Laws

Linear and angular motion are pretty close bedfellows! What goes for linear motion also goes for angular motion. Consequently Newton's Laws that govern linear motion also underpin rotational movement.

- **Newton's First Law:** A rotating body will continue to turn about its axis of rotation with constant angular momentum unless an external couple or eccentric force is exerted upon it.
- **Newton's Second Law:** The rate of change of angular momentum of a body is proportional to the torque (force) causing it and the change takes place in the direction in which the torque acts.
- **Newton's Third Law:** For every torque that is exerted by one body on another there is an equal and opposite torque exerted by the second body on the first.

Figure 5.16 demonstrates that the action of bringing the legs upwards (clockwise) during the long jump causes a reaction of the arms coming forwards and downwards (anti-clockwise).

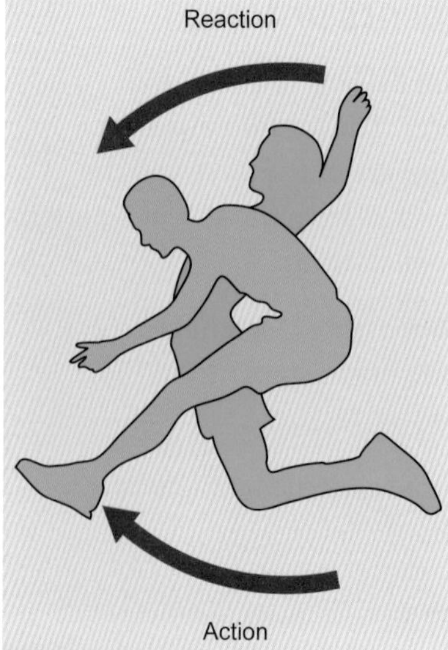

Fig 5.16 The angular analogue of Newton's Third Law of Motion

Moment of inertia (MI)

The **moment of inertia** is a measure of the resistance of an object to rotation and the desire of a body to want to continue to rotate once it has been set in motion. It is dependent upon two key factors – the mass of an object or body and the distribution of its mass around the axis of rotation.

- **The mass of the object:** The greater the mass of an object the greater its moment of inertia. A ten pin bowling ball is therefore more difficult to roll along the ground than a volleyball.
- **The distribution of the mass from the axis of rotation:** The further the mass is distributed away from the axis of rotation the greater the moment of inertia. A 4kg medicine ball should have a higher moment of inertia than a 4kg shot as its mass is spread further away from the axis of rotation. The shot has its mass concentrated about the axis, the moment of inertia is therefore lower and the shot will rotate faster. We can apply this to rotating humans too!

Applying moment of inertia to sport

Take for example a trampolinist. When performing a tucked back somersault the speed of rotation is much quicker than when performing a straight back somersault. This is because the mass of the trampolinist is spread further away from the axis of rotation when performing the straight back which in turn increases the moment of rotation and reduces angular velocity.

By altering body shape, it is possible to change the moment of inertia of the performer and either speed up or slow down rotation. Nowhere more so do we see this than when an ice skater performs a spin. Initially the skater may have limbs outstretched so that the moment of inertia is large; as they bring their limbs in closer to the body, the mass is brought in closer to the axis of rotation and the angular velocity increases.

This same principle is used by swimmers when swimming front crawl. After the propulsive phase, the arm exits the water and flexes at the elbow this reduces the moment of inertia and helps increase the speed of the recovery phase so that the arm can enter the water as quickly as possible, ready for the next arm pull.

Angular momentum

The relationship between angular velocity and the moment of inertia is inversely proportional. So that when one goes up the other goes down proportionally. This means that **angular momentum** must remain constant when an object or body is in flight and cannot change until an external force is applied. This is known as the law of conservation of angular momentum and is related to Newton's First Law.

Fig 5.17 A slalom skier initiates the turn in a low tucked position. MI is high and AV low. As he rounds the gate he straightens up, effectively halving MI and doubling AV. As he comes out of the turn he tucks once more, returning to a state where MI is high and AV low. This enables him to prepare for the next gate

Fig 5.18 An ice skater speeds up rotation by pulling body parts (head and limbs) in towards the axis of rotation

KEY TERMS

Moment of inertia (MI):
a measure of the resistance of a body to change its state of angular motion, measured in kgm^2

Angular momentum:
the quantity of angular motion or rotation a body possesses measured in kgm^2/sec which reflects the moment of inertia and angular velocity characteristics of the parameter,
i.e. Angular momentum = Moment of inertia × Angular velocity

The law of conservation of angular momentum

Angular momentum cannot be changed during flight. This has important implications for sporting activities that require many rotations to be performed such as in high diving and figure skating. Currently many figure skaters are attempting quadruple jumps in their routines. To ensure maximal angular momentum at take-off the skater prepares for the jump so that at take-off the arms are out to the side and one leg extended behind them. The idea is to generate as great a torque (turning moment) as possible. The larger the force or the farther the force is from the axis of rotation, the larger the torque. The larger the torque, the greater the angular momentum. Once in flight the skater pulls their arms and legs in as close to the longitudinal axis as possible which decreases moment of inertia and increases angular velocity enabling the skater to rotate very quickly. Upon landing the skater spreads arms out once again to increase moment of inertia and decrease angular velocity.

TASK 5.10

Perform a full twisting jump using the following methods:

a) arms by side at take-off
b) arms outstretched at take-off and brought in close to the body during flight.

In which jump could you perform the most rotation? Use your understanding of angular momentum to explain your observations.

TASK 5.11

Use Figure 5.19 to explain how a sprinter can use the concept of moment of inertia to improve technique and sprint times.

Fig 5.19 A sprinter can use the concept of moment of inertia to improve leg technique

STRETCH AND CHALLENGE

Use Figure 5.20 to explain how a diver can use knowledge of moment of inertia and the law of conservation of momentum to help maximise performance.

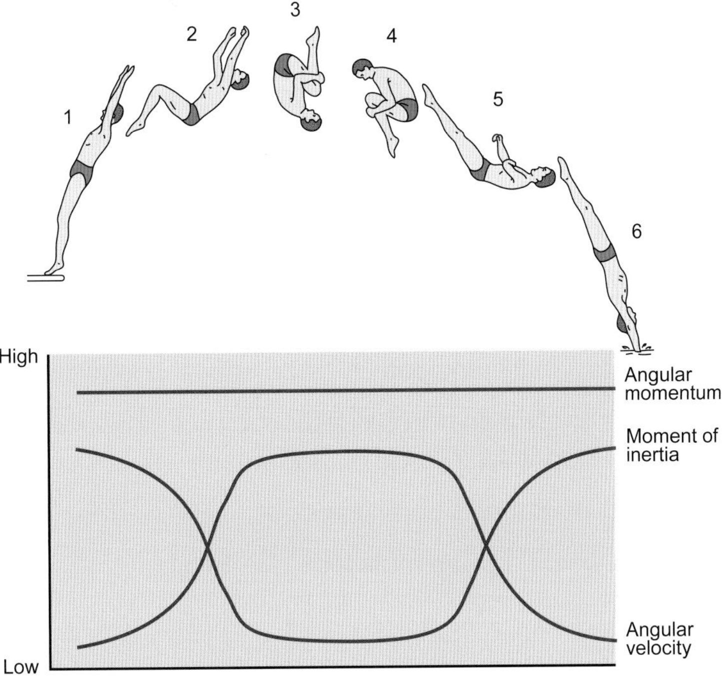

Fig 5.20 The relationship between angular velocity , moment of inertia and angular momentum during a dive

Exam**Café**

Relax, refresh, result!

Refresh your memory

Revision checklist

Make sure you know the following:

- ▷ A scalar quantity is one which can only be described by magnitude alone. Examples of scalar quantities include distance, speed and mass.
- ▷ A vector quantity is one which can be described by magnitude and direction. Examples of vector quantities include displacement, velocity and weight.
- ▷ Mass is the quantity of matter a body possesses.
- ▷ Weight is the force which a given mass feels due to gravity.
- ▷ Inertia is the reluctance of a body to change its state of motion.
- ▷ Distance is a measure of the path a body takes in moving from one position to another. It is a scalar quantity.
- ▷ Displacement is the shortest route possible between the starting and finishing point of a body that has moved. It is a vector quantity.
- ▷ Speed is a body's movement per unit of time with no consideration for direction. It is a scalar quantity. Speed = distance/time and measured in m/s.
- ▷ Velocity is the rate of change of displacement. It is a vector quantity. Velocity = displacement/time and measured in m/s.
- ▷ Acceleration is the rate of change of velocity. It is a vector quantity. Acceleration = change in velocity/time and measured in m/s^2.
- ▷ Momentum is the amount of motion a moving body possesses.

  Momentum = mass × velocity and measured in kgm/s.
- ▷ Newton's First Law of Motion is known as the law of inertia. It states that 'Every body at rest or moving with constant velocity in a straight line will continue in that state unless compelled to change by the application of an external force exerted upon it.'
- ▷ Newton's Second Law of Motion is known as the law of acceleration. It states that: 'The rate of change of momentum of a body (or the acceleration for a body of constant mass) is proportional to the force causing it and takes place in the direction in which the force acts.'

- Newton's Second Law can be summarised as F = ma.
- Newton's Third Law of Motion is known as the law of reaction. It states that: 'For every action, there is an equal and opposite reaction.'
- Force is the push or pull exerted on an object.
- Forces can cause a body at rest to move, a moving body to accelerate, a moving body to decelerate, a moving body to change direction, a body to change shape.
- Force is measured in Newtons. A Newton is the force required to give a 1kg mass an acceleration of $1 m/s^2$.
- Net force is the resultant force acting on a body having considered all other forces acting.
- Zero net force is a situation where forces acting cancel each other out.
- To calculate the size and direction of a net force, a parallelogram of forces can be constructed.
- When describing a force it is important to show the point of application, the direction and the magnitude or size.
- Vertical forces include weight and normal reaction.
- Horizontal forces include friction (thrust in water) and air resistance (drag in water).
- Friction is a resistive force encountered when two or more bodies in contact move past one another. Friction opposes motion.
- Factors affecting friction include: the roughness of the surfaces in contact, the mass of the object or body, the warmth of the surfaces in contact.
- Air resistance is a form of fluid friction that acts in the opposite direction to the direction of motion.
- Free body diagrams can be constructed to illustrate all the forces acting on an object or body.
- Impulse relates to the length of time a force is applied to an object or body: Impulse = force x time. Impulse is measured in Ns.
- Impulse can be used in sporting activity to increase the speed of an object or body and to slow down a moving body.
- Projectile motion occurs whenever a body or object is in flight.
- The horizontal distance covered by a projectile is dependent upon the velocity of release, the height of release and the angle of release.
- Where release height = landing height the optimal angle of release is 45°.
- Where release height > landing height the optimal angle of release <45°.
- Where release height < landing height the optimal angle of release > 45°.

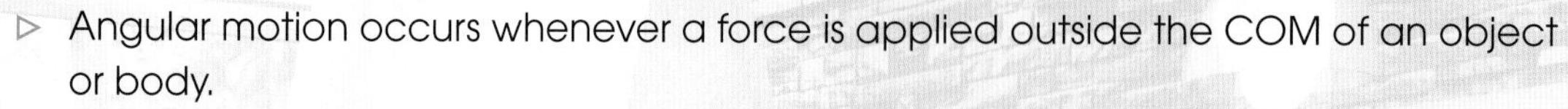

- Angular motion occurs whenever a force is applied outside the COM of an object or body.
- A force that is applied outside the COM of an object or body is known as an eccentric force.
- Angular motion occurs about one or more of the three axes of rotation in the body: the longitudinal axis which runs through the body from top to bottom; the horizontal axis which runs through the body from side to side; the frontal axis which runs through the body from front to back.
- Each of Newton's Laws of linear motion have an angular counterpart called analogues of Newton's Laws.
- The moment of inertia is a measure of the resistance of a body to change its state of angular motion. Moment of inertia is measured in kgm^2.
- The moment of inertia is dependent upon the mass of the object and the distribution of the mass from the axis of rotation.
- By altering the shape of the body it is possible to change the moment of inertia of a performer.
- Moment of inertia and angular velocity are inversely proportional. If moment of inertia increases angular velocity decreases accordingly and vice versa.
- The inverse proportional relationship between moment of inertia and angular velocity means that angular momentum must remain constant in flight.
- The law of conservation of momentum explains the constancy of momentum in flight due to the inverse proportional relationship between moment of inertia and angular velocity.

Revise as you go

1. Use Newton's three laws of motion to explain the motion of a high jumper at take-off.
2. Draw a stick figure diagram showing the vertical forces acting on a high jumper at take-off. With reference to your diagram explain what is meant by a net force.
3. Define momentum. Calculate the momentum of a downhill skier who has a mass of 85kg and is travelling at a velocity of 42m/s.
4. Air resistance is a force that acts against a moving body. How might a track cyclist attempt to reduce the size of this force?
5. Sketch a diagram to show the flight path of a shot from the moment it leaves the putter's hand to the moment it lands. Add arrows to the sketched flight path to represent the horizontal and vertical components of the shot at the following points:
   a) as it leaves the shot putter's hand
   b) the highest point of the flight path
   c) the point of the flight path that is level to release
   d) the point just before landing.
6. How does the angle of release, height of release and velocity of release affect the horizontal distance travelled by a shot?
7. The follow-through is an important aspect of the stroke in all racquet sports. Sketch a graph of the force applied by a squash racquet against time:
   a) with no follow-through
   b) with a follow-through.
8. Name the three axes of rotation. Give an example of a skill from sport where rotation about each of these three axes occurs.
9. Define the moment of inertia. With reference to a bent leg recovery, explain how a long jumper uses the concept of moment of inertia during the run up.
10. Trampolinists are now regularly performing triple front somersaults in their optional routines. State the relationship between angular momentum, moment of inertia and angular velocity. Sketch a graph to demonstrate this relationship during a tucked back somersault.
11. How does an ice skater maximise angular momentum at take-off?

Get the result!

Examination question

In order to optimise performance, athletes may take supplements. Discuss the potential benefits and harmful effects to an athlete in taking caffeine, creatine and sodium bicarbonate supplements (14 marks)

Model answer

Student answer (A grade)

There is a wide range of sports supplements available to sports performers, who will take them in the hope of optimising their performance. Creatine, caffeine and bicarbonate of soda are just three of the supplements that may benefit performers. However most supplements come with some harmful side effects, so the athlete will need to weigh up the pros and cons of using them in supplementing their diet before taking them.

Creatine supplementation involves the consumption of creatine monohydrate in powder, capsule or liquid form, which can increase the levels of phosphocreatine stored in the muscle cell by up to 50%. As it delays the alactic/lactic threshold using supplements of creatine is common among performers such as sprinters and weightlifters where short bursts of energy and explosive strength are required. As ATP-PC/lactic acid threshold is delayed it means that performers can train and compete maximally for longer, leading to increased performance. Consequently some athletes have noted gains in maximum and elastic strength. Reported drawbacks of creatine use include weight gain (often mistaken for muscle mass!), water retention, stomach cramps and diarrhoea and muscle cramps.

Caffeine is a mild stimulant that occurs naturally and is predominantly found in coffee, tea and colas. It is probably the most widely available and accessible pharmacological aid. Until 2004, caffeine was listed as a banned substance by WADA, the World Anti-doping Agency as its consumption was deemed to give performers an unfair advantage. Some studies cite that caffeine reduces the athlete's perception of

Model answer

muscle fatigue and results in an increased ability of the muscle to mobilise and utilise fat as a fuel. Consequently, caffeine is deemed to be of particular benefit to endurance performers such as runners and cyclists. The enhanced nervous stimulation associated with caffeine increases mental alertness and concentration levels. Consequently the athlete or games player will be able to react more quickly to situations that arise on the field of play. Reported side effects of caffeine include dehydration (caffeine is a diuretic), sleep deprivation and muscle and abdominal cramping.

Some athletes seek to enhance the buffering capacity of the body by drinking a solution of bicarbonate of soda an hour or so before an event or training, which increases the amount of bicarbonate ions (HCO_3^-) in the blood. Bicarbonate ions act as buffers to maintain the pH of the blood by attracting hydrogen ions from lactic acid therefore neutralising it. In this way soda loading helps to improve the athlete's tolerance to lactic acid, thereby delaying OBLA (onset of blood lactate accumulation) and enabling the performer to work harder for longer. Soda loading appears to be of benefit particularly to those activities that operate at near maximum intensities of between 1 and 7 minutes including 400m runners, 1Km track cyclists and rowers although some endurance athletes favour its use in training. Reported side effects of soda loading as it is commonly known include stomach cramping and diarrhoea and vomiting (due to the unpleasant taste).

There is therefore a plethora of sports supplements available to the sports performer. In the case of creatine, caffeine and soda loading all three come with potential performance benefits but they also come with additional side effects or health risks. The athlete cannot take these lightly and must weigh up the performance benefits and the possible health risks (as well as discuss with their coach and nutrition experts) before considering using any of the sports supplements that are widely available on the market.

Examiner says

This is a really good answer. It is well-structured and has clear explanations with examples from sport.

Mark scheme

The band descriptions for this 14-point question are illustrated below. Once you have studied the mark scheme have a go at marking the model answer yourself.

Band range	Band descriptors
11–14	• Addresses all aspects of the question, demonstrating a wide range of depth and knowledge • Expresses arguments clearly and concisely • Good use of examples to support answer • Few errors in spelling, punctuation and grammar, and correct use of technical language
7–10	• Addresses most aspects of the question whilst demonstrating a clear level of depth and knowledge • Attempts to express arguments clearly and concisely • Uses examples to support answer • Few errors in spelling, punctuation and grammar, demonstrates use of technical language although sometimes inaccurately
3–6	• Addresses some aspects of the question but lacks sufficient depth and knowledge • Limited attempt to develop any arguments or discussions, normally vague or irrelevant • Attempts to use examples although not always relevant • Errors in spelling, punctuation and grammar and limited use of technical language
0–2	• Addresses the question with limited success • Little or no use of examples • Major errors in spelling, punctuation and grammar, with no use of technical language

Caffeine

1. Primarily used by endurance athletes/games players

Benefit

2. Stimulant
3. Increased mental alertness
4. Reduces effects of fatigue
5. Allows performer to continue at higher intensity for a longer duration
6. Reacts quicker to aspects on the track/pitch
7. Overall leading to a higher level of performance

Drawback

8. Loss of fine control
9. Against rules of most sports in large quantities

Creatine

10. Sprinters/ intense exercise/sprinting/weight-lifting

Benefit

11. Increase phosphocreatine stores
12. Increases the amount of energy supply from this system
13. Able to perform maximally for longer, leading to increase in performance

Drawback

14. Water retention
15. Vomiting, diarrhoea

Sodium bicarbonate

16. Sprinters/ endurance athletes

Benefit

17. Increases buffering of lactate
18. Delays in the onset of blood lactate accumulation
19. Enables performer to maintain intensity for a longer duration

Drawback

20. May cause vomiting

Examiner's tip

Question 1a (for Section A) will always be marked using banded criteria so it is important that you produce an extended piece of writing that addresses all parts of the question, uses terminology appropriately and uses a wide range of sporting examples to support your answer. In this example the candidate has clearly outlined the potential performance benefits of taking each of the supplements creatine, caffeine and bicarbonate of soda, together with due consideration of possible side effects or health risks associated with taking them. Regular referencing and application to sport and physical activity is used successfully to support the points being made.

Get the result!

Examination question

Elite athletes may train in different climates, in order to acclimatise prior to competition.

a) How does the body regulate temperature, when an elite performer is exercising in a warm climate?

b) What are the effects of dehydration on an athlete and how does this affect performance? (7 marks)

Model answer

Student answer (A grade)

a) Temperature regulation is essential for an athlete, particularly when exercising for long periods of time in a warm environment. To prevent the body from overheating, thermoreceptors located around the body monitor body temperature and the hypothalamus (the thermoregulatory centre) responds to changes in the body's core temperature. If temperature rises the body responds by increasing the flow of blood to the skin, which transfers heat from the core towards the surface of the body. The blood vessels carrying the blood also vasodilate, which increases the volume of blood reaching the skin, in doing so the body is able to lose heat through the processes of evaporation (sweating), convection, conduction and radiation.

b) Dehydration can have a number of effects on a performer which can be detrimental to their performance. Losing the equivalent of 2% of your body weight as sweat can impair performance by up to 10-20%. If you do not replace the lost water then core body temperature will rise which brings with it a number of performance inhibitors. The blood becomes 'thicker' or more viscous which slows down the flow to the working muscles. To try and compensate, the heart beats faster putting the body under greater stress, a phenomenon known as cardiovascular drift. In an attempt to preserve water the body reduces its sweating response which increases the core temperature of the body however this has a destructive impact on muscle contraction as the contractile proteins of the muscle become inactivated and the enzymes that facilitate energy release become de-natured in such a hot environment. Consequently the performer becomes

Model answer

unable to meet the demands of the exercise and performance deteriorates. Furthermore, the loss of electrolytes through sweating can cause fatigue and cramps so it is essential that performers remain hydrated. As a general rule it is recommended that approximately 15 minutes before training or competition performers should drink between 400-500ml of fluid whilst during exercise 150-200ml should be drunk every 15-20 minutes.

Examiner's tip

For these shorter answers it is essential that you take note of the mark allocation for the question. The two parts of this question together have a total mark allocation of 7 marks. In order to achieve maximum marks, you must therefore ensure that each part of the question is answered in similar depth and detail with at least four separate points made in each part. Try to give two or three additional points over and above the stated mark allocation.

Mark scheme

This mark scheme will give you an idea of how the marks are allocated.

(a) max 4 marks

1. Transfer heat away from core
2. Vasodilation of blood vessels to the skin
3. Sweating/evaporation
4. Reddening to skin to radiate heat away
5. Conduction and convection
6. Maintains blood plasma volume through kidney function

(b) max 4 marks

1. Increase blood viscosity
2. Reduced blood pressure
3. Reduced cardiac output
4. Reduced sweating to prevent water loss
5. Increased core temperature
6. Enzymes become denatured and do not perform to optimum
7. Unable to meet demands of exercise
8. Decreased performance

Max 7 marks

Optimising performance and evaluating contemporary issues within sport

Section B: Psychological aspects that optimise performance

Introduction to Section B

During the AS course you studied the nature of skilled performance, methods to optimise the learning of skills, and how a performer processes the information available to him or her in order to produce an efficient performance. The psychological aspect of the course for A2 builds on that knowledge but focuses on the factors which influence an elite performer during competition.

The aim of this theoretical section is to develop your understanding of how an elite performer prepares him or herself mentally for intense competition. In the modern world of sport, where events are won by the narrowest of margins, it is often the performer who can consistently control his or her emotions and concentration levels most effectively who will emerge victorious. There may be the odd occasion where a performer may find themselves in the 'zone', allowing the performer to produce the performance of a lifetime, but the ultimate champions are those who can repeat that level of performance again and again when under pressure.

The vast majority of elite performers now have access to high quality preparation including: state of the art facilities, funding, high quality coaching, technology allowing detailed analysis of movement, physiologists, physiotherapists and a variety of other resources at their disposal. As a result there may only be minor differences in the physiological capabilities of the athletes. The margin between winning and losing is minimal but the consequences of victory are enormous, both in terms of recognition and rewards.

The relatively new field of 'sports psychology' is one way in which performers can attempt to gain an advantage over their opponents. Many elite athletes now employ various aspects of psychological techniques as an integral aspect of their preparation, and devote time to mastering those techniques in a competitive environment.

Think how often you have heard coaches and performers refer to their mental ability or the need to win using the 'top two inches'. The mind exerts a powerful influence during competition: it can either allow you to be full of confidence, totally focused and ready, or it can cause you to feel anxious, worry about the consequences of failure and ultimately be the major factor causing failure.

EXAM TIP:

In order to answer the examination questions, each topic should be approached in a similar manner. After reading each chapter you should be able to answer questions which focus on the following areas:

- What are the various theories linked to this area?
- How might this information affect my performance?
- How can this knowledge be used and what strategies can be employed to improve performance?

What you have learned can then be applied to your own sporting experiences, allowing you to become a better performer.

CHAPTER 6

Aspects of personality

LEARNING OBJECTIVES:

By the end of this chapter you should be able to:

- understand the term 'personality' and outline its relationship to sport, including its use as a predictor of performance
- outline the trait approach and explain its limitations
- outline the interactionist approach and explain its relationship to performance
- discuss the various methods used to measure personality and evaluate their effectiveness
- explain the profile of mood states, or iceberg profile, and evaluate its relationship to performance
- explain the concept of achievement motivation
- outline the characteristics of the personality types classified as 'need to achieve' and 'need to avoid failure'
- suggest factors which contribute to the adoption of each behaviour pattern, including 'incentive value' and 'probability of success'
- discuss the effect that approach behaviour and avoidance behaviour has on performance
- suggest strategies to develop approach behaviour.

Introduction

Many psychologists have completed research in an attempt to find the personality most suited to becoming an elite performer. As a component of a talent identification programme, some form of psychological testing may often take place. This may be helpful to determine levels of motivation, reaction to pressure situations, suitability towards specific forms of training, and the ability to deal with failure.

In order to be successful, are certain traits required such as competitiveness, self-confidence and the ability to deal with crowds and media attention? If they are, can they be identified? Do certain sports benefit from a performer having a specific personality? If they do, can this allow us to predict a person's personality and their subsequent behaviour? This may help us when attempting to identify potential elite performers.

Fig 6.01 Do all elite performers have similar personalities which make them successful?

Understanding the personality of a performer also allows the coach, other team members and anyone linked with him or her to better identify potential weaknesses when placed in a competitive situation and implement strategies to overcome those deficiencies.

This section will focus on a basic proposition – that of **nature** versus **nurture**. In other words, are we born with the **traits** which allow us to be successful or do we develop personality based on our experiences?

KEY TERMS

Nature:
individuals are a product of the genes of their parents. A genetically inherited disposition

Nurture:
a learned pattern of behaviour acquired through reinforcement, imitation of the behaviour of others and general environmental influences

Trait:
an innate, enduring characteristic possessed by an individual that can be used to explain and predict behaviour in different situations

Definitions of personality

Before we study the different theories in more depth, we need to develop an understanding of the term 'personality'.

TASK 6.01

With a partner, devise a definition of personality and attempt to describe the characteristics of your own personality. Discuss with other students and compare your definition with those on this page.

Different psychologists have given definitions of personality but many have common characteristics, as illustrated below.

Gross (1992)
'Those relatively stable and enduring aspects of individuals which distinguish them from other people, making them unique but at the same time permit a comparison between individuals.'

Eysenck (1995)
'Personality is the more or less stable and enduring organizations of a person's character, temperament, intellect and physique, which determines the unique adjustment the individual makes to the environment.'

Hollander (1971)
'Personality is the sum total of an individual's characteristics which make him unique.'

The key factor in each of these definitions is that personality is unique to the individual. The work of Hollander (1967) provides an easy structure which allows a clear understanding of personality. He sub-divided personality into three separate but inter-related levels (see Figure 6.02):

- **Psychological core** – this is the inner core of your personality; it can be described as 'the real you'. It comprises your beliefs, values, attitudes and self-worth, all of which are relatively permanent and tend to be resistant to change.
- **Typical responses** – as the term suggests, this layer of the model represents our usual response to a situation, which is often learned. Such responses can be a good indicator of the psychological core. For example, one player may react to a defeat by training harder and viewing the experience in a positive manner, whilst another may feel that her or she is unable to improve and give up easily.
- **Role-related behaviours** – refers to our behaviour at any given time depending on the specific circumstances and our perception at that time. This is the most changeable aspect of our personality. In other words, our behaviour alters to suit the situation and at times may appear 'out of character' and may not be a true reflection of

our psychological core. For example, a player may normally be controlled during a game but may resort to an aggressive act if provoked.

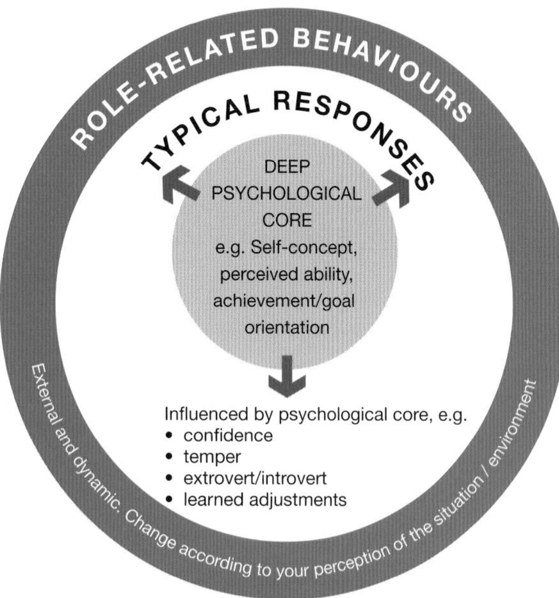

Fig 6.02 The structure of personality (Hollander, 1971)

Trait theories

Trait theories of personality represent the 'nature' approach. They suggest we are born with inherited characteristics which do not alter over time and which cause us to react in a similar fashion irrespective of the situation. Traits are seen to be stable, enduring and consistent. For example, if a person has an aggressive nature then he or she will be aggressive in all situations or may display behaviour patterns of extreme competitiveness.

If the concept of the trait theories is correct it would allow us to predict behaviour patterns in all situations. This would obviously be useful in terms of sporting performance as it would help identify potential performers who could cope with the pressure of intense competition without becoming over-aroused or aggressive. Similarly, potential leaders or captains could be identified if they possessed the necessary traits required to fulfil such roles of responsibility.

The measurement of traits using questionnaires provides a quick and straightforward assessment of personality (measurement of personality traits will be covered in more detail later). However, as you may gather from your own experiences, behaviour patterns may alter from one situation to the next and as a result merely using traits to predict behaviour is unreliable. Also, despite numerous attempts to classify the characteristics required to perform at elite level, there are no common traits, with many performers displaying wide-ranging differences in personality despite being highly successful.

EXAM TIP:

Make sure you can outline the various theories and evaluate their strengths and weaknesses.

STRETCH AND CHALLENGE

Although trait theories will not be examined directly, it is worthwhile gaining an understanding of the topic to fully appreciate why the interactionist theory (which will be discussed later in this chapter) has been developed.

Eysenck's personality dimensions

Hans Eysenck suggested that individuals possess stable traits based on two broad dimensions which are derived from biological factors.

1. Extrovert–Introvert dimension
   This dimension is based on the assumption that individuals attempt to maintain a certain level of stimulation or arousal suitable for them. The level of stimulation is controlled by the Reticular Activating System (RAS), which is located in the central cortex of the brain.

   - **Extroverts** need more arousal and stimulation as the RAS inhibits or dampens down information received via the sensory system. In other words it needs extra stimulation to maintain optimum levels of attention.
   - **Introverts** need less arousal and stimulation as their RAS is already stimulated and additional excitement will cause the individual to become over-aroused.

2. Stable–Neurotic dimension
   The second dimension is based on emotionality and the reaction of the autonomic nervous system (ANS) to stressful situations.
   - **Stable** individuals tend to possess a fairly slow and less vigorous response to stressful situations.
   - **Neurotic** individuals have a rapid reaction to stressful situations. Obviously a performer with this response would not ideally be suited to the high pressure environment of the modern day sporting arena.

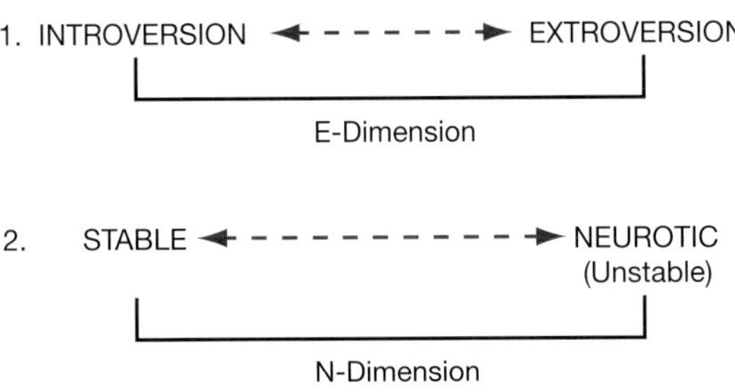

Fig 6.03 Eysenck's personality dimensions

The two personality dimensions are independent of each other and an individual can be a combination of the differing traits. For example, overall personality may lie in any one of the four quadrants shown in Fig 6.04.

A third dimension of Psychotism–Intelligence (the P-Dimension), relating to how far a person was prepared to conform to society's rules and conventions, was added later, in 1976.

KEY TERMS

Extrovert:
sociable outgoing, talkative, active and optimistic

Introvert:
quiet, passive, unsociable, reserved and careful

Stable:
calm, even-tempered, reliable, controlled and logical

Neurotic:
moody, anxious, touchy, restless and aggressive

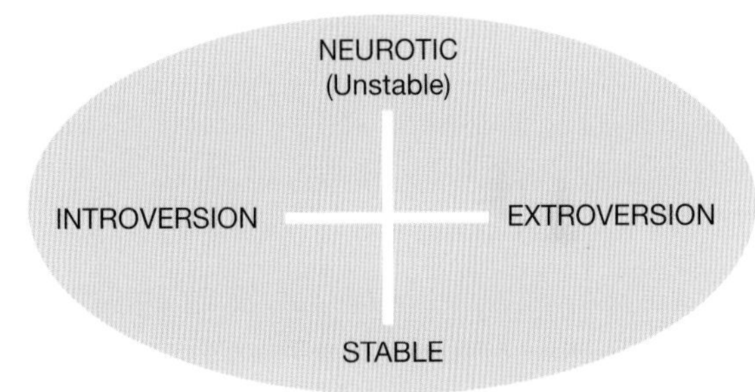

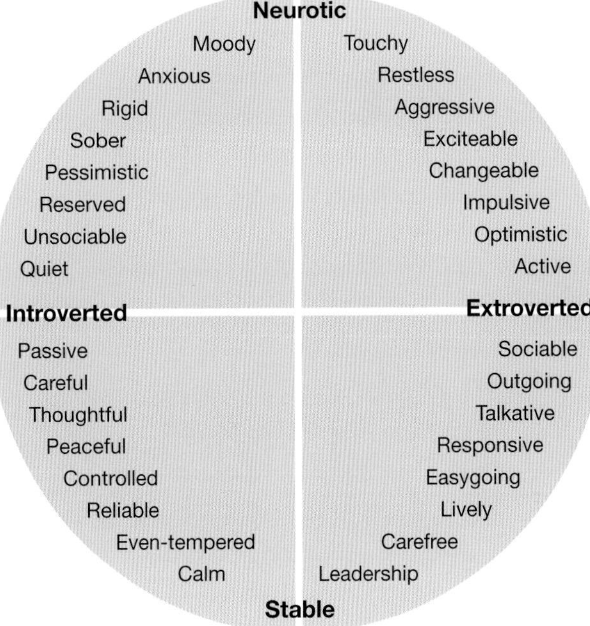

Fig 6.04 Eysenck's circular diagram of personality characteristics

TASK 6.02

1. Copy Figure 6.03 and place a cross in the section which you feel best matches your personality based on the characteristics listed in Figure 6.04.
2. Complete Eysenck's Personality Inventory (EPI) in Table 6.01 and plot your results on the graph.
3. Compare your results with a partner and discuss the relationship between your personality and choice of sports.

Complete the questions below answering either Yes or No.

		Yes	No
1.	Do you often long for excitement?		
2.	Do you often need understanding friends to cheer you up?		
3.	Are you carefree?		
4.	Do you find it hard to take 'no' for an answer?		
5.	Do you stop to think things over before doing anything?		
6.	If you say you will do something do you always keep your promise, no matter how inconvenient it might be to do so?		
7.	Does your mood often go up and down?		
8.	Do you generally do things quickly without stopping to think?		
9.	Do you ever feel 'just miserable' for no good reason?		
10.	Would you do anything for a dare?		
11.	Do you suddenly feel shy when you want to talk to an attractive stranger?		
12.	Once in a while do you lose your temper and get angry?		
13.	Do you often do things on the spur of a moment?		
14.	Do you often worry about things you should not have said or done?		
15.	Generally do you prefer reading to meeting people?		
16.	Are your feelings rather easily hurt?		
17.	Do you like going out a lot?		
18.	Do you occasionally have thoughts and ideas that you would not like other people to know about?		
19.	Are you sometimes bubbling over with energy and sometimes very sluggish?		
20.	Do you prefer to have a few but special friends?		
21.	Do you daydream a lot?		
22.	When people shout at you do you shout back?		
23.	Are you troubled by feelings of guilt?		
24.	Are all your habits good and desirable ones?		
25.	Can you usually let yourself go and enjoy yourself a lot at a lively party?		
26.	Would you call yourself tense or highly strung?		
27.	Do other people think of you as being lively?		
28.	After you have done something important, do you often come away feeling you could have done better?		
29.	Are you mostly quiet when you are with other people?		
30.	Do you sometimes gossip?		

Table 6.01 Eysenck's Personality Inventory (EPI)

TASK 6.02

31. Do ideas run through your head so that you cannot sleep?		
32. If there is something you want to know about, would you rather look it up in a book than talk to someone about it?		
33. Do you get palpitations or jumping in your heart?		
34. Do you like the kind of work that you need to pay close attention to?		
35. Do you get attacks of shaking or trembling?		
36. Would you always declare everything at customs, even if you knew that you could never be found out?		
37. Do you hate being in a crowd who play jokes on one another?		
38. Are you an irritable person?		
39. Do you like doing things in which you have to act quickly?		
40. Do you worry about awful things that may happen?		
41. Are you slow and unhurried in the way you move?		
42. Have you ever been late for an appointment or work?		
43. Do you have nightmares?		
44. Do you like talking to people so much that you never miss a chance of talking to a stranger?		
45. Are you troubled by aches and pains?		
46. Would you be unhappy if you could not see lots of people most of the time?		
47. Would you call yourself a nervous person?		
48. Of all the people you know are there some who you definitely do not like?		
49. Would you say you were fairly self-confident?		
50. Are you easily hurt when people find fault with you or your work?		
51. Do you find it hard to really enjoy yourself at a lively party?		
52. Are you troubled by feelings of inferiority?		
53. Can you easily get some life into a party?		
54. Do you sometimes talk about things you know nothing about?		
55. Do you worry about your health?		
56. Do you like playing pranks on others?		

Table 6.01 continued

Follow the instructions below to assess your answers:

1 Obtain a score out of 13 for the Extrovert–Introvert dimension (E):
- 1 point for answering 'yes' to questions 1, 3, 17, 39, 44, 46, 49 & 53
- 1 point for answering 'no' to questions 15, 29, 32, 41 & 51

2 Obtain a score out of 3 for the Neurotic–Stable dimension (N):
- 1 point for answering 'yes' to questions 19, 35 & 52

3 Obtain a Lie score (L):
- 1 point for answering 'yes' to questions 6 & 24, and 'no' to questions 42 & 54

4 Plot your results on Figure 6.03.
Extreme extrovert = 13; Extreme introvert = 0;
Extreme neurotic = 3; Extreme stable = 0.

If your 'lie' score is 3 or 4 your answers for the test will not be valid. Look at those questions again and think why this might be the case.

TASK 6.03

Discuss the strengths and weaknesses of using a self-report questionnaire such as the EPI to evaluate personality.

Eysenck later included a third dimension of Psychoticism–Intelligence, which indicted how tough-minded or tender a person may be. This was measured by using a modified version of the questionnaire known as the Eysenck Personality Questionnaire (EPQ).

Based on these claims it was suggested that certain personality types would be suited or drawn towards specific activities. It was generally claimed that most elite performers possessed stable, extrovert characteristics. Other claims included:

- Extroverts would be more likely to play high-action sports such as rugby and football.
- Stable individuals were more likely to participate in sport compared to the general population.
- Introverts would be drawn to individual activities, such as running.

However, despite these claims, numerous other researchers have been unable to prove conclusively that a particular personality type is required to participate in particular sports or needed to reach elite standard.

Cattell's Theory – 16 personality factors

Raymond Cattell (1965) also suggested that personality was based on stable traits but thought Eysenck's theory to be too simplistic. He proposed that personality could be profiled into 16 categories which give a more accurate picture of people's characteristics and behaviour patterns. He measured these traits using the 16PF questionnaire, but accepted that responses may be different each time depending on motivation, mood and situational factors.

While this allowed for a more dynamic approach to personality there was still no clear evidence to suggest particular personalities were more likely to be successful performers than others.

Evaluation of trait theories

The research completed by psychologists such as Eysenck and Cattell was widely criticised but provided a framework for further study and debate. Numerous studies have attempted to find correlations between choice of activity and personality type and, whilst there may be some evidence, there is no conclusive proof that people with particular traits are drawn to certain sports. However, there are some serious criticisms, some of which you may have already thought of and discussed based on your completion of the EPI.

Criticisms of the trait theories include:

- too simplistic
- they do not account for personality changing over time
- they do not fully account for environmental or situational factors
- they fail to allow for individuals actively shaping and understanding their own personality
- they are not an accurate predictor of sport preference
- they have limited value as a predictor of sporting success.

However, the identification of personality traits may be useful to a coach in order to highlight potential difficulties an individual might encounter and employ strategies to reduce any negative behaviour patterns that may occur.

EXAM TIP:

Ensure you can outline the most commonly used personality tests and critically evaluate them.

Interactionist theories

Interactionist theories propose that personality is a mixture of inherited traits and a person's current situation. This idea was first proposed by Bowers (1973). Interactionist theories may be viewed as a more dynamic approach and possess greater validity because they explain why we alter our behaviour from one moment to the next. They are a combination of the trait theory and the social learning theory (refer back to your AS course and the work of Bandura). The dominance of either the personality or the situation depends on their specific relative strengths at the time.

For example, if the situational factors are strong, such as in a highly competitive match with a high extrinsic reward for success, these factors may be more influential on behaviour than personality. However, if the situational factors are not strong, such as in a recreational game, personality is more likely to control behaviour.

A common equation used to understand this approach was put forward by Lewin (1936):

$$B = f\ (PE)$$

Where:

B = Behaviour, f = function, P = Personality and E = Environment.

The work of Hollander outlined earlier in the chapter is an example of the interactionist theory.

Consider similar situations in which you have found yourself and think how your behaviour may have altered as a result of differing factors. For example, has your behaviour changed if:

- a crowd or **significant other** has been watching
- the match is against an old adversary or a derby match
- the final outcome is of great importance or you have been provoked by the opposition?

The coach or sports psychologist can use this dynamic approach and attempt to identify characteristic behaviour patterns in specific situations. For example, if a player becomes over-aroused or aggressive in the final stages of a match if the result is close, various stress management strategies can be developed. Similarly, if the performer can pinpoint specific situations that have a negative impact on his or her performance, attempts can be made to alter behaviour patterns. However, this does mean the coach must recognise that each performer is unique, must devote time to developing an understanding of each person, and must treat them accordingly.

KEY TERMS

Significant other:
a person who is held in high esteem by the individual. Significant others may include family, peer group, teachers, coaches and role models

EXAM TIP:

Make sure you are able to explain the different theories of personality and evaluate their strengths and weaknesses.

APPLY IT!

Negative effects of over-arousal

As a young international player Wayne Rooney has on occasions become over-aroused and displayed signs of frustration and aggression towards opposing players. One notable incident occurred in a World Cup match against Portugal, which resulted in a red card. England went on to lose the match and were eliminated from the tournament. However, Rooney appears to have learned from this experience and, with the help of his coaches, has developed strategies to channel his frustrations in a positive manner. While he still occasionally displays signs of frustration, he rarely loses his temper and competes in a fully committed manner.

Fig 6.05 Players can learn from their experiences and alter their personality and behaviour patterns in specific situations

Measurement of personality

As you may have found from completion of the EPI, measuring personality is not straightforward. The two main forms of evidence collection used are self-report questionnaires and observation.

Self-report questionnaires such as the EPI, Cattell's 16PF, and the Athletic Motivation Inventory (AMI) developed by Ogilvie and Tutko, are widely used because they are easy to administer, collection of data is straightforward, and large numbers can be accommodated in a short space of time. However, they have all been criticised on several counts:

- their validity may be questioned as there is no agreed definition of personality
- their reliability may be questioned as the results may vary when the test is repeated
- participants' responses may be affected by their mood, situation and attitude towards the test
- respondents may lie or not answer accurately as they may be tempted to give socially acceptable answers
- participants may not fully understand the questions as they may be ambiguous or be interpreted differently
- possible response options, for example, 'yes' or 'no', may be too limited to provide a complete picture of the individual to emerge
- the ethics of personality testing have been questioned. Respondents should be fully informed of the purpose of the test and have the right to withdraw at any time.

Many sports psychologists now utilise more sport-specific objective questionnaires, such as the Sport Competition Anxiety Test (SCAT) and the Competitive State Anxiety Inventory (CSAI–2), as they provide more reliable evidence. (These tests will be covered in detail in Chapter 8.)

Observation techniques involve the performer's behaviour being recorded in specific situations over a period of time. Similarities of behaviour are noted and a personality profile can be constructed. Whilst this method is useful as it observes relevant behaviour, it is time consuming and, subjective, and the recorder must ensure that her or she collects the data using the same criteria on each occasion.

Interviews can also be used, with a series of questions devised to reflect behaviour patterns in different situations. The questions could be similar to those found in the EPI and other questionnaires. The major problems associated with this method are the same as for questionnaires.

EXAM TIP:

Ensure you can name, describe and evaluate different methods of testing related to personality.

Profile of Mood States (POMS)

The personality of a performer can change from moment to moment, but it has been suggested by Morgan (1979) that mood states are more useful in the identification of successful athletes. Rather than stable personality traits being the most important factor, mood states are temporary and change with the situation. Consequently this might be seen as a better predictor of performance and behaviour.

McNair, Lorr and Droppleman (1971) developed the Profile of Mood States (POMS), which measures six mood states:

- tension
- depression
- anger
- vigour
- fatigue
- confusion

Morgan compared the mood states of successful and unsuccessful athletes and suggested that to be a successful performer the score for vigour should be high, whilst the tension, depression, fatigue and confusion scores should be lower. This pattern is known as the **Iceberg Profile** as shown in Figure 6.06. The more pronounced the profile, the more successful the individual.

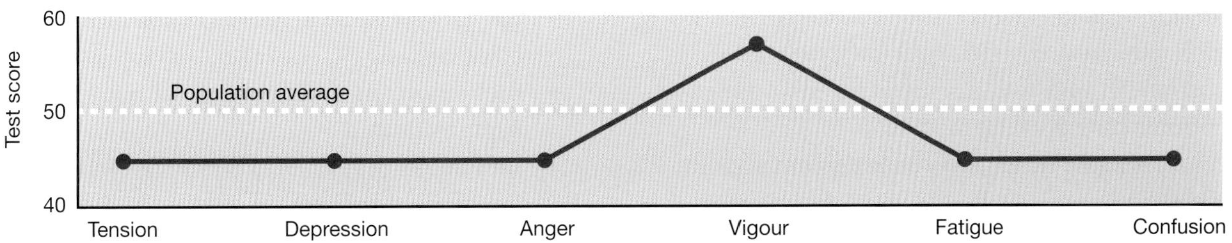

Fig 6.06 Iceberg Profile

While there has been extensive research to support this suggestion, there has also been evidence to demonstrate it is possible to reach elite level without displaying the Iceberg Profile. Some psychologists have also put forward the notion that as success is achieved this contributes to a positive self-image, high confidence levels and positive mood states, rather than this being a prerequisite for success initially.

EXAM TIP:

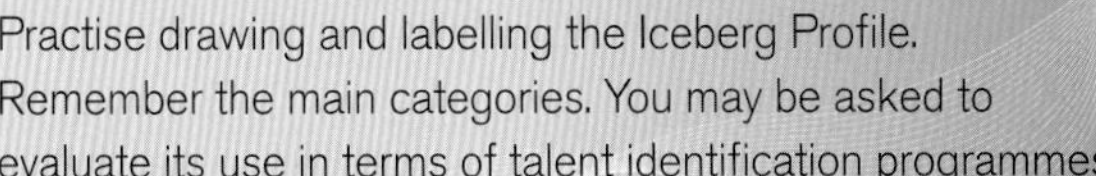

Practise drawing and labelling the Iceberg Profile. Remember the main categories. You may be asked to evaluate its use in terms of talent identification programmes.

Personality and sporting performance

Based on the research evidence, is it possible to identify links between personality and sporting performance? Many of the theories appear to contradict each other. Some psychologists adopt the **sceptical approach**, which questions the link between the two, whilst other adopt the **credulous approach**, believing there is a link between success and personality type.

Some key factors have emerged:

- there is no clear link between personality type and success in sport
- there is no clear link between personality and choice of sport
- personality can be affected by the situation and the environment.

KEY TERMS

Iceberg Profile:
on Profile of Mood Status (POMS) score successful athletes were above the waterline (population norm) on vigour but below the surface on the more negative moods, thus creating the profile of an iceberg

Sceptical approach:
based on the approach which questions the link between personality and sports performance

Credulous approach:
based on the approach which supports the link between personality and success in sport

Achievement motivation

Sports performers have to endure many hardships in order to be successful. Their innate ability and high skill levels will be insufficient to guarantee them a place on the victory podium. Throughout their training there will be times when motivation will be low because progress is not as fast as they initially hoped. During competition, results may be poor or emotions may have taken over causing a sub-standard performance. The following pages will study aspects of sports psychology which help to explain the reasons why this may occur and also outline strategies to deal effectively with emotional problems which the performer may encounter.

During your AS level studies the topic of motivation was covered. Refer back to this area and refresh your memory about the importance of developing intrinsic motivation and the considerations which must be taken into account when using extrinsic motivation. This knowledge will help to develop a greater understanding of the topics discussed in the following pages.

The motivation level of an individual is a key factor in his or her desire to strive for success and directly affects his or her behaviour. It influences the performer in many ways; it ensures he or she persists even if he or she fails or finds tasks difficult, and may also encourage challenges to be taken even if the attempt is not successful. The theory of achievement motivation attempts to link personality with competitiveness and to explain why a performer may behave in a specific manner when faced with a particular task.

Theory of Achievement Motivation

McCelland and Atkinson (1964) viewed achievement motivation as a stable aspect of personality. They suggested we all have two underlying motives when placed in a situation in which some form of evaluation takes place:

1. The motive to succeed/need to achieve (**n.Ach**) – performers display the following characteristics:
   - a sense of pride and satisfaction from competing
   - perseverance
   - quick completion of the task
   - they welcome feedback
   - optimism
   - confidence
   - they take responsibility for their own actions
   - they attribute performance to internal factors (see Attribution theory, Chapter 12)
   - they are prepared to take risks and face challenges
   - they enjoy performing in front of others and being evaluated
   - they do not mind if they fail as it is seen as a learning experience.
2. The motive to avoid failure/need to avoid failure (**n.Af**) – performers display the following characteristics:
   - attempt to avoid shame and humiliation
   - worry about failure
   - avoid situations with a 50–50 chance of success
   - choose tasks which are very easy or very hard
   - dislike personal feedback
   - attribute performance to external factors (see self-serving bias on page 188)
   - their performance tends to deteriorate when being evaluated
   - they give up easily.

KEY TERMS

Theory of Achievement Motivation:
a theory which proposes that the behaviour of an individual is based on his or her interaction with the environment and desire to succeed

n.Ach:
abbreviation for 'need to achieve'

n.AF:
abbreviation for 'need to avoid failure'

Interactionist:
the behaviour of an individual is a combination of his or her personality and the environment or situation at the time

When faced with a competitive situation we make a decision based on the relative strengths of each aspect of our personality. This can be expressed as: *Achievement motivation = desire to succeed – fear of failure.*

APPLY IT!

N.Ach v n.Af

To put these characteristics into context, consider the following example. A club standard tennis player with a motive to achieve is given the opportunity to play someone of a similar or better ability. He will rise to the challenge and use the experience he may gain in the future, irrespective of the result. However, a player with a motive to avoid failure will tend to choose opponents who are better or worse than himself, because he is not expected to win or should do so easily. As a result, the outcome will not be a reflection of the player's ability.

EXAM TIP:

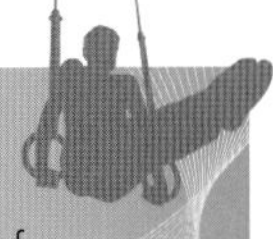

Be able to explain the different characteristics of a n.Ach and n.Af performer.

The theory of achievement motivation, an interactionist perspective, also takes into account the situation in which the performer finds him or herself. Our level of achievement motivation is a combination of personality and an evaluation of the situational factors. The evaluation assesses two aspects:

- the probability of success (this relates to the difficulty of the task)
- the incentive value of the success (this relates to the relative feelings of pride or shame following the final result).

This can be expressed as:

$$(Ms - Maf) \times (Ps \times \{I - Ps\})$$

Where:

- *Ms* = motive to succeed
- *Ps* = probability of success
- *Maf* = motive to avoid failure
- *I* = incentive value of success

Performers who have a higher motive to achieve (n.Ach) will tend to have **approach behaviour** patterns. They will be prepared to take risks and rise to the challenge, gaining feelings of satisfaction from the task even if it is difficult in nature. Those who have a higher motive to avoid failure (n.Af) will have **avoidance behaviour**, as they will tend to opt for the easier choice or not even attempt the task, since they wish to protect their self-esteem. As a coach the aim should be to encourage performers to adopt approach behaviour.

EXAM TIP:

Be able to explain, with the aid of practical examples, how the different types of personality will approach a specific situation.

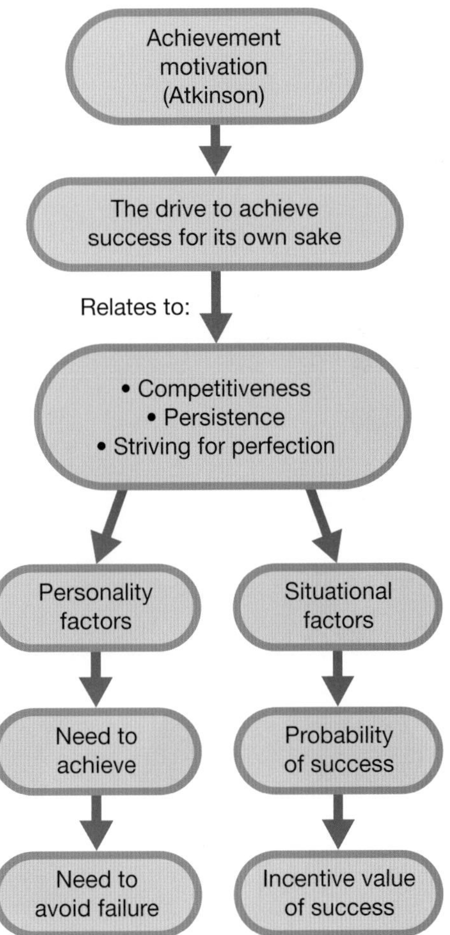

Fig 6.07 Atkinson's components of achievement motivation

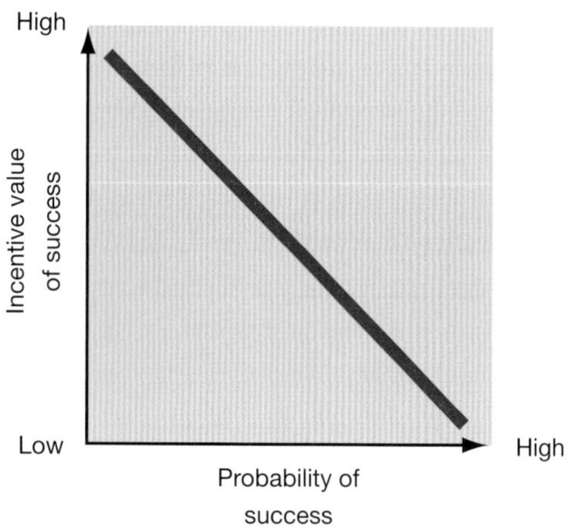

Fig 6.08 Relationship between probability of success and incentive value

KEY TERMS

Approach behaviour:
the performer is motivated to attempt a challenging situation even if he or she may fail

Avoidance behaviour:
the performer is motivated to protect his or her self-esteem and may not place him or herself in a situation where he or she may be evaluated

Fig 6.09 Performers with a high need to achieve will be prepared to challenge themselves in highly competitive situations

When evaluating this theory, several critical points can be highlighted:

- It is most useful when the task involves a 50–50 chance of success.
- 'Success' may mean different things and can be interpreted in various ways by individuals. For example, the end result may not be as important to one performer if their technique improves and the goal set before the event is achieved.
- Measuring achievement motivation using attitudes and anxiety scales may be unreliable.
- Achievement motivation is not a global concept – performers may react in different ways depending on the sport-specific situation and it may be more appropriate to consider an individual's level of competitiveness.
- No clear relationship between achievement motivation and performance has been established. However, it is useful when attempting to predict long-term motivation.

TASK 6.04

Explain with reference to Achievement Motivation Theory the decision of each of the players in the following scenario:

'In a cup final the scores are level at the end of full time. The coach asks different players to participate in a penalty shoot-out. Some agree and others refuse.'

Achievement Goal Theory

More recently sports psychologists including Duda (1993) and Roberts (1993) have proposed the Achievement Goal Theory which suggests that a performer's level of achievement motivation will differ depending on the reasons for his or her participation, the goals set and the relative meanings of those goals. The performer may be set different types of achievement goals such as:

1. **Outcome goal** – a goal that is set to judge the performance of the individual against others and the end result. For example, a cyclist may be set the goal of either winning the race or finishing in the top three places to qualify for the next round. The efficiency and manner of the performance is not relevant, only the final result. If the goal is realistic and within the performer's capability, and he or she achieves the aim, motivation and feelings of pride and self-esteem are increased. However, it can be demotivating if the performer is unsuccessful, especially after repeated attempts. The performer may feel shame and attribute the failure to his or her own ability, causing him or her to adopt avoidance behaviour patterns in the future.
2. **Task-oriented goal** – a goal that is used to judge the performance of the individual against his or her own standards, rather than in comparison with competitors. For example, a cyclist may set a number of goals for a race including:
    - applying the tactics as agreed with the coach
    - using effective slipstreaming behind another rider
    - comparing how close he or she rode to a personal best time, rather than the finishing position.

If the goal of the coach is realistic, the performer can evaluate his or her own actions and not worry about comparison with others. This helps to reduce anxiety, allowing the cyclist to remain motivated wherever he or she finishes. This type of goal may be an effective method of developing a performer's approach behaviour and encouraging a positive motive to succeed. (For more on goal setting, refer back to your AS textbook.)

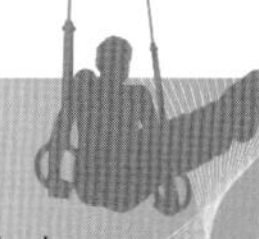

EXAM TIP:

1. Learn the characteristics of each personality type and how it may influence the type of goal setting to be used.
2. Be able to outline, with practical examples, the different types of goals that can be used. Be able to state which is the most appropriate with each type of personality.

STRETCH AND CHALLENGE

You are the coach of a team for a sport of your choice. Give examples of team and individual goals you may set at the start and mid-way through the season. For each you should set both outcome and task-orientated goals. Discuss your goals with a partner.

Development of approach behaviour

The aim of the coach must be to develop performers who possess a high level of achievement motivation, with a high motive to succeed and approach behaviour. There are various strategies which can be used to fulfil this aim including:

- providing positive childhood experiences and encouraging feelings of pride and satisfaction through success
- reducing punishment and negative feelings
- gradually increasing the task difficulty but ensuring that challenging tasks are set
- catering for all levels of ability
- raising levels of **self-efficacy** (see page 174) and avoiding **learned helplessness** (see page 190)
- setting appropriate outcome or task-orientated goals
- considering cultural differences
- using **attributions** (see page 186) correctly
- providing encouragement from significant others.

KEY TERMS

Self-efficacy:
the degree of self-confidence experienced by a performer when placed in a specific situation

Learned helplessness:
feelings experienced by an individual when he or she believes that failure is inevitable because of negative past experiences

Attributions:
the perceived reasons a performer gives for his or her performances, both success and failure

TASK 6.05

Copy the table below and place each of the following characteristics in the appropriate column, either Need to Achieve (n.Ach) personality or Need to Avoid Failure (n.Af) personality.

- a sense of pride and satisfaction from competing
- quick completion of the task
- optimistic
- perseverance
- attempt to avoid shame and humiliation
- avoid situations with 50–50 chance of success
- take responsibility for their own actions
- dislike personal feedback
- attribute performance to external factors
- performance tends to deteriorate when being evaluated
- welcome feedback
- confident
- worry about failure
- choose tasks which are very easy or very hard

Need to achieve	Need to avoid failure

TASK 6.06

Complete the following passage using the words in the list given.

avoidance	approach	satisfaction
easier choice	self-esteem	risks

Performers who have a higher motive to achieve (n.Ach) will tend to have ___________ behaviour patterns. They will be prepared to take ___________ and rise to the challenge, gaining feelings of _____________ from the task even if it is difficult in nature. Those who have a higher motive to avoid failure (n.Af) will have ______________ behaviour, as they will tend to opt for the ___________ or not even attempt the task, as they wish to protect their _____________.

APPLY IT!

During a school netball match the teachers from the teams approach the game from different perspectives. One teacher encourages the players to shoot to score a goal when they have a suitable opportunity and if they miss, encourages them saying *'not to worry it was a good attempt'.* The other teacher shouts criticism at the players if they miss a shot or do not shoot when they have the opportunity.

Consider the different approaches adopted by each teacher. One team know that they have the support of the teacher and are willing to attempt to score even if they miss (encouraging approach behaviour). However the other team are more likely to develop avoidance behaviour, resulting in them only attempting to score when they have an easy shot or making sure they do not get into positions where shooting is an option. The players are too concerned with the consequences of their actions rather than playing to the best of their ability.

ATHLETE PROFILE

In 2008, at the age of 17, Claire Vigrass became the US Open Ladies Real Tennis Champion. She built on this success throughout the year producing a series of highly commendable results in major competitions. In terms of her personality she could be classed as a stable extrovert with a lively sense of humour who is not afraid to challenge herself and learn from her experiences. While Claire possesses these core personality traits, she has learnt through experience how to alter her behaviour patterns to suit the situations (**interactionist theory**). Through her continued success and ability to reach the final stages of major tournaments, for example the 2008 British Open Final and French Open Semi-final, she is now much less carefree during important matches, becoming more serious and assertive. For example, she has developed more confidence to challenge umpires' decisions. In terms of her achievement motivation, she clearly has the characteristics of a 'need to achieve' performer, displaying approach behaviour, as she is not concerned about playing against those of equal or higher standard. As a result of this committed approach Claire has risen to number 2 in the World Rankings.

Fig 6.10 Claire Vigrass – holder of Real Tennis 2008 United States Ladies Open Singles title

ExamCafé

Relax, refresh, result!

Refresh your memory

Revision checklist

Make sure you know the following:

Personality

- ▷ Personality is the combination of those characteristics which make a person unique.
- ▷ Personality refers to those relatively stable and enduring aspects of an individual's behaviour.
- ▷ The study of personality has tended to consider is it as a result of 'nature' or 'nurture'.
- ▷ *Trait theories* see personality as being innate and stable predispositions, enabling behaviour patterns to be predicted in all situations.
- ▷ *Interactionist theories* see personality as being a combination between traits and the environment: $B = f(PE)$
- ▷ A variety of methods can be used to test personality, the most common being questionnaires, observation and interviews.
- ▷ Personality tests should not be used in isolation to identify potential talented performers as there are question marks over their validity.
- ▷ There are no definite findings suggesting different personalities lead to more successful athletes or specific types of sport.
- ▷ The closest we can get to predict the behaviour of an individual is through 'mood states' which link to the suggested Iceberg Profile.
- ▷ For success in sport each individual must be viewed differently by the coach according to the three levels of personality made up of psychological core, typical response and role related behaviour.

Achievement motivation

- ▷ Achievement motivation is a predisposition to strive for success, persist and experience pride in one's success.
- ▷ Two types of motives which are likely to exist in evaluative situations have been identified: need to achieve (n. Ach); need to avoid failure (n. Af).
- ▷ Whether a person is a high achiever or low achiever has been found to affect task selection, effort and persistence.

- Performers also evaluate the probability of success (this relates to the difficulty of the task) and the incentive value of the success (this relates to the relative feelings of pride or shame following the final result).
- Goal setting is seen as an important tool in developing achievement motivation.
- The adoption of task orientated goals emphasising comparisons with personal performance rather than outcome or ego orientated goals has been found to be more effective in developing achievement motivation.
- Coaches should aim to develop approach behaviour rather than avoidance behaviour.

Revise as you go

1. What is a trait?
2. What do trait theories suggest about personality and choice of sporting activity?
3. Interactionist theories propose that specific personality types are suited to particular sports – true or false?
4. Explain the characteristics of the deep psychological core as suggested by Hollander.
5. What does Hollander suggest influences the outer layer of his model (the role-related behaviour)?
6. Trait theories are a good predictor of sporting success – true or false?
7. Explain the formula $B = f(PE)$.
8. How can a coach use the knowledge gained from observing particular behaviour patterns?
9. Name the three most common methods used to measure personality.
10. Outline Eysenck's Personality Inventory (EPI).
11. Suggest two advantages of using self-report questionnaires.
12. Suggest two disadvantages of the observational method of data collection.
13. The POMS for a performer with positive mental health is commonly known as the I__________ P__________.
14. All successful elite athletes display a positive profile – true or false?
15. Which aspect of mood states gives the shape of the POMS graph in Fig 6.06 the distinctive peak?
16. Name the two factors that influence a performer's achievement motivation.
17. List five characteristics of a need to achieve (n.Ach) performer.
18. What are the two types of achievement goal suggested by the Achievement Goal Theory?
19. Suggest why it is important to develop n.Ach performers with approach behaviour.
20. Suggest two strategies a coach could employ to improve the n.Ach characteristics of a performer.

CHAPTER 7

Arousal

LEARNING OBJECTIVES:

By the end of this chapter you should be able to:

- explain the term 'arousal'
- outline and evaluate different theories of arousal, including the Drive theory, Inverted-U theory and Catastrophe theory
- discuss the relationship between arousal levels and sporting performance
- outline the concepts of the zone of optimal functioning and peak flow experience
- explain the term 'attentional narrowing'
- suggest strategies to control arousal levels.

Introduction

The key to success in sport is often linked to the effective ability of an athlete to control the emotions experienced when faced with extreme pressure. The perceived pressure may be due to a number of factors, many of which you will be able to associate with. For example, the pressures may include:

- an audience
- the expectations of teammates, the coach or parents
- the importance of the event and personal aims.

Often the performer will become anxious and this in turn will hinder his or her performance. The ultimate champion will usually be the one who is able to control feelings of negativity and focus his or her attention on the task at hand. Arousal affects individuals in different ways: some need to reduce their levels to perform at their best, whilst others need to be more 'psyched up'. During this section we will explore the concept of arousal and outline strategies that can eliminate its negative effects on performance.

What is arousal?

Arousal should be thought of as a multi-dimensional state. It has been defined as:

Gould and Krane (1992):
'A general physiological and psychological activation of the organism (person) that varies on a continuum from deep sleep to intense excitement.'

From this definition we can see that arousal may be cognitive, involving thought processes, or **somatic**, causing a change in the body's response such as an increase in heart rate or sweat production. Arousal also involves a variety of states, ranging from sleeping to normal everyday responses and highly energised states with high levels of excitement, such as the feelings created by taking part in competitive sporting events. If we become over-aroused this usually has a negative effect on performance, caused by anxiety and stress (see Chapter 8 for more information). The level of arousal is controlled by the **reticular activating system (RAS)**, which interprets the level of stimulation entering the body and initiates an appropriate response. The primary aim of the performer is to control his or her arousal to an optimal level suitable for the activity undertaken, so that concentration and decision-making are not impaired.

Fig 7.01 Increased levels of physiological and psychological arousal of are needed for individuals to perform at their best

KEY TERMS

Arousal:
the energised state of readiness of the individual to perform a task, motivating him or her to direct his or her behaviour in a particular manner

Somatic:
refers to the physiological changes which the performer experiences

Reticular activating system (RAS):
a cluster of brain cells located in the central part of the brain stem, which maintains levels of arousal

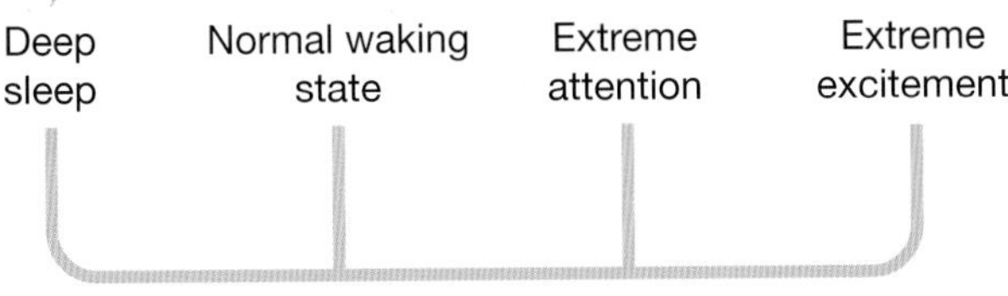

Fig 7.02 The arousal continuum

Theories of arousal

There are three theories of arousal with which you need to be familiar:

- Drive Theory (Hull, 1943; Spence and Spence, 1966
- Inverted-U Theory, Yerkes and Dobson, 1908
- Catastrophe theory Hardy and Fazey, 1987.

Drive Theory

The original Drive Theory (Hull, 1943) suggested a linear relationship between arousal and performance. Figure 7.03 shows that as the level of arousal increases, the level of performance also increases. Therefore the more aroused a performer becomes, the better the performance.

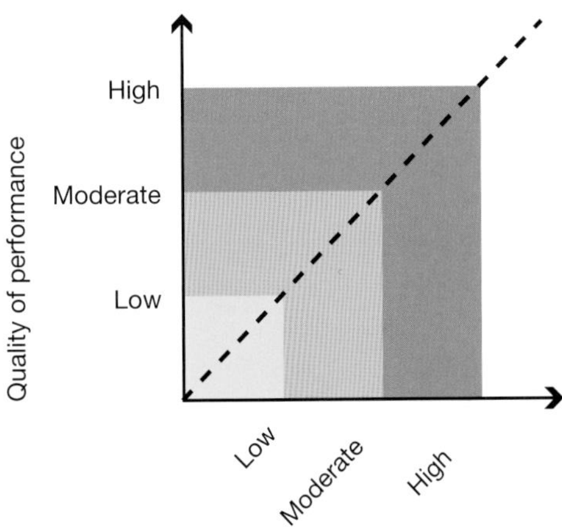

Fig 7.03 Original Drive Theory

KEY TERMS

Drive Theory:
a theory suggesting a linear relationship between arousal and performance

Dominant habit or response:
the typical behaviour pattern of an individual, either skilled or non-skilled, in the execution of a task

EXAM TIP:

Ensure you are able to draw each of the arousal graphs and label them correctly.

Later research by Spence and Spence adapted the theory, proposing that the performer's **dominant habit or response** would be more evident as his or her arousal level increased. This relationship is expressed as:

$$P = f\ (H \times D)$$

Where:

- P = performance
- H = dominant habit or response
- f = function
- D = drive or level of arousal

The effect of arousal on performance is therefore linked to the task and the experience of the performer. It is suggested that as arousal increases the following will occur:

- an experienced performer will complete the skill well because his or her dominant habit is well learned
- an inexperienced performer will execute the skill poorly as his or her dominant habit is not well learned.

APPLY IT!

During training a young badminton player has learned the technique of a smash shot and is able to execute the skill reasonably well in practice. During a game situation, the pressure increases and the new skill that is not yet fully learned is unsuccessful. However, an experienced player's smash would be executed properly during a match. The Drive Theory is closely related to the concept of social facilitation (see Chapter 11). If this suggestion is accepted, novices must be able to develop their skills during practice situations with lower levels of arousal if learning is to be optimised.

KEY TERMS

Social facilitation:
the influence of the presence of others on performance, which may be positive or negative

Autonomous phase of learning:
stage reached by an athlete when he or she has learned a skill so that it becomes automatic, involving little or no conscious thought or attention when performing the skill

Somatic or cognitive anxiety:
a negative stress response which affects a performer's physiological responses, such as heart rate, or thoughts

Inverted-U Theory:
a theory proposing that as arousal levels increase so does the performance, but only up to an optimum point after which performance deteriorates

Critics of Drive Theory question some of the proposals as they do not explain the reasons why skilled performers in the **autonomous phase of learning** often fail to complete skills in situations of high arousal. For example, consider how often a professional player appears to make an easy mistake, such as missing a penalty or dropping a catch. According to the theory, an increased level of arousal should help the player's performance not cause it to deteriorate. The theory also takes no account of different types of arousal which may occur, such as **somatic or cognitive anxiety**.

Fig 7.04 Even the most skilful of players when over-aroused may not play to their potential, as shown when Cristiano Ronaldo missed a penalty in the 2008 Champions League Final despite scoring earlier in the match

Inverted-U Theory

The **Inverted-U Theory** (Yerkes and Dobson, 1908) counters some of the problems of the Drive Theory by proposing that as arousal levels increase, so does the level of performance, but only up to an optimum point. The optimum point of arousal is usually reached at moderate levels of arousal. After this point further increases will cause the performance to deteriorate, as shown in Figure 7.05 below:

- **A: Under-aroused** – performer may show a lack of concentration and attention.
- **B: Moderate level of arousal** – optimal level of arousal, good selective attention and level of concentration.
- **C: Over-aroused** – performer may lose focus, miss cues, become anxious, experience muscle tension, make poor decisions and possibly display aggressive behaviour.

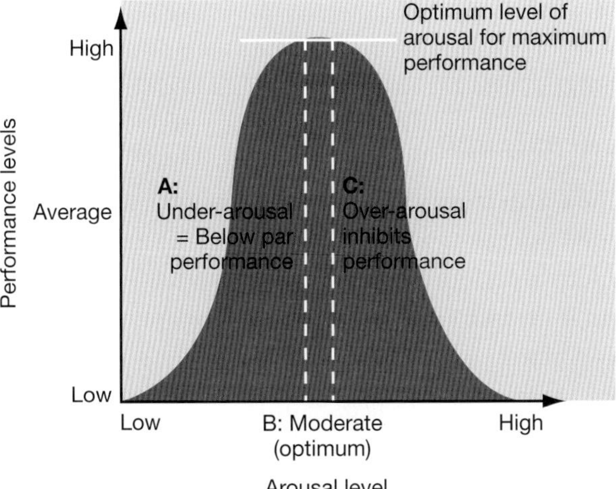

Fig 7.05 Inverted-U Theory of arousal

Each individual will have a different optimal level of arousal. Several factors need to be considered when attempting to determine the personal optimum level of arousal, including:

- **Nature of the task** – skills that are classified as complex or involve fine muscle movement (such as snooker, golf putting and archery) require a lower level of arousal than those of a gross or simple nature, for example, running, weightlifting or contact sports such as rugby.
- **Skill level of the performer** – performers who are experienced may be able to cope with higher levels of arousal as their movements are autonomous; in comparison, novice performers need to focus more carefully on relevant cues. For example, a novice basketball player will need to concentrate on the basic shooting action and may become over-aroused when faced with a defender, whereas an experienced player will be able to execute the skill under such pressure.
- **Personality of the performer** – performers who are more extrovert tend to be able to cope more effectively with higher levels of arousal and excitement when compared to introverted individuals.

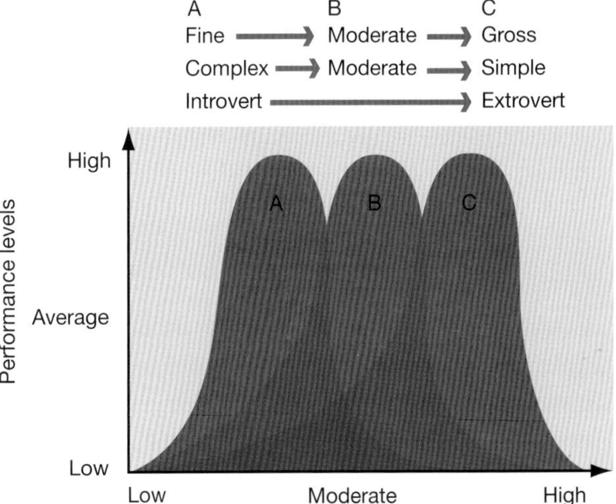

Fig 7.06 Relationship between arousal levels, the task, skill level and personality of the performer

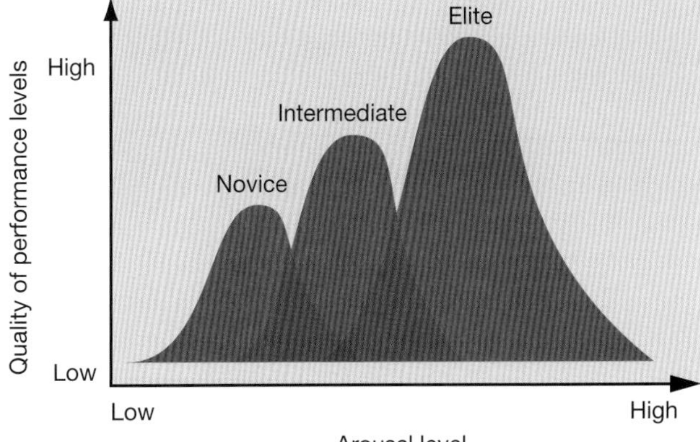

Fig 7.07 Relationship between arousal and experience

The coach must take all these factors into account and attempt to ensure the learning conditions are suitable for development to occur. The coach must also work with the performer to ensure that he or she recognises how different levels of arousal are required at various times during competition.

EXAM TIP:

Make sure you understand that the optimum level of arousal can alter for each performer, depending on his or her experience, personality, the task and the situation. Reinforce your answers with practical examples.

APPLY IT!

Rugby players, such as Jonny Wilkinson, may have to change their level of arousal from moment to moment as they may be required to execute a tackle and immediately afterwards attempt a penalty kick. As you can see, each skill requires a different level of arousal and unless the performer can make these adjustments, his or her performance may deteriorate.

A weakness of Inverted-U Theory is that it does not explain how an individual may become over-aroused at some point during the performance yet still recover sufficiently to compete effectively. It assumes that when over-arousal occurs performance will continue to deteriorate.

TASK 7.01

Rank the following activities in order (1 to 10) of importance for high levels of arousal. Justify your decision.

• golf putt	• 100m sprint
• high jump	• rugby
• hockey penalty flick	• pistol shooting
• boxing	• weightlifting
• archery	• gymnastic vault

Fig 7.08 Jonny Wilkinson needs different skills for taking a conversion than for tackling an opponent

Catastrophe Theory

The **Catastrophe Theory** (Hardy and Fazey, 1987) suggests an increase in cognitive arousal will improve performance (as in the Inverted-U Theory), but if over-arousal occurs one of two options may take place:

- If arousal levels drop slightly, caused by an increase in cognitive anxiety, a performer could recover sufficiently and regain his or her optimal arousal level. This may be achieved using supportive words from a coach or teammates, as well as the implementation of effective stress management techniques.

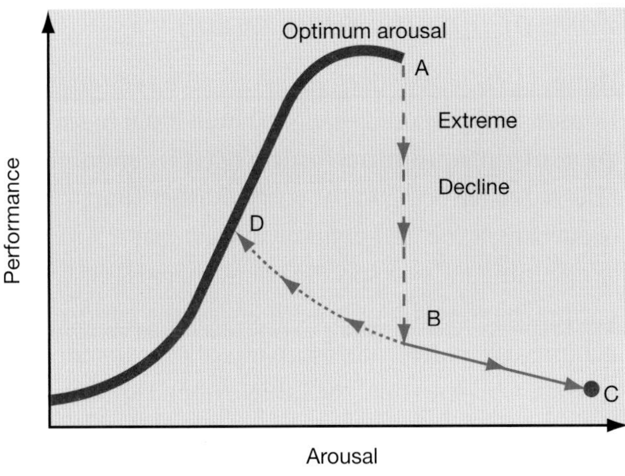

Fig 7.09 Catastrophe Theory

- If arousal levels continue to increase, both in terms of cognitive anxiety and somatic anxiety (physiological responses), the performer will not be able to recover and a catastrophe will occur. In other words, his or her performance will continue to decline and the performer will not be able to recover. This is illustrated by Figure 7.09.

A – Over-arousal, threshold of catastrophe
B – Arousal level after catastrophe
C – Continued deterioration of performance
D – Recovery of arousal levels and gradual return to optimum arous

STRETCH AND CHALLENGE

There are many examples during training when a golfer will have low levels of arousal and complete shots successfully, but in a competition they may become over-aroused causing a dramatic reduction in performance, including loss of concentration, ineffective decisions and poor execution of shots. The player may take time to recover from this position and return to an optimum level of arousal or his or her performance may continue to deteriorate. The final stages of the 2007 Open Championship held at Carnoustie illustrate this point.

Luck or skill?

Padraig Harrington beat the long-time leader of the match, Sergio Garcia, by one shot in a four-hole play-off after a final round of excitement in which the lead was held by three different players at various times.

But the match was made great by the real drama of the final few holes as first one, and then another, hopeful challenger fell by the wayside. Garcia, who had led from the very first round, journeyed to hell and back four times before taking advantage of an unbelievable string of errors by Harrington on the last green. After seven holes the Spaniard was four ahead and looking comfortable. By the 16th he was two down, then one up again before a dramatic finale unfolded on the last two holes.

The young Argentinian Andres Romero, who had only ever won three minor tournaments in South America before, was stringing together a remarkable round that included 10 birdies. By the time he reached the 16th, he was two shots ahead of the field at nine-under par. Then it all went pear-shaped. Had he been able to finish the last two in par four he would have won the title. Instead, he concocted a six and five cocktail that not only knocked him sideways but out of the reckoning.

That left Harrington one shot ahead of Garcia (who was a hole behind him) coming up to the 18th. And that was when his luck ran out. He finished up in a stream, not once but twice, and also dropped two shots, giving Garcia a chance to snatch the coveted Claret Jug.

But drama continued to heap on drama and Garcia could only respond with a five. This meant they were all square and had to perform four extra play-off holes to decide the winner. After his 18th-hole disaster Harrington pulled his game back together, went in to a two-shot lead with a birdie against Garcia's bogey at the first extra hole, and held on over the remaining, tormenting minutes.

1. In pairs discuss the events outlined in the golf tournament above and draw annotated graphs to explain the possible effects of arousal on each of the three golfers.
2. In pairs, discuss a sporting situation in which you have participated where you performed well. Explain how you felt performing and identify how you maintained your correct level of arousal. Compare this situation to one when you became over-aroused. Discuss if you were able to recover and if so explain how this was achieved.

EXAM TIP:

1. You will need to be able to sketch a graph of Catastrophe Theory and interpret its shape when linked to a practical example.
2. You need to understand the relationship and limitations of the different theories of arousal and be able to outline methods to control arousal levels.

KEY TERMS

Catastrophe Theory:
a theory suggesting an increase in arousal levels will have a positive effect on performance, and that over-arousal may cause deterioration in performance but the individual may recover his or her optimum levels of arousal

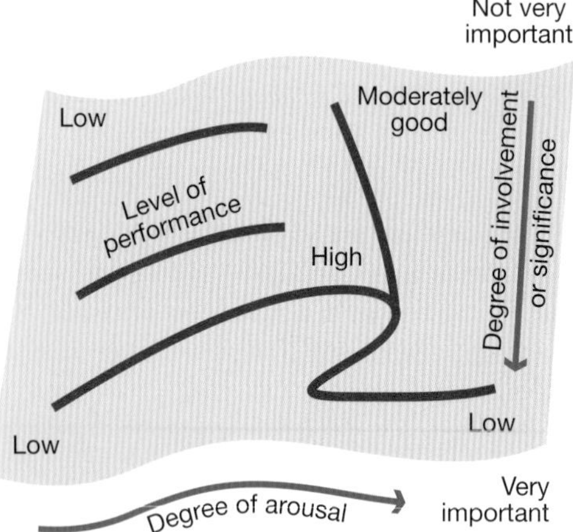

Fig 7.10 A three-dimensional model of arousal and performance in sport

Zone of optimal functioning

Hanin (1980) developed the work of Yerkes and Dobson and proposed that each individual has a **zone of optimal functioning (ZOF)**, commonly referred to as 'being in the zone'. Rather than occurring at the mid-point of the arousal continuum and at a specific point, there is an optimal band width or area in which the performer achieves his or her maximum attention capacity.

When 'in the zone' the athlete often experiences:

- the feeling of the movement being effortless, without conscious control
- the ability to select the correct cues and make decisions quickly and effectively, in addition to remaining focused on the task without being distracted by other players or the audience.

It must be remembered that each individual will have his or her own zone of optimal functioning, as illustrated in Figure 7.11.

KEY TERMS

Zone of optimal functioning:
the unique level of arousal for each athlete, which allows the athlete to perform with maximum concentration and effort

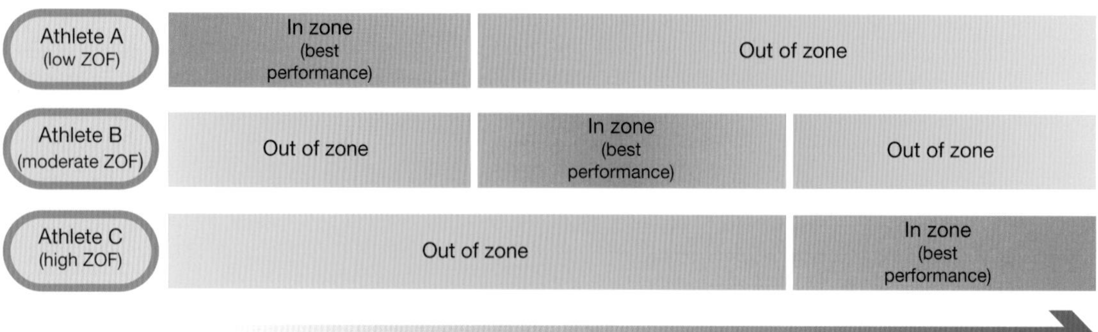

Fig 7.11 Zone of optimal functioning for different performers

Hanin's concept although similar to the Inverted U Theory differs in two major aspects.

1. The optimum level of arousal does not always occur at the midpoint of the arousal continuum. Variable factors such as the situation and the performer will cause the ZOF to alter.
2. The optimum level of arousal does not occur at a specific point but over a 'band width'.

The implications for the coach and performer are that work must be done to allow the individual to recognise when they are both within and outside the ZOF, either needing to relax or become more psyched-up. Also the coach must be aware that within a team there may be performers who have different ZOFs and simply competing a pre-match psyching-up session involving everyone may actually be detrimental to the group productivity and final result.

Critics of the theory claim it does not differentiate between cognitive and somatic anxiety. Also some studies have found that there is no significant difference in performance whether the athlete is in their zone or not.

Attentional narrowing

During competition the aim of every performer is to ensure they select the appropriate cues and make the correct decisions as quickly as possible. When optimal arousal levels are reached the performer should be able to detect the correct stimuli easily. The **cue-utilisation theory** suggests that we detect the cues required to complete the task successfully. However, if arousal increases, the performer may actually begin to miss vital cues and signals which will lead to a reduction in his or her performance level.

Attentional narrowing links arousal levels directly to the individual's ability to focus on relevant cues and stimuli. If the performer reaches his or her optimal arousal level, he or she will identify the appropriate cues, but over-arousal will hinder the process. As attentional narrowing continues, vital cues will be missed, known as **attentional wastage**, leading to a decrease in performance. For example, a basketball player may not detect a teammate in an open shooting position or may fail to see a defender closing down his space as he moves in to shoot.

The attentional wastage occurs when the performer's concentration is misdirected to cues that are irrelevant, causing a decrease in performance. For example, as the performer becomes over-aroused during a game of basketball, he may listen to shouts from the crowd rather than focus on the position of players on court.

To ensure the correct level of arousal is reached and maintained, the performer and coach must work together to identify potential causes of weakness and over-arousal. They must then implement various stress management techniques (see Chapter 8) and other psychological strategies to minimise the factors which may lead to over-arousal.

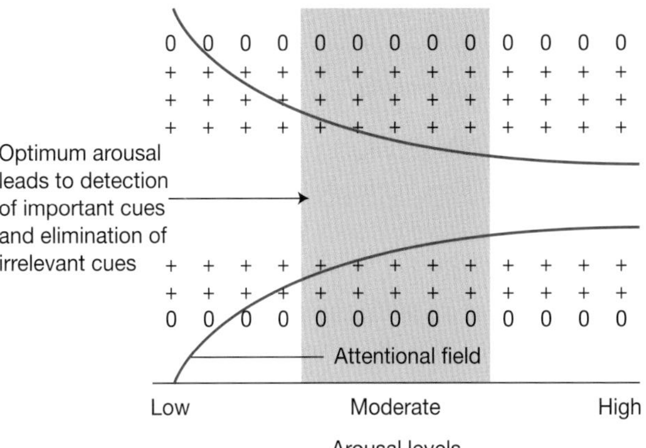

Fig 7.12 Attentional narrowing

KEY TERMS

Cue-utilisation theory:
this involves the use of relevant cues to focus the performer's attention as arousal levels increase in order to complete the task successfully

Attentional narrowing:
this links arousal theories directly to the individual's ability to focus on relevant cues

Attentional wastage:
this occurs when the performer's concentration is misdirected to cues that are irrelevant, causing a decrease in performance

Peak flow experience

Sports performers sometimes experience a situation when the timing of movements and actions appears perfect. They seem unable to do wrong and everything they do seems to work. Performers report to be experiencing the ultimate intrinsic experience when this happens. Csikszentmihalyi (1975) describes this as the 'flow experience'; in his research he identified the common characteristics of such feelings are:

- total ability to complete the challenge successfully
- complete absorption in the activity
- clear goals
- totally focused on task
- apparent loss of consciousness
- an almost subconscious feeling of self-control
- effortless movement.

Many psychologists when researching this area have tended to concentrate on analysing the factors which have a negative impact on intrinsic motivation whereas Csikszentmihalyi (1990, 1999) focused on what makes a task intrinsically motivating. Although it cannot be consciously planned for, the development of 'flow' has been linked to the following factors:

- positive mental attitude with high levels of confidence and positive thinking
- the performer being relaxed, controlling anxiety, and enjoying optimum arousal
- focusing on appropriate specific aspects of the current performance
- confidence in personal physical readiness, i.e. training and preparation
- optimum environmental and situational conditions, including a good atmosphere
- a shared sense of purpose (team games), good interaction
- performer has a balanced emotional state.

It is suggested there is a link between somatic arousal (physiological response) and cognitive arousal (thought processes). When the performer has reached the correct level of somatic arousal and the cognitive arousal is low, peak flow is more likely to occur. The diagram below illustrates the relationship and emotional states that may occur depending on the different levels of arousal at the time.

By focusing on aspects of their preparation which can help the development of the above factors, especially self-confidence, elite performers can increase the probability of the 'flow experience' occurring. As a result it can be argued that the psychological preparation of an athlete is just as important as physiological performance.

A number of factors may interfere with the experience, resulting in 'disrupted flow'. Such factors include:

- injury
- fatigue
- crowd hostility
- uncontrollable events
- worrying about end result or personal performance
- lack of challenge
- not at optimal arousal levels
- limited cohesion within the group or team
- negative self talk
- poor officials
- poor preparation
- poor performance.

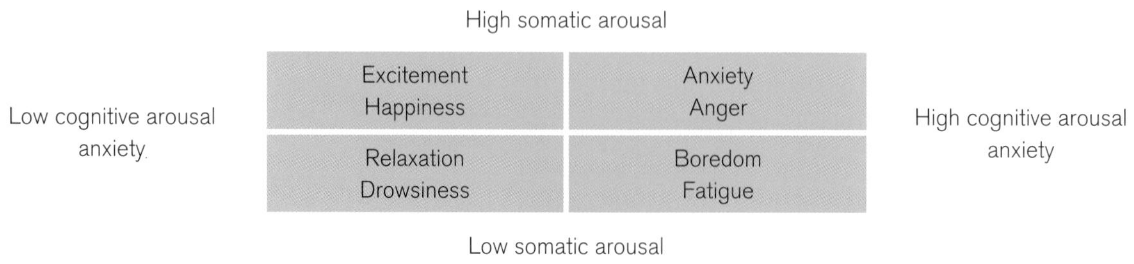

High somatic arousal

Low cognitive arousal anxiety	Excitement Happiness	Anxiety Anger	High cognitive arousal anxiety
	Relaxation Drowsiness	Boredom Fatigue	

Low somatic arousal

Fig 7.13 Peak flow experience – the interaction of somatic and cognitive arousal

APPLY IT!

At the 2008 Beijing Olympics, Ben Ainslie became the most successful British sailor by winning his third consecutive gold medal. Ainslie's closest rival for the gold medal was the American, Zach Riley, and as long as he finished ahead of Riley he would win the gold medal. The following quotes show not only how Ainslie was able to adjust his tactics depending on the weather and the requirements of the races, but indicates he was able to remain totally focused and ignore irrelevant factors which may have hindered his performance.

Ben Ainslie 'in zone'

During the final medal race Ainslie ignored all the other competitors and maintained his position just ahead of Riley at the back of the field, blocking every attempt he made to pass him.

'I had to string together some top-five finishes and with wins in the second, fourth and fifth races, I was doing well but then I was tenth again. You discount your worst finish, but I had had two bad runs. But in the frustratingly light wind everyone was being erratic. It was really only Zach Riley, the American, who was staying with me. As we got near the end of the regatta, it was all about keeping an eye on him, and hanging on to my lead.

We spent a long time hanging around before starting and had raced two legs when the wind just disappeared and the race was abandoned. I had one hand on the gold medal, but had to stay focused.'

However as the race was abandoned the sailors had to return the following day, but this time required a different approach.

'On Sunday, the conditions were completely opposite. It was pouring with rain and we had to come in for a while because visibility was so poor. But when we went back out, the windy conditions allowed me to control the race and finish first.'

Ainslie was able to completely focus on the task and concentrate on his own performance, rewarding him with a gold medal for his efforts.

Fig 7.14 Ben Ainslie stayed focused to win his gold medal at the 2008 Beijing Olympics

ATHLETE PROFILE

Claire Vigrass has experienced the effects of being 'in the zone' and being 'outside the zone', in terms of being under-aroused and over-aroused during competitive Real Tennis matches. During the 2008 US Ladies Open Championships she reported feelings of confidence and playing shots effortlessly, without seeming to consciously think about the type of shot she should be playing. She was at the 'optimum level of arousal' (**Inverted-U Theory**). However in other tournaments the same feelings did not occur. Claire lost the semi-final of the 2008 French Open and felt she was not suitably aroused due to a lack of focus caused by a last-minute change in playing order, playing an opponent she had recently beaten and thinking about who she would play in the final. In the 2008 British Open Final Claire was runner-up being defeated by the World Number 1 player. Over-arousal rather than under-arousal was the issue on this occasion. After the match she said she felt tense and unable to focus on the cues, becoming distracted by the crowd and the possible consequences of winning the match.

In the National League Final, where Claire represented her club, Prested Hall, Essex, she lost the opening game 1–6 and could easily have crumbled to lose the match (**Catastrophe Theory**). However she regained her composure quickly and went on to win by two games to one.

ExamCafé

Relax, refresh, result!

Refresh your memory

Revision checklist

Make sure you know the following:

Arousal

- Arousal is a physiological state of alertness and anticipation which prepares the body for action.
- The reticular activating system (RAS) is responsible for maintaining the general level of arousal within the body.
- Drive Theory states that there is a linear relationship between arousal and performance. As the level of arousal increases so does the likelihood of the dominant response occurring.
- Inverted-U Theory suggests that the relationship is curvilinear. Increased arousal improves performance up to a certain point after this any increases in arousal level will have a detrimental effect on performance.
- Levels of optimum arousal will be different according to the complexity and nature of the specific task, the level of experience of the performer and their personality.
- Increased arousal leads to attentional narrowing but over arousal can create attentional wastage.
- Catastrophe Theory suggests that increased levels of arousal will have a positive effect on performance and that over-arousal may cause deterioration in performance but individuals may recover to regain their optimum level of arousal.

Zone of optimal functioning (ZOF)

- ZOF suggests that each individual performer has a zone of optimal state anxiety in which their best performance occurs.
- Variable factors such as the situation and the performer will cause the ZOF to alter.
- The optimum level of arousal does not occur at a specific point but over a 'band width'.

Peak flow experience

- Emotional state that a performer may experience during sport when the timing of movements and actions appears perfect.
- This emotional state is more likely to occur when the performer has reached the correct level of somatic arousal and the cognitive arousal is low.

Revise as you go

1. Explain the term 'arousal'.
2. What is the purpose of the RAS?
3. Explain how the RAS differs depending on the personality of the performer.
4. What does Drive Theory suggest will happen as arousal levels increase?
5. With reference to Drive Theory, how will increased arousal levels affect the performance of experienced and novice performers?
6. What is the main criticism of Drive Theory?
7. What are the characteristics of a performer who is over-aroused?
8. What is the term given to the optimal level of arousal that will produce the best performance?
9. According to the Inverted-U Theory, at what level of arousal does optimal performance occur?
10. How does the skill level of a performer affect the optimum arousal level?
11. Explain how the personality of a performer may influence the optimum level of arousal.
12. How does the Catastrophe Theory differ from the Inverted-U Theory?
13. How can a performer recover his or her arousal levels and avoid catastrophe?
14. Explain the term attentional narrowing.
15. When does 'attentional wastage' occur during a performance?
16. What is the zone of optimal functioning and explain the impact on the performer?
17. How does the ZOF differ from the Inverted U Theory?
18. Explain the concept of the 'peak flow experience'.
19. When is the peak flow experience more likely to occur?
20. Outline four factors which may lead to 'disrupted flow'.

CHAPTER 8

Controlling anxiety

LEARNING OBJECTIVES:

By the end of this chapter you should be able to:

- identify the characteristics and causes of stress
- understand the impact of stress on sporting performance
- explain the different forms of anxiety including somatic, cognitive, trait and state anxiety
- outline methods to measure anxiety levels for individual performers
- suggest strategies to combat cognitive anxiety and control arousal levels
- suggest strategies to combat somatic anxiety and control arousal levels
- outline how to use goal setting effectively to help reduce levels of anxiety.

Introduction

A key element in most topic areas of sports psychology is the ability of the performer to control his or her emotions, which then allows him or her to execute the appropriate skills and tactics to the best of his or her ability. In the modern world of sport the difference between success and failure is measured in hundredths of a second or a moment of inspiration from a player. All performers are physically well prepared and there is little to separate individuals. Coaches often highlight the importance of emotional control as a key factor in victory or defeat. The ability to manage stress levels can make the significant difference in the final result.

EXAM TIP:

Throughout this chapter think about your own experiences while playing sport and attempt to relate the theoretical explanations to your own feelings and actions.

Definitions of stress

The term '**stress**' is often used to describe the negative feelings a person experiences when placed in a potentially threatening situation. However, a clear distinction must initially be made between stress which has a positive effect and stress which has a negative effect on the individual.

The definitions below explain in broad terms the reaction of an individual:

Seyle (1956):
'The non-specific response of the body to any demand made on it.'

According to McGrath (1970) stress occurs due to:

'A substantial imbalance between demand (physical and/or psychological demands) and response capability, under conditions where failure to meet the demands has important consequences.'

Therefore, if we are placed in a situation in which we feel pressurised, unable to meet the task or worried about the consequences, we may experience a stress reaction. This may differ from one person to another. Because individuals react differently we have to recognise this fact and implement specific strategies to allow them to cope.

The stress experience, which is initiated by a **stressor**, may be positive or negative, as outlined below:

- **Eustress** is a positive form of stress which performers actively seek to test their abilities to the limit and provide them with an adrenalin rush. It can enhance their performance and heighten their emotions; if successfully completed it can lead to intrinsic satisfaction and boost confidence levels. Examples of eustress may include participation in adventurous activities, such as abseiling or performing in front of significant others. You may have experienced this form of stress when preparing to ride on a roller-coaster at a theme park or when playing in an important match.
- **Anxiety** is the negative form of stress which can lead to an increase in arousal and a potential decrease in performance levels. Often performers experience loss of concentration, feelings of apprehension or an inability to cope, attentional narrowing and fear of failure (**cognitive responses**). They may also suffer from sweating, increased muscle tension, feelings of nausea, increased heart rate and other physiological reactions (**somatic responses**).

Fig 8.01 The same activity can cause different stress reactions depending on the perceptions of the individual person

When the performer is placed in a stressful situation, McGrath (1970) suggested that he or she responds by progressing through four stages, as outlined in Fig 8.02.

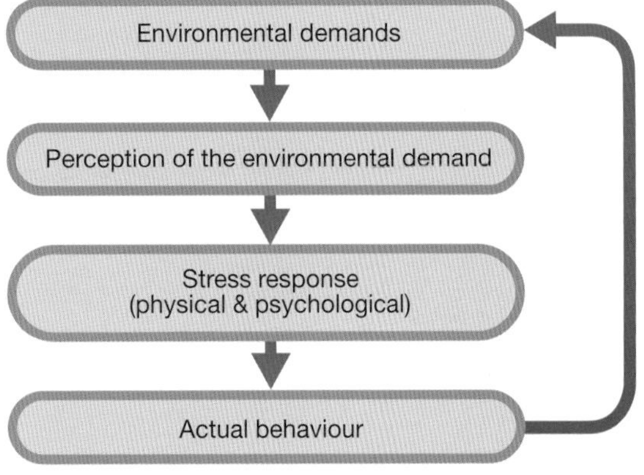

Fig 8.02 The stress process

- **Stage 1: Environmental demands** – this involves the individual having to cope with either a physical or psychological demand. For example, performing a difficult skill in front of a large audience.
- **Stage 2: Perception of the demands** – the individual then makes a judgement about the specific requirements of the task and his or her ability to deal with them. For example, more anxiety will occur if the performer has never competed in front of a large crowd (social facilitation).
- **Stage 3: Stress response** – once a judgement of the situation has been made the individual experiences a specific reaction as outlined above, which may be physical (somatic) or psychological (cognitive). For example, the performer becomes apprehensive, worries about failure and doubts his or her ability to complete the task.
- **Stage 4: Behaviour** – the performer then attempts to execute the skill. The performer's behaviour will often reflect his or her psychological attitude to the task. For example, the performer is worried and as a result suffers from muscle tension and poor selective attention, causing him or her to execute the skill poorly.

KEY TERMS

Stress:
the perceived imbalance between the demands of the task and the individual's ability to complete the task

Stressor:
any demands that are placed on the performer that initiate stress

Cognitive response:
any change in the performer's thoughts (which are often negative), e.g. worry or feelings of failure

Somatic response:
any change in the physiological response experienced by the performer, e.g. an increase in heart rate

Causes of stress

There are numerous causes of stress and different people will perceive each one differently. Any factor which initiates the stress response is known as a stressor. Within sport there are many such stressors, as outlined in Table 8.01. There may also be other stressors which you may have experienced or can identify.

Factors that initiate stress	
Nature of the game – conflict	Fear of failure (n.Af/avoidance)
Injury of fear for personal safety	Naturally high trait anxiety
Importance of the event	Attitude of coach
Status of the opposition	Parental pressure
Extrinsic rewards	Media pressure
Climate	Personal expectations
Frustration with own performance or that of others or officials	Nature of the crowd, e.g. size, proximity, knowledge

Table 8.01 Types of stressor

TASK 8.01

Select an event in which you have participated and identify potential stressors that may have affected you. Watch a professional sporting event and make a similar list. Compare the potential stressors and consider what the differences may be.

Stress response: General Adaptation Syndrome

When stress is experienced, either positive or negative, the body responds in a similar manner. Seyle (1956) proposed that whatever the stressor may be, all individuals have the same physiological reaction. This is known as the General Adaptation Syndrome (GAS).

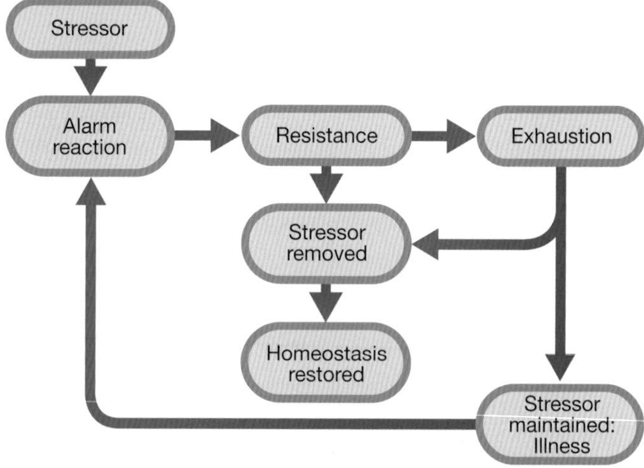

Fig 8.03 The three main stages of General Adaptation Syndrome

Seyle outlined three main stages of the GAS, as shown in Figure 8.03.

1. **Alarm reaction stage** – this is initiated when the perceived stressful situation occurs. The sympathetic branch of the **autonomic nervous system** (ANS) is activated causing increases in heart rate, blood sugar level, adrenalin and blood pressure. This is also linked to the emotional experiences of the 'fight or flight' response.

2. **Resistance stage** – the body systems attempt to cope with the stressors if they are not removed by reverting to normal functioning levels if possible or a state of **homeostasis**. The body will attempt to resist the effect of the sympathetic nervous system.
3. **Exhaustion stage** – the continued presence of the stressors will prove too much for the body to cope with, causing heart disease, stomach ulcers and high blood pressure. The body fails to deal with the continued demands placed upon it and is unable to fight infection and ultimately death may occur.

EXAM TIP:

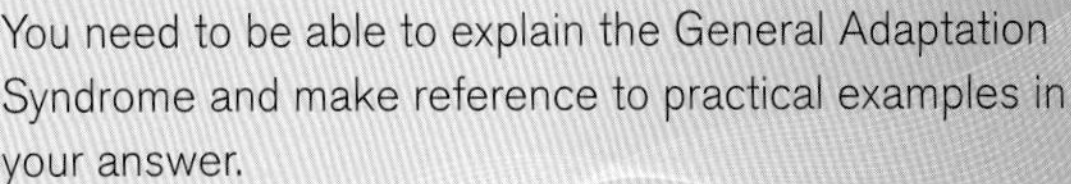

You need to be able to explain the General Adaptation Syndrome and make reference to practical examples in your answer.

KEY TERMS

Autonomic nervous system (ANS):
the ANS works automatically to co-ordinate the body. The sympathetic branch of the ANS is stimulated by strong positive or negative emotions

Homeostasis:
the process by which the body maintains its constant internal physiological state

Anxiety

There are several specific types of anxiety which affect a performer and each may influence performance in a different way. There are two broad categories of anxiety:

- **Cognitive anxiety** involves the performer's thoughts and worries concerning his or her perceived lack of ability to complete the task successfully. The individual will often experience feelings of nervousness and, apprehension, and have difficulty concentrating before and during competition. Cognitive anxiety is usually experienced prior to the event – even several days beforehand.
- **Somatic anxiety** involves the individual's physiological responses when placed in a situation where he or she perceives an inability to complete the task successfully. The performer may experience an increase in heart rate, sweating, blood pressure, muscle tension and feelings of nausea. All of which could hinder performance initially; however, these symptoms often reduce when the event has started.

Figure 8.04 illustrates how a performer's cognitive and somatic anxiety levels may vary before, during and after competition. This graph does not apply to all performers but is an example of how anxiety levels may alter depending on the situation.

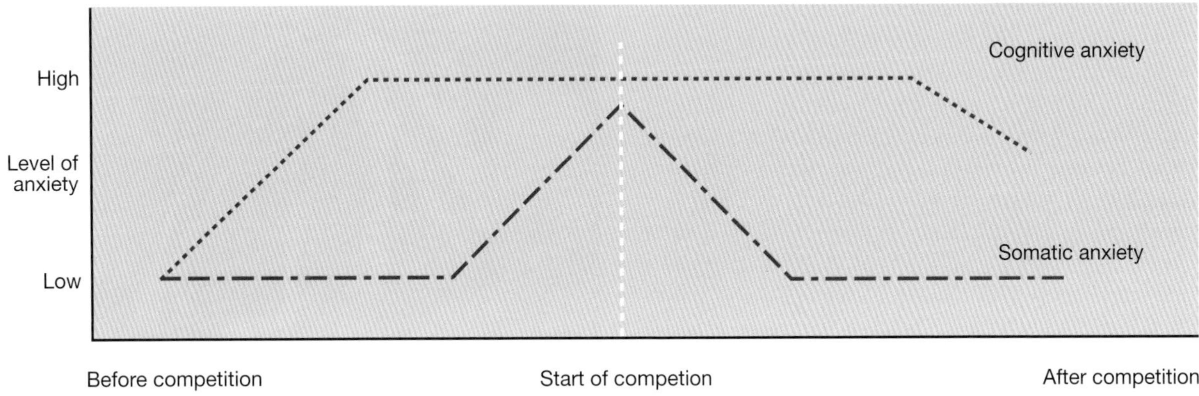

Fig 8.04 Example of changing anxiety levels, before, during and after performance

Individuals may react differently depending on the situation and their personality. Speilberger (1966) identified two types of anxiety which may account for such differences:

- **Trait anxiety** refers to the general disposition of an individual to perceive situations as threatening. As with other traits this disposition is stable and genetically inherited. If a performer possesses this characteristic he or she is more likely to become anxious in a wide variety of situations, experiencing a higher state of anxiety than those with low levels of trait anxiety. This is also referred to as 'A-trait'.
- **State anxiety** is a form of anxiety which occurs when the performer is placed in a particular situation. It is linked to the performer's mood and can literally alter from moment to moment. At times anxiety may be high, such as before the event, but may reduce when the event has started and increase again when faced with a new challenge, such as taking a penalty. Both cognitive and somatic anxiety may be experienced during this time. This form of anxiety is also known as 'A-state'.

APPLY IT!

The account below illustrates how both cognitive and somatic anxiety may affect performers. Team GB's cyclist, Victoria Pendleton, at the 2008 Beijing Olympics had to wait until the end of the cycling programme to compete, while watching her teammates excel, winning numerous medals.

Nerves versus will

Victoria Pendleton has a very clinical racing style but yet she regularly admits that she is a bag of nerves. The man who has enabled her to master her emotions at the times that matter is the team psychiatrist, Steve Peters. She claims he is the key to her success and has said: *'The psychology of what drives me as a person has been essential, getting everything in perspective, getting me in the right mind-frame. My expectations were too high. I was beating myself up psychologically at every moment. It was knocking me back.'*

Peters whispered words of encouragement to Pendleton before she set off to face Anna Meares of Australia in the second of the two rounds. It looked straightforward as she made a jump down the penultimate banking to take the lead going down the back straight. She accelerated down the straight to gain a narrow lead on the final banking and then a chasm between the two of them by the line. After a few laps warm down, she collapsed into the arms of the tactics coach for the cycling team, Jan van Eijden. He's the man who takes her round the velodrome in Manchester elbowing and shoulder barging her to get her used to the physical stuff. This emotion was understandable. She had endured a nerve-jangling two days before taking to the track.

Once she had the gold medal around her neck, she said, *'Seems like I've been waiting for ever.'* When asked how she spent the wait, she replied: *'I painted my nails a few times, watched the TV, struggled to find something to eat because obviously you haven't much of an appetite, went on the rollers, just biding my time. It was very tough, harder than I anticipated, especially with the success of the team. On some days I was very emotional in a good way because it's good to see your team win and it was awesome to see my team-mates win.*

'The pressure was mounting because I wanted to do what they've done and win a medal. It was important to be part of that. This week, watching the guys perform gave me some experience of what it must be like being a parent. I was a mess watching them and there was nothing I could do because they were on TV. I was like 'woh, is that how my mum and dad feel, because that is awful' and I felt quite guilty. How dare I inflict that on someone else?'

Fig 8.05 Victoria Pendleton after she won her gold medal

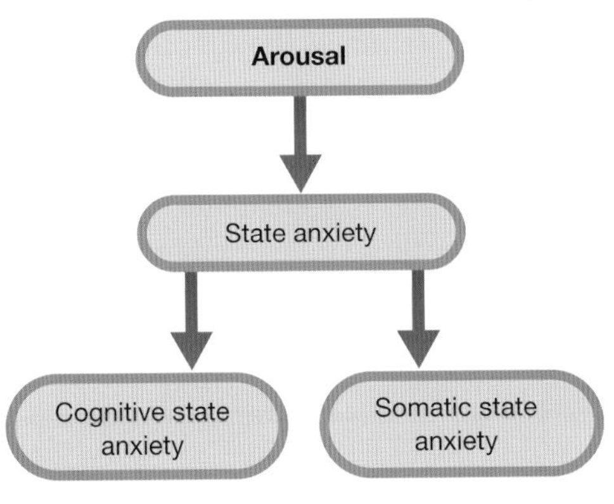

Fig 8.06 Relationship between types of anxiety

Further research by Martens (1977) also suggests there may be a specific trait named **competitive trait anxiety**. This involves the tendency of the performer to perceive competitive situations as threatening and to respond with feelings of apprehension or tension. An individual with high trait anxiety is more likely to experience a high state of anxiety when faced with stressful situations, such as competition, where he or she feels others may evaluate his or her performance (**evaluation apprehension**). The same person may not become as anxious in training as the performer may feel that he or she is not being judged and evaluated.

The causes of stress as previously outlined contribute to state anxiety levels prior to and during competition. This interactionist approach to anxiety is illustrated in Figure 8.07.

EXAM TIP:

Familiarise yourself with the most commonly used methods of stress measurement. Be able to explain the techniques, their methodology, and evaluate their effectiveness.

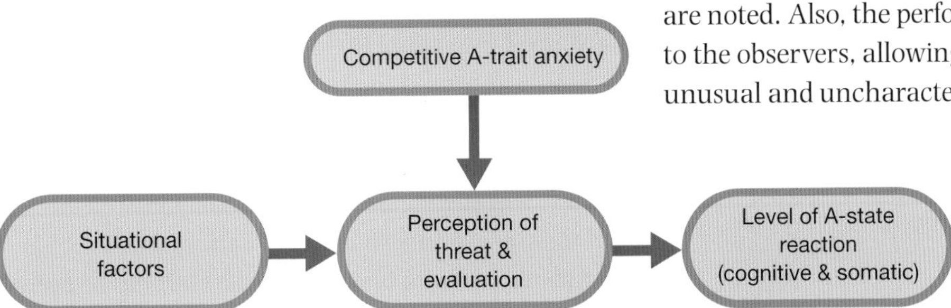

Fig 8.07 The interactionist approach to anxiety

Measurement of stress levels

The measurement of stress levels is an important aspect of a performer's preparation. If patterns of behaviour can be identified and linked to specific situations, the coach can implement various strategies to reduce the performer's anxiety, control arousal levels and allow the athlete to operate in his or her zone of optimal functioning.

There are three methods generally used to gather such information:

1. observation
2. biofeedback
3. self-report questionnaires.

Observation

Observation of performance, while subjective, does allow the performer to be assessed in the actual performance situation. The observer will record two types of data:

- **Individual behaviour:** i.e. those behaviours usually associated with nervous actions, such as fidgeting, changes in speech patterns, acts of increased aggression, etc.
- **Aspects of performance**, i.e. execution of skilled actions such as accuracy of passing, decision-making, speed of reaction, etc.

The information is analysed and repeated behaviour patterns are noted. Detrimental aspects of performance are highlighted during specific situations and relevant stress management techniques are implemented.

There are several drawbacks to using this method. In order to fully assess the performer, several observers should be watching to ensure all actions are noted. Also, the performer should be well known to the observers, allowing them to identify any unusual and uncharacteristic behaviour patterns.

Biofeedback

Biofeedback involves monitoring the physiological responses of the performer. Data is collected on changes in heart rate, muscle response, respiration rate, sweat production and levels of hormone secretion.

While this provides accurate data there are several drawbacks including the difficulty of recording information during an actual competitive performance (as the athlete has to be 'wired-up' to obtain the results). The potential changes caused as a natural reaction to being evaluated and the replication of the competitive environment is difficult in the laboratory situation.

Self-report questionnaires

These involve performers answering a series of questions concerning their emotions in specific situations. There are numerous advantages to using this method including:

- ease of administration
- large numbers can be assessed quickly
- cheap to administer.

However, there are some drawbacks too:

- misinterpretation or lack of understanding of the questions
- the respondents may not answer honestly as they may wish to appear in a positive light or they may give the answers they think are required or socially desirable
- inappropriate questions may be used, which may lead to biased results
- the actual time of completion may influence the responses
- the available responses may not cater for the exact emotions being experienced.

EXAM TIP:

Understand the value and limitations of the different techniques of measuring stress and be able to explain the most appropriate times for them to be employed.

State Trait Anxiety Inventory (STAI)

This self-report inventory, devised by Spielberger (1966) consists of 20 statements to assess state anxiety and another 20 statements to assess trait anxiety. In theory those individuals with a high trait anxiety rating (i.e. enduring characteristic) are more likely to experience high state anxiety (i.e. anxiety at a specific time).

Sport Competition Anxiety Test (SCAT)

Later work by Martens (1977) developed the Sport Competition Anxiety Test (SCAT) which is used to measure the competitive trait anxiety of a performer when placed in a pre-competitive sporting environment. The questionnaire consists of 15 statements and the performer is required to state how he or she generally responds to each. Examples of the statements are shown below:

1.	Before I compete I feel uneasy.	hardly	sometimes	often
2.	Before I compete I am calm.	hardly	sometimes	often
3.	Before I compete I get a queasy feeling in my stomach.	hardly	sometimes	often
4.	Before I compete I am nervous.	hardly	sometimes	often

Psychologists can then use this information to assess if the performer is prone to experiencing high levels of anxiety before the competition. To obtain a more accurate prediction, the performer should complete the SCAT several times before competing in different events, to develop a clear pattern of emotions.

Competitive Sport Anxiety Inventory (CSAI-2).

To identify the type of anxiety a performer may experience, Martens (1990) refined the SCAT and developed the Competitive Sport Anxiety Inventory (CSAI-2). It is used to assess an individual's state anxiety and corresponding behaviour patterns. This questionnaire measures levels of both cognitive anxiety and somatic anxiety as well as self-confidence in a sporting situation. It is completed up to an hour before the start of the event.

1.	I have self-doubts.	not at all	somewhat	moderately	very much so
2.	My body feels tense.	not at all	somewhat	moderately	very much so
3.	I feel at ease.	not at all	somewhat	moderately	very much so
4.	My heart is racing.	not at all	somewhat	moderately	very much so
5.	I am concerned about reaching my goal.	not at all	somewhat	moderately	very much so

As you can see from the examples above, each question specifically refers to either a cognitive or somatic stress response.

After evaluating the data the coach is able to identify trends in a performer's stress response and particular weaknesses that may hinder performance. However, it must be remembered that some somatic responses prior to competition are natural and may aid performance. However, high levels of cognitive state anxiety may adversely affect the performer and should be dealt with utilising stress management techniques.

Stress management techniques

The development of self-confidence is a key element in a performer's approach to an event. Throughout your studies in this section there are numerous examples of how a performer's personal belief in his or her own abilities can be developed. The factors contributing to an individual's self-efficacy (see Chapter 11), via past experiences, vicarious experiences and verbal persuasion, all contribute significantly. So too do the correct use of both intrinsic and extrinsic motivational factors, the appropriate use of attributions (Chapter 12) and the encouragement of approach behaviour. If all the theoretical aspects discussed are implemented correctly there is an increased chance the performer will perceive the competitive situation as challenging rather than as a threat.

Following evaluation of the stress response and the identification of particular types of anxiety, the performer must be taught how to recognise the symptoms of an increased state anxiety. These may be either physiological, psychological or behavioural. Various techniques can be employed, all of which need practice. This aspect of a performer's preparation is vital if he or she is to achieve his or her potential, and as such it should form an integral part of the performer's training regime.

Remember, stress is caused by an imbalance between the perceived demands of the task and the individual's ability. The aim of all the techniques is to lower the arousal levels, allowing the athlete to feel in control of his or her emotions and actions, so that he or she feels able to complete the task successfully.

There are numerous stress management methods which can be used and they fall into two broad categories:

1. cognitive strategies
2. somatic strategies.

Some techniques, however, do combine elements of both.

Cognitive methods

Imagery involves the formation of mental pictures of successful performances. It can be used in a variety of ways to either create the expected experience of a new situation or recall the feelings of a past situation. The performer can use the technique to develop a variety of sensations. The performer may:

- create a place where he or she can retreat which has a calming atmosphere, away from the pressure of competition
- recreate the kinaesthetic feeling of a successful movement
- create images of what may happen and how to deal with them, e.g. a situation within a game when confronted with two defenders
- create emotional feelings that may be experienced when placed in a stressful situation, such as success, victory and control

- create the sounds experienced in the situation, for example, either the ball on the bat or external sources that may be distracting, such as the crowd during the execution of a vision penalty kick.

Imagery can be either **internal** or **external**. Internal imagery involves a sportsperson seeing him or herself from within, completing the action or in the situation, experiencing the kinaesthetic feelings. External imagery involves the sportsperson seeing him or herself as if he or she were a spectator or on film.

TASK 8.02

Select a sports skill in which you have previously completed well in a pressurised situation. Using internal imagery, attempt to recreate the feelings you experienced during the performance. Attempt to remember any visual and auditory cues as well as the kinaesthetic feeling involved. Repeat the action in your mind several times. Before your next event, repeat this process if you feel yourself becoming anxious and practise its use as a stress management control method.

APPLY IT!

Often during competition you may have observed athletes closing their eyes and appear to recreate what they are about to attempt in their mind. This is often seen when long jumpers and bobsleigh drivers are preparing to start.

These techniques are also used in training and transferred to the competitive environment. This extract explains how Jonny Wilkinson prepares using such a technique, but not in the way you might expect:

Dealing with stress

Jonny and Alred (Wilkinson's kicking coach) have devised a set of techniques aimed at giving accuracy, power and consistency. In one, in which he tries to land the ball on the crossbar, he pretends that he is a golfer and that his foot is a seven-iron. In another, he imagines a jeering mouth behind the goal and attempts to send the ball down its throat. The funniest technique involves an imaginary woman called Doris, who sits in a particular seat in the stand behind the goal, holding a can of drink. As Wilkinson prepares to kick, he visualises the flight of the ball ending up in Doris's lap, knocking the drink out of her hands. *'The idea was that, instead of aiming at the posts, you were aiming at something specific 30 yards back,'* he said. *'That way we changed the emphasis of where I was aiming and it made me really kick through the ball.'*

APPLY IT!

A netball player who has missed several shots and is beginning to have doubts about the next shot, might click her fingers or say 'focus' to herself. As a result she concentrates on the action, technique or tactic for the next attempt, rather than thinks about the previous attempts.

Moving on

Jonny Wilkinson, when preparing for a kick employs a similar technique which he has practised in training. This report explains how he prepares:

Kicking through the ball is just one element of a complex technique, which is built up step by step (as described above). Another element is 'hardening' the kicking foot, which Wilkinson does by tapping his left toe on the grass before he kicks, usually in two sets of three taps, thus helping the foot to adopt the shape and the tension he wants when he hits the ball. Other elements are the need to focus on the precise point of the ball he is going to strike, and the importance of allowing the foot to follow through along the line of the ball for as long as possible, like a golfer. Trying to hit it hard, he says, is no good. Hitting it sweetly is the way to project it 40 metres or more, as he routinely does against his opponents.

Thought-stopping involves the individual recognising when he or she is starting to worry or develop negative thoughts about his or her performance. When this occurs a cue, action or word is used to redirect the attention to positive thoughts.

Attentional control involves performers developing their ability to alter their perceptual field. This will allow them to vary the amount and type of information that enters the body depending on the situation and the requirements of the task. In other words they will alter their selective attention depending on the specific needs at the time. During practice and through observation of competitive situations the coach should attempt to identify the attentional style required in a particular situation. If the performer has a specific weakness and fails to detect the appropriate cues during a particular phase of play it can be developed through practice. Unless the skill being performed is a 'closed skill' the performers will often be required to 'switch' between different styles to maximise their performance.

STRETCH AND CHALLENGE

Nideffer proposed his Model of Attentional Focus (1976) suggesting that attentional style varies along two dimensions:

1. **Width** – which refers to the number of stimuli requiring attention at particular times
   - **narrow** – focuses on a limited range of stimuli e.g. when serving the player focuses on the place where they wish to hit the tennis ball
   - **broad** – focuses on a wide range of stimuli e.g. the tennis player needs to detect their own and opponents position on court, as well as the location, flight and speed of the tennis ball.
2. **Direction** – refers to the focus of the thought processes of the performer
   - **external** – focuses on stimuli in the environment e.g. the location of the players and tennis ball or the type of shot being played by the opponent
   - **internal** – focuses on their own thoughts and feelings e.g. the player mentally rehearsing the correct movement pattern or applying the correct stress management techniques to control their level of arousal.

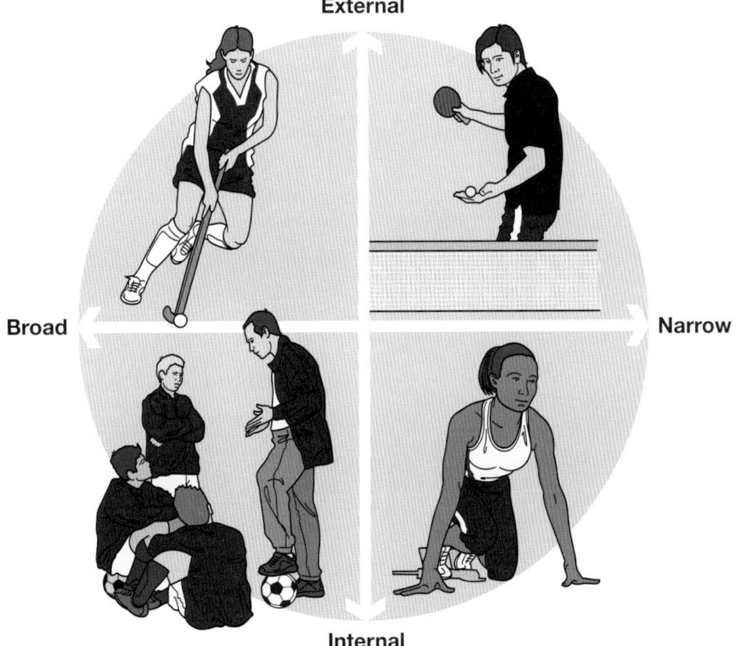

Fig 8.08 The four attentional styles

Based on Figure 8.08 you can see that Nideffer identified four attentional styles:

1. **Broad/external** – used by players during games to detect fast changing situations and identify the best option
2. **External/narrow** – used by players to concentrate on specific objects or tasks, possibly with limited number of cues
3. **Narrow/internal** – used by players to mentally rehearse a skill or task
4. **Internal/broad** – often used by coaches to analyse performance and plan future strategies and tactics.

APPLY IT!

The players involved in a tennis doubles match will need to detect different stimuli when serving compared to a rally where more information needs to be processed. When serving they will need to adopt a narrow/internal style to imagine how they are going to play the serve, but then immediately switch to a broad/external style when the rally begins.

Imagine the differing attentional style required by Jonny Wilkinson. One moment he is faced with kicking a penalty and his entire attention has to be on executing the skill he has practised thousands of times; the next he may be required to tackle an opponent but be aware of his position in relation to other players in his team to maintain their defensive strategy. Immediately after he may be in possession of the ball and be required to assess the whole field of play and decide in a split second should he pass, run or kick the ball or even take it into contact to retain possession. Having the ability to switch his attentional control is vital to maintain his optimal arousal level.

Self-talk involves the individual developing positive thoughts about his or her actions and performances. The aim is to eradicate any negative thoughts and replace them with positive statements.

APPLY IT!

A sprinter at the start of a race may change thoughts such as *'Am I ready for this?'* to *'My training has gone well and I'm prepared!'* Similarly, a rugby team who are losing by two points towards the end of a match may have been conditioned to think 'We have plenty of time left' rather than 'We've only got two minutes left to win the game'.

Go to the BBC Sport website to find out more about the emotions and feelings that Olympic gold medallist Sir Chris Hoy experiences before, during and after a race.

http://news.bbc.co.uk/sport1/

Somatic methods

These methods all involve techniques to reduce the negative physiological effects associated with anxiety. This includes reducing the heart rate, respiration rate and relaxation of the muscles. They can be used at different times depending on the situation and time available. However, like all training methods they must be practised on a regular basis if they are to be successfully used in competition.

Centring/breathing control involves the performer relaxing the chest and shoulder muscles, then focusing on the movement of the abdominal muscles whilst taking slow, deep breaths. The technique is beneficial as it can redirect attention, can be performed anywhere and if practised can be completed quickly and privately.

APPLY IT!

Jonny Wilkinson also uses breathing to control his arousal levels.

Jonny is reported to have said his hands are like a barrier erected against the outside world, helping him to cut out the tens of thousands of opposing fans who are likely to set up a barrage of whistles and jeers in an attempt to disturb his intense concentration. *'As I got more into kicking,'* he said, *'I became more involved in looking at other aspects, and one area I looked at was focusing from the inside, slowing down the breathing, relaxing,* 'centring', *which is a way of channelling my power and energy from my core, just behind my navel, down my left leg and into my left foot to get that explosive power. When I was doing this, the position with the hands happened to be the one I adopted. Look at pictures from 1998, and you will see my hands are further apart. Each year they have gradually got closer. For whatever reason, it has become a very strong position for me.'*

Biofeedback involves the measurement of the body's physiological responses to stress using objective techniques. The performer is made aware of the physiological responses that are occurring and then focuses his or her thoughts to calm him or herself. The effectiveness is viewed immediately and accurately due to the machines' biological feedback. Eventually the performer can recognise the physiological changes taking place without the aid of machinery and implement other stress management techniques during competition. Commonly used methods are:

- Galvanic skin response, which measures the skin's electrical conductivity when sweating. If tense, more sweat is produced to remove the heat generated by the muscles.

APPLY IT!

This report illustrates how these techniques have been used in an attempt to improve performance.

Biofeedback impacts on performance

The Italian football giants AC Milan are reported to be the first professional football club to successfully create a 'Mind Room' to train their players' brains to help reduce the chances of choking at the crucial stages of a game.

In the Mind Room, the athletes lie on reclining chairs, their bodies strapped to a device that measures physiological factors – from their brain waves and muscle tension to their breathing and heart rate. The club sports psychologist then trains them to use their minds to reach a meditative state. The next step is to teach the athletes to maintain that state while visualising in their minds their athletic performance. They often watch videos of themselves in action on the pitch.

If they have a particular problem – like missing a penalty kick or hitting the crossbar – the psychologist will train them to relax mentally. He does this by first getting them into the meditative state, then showing them a video of their flawed performance for a couple of seconds. Naturally, their muscles will immediately tense and their blood pressure will go up as they watch the missed goal, but the psychologist will get them to relax again. The treatment is repeated until the player can watch the flawed performance from start to finish while maintaining the meditative state.

The idea is that when they go out on the pitch and have to make the penalty kick, they'll be so focused, so prepared mentally, that they won't miss. They'll be able to bring down their heart rate when they don't have to run to conserve energy, and they'll do that without even thinking.

Biofeedback trains the athlete's mind to maintain a meditative state to reduce the chances of a brain explosion during a game.

- Electromyography (EMG) measures muscle tension via a series of electrodes taped to the skin, emitting a louder sound when tension is high.
- Skin temperature is measured via thermometers attached to the skin; reading are lower during times of stress.

Relaxation involves actively causing the muscles to become less tense or rigid. This can be achieved using either cognitive methods, which utilise thoughts to induce a calmer state, or somatic methods involving the control of muscle tension. Either can be used in training or competition, but care should be taken with some techniques – if employed too close to an event this may lead to under-arousal.

Progressive muscle relaxation technique involves the performer being aware of the alternating sensations of tension and relaxation of the muscles. Specific muscle groups are identified in succession, gradually reducing the tension throughout the body. Initially this may take time, but with practice athletes can focus and relax the whole body almost immediately. This is particularly useful prior to competition, to help facilitate sleep.

STRETCH AND CHALLENGE

Investigate how elite athletes prepare mentally for competition. Select two performers from different sports and answer the following questions:

1. What specific techniques do they use?
2. How often do they use the techniques?
3. What has been the impact on their performance?
4. Discuss your findings with the rest of the group.

Goal setting

Another effective method used to control anxiety levels is goal setting. Often this method allows the performer to direct his or her attention away from the source of stress and focus on an achievable target. If goals are set correctly they can have several effects, including:

- development of self-confidence and self-efficacy
- increased motivation levels
- improved selective attention
- approach behaviour
- persistence
- a reduction in anxiety.

The coach must take care when setting goals to ensure the performer's motivation is maintained whilst simultaneously not pushing the performer too far. The type of goal set will depend on the nature of the task, the level of ability of the performer and his or her anxiety levels. There are two types of goal which should be considered:

1. outcome goal
2. performance goal.

Outcome goal

An **outcome goal** judges the performance of the individual against others and the end result. The performer is being compared to others and a social comparison is being made. For example, a swimmer may be set the goal of either winning the race or finishing in the top three places to qualify for the next round. The efficiency and manner of his performance is not relevant – only the final result. If the goal setting is realistic and within the performer's capability, and if he achieves the aim, his motivation is increased. Performers of this nature are said to be 'outcome goal orientated.' However, it can be demotivating if the performer is unsuccessful, especially after repeated attempts, and this can lead to an increase in anxiety levels. Therefore, with novice performers or those who tend to have avoidance behaviour, performance goals are more appropriate.

Performance goal

This type of goal judges the **performance** of the athlete against his or her own standards, rather than making a social comparison with his or her competitors. For example, the swimmer may be set a number of goals for a race, including a good reaction to the starter's gun, and effective breathing action, and his performance may be evaluated with reference to his personal best time rather than his finishing position. If the goals set are realistic the performer can evaluate his own actions and not worry about comparison with others. This helps to reduce anxiety, allowing the swimmer to remain motivated irrespective of his finishing position.

TASK 8.03

You are the coach of a team. During the pre-season you decide to set both outcome and performance goals. For a sport of your choice, give examples of each type of goal which may be set for the team and individual performers.

The coach may also set specific **process-orientated goals** which relate to the development of the tactics or technique of the performer and contribute to the overall performance goal. For example, the swimmer may set the goal of a tighter tumble turn with greater leg drive off the wall in order to improve his overall performance.

Another factor which needs to be considered is the time span of the goal. It is generally accepted that both long-term goals and short-term goals should be set to maximise their use. Many performers will use major competitions as their focus for long-term goals and sub-divide their preparation into short-term goals. For example, an international performer may base her preparation on the timing of the Olympic Games or World Championships and set her outcome goals in relation to these events. Throughout the season intermediate goals are set (which may be performance goals) allowing the performer to monitor and evaluate her progress. This not only maintains the performer's motivation levels but ensures the performer does not become anxious unnecessarily if her ultimate target appears to be beyond her reach. If the performer achieves her short-term goal, positive feelings are generated, contributing to an increased level of self-efficacy. Goals should even be set for individual training sessions and evaluated afterwards.

Method and principles of goal setting

In order for goal setting to be effective, in addition to the points outlined previously, many performers ensure their goals fulfil the following criteria, as proposed by Sportscoach UK, and referred to as the 'SMARTER' principle:

- **Specific** – the goal must be related to the individual performer and include precise aims, rather than simple statements such as 'you must put more effort into the race'. Ideally the goals should be clear and unambiguous, with a clear relevance to the ultimate outcome goal.
- **Measurable** – the goal must be able to be assessed and recorded to allow the performer to see his or her progress. Ideally this should be a relatively quick process. It may not always be possible to use objective evidence such as times or passes completed, but any subjective feedback must be as precise as possible.
- **Accepted** – the goal must be agreed between the performer and the coach. Ideally the athlete should be part of the discussion process to establish the goal, which will increase motivation levels and he or she will be more likely to commit him or herself to achieving the end result.
- **Realistic** – any goal must be within the performer's capabilities otherwise his or her anxiety will actually increase because of worry about not meeting expectations.
- **Time phased** – each goal must have a fixed deadline for evaluation, otherwise the performer may lose motivation. The length of time allowed to achieve the goal will depend on the difficulty of the task.
- **Exciting** – the goal must be viewed as a challenge to the athlete and he or she must be motivated to achieve success and to gain intrinsic satisfaction. This aspect of goal setting must be considered carefully because a target that may seem exciting initially may then lose its impact if success is not achieved; it may then appear unobtainable thus causing anxiety.
- **Recorded** – all goals should be recorded for evaluation. If a goal has been set several months before and there is no fixed record of the agreed target, disputes may arise and again there will be a negative effect on the performer's anxiety level.

If these guidelines are followed, goal setting can be highly effective in the development of a sport performer's career. It allows the performer to remain focused but be constantly challenged, always believing that he or she can improve his or her performance.

TASK 8.04

Before your next competitive event set yourself either an outcome goal or a performance goal. The goal must be SMARTER. For the next event set the other type of goal. Discuss your results with a partner and evaluate which type of goal was the most effective for you.

ATHLETE PROFILE

During recent years, as Claire Vigrass has played in more prestigious Real Tennis tournaments, the pressure and expectations have increased as the status and rewards for winning have also increased. Initially she found she was overawed by the new experiences and suffered from anxiety. This was evident as she was unable to focus during rallies and frequently lost points at crucial times because she doubted her ability and was concerned about making a mistake (**cognitive anxiety**). Occasionally she also became very tense, feeling nauseous (**somatic anxiety**), before games against players who were highly ranked. In order to overcome anxiety she has employed several methods including goal setting, where she has agreed with her coach either outcome or performance goals depending on the nature of the competition. Initially the more difficult the tournament the goals tended to be more performance based. Claire also practised imagery techniques both in training and in competition, where she attempted to place herself in particular situations, such as serving to win game point, and recreated the feelings she might experience and how she would cope with them. Finally Claire learnt the technique of thought stopping, which involved thinking about the cue word, 'contact', before she served to focus her mind on the correct technique. All of these techniques took time to master but each is now used regularly, at different times during matches, and have proved effective in controlling her anxiety levels.

ExamCafé

Relax, refresh, result!

Refresh your memory

Revision checklist

Make sure you know the following:

Stress & anxiety

- ▷ Stress can be either positive (eustress) or negative (anxiety).
- ▷ Stressors is the term given to anything that causes stress to be experienced.
- ▷ Stressors can be very specific or general. The level of their effect depends on a person's perceptions of them in relation to their own perceived capabilities.
- ▷ Examples of sporting stressors include competition, frustration, conflict, and environmental factors.
- ▷ The General Adaptation Syndrome explains how the body responses to stress.
- ▷ The GAS occurs in three stages: alarm/reaction, resistance and exhaustion.
- ▷ Anxiety is a negative emotional state associated with feelings of apprehension and worry caused by over arousal as a result of being stressed.
- ▷ There are two types of anxiety:
  - Trait anxiety is a predisposition to perceive situations as potentially more threatening than they are.
  - State anxiety is the changing emotional state a person experiences in specific situations.
- ▷ A person with high levels of A-trait anxiety is likely to respond with potentially higher levels of A-state anxiety.
- ▷ State anxiety responses can be somatic (physiological) or cognitive (psychological).
- ▷ Performers who display high competitive A-trait have been found to perceive competitive situations as highly threatening and to respond disproportionately with higher levels of state anxiety.
- ▷ Stress can be measured by observation, self-report questionnaire and biofeedback.

Managing stress

- Stress management techniques help reduce somatic and cognitive anxiety.
- A key issue to reduce stress is personal control.
- Cognitive stress management techniques include imagery, attentional control, cue utilisation, thought stopping and positive self-talk.
- Somatic techniques involve various types of 'relaxation' such as progressive relaxation, centring or breathing control biofeedback.
- All psychological skills training techniques require regular practice and inclusion in the normal preparation routines of performers.
- Goal setting should follow the SMARTER principle.

Revise as you go

1. What is the difference between anxiety and eustress?
2. Explain the term 'stressor'.
3. Give three examples of possible stressors that may affect a performer during competition.
4. Name the three stages of the General Adaptation Syndrome.
5. What is the difference between cognitive anxiety and somatic anxiety?
6. Explain the difference between state anxiety and trait anxiety.
7. Outline the Competitive State Anxiety Inventory (CSAI-2).
8. How do the State Trait Anxiety Inventory and the Sport Competition Anxiety Test vary?
9. Name two physiological tests commonly used to measure levels of stress.
10. Give three examples of how a performer may display signs of somatic anxiety.
11. Outline how a performer can alter his or her attentional control.
12. Explain the difference between somatic and cognitive methods of stress management.
13. What is the difference between internal imagery and external imagery?
14. What does the technique of centring involve?
15. Explain the term 'self-talk'.
16. What is thought-stopping?
17. How is biofeedback used to control levels of stress?
18. What do the letters SMARTER represent?
19. Explain the difference between an outcome and a performance goal.
20. Why is it important to set short- and long-term goals?

CHAPTER 9

Attitudes

LEARNING OBJECTIVES:

By the end of this chapter you should be able to:

- explain what is meant by the term 'attitude'
- describe the components of an attitude
- outline the factors influencing the formation of an attitude and how they influence behaviour
- understand the importance of developing positive attitudes towards specific attitude objects and the impact a negative attitude can have on performance
- describe the methods used to assess attitudes and evaluate their effectiveness
- explain the methods used to change an attitude including cognitive dissonance and persuasive communication.

Introduction

The development of a positive attitude in an elite performer is vital if he or she is to achieve success. All athletes are motivated to win but they must also possess a positive approach and consistent behaviour pattern to training, preparation and competition, to compete at the highest level (see achievement motivation and approach behaviour in Chapter 6). While an individual may strive to produce his or her maximum performance in the competitive environment, he or she may not be so committed to training. It is the role of the coach to ensure the high level of motivation is maintained in all aspects of the individual's training programme. If the performer has a positive attitude and this can be maintained, he or she is more likely to engage in activities enthusiastically and display persistent behaviour patterns in order to master the skills being developed. It is therefore vital that the factors influencing the formation of an individual's attitude can be identified and, if required, systems implemented to modify that attitude, thereby leading to more productive behaviour.

Definitions of attitude

As with many aspects of psychology there are numerous definitions of attitude, but they all have common elements.

TASK 9.01

With a partner devise a definition of attitude and attempt to describe the characteristics of your own attitude. Discuss with other students and compare your definition with those outlined below.

Several definitions of attitude are outlined below:

Aronson et al (1994):
'An enduring evaluation – positive or negative – of people, objects and ideas.'

Triandis (1971):
'Ideas charged with emotion (positive or negative) which pre-disposes a class of actions to a particular social situation.'

Allport (1935):
'A mental and neural state of readiness, organized through experience, exerting a directive or dynamic influence upon the individual's response to all objects and situations with which it is related.'

Based on these three definitions there are common threads:

- attitudes can be positive or negative
- they are generally stable and enduring
- they are focused to a particular item or situation (see attitude object)
- attitudes are evaluative, subjective or beliefs.

Consider your own attitudes: are they all positive? The truthful answer is probably not. It is important to realise that we possess both positive and negative attitudes and that they are each the focus of specific attention. Attitudes influence our behaviour towards certain situations; are based on our evaluation or beliefs our thoughts towards an **attitude object**. Our attitude may alter dramatically from one attitude object to another. For example, we may have a positive attitude towards sport in general but a negative attitude towards sports which may involve physical violence. Similarly, it may be argued that just because a performer has a positive attitude towards a particular activity and regularly participates, it does not mean that he or she will always display a fully committed behaviour pattern in training or competition; other factors may have a more influential effect at that particular time. Therefore, we can say that whilst generally a positive attitude can lead to positive behaviour patterns, this cannot be guaranteed.

KEY TERMS

Attitude object:
the focus of an individual's attitude. The object may be training, people., events, ideas or specific objects

EXAM TIP:

Make sure you can explain: how an attitude is formed; its components; methods to measure an attitude; implication for the coach; and methods to alter a negative attitude.

TASK 9.02

Discuss with a partner specific attitude objects to which you have a positive and negative attitude. Select an activity for which you have a positive attitude. Have there been occasions when you displayed a negative attitude? Why did this occur and how did your behaviour alter?

Components of attitude

Attitudes often form our beliefs and values, which in turn may influence our behaviour (though not always). To illustrate this it is useful to study Triandis' proposal that our attitude comprises three components: cognitive, affective and behavioural components. This is known as the **Triadic Model**.

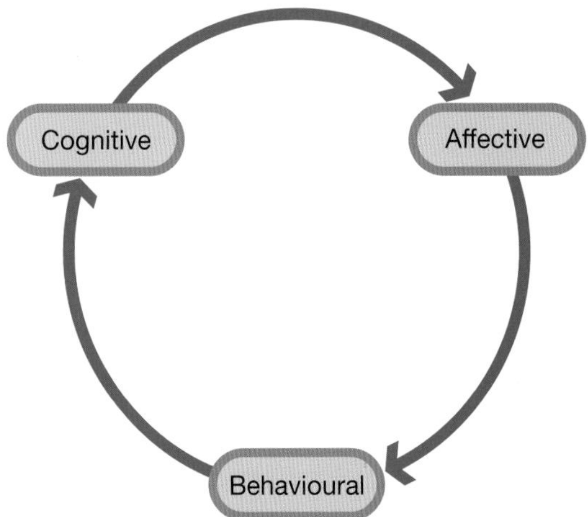

Fig 9.01 The Triadic Model

Cognitive component

This aspect of attitude reflects our beliefs, knowledge, thoughts, ideas and information we have regarding an attitude object. For example, based on information received from our parents and physical education lessons, we may think swimming is good for us in terms of our health and safety.

Affective component

This involves our emotional response or feelings to the attitude object. For example, in the past we may have enjoyed swimming lessons and visited a local pool with friends. This may have led to positive feelings towards future participation. However, if the experience has been negative (possibly due to feelings of fear for personal safety) then future participation may be affected.

Behavioural component

The final component involves our intended or actual behaviour towards an attitude object. This is often based on our evaluation of the first two components. For example, because of positive beliefs and experiences about swimming, we actually participate regularly.

Whilst this structural analysis of attitude is a good starting point for discussion, it also shows that cognitive and affective components are not always an accurate predictor of behaviour. For example, how many of you think swimming is good for you and enjoy going but fail to actually visit a pool on a regular basis and complete a worthwhile exercise session?

Formation of attitudes

An understanding of how attitudes are formed is vital if we are to develop desirable positive attitudes and suppress negative attitudes. This not only

APPLY IT!

In order to prepare athletes for the Olympics and World Championships several sports in recent years have modified their development and support systems. The Royal Yachting Association has established a central training venue in Weymouth and Portland where the majority of the squad train together throughout the year. The facilities are being extended with a £4 million investment as part of the preparation for the 2012 Olympics. This has enabled the best sailors to not only train together but learn from each other. The fact that they are all together has helped to create positive attitudes in each of the components of the Triadic Model. Not only do they enjoy preparing in a competitive but supportive atmosphere, but they also are motivated to push themselves to their limits in order to achieve success. All of their training is closely monitored on a regular basis and new targets set to ensure positive attitudes are maintained.

British Cycling have established a similar system based in Manchester, also with the aim of developing performers with a positive attitude who are prepared to dedicate the time to develop their fitness and skill levels in order to win goal medals.

Fig 9.02 Team GB cyclists train together and learn from each other to maintain and develop positive attitudes

helps to create an environment in which healthy attitudes are created but can also break down the negative **stereotyped** opinions which may restrict participation and lead to **discrimination** and **prejudice**.

KEY TERMS

Stereotype:
a standardised image or concept shared by all members of a social group

Discrimination:
unjust or prejudicial treatment of different categories of people, especially on the grounds of race, age or sex

Prejudice:
a formed opinion, especially an unfavourable one, based on inadequate facts, often displaying intolerance or dislike towards people of a certain race, religion or culture that may be different from their own

TASK 9.03

Discuss with a partner the reasons how you know you have a positive attitude towards your chosen practical activity (refer to the three components of attitude). Suggest how this attitude has developed.

From your discussion many of you will have mentioned that the major factor in attitude development is your past experiences. Those situations which have been enjoyable and successful will undoubtedly have meant your future participation, whilst those that have involved failure, disappointment or possibly injury will have had the opposite effect.

Most attitudes are developed through learning, either socialisation/social learning (watching others) or operant conditioning (positive reinforcement). (For each of these refer back to your AS studies to remind yourself of their full meaning.) Linked to these areas, other influences may have included parents, family, peer group, teachers, coaches, the media and role models. Some of these factors will be more influential than others and may change over time.

TASK 9.04

Discuss with a partner how you know you have a negative attitude towards an attitude object. Suggest why this attitude has developed.

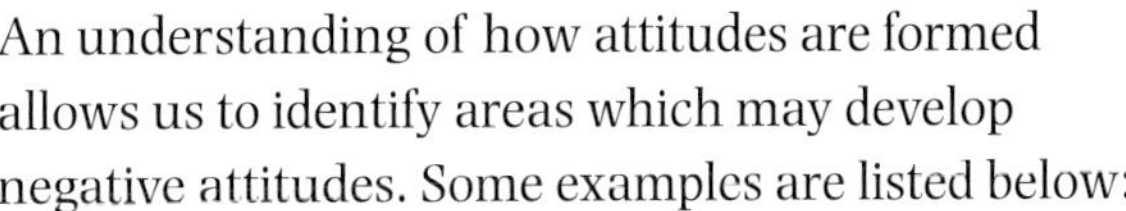

An understanding of how attitudes are formed allows us to identify areas which may develop negative attitudes. Some examples are listed below:

- negative experiences/failure
- fear of failure
- fear of injury/personal safety
- negative role models
- high task difficulty
- low self-confidence
- lack of support from family and friends/peer group
- cultural beliefs
- low status of activity in society
- stereotypical images.

Later in this chapter we will use this information to look at how a negative attitude can be changed.

Measurement of attitudes

It is important for psychologists to ascertain the attitude of an individual in order to understand his or her beliefs and emotions. If these do not meet the expectations, required strategies may have to be implemented in an attempt to change negative aspects and to ensure positive behaviour patterns. There are several direct and indirect methods in which a person's attitude may be measured. The former includes interviews and questionnaires, whilst the latter involves observation of behaviour and physiological responses. The most popular methods are interviews and self-report questionnaires, as they are less subjective and therefore less interpretation is required on the part of the researcher.

Whichever method is utilised, the **validity** and **reliability** of the data is important to identify specific issues and monitor future changes.

The three major types of self-report questionnaires are:

- Thurston Scale (1931)
- Likert Scale (1932)
- Osgood's Semantic Differential Scale (1957).

Thurston Scale

The questionnaire is made up of a number of statements covering a range of opinions towards an attitude object. Initially about 100 statements are issued to a panel of judges. Each statement is given a rating on their favourableness or unfavourableness on an 11-point scale. The statements with scores which vary widely are rejected until there are 11 favourable and 11 unfavourable items left. The remaining statements form the attitude scale. The average of the judges' rating becomes the scale value for the statement. Therefore, a statement with a value of 6 shows a neutral opinion, whilst a statement with a score of 10 indicates a favourable opinion and a score of 2 indicates an unfavourable opinion. This type of scale allows comparisons with other individuals but:

- is time consuming
- requires a large number of experts to construct the scale initially
- because the average show (or value) is used it can hide extreme attitudes.

Likert Scale

This is a simplified version of the Thurston Scale but still provides valid and reliable data. As a result this is the most frequently used form of attitude scale.

A series of statements is constructed showing both favourable and unfavourable opinions towards the attitude object. The participant is required to respond to a statement on a 5-point scale, for example where:

5 = strongly agree, 4 = agree, 3 = undecided, 2 = disagree, 1 = strongly disagree

Favourable statements score 5 for 'strongly agree' with unfavourable statements 1 for 'strongly disagree'. The scores are then totalled to provide an overall attitude score.

For example:

Gymnastics is good for you.
5 strongly agree, 4 agree, 3 undecided, 2 disagree, 1 strongly disagree

Gymnastics is dangerous.
1 strongly agree, 2 agree, 3 undecided, 4 disagree, 5 strongly disagree

Advantages of using scales such as these include:

- allows for a range of answers
- easy to administer
- cheaper and easier to construct
- produces reliable results.

Osgood's Semantic Differential Scale

The participant is required to give the attitude object a 7-step rating based on two opposing adjectives. The individual has to select a point which best reflects his or her feeling.

For example:

Rate how you feel about the safety of performing gymnastics.
Dangerous +3 +2 +1 0 −1 −2 −3 Safe

Whilst this is a quick and simple method to use, the selection of the word pairs may not allow the individual much choice and could be interpreted differently.

TASK 9.05

Construct an attitude questionnaire on a topic of your choice, for example, the value of exercise or media portrayal of sport. Ask a group to complete it and evaluate the results and its effectiveness.

Evaluation of attitude scales

These types of questionnaires are useful but the results must be viewed cautiously as there can be several problems with collection of the data. These include:

- individuals not responding truthfully
- people providing socially acceptable answers
- misunderstanding of the question/ambiguous questions

- attitudes may be difficult to express in words
- wording of the statement may lead to respondents answering in a certain manner.

Changing attitudes

It is important that we understand how to change an attitude if this will lead to a more positive approach and behaviour. If a performer has a positive attitude the coach generally has fewer problems to overcome in terms of motivation and task persistence. The two most commonly used methods are:

- persuasive communication
- cognitive dissonance.

Persuasive communication

This method involves the attitude being altered by persuasion. There are four factors which need to be considered in order for this to be effective:

- **The status of the messenger or person delivering the new ideas:** if this person has certain characteristics then he or she is more likely to be successful. For example, the person should be of high status/a significant other, seen as an expert, likeable with good intentions and be attractive to the individual.
- **The quality of the message:** the message should make the individual want to change his or her attitude. Therefore it should be clear, unambiguous, appeal to the recipient's sense of fear/failure, and be presented in a confident and logical manner. The higher the quality of the message the more likely the chance of success.
- **The strength of the current attitude and the resistance to change:** the characteristics of the recipient can influence the degree of resistance to change. Factors to consider include original formation of the attitude, the strength of current belief and the level of education.
- **The situation or context in which the message is being delivered:** different situations require different approaches, for example, when considering the formality of the environment, the level of support from other people, and the time and resources available.

APPLY IT!

In an attempt to change the attitudes of young people towards participation in sporting activities, high profile sports champions are used in persuasive communication.

Dame Kelly as role model

Dame Kelly Holmes has been named the first national 'school sport champion' as part of a drive to get more children interested in PE. The double Olympic champion said she wanted to help discover and inspire the sports stars of the future in the years leading up to the London games in 2012.

Her appointment comes as part of the government's attempt to involve more youngsters in PE and school sport amid concerns over childhood obesity levels. Dame Kelly said she was *'proud and delighted'* to have been given the job. *'I believe I can help to encourage young people to get more involved and also make this a greater priority for everyone,'* she said.

'I want to see real change and for more children to take part in more activities.

'We need to be a sporting nation and for that to happen we have to inspire, motivate, encourage and capture the imagination of all our young people so that sport becomes a part of their day-to-day lives.

'Winning the right to stage the Olympic and the Paralympic games in 2012 has given British sport a tremendous boost and hopefully we can use this new opportunity to discover a few champions.'

Dame Kelly will visit schools and sports events *'to promote the government's strategy for school sport and help inspire and motivate young people',* officials said.

Sue Campbell, the chairwoman of the Youth Sport Trust, said Dame Kelly was a 'fantastic' role model.

'She, more than anyone, has the ability to reach young people and motivate them to participate in sport and adopt a healthy lifestyle.'

Fig 9.03 Dame Kelly Holmes has been appointed national 'school sport champion'

Consider how often the media use role models to promote positive messages of healthy lifestyle, fair play and sportsmanship, and to advertise sporting goods and numerous other products.

EXAM TIP:

The topic of changing attitudes appears regularly. Ensure you know the theoretical basis and be able to apply it to a practical situation.

TASK 9.06

Select a high profile sports performer who has been used in an attempt to promote a positive attitude. Using the variable factors listed previously, identify how this has been achieved. Discuss your findings with a partner. Has one advertising campaign been more successful than another?

Cognitive dissonance

Festigner (1957) proposed that an individual's beliefs and thoughts have a direct influence on his or her behaviour. If these ideas or cognitions are challenged with new information then a person will experience a sense of psychological discomfort and will attempt to restore the balance of harmony. Such a conflict of beliefs is known as **dissonance**.

KEY TERMS

Dissonance:
an emotional conflict

Triadic Model:
an attitude that consists of three components – affective (emotions), behavioural (actions) and cognitive (thoughts)

The aim of this method to change an attitude is based on the assumption that one of the components of the **Triadic Model** (see pages 157–158) can be manipulated to create dissonance. After reviewing the new information or experience the individual either then develops a new attitude or retains the existing approach. If dissonance does occur the feelings of discomfort can be dispelled by following three stages:

- making the cognition/thought less important
- changing the cognition
- replacing the cognition.

EXAM TIP:

Be able to apply the methods of changing an attitude to actual practical situations with relevant examples.

To alter the cognitive component of an attitude, new information can be provided. For example, the performer who thinks training is not required is given detailed benefits of adopting a more committed approach in terms of skill, fitness levels and possible future extrinsic rewards; he or she may be shown examples of others who have comparable ability but have wasted their talents by not training, or discuss the consequences of his or her actions with a respected significant other.

STRETCH AND CHALLENGE

With reference to the cognitive dissonance theory, explain how you would change the attitude of a group of young people who have a negative attitude towards one of the following scenarios:

- swimming
- attending training sessions
- physical exercise.

Include practical examples to illustrate your suggestions. Compare your strategies with those of the rest of the group

The affective component may be changed by giving a different experience, which may be viewed as more positive. For example, the performer is given more praise during training, set challenging targets, the activities are made more enjoyable and possibly less repetitive. Also, he or she may be given feedback based on knowledge of performance rather than being compared to others or focusing on the outcome. If the performer is concerned about his or her safety, manual or mechanical guidance may be used to alleviate such fears. Other methods may include giving roles of responsibility and encouraging the peer group to be supportive or apply pressure to conform, i.e. a sense of group/shared responsibility.

The behavioural component can be altered by ensuring the skill is simplified, success is achieved and subsequently reinforced, thus causing a positive affective component of attitude.

Often negative attitudes to an attitude object can be altered dramatically by the change of opinion within the peer group or society generally. For example, people's attitudes towards a sport which has declining interest due to indifferent results, lack of role models or stereotypical images can quickly change if:

- the team is successful
- high profile stars emerge
- non-stereotyped performers are involved.

The success of Team GB at the 2008 Beijing Olympics bears this out. Many sports received huge amounts of media coverage due not only to the success of one particular sport but over a whole range of sports. Subsequently there has been an increase in the number of players and spectators in all kinds of sport and from all sections of society.

APPLY IT!

During recent years the Sport Relief Mile has grown in popularity for a variety of reasons. It has been used to raise money for charity and increase the number of people actively involved in some form of exercise. The message is clear: everyone can either run or walk at least a mile and participate in some form of exercise. To support this claim a host of celebrities and sports stars participate, explaining the reasons for their involvement. This campaign, which is similar to the Cancer Research UK Race for Life, which aims to highlight breast cancer, is aimed at fun runners and people who are not inclined to run, for example, the London Marathon. The consequences of such events have been not only to raise the awareness of the charities but to promote the benefits of health and show how easy and enjoyable it can be to participate in some form of exercise.

Fig 9.04 The Sport Relief Mile attempts to change people's attitude towards exercise by giving them new information which encourages participation

ATHLETE PROFILE

Claire Vigrass displays a **positive attitude** towards her Real Tennis, both in terms of preparation and competition. She loves the sport and enjoys training and playing (**affective component**); she thinks playing is beneficial to her, both physically and as a potential career (**cognitive component**), and she trains six days a week (**behavioural component**).

However this was not always the case. Several years ago she played Real Tennis socially, trained occasionally and won a few competitions without exerting herself too much. But with the support and encouragement of her parents and coach, Ricardo Smith, she developed a much more committed approach to the sport when they showed her the possibilities of what she might be able to achieve. They used persuasive communication and cognitive dissonance to change her attitude and convince her she had the potential to excel. While Claire has a very positive attitude towards playing in singles competitions the same cannot be said about doubles events. For various reasons she does not have the same attitude and as a result does not approach competitive events with the same commitment and passion as her favoured singles event.

Exam**Café**

Relax, refresh, result!

Revision checklist

Make sure you know the following:

- Attitudes are usually subjective beliefs and values.
- Attitudes are specific and related to an attitude object.
- Attitudes are largely formed through experiences.
- The Triadic Model suggests that attitudes have three components: cognitive, affective and behavioural.
- Attitudes can influence behaviour in sport but are not necessarily a predictor of behaviour.
- Stereotyping is not necessarily 'bad' in itself, but it is important for teachers and coaches to understand the implications of inaccurate stereotypes and challenge them.
- Attitudes can be resistant to change and can lead to prejudice.
- Attitudes can be changed by persuasive communication and cognitive dissonance.

Revise as you go

1. Explain the term 'attitude object'.
2. Name two common forms of questionnaires used to measure the attitude of an individual.
3. Attitudes can be used to predict behaviour – true or false?
4. Explain the three components of Triandis' model.
5. Give three factors that may influence the formation of an attitude.
6. Outline the term 'stereotype'.
7. Explain the cognitive dissonance theory.
8. Suggest three strategies to improve the attitude of a performer.
9. How can the effectiveness of the persuasive communication technique be maximised?
10. Give two reasons why a performer's attitude may need to be changed.

CHAPTER 10

Aggression

LEARNING OBJECTIVES:

By the end of this chapter you should be able to:

- *differentiate between an aggressive and an assertive act*
- *understand the difference between hostile/reactive aggression and channelled/instrumental aggression*
- *outline the reasons why performers may become aggressive with specific reference to the Instinct theory, the Frustration–Aggression hypothesis, the Cue Arousal theory/Aggressive Cue hypothesis and the Social Learning theory*
- *explain the consequences of aggressive actions*
- *suggest strategies to control reactive aggressive behaviour.*

Introduction

The term 'aggression' is commonly used during modern sports commentary, but for the purpose of your studies it is often used in the wrong context. A performer is often said to be 'aggressive in their tackle' or 'playing aggressively in order to exert his dominance'. In fact the performer may actually just be displaying forceful behaviour rather than being aggressive. There is a grey area between acceptable and unacceptable behaviour and it is the role of the officials to determine when a player's behaviour has crossed this boundary. Many of these decisions are subjective and have to be made in a split second, the consequence of which may have a significant impact on the final result and manner in which the remainder of the contest takes place. It is also important to realise that acts of aggression may be interpreted differently depending on the nature of the sport. For example, during a tennis match punching an opponent is clearly unacceptable, but within a boxing match it is an integral aspect of the sport.

The ability of the performer to control his or her aggressive behaviour is vital, not only for his or her own performance but because it may directly affect others if involved in a team activity. As a result it is important to identify potential causes of aggressive behaviour and implement appropriate strategies to deal with over-arousal.

Fig 10.01 The term 'aggression' is often used in the wrong context

Definitions of aggression

There are numerous definitions of aggression but they all have similar characteristics, as shown below:

Baron (1977)
'Aggression is any form of behaviour directed toward the goal of harming or injuring another living being who is motivated to avoid such treatment.'

Bull (1991)
'Any behaviour intended to harm another individual by physical or verbal means.'

Gill (1986) identified key features for an act to be aggressive:

- It must actually happen (behavioural), either physically or verbally. The mere act of thinking you may hurt someone is not enough.
- It must harm another person either physically or emotionally, for example, kicking a ball in anger or smashing a racket would not be classed as aggressive.
- It must be intentional, for example, an accidental collision which causes an injury is not deemed to be aggressive.

Other psychologists also suggest that an aggressive act is outside the rules of the activity.

Fig 10.02 Aggressive acts have common characteristics

Sporting actions which possess these characteristics can be classified as hostile or reactive aggression.

The terms commonly used to describe actions that are acceptable are **channelled aggression** or **instrumental aggression** and **assertive behaviour**. However, there are subtle differences between these terms.

Channelled (or instrumental) aggression involves behaviour that is within the rules of the activity and aims to successfully complete the skill but has the side effect of inflicting harm or physical pain. For example, a rugby player will attempt to tackle an opponent legally but also as physically as possible.

In contrast, Husman and Silva (1984) suggested that **assertive behaviours**:

- are not intended to cause injury or harm
- are goal-directed
- are within the rules, laws and spirit of the game
- only use legitimate force.

For example, a rugby player competing for a 50–50 ball on the ground who collides with another player would be assertive, as would a basketball player driving for a lay-up. As a result these actions would not be classed as aggressive.

KEY TERMS

Channelled aggression – instrumental aggression:
the actions of the performer are within the laws of the game, with no intention to harm another player and are goal-directed

Assertive behaviour:
a form of aggression where the aim is to achieve a goal and any injury which may be caused is incidental

TASK 10.01

For a sport of your choice, list two acts of reactive aggression, two acts of instrumental aggression and two assertive acts.

As you can see, there are clear differences between the terms aggression and assertion. However, in many sporting situations there is an area of doubt involving intention and this increases if the nature of the sport involves physical contact. The subjective decisions of the officials are important if the sport is to be played in the correct spirit, allowing the players to participate fairly, safely and to the best of their ability.

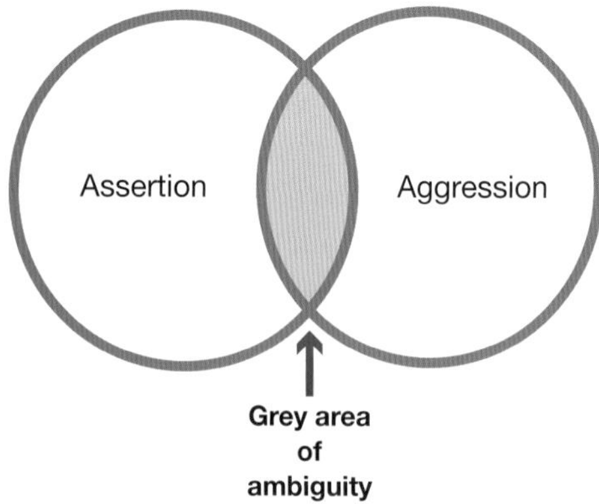

Fig 10.03 Aggression or assertion? – an area of doubt

APPLY IT!

During the 2008 Premiership football match between Arsenal and Birmingham City, a tackle by the Birmingham City defender Martin Taylor resulted in Eduardo da Silva suffering a broken ankle. The referee immediately issued Taylor a red card and he was sent off as the tackle had broken the rules and been classed as aggressive.

In contrast, during a match several seasons before the Liverpool striker Milan Baros also suffered a broken ankle after a tackle from Blackburn Rover's Markus Babbel, but no action was taken by the referee. All those concerned were not upset by this incident as shown by the Liverpool manager at the time, Gerard Houllier's reaction after the match, when he said:

'The referee did the right thing – it was not even a foul, Markus tackled properly and got the ball and it probably happened when he fell over on the floor.'

As we can see from these two incidents, which both resulted in serious injury to the players involved, it was up to the referee to decide if the cause was aggressive or assertive play.

TASK 10.02

For each of the situations outlined below state if you consider them to be 'aggressive' or 'assertive' acts.

1. Two boxers fighting for a World title.
2. An American footballer punches an opponent following a hard tackle.
3. During a cricket match the fielders 'sledge' the batsman.
4. A goalkeeper slides into an attacker during the save and accidentally cuts his leg with the studs.
5. A tennis player swears at an official after a bad line-call.
6. A rugby player 'handing off' an opponent.
7. A runner hopes an opponent will become injured before the race.
8. A footballer, after being fouled, kicks an opponent but misses.
9. A basketball player drives for a lay-up and collides with an opponent after shooting.
10. Two cyclists collide and crash during the final sprint for the line.

TASK 10.03

Watch a sporting event which involves physical contact, e.g. a rugby or football match, and list:

1. possible acts of aggression
2. possible causes
3. consequences of aggressive acts
4. acts of assertion .

Discuss your observations with the rest of the group, do they agree with you?

EXAM TIP:

Be able to give examples of aggressive and assertive acts and justify your reasons for each.

Causes of aggression

Before studying the theoretical basis of aggressive behaviour we should consider the specific causes within a competitive situation. The list below is not exhaustive and might not apply to all performers. It might also vary depending on the situational factors. Compare your list from Task 10.01 and your own experiences of sport to the factors listed below:

- nature of the sport – contact or non-contact
- rivalry between teams or players, e.g. local derby match
- high arousal levels
- importance of the event and expectation from peers, coaches, managers, the media
- nature and proximity of the crowd
- venue – home or away
- frustration at personal performance or that of others
- score line – large difference may lead to more aggression
- poor officiating
- copying other players, especially role models/ significant others
- extrinsic rewards – financial gain, status, fame, selection to higher level team.

Theories of aggression

Many of the causes of aggression listed above can be applied directly to the theories outlined below. As you saw in Chapter 6, discussions focus on the nature versus nurture debate.

Instinct theory

As the name suggests, this theory is based on the nature approach. It argues that aggressive behaviour is innate, genetically inherited and, as a result, inevitable. Freud proposed aggression is due to our evolutionary development; our need to dominate and our death instinct (a trait directed towards self-destruction but balanced by our life instincts). The energy that builds up within us has to be released to maintain our well-being, and sporting participation allows this to occur in an acceptable manner – it is a cathartic release.

It is also suggested that displacement may occur via sport. Rather than display aggression in an inappropriate situation, such as the workplace, an individual will wait for a more suitable time, such as during a sporting contest.

Evaluation of the instinct theory: Numerous psychologists have criticised the theory because:

- human aggression is often not spontaneous
- aggression is often learnt and linked to culture – cultural norms can influence the levels of acceptable aggression displayed by individuals
- levels of aggression tend to increase during sporting participation rather than decrease
- performers in sports of an aggressive nature do not tend to display similar characteristics away from the sporting environment
- no biological innate characteristics have been identified
- rather than being warriors, early humans were hunter-gatherers.

Frustration-Aggression hypothesis

Dollard (1939) suggested an interactionist approach to aggression (see also page 170–171). He argued that individuals display aggressive behaviour due to innate characteristics and learning from others, becoming aggressive when their goal is blocked leading to frustration. He proposes that frustration will always lead to aggressive behaviour and aggression will always be caused by frustration. Figure 10.04 shows that if the performer is able to release his or her frustration via an aggressive act, it has a cathartic effect. However, if the aggressive act is punished the frustration levels are increased. The performer's drive may increase due to a number of factors (as outlined previously), such as an opponent playing well against him or her. This causes an increase in frustration and a bad tackle may be the result. As the frustration has been released the player feels satisfied, but if he or she is punished, further aggressive acts may follow.

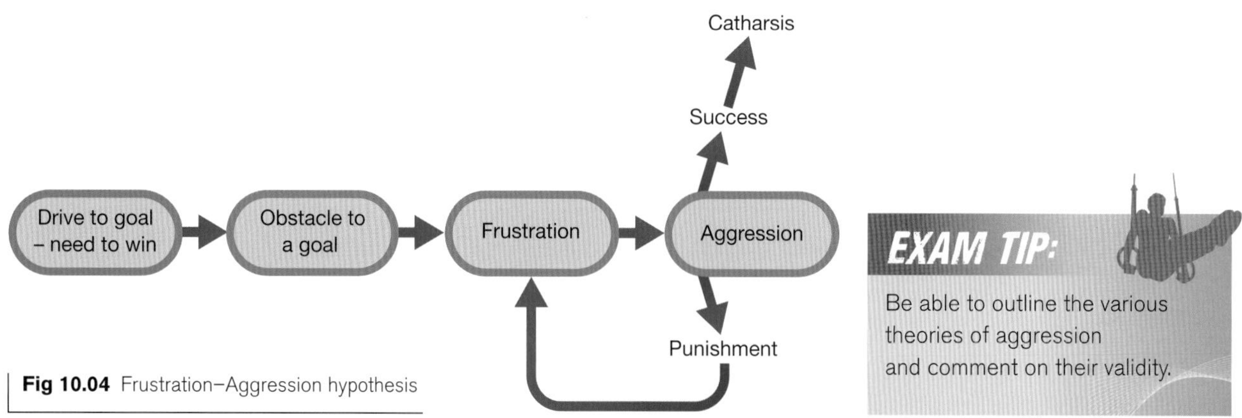

Fig 10.04 Frustration–Aggression hypothesis

> **EXAM TIP:**
> Be able to outline the various theories of aggression and comment on their validity.

Evaluation of the Frustration–Aggression hypothesis:

- Not all frustration leads to aggression.
- Not all aggression is caused by frustration – it can be learned.
- It does not account for situational factors or individual differences.

Cue Arousal theory/Aggressive Cue hypothesis

The work of Dollard formed a basis for other research and Berkowitz (1969) proposed the Aggressive Cue hypothesis, also known as the Cue Arousal theory, which incorporates learning and arousal into the explanation for aggressive behaviour. The theory suggests that frustration will cause **arousal** to increase but aggression will only occur if there are socially acceptable **cues** present. For example, a player may commit a dangerous tackle if the player's team or coach reinforces such behaviour. Similarly, a player may commit such an act if he or she thinks the official is not watching. Some sports-related cues are more likely to lead to aggression than others; for example:

- people associated with aggressive acts (a coach, player or fans)
- sports associated with aggression (contact sports)
- places associated with aggression (a venue linked to previous experience of violent acts)
- objects associated with aggression (bats, boxing gloves, etc).

> **KEY TERMS**
>
> **Arousal:**
> the energised state of readiness of the individual to perform a task, motivating him or her to direct his or her behaviour in a particular manner
>
> **Cue:**
> signal, action or situation which will act as a trigger to perform a specific type of behaviour
>
> **Vicarious experience:**
> the process of watching other performers and copying their actions. More likely to be successful if the model is a significant other or similar standard to the observer

If this theory is correct it may explain why some players are able to maintain their composure and control their arousal levels and not act aggressively.

Evaluation of Cue Arousal theory/ Aggressive Cue hypothesis: Berkowitz's theory is a more valuable explanation of aggression than earlier theories. Rather than simply being an innate response to an external stimulus, aggression is actually linked to learning and will occur only when suitable environmental cues are present.

Social Learning theory

Bandura's Social Learning (1966) theory adopts the nurture approach, rejecting the idea that aggression is innate. It proposes that aggressive behaviour is learned through observation of others and copying their actions. If reinforced, the copied actions are repeated in similar situations. This is known as a **vicarious experience**.

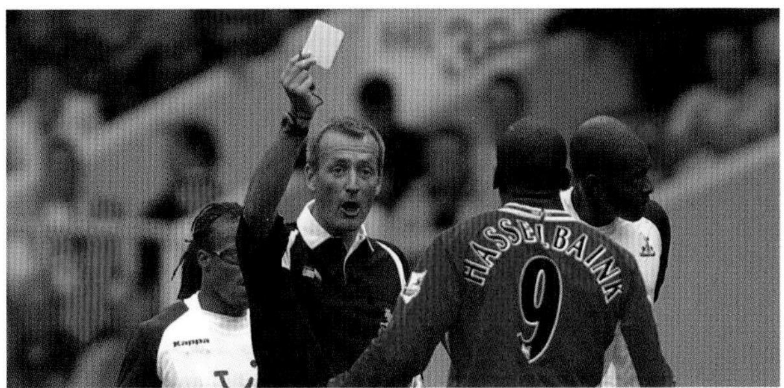

Fig 10.05 Social learning theory suggests that referees should punish aggressive acts and ensure they apply the rules consistently

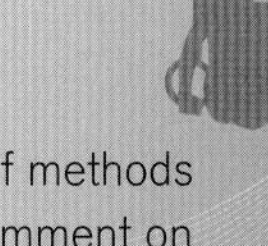

EXAM TIP:

1. Be able to give practical examples of methods to control aggressive players and comment on the implications these methods may have on their performance.
2. Questions may require you to explain how aggression can be controlled from the perspective of different people. For example, what strategies can the player, the coach or the official use to combat aggressive behaviour?

There are many examples of vicarious experience in modern day sport. Due to the extensive media coverage of sport, many players see their role models or significant others displaying acts of aggression. Often such behaviour is not punished and consequently others copy their actions believing it is acceptable to act in this manner. The player may receive many forms of reinforcement which encourage such behaviour, from spectators, coaches, teammates and parents.

While there are negative aspects to this proposal, it should also be viewed that if players can be taught unacceptable behaviour they can also be taught acceptable behaviour. If this is the case it is possible to control arousal levels and modify behaviour if the correct reinforcement is provided.

Evaluation of Social Learning theory: While it is clear that many aggressive actions are copied from significant others and are more likely to be repeated if reinforced, the Social Learning theory does have some critics. It does not fully explain how some people may be aggressive without observing others if placed in a particular situation.

Reducing and controlling aggressive behaviour

As we have seen there are numerous causes of aggressive behaviour and each may be specific to the individual. As a result the strategies outlined below may not be suitable for all performers but must be applied differently depending on the situation. The responsibility for eliminating aggressive behaviour should be shared between the player, teammates/ peer group, coaches, officials, spectators, the media and even sponsors.

Possible solutions to reduce aggressive behaviour include:

- Punish aggressive acts using penalties such as booking, sin bins, sending-off, bans and fines.
- Increase peer group pressure and highlight responsibility to the team.
- Remove the offending player from the situation by the coach (either a substitution or a change of position).
- High quality officials who offer consistent interpretation of the laws.
- Positive reinforcement and rewards for non-aggressive play, e.g. fair play awards.
- Highlight non-aggressive role models.
- Reduce the importance of the event and the emphasis on winning.
- Increase personal fitness levels to delay the effects of fatigue.
- Set performance goals rather than outcome goals.
- Develop effective stress management techniques, such as positive self-talk, thought-stopping and imagery (see Chapter 8, page 147–148).
- Lower levels of arousal via relaxation methods.
- Educate players on the difference between aggression and assertion.

STRETCH AND CHALLENGE

Observe either a live or televised match. Note any instances when a player becomes aggressive. Outline strategies used by various people to limit aggressive behaviour and evaluate their effectiveness. Suggest alternative strategies which could have been used.

ExamCafé

Relax, refresh, result!

Refresh your memory

Revision checklist

Make sure you know the following:

- The characteristics of aggressive behaviour include; intentional behaviour which is outside the rules and directed towards the goal of harming or injuring another living being, when they are motivated to avoid such treatment.
- Assertive behaviour and channelled aggression are deemed as acceptable behaviour.
- The main theories associated with the study of aggression are: instinct theory; Frustration-Aggression hypothesis; Aggressive Cue hypothesis and Social Learning theory.
- The revised Frustration-Aggression hypothesis is seen as having some credibility, particularly when it is linked to Social Learning theory.
- Social Learning theory suggests that reinforcement and modelling either of or by significant others are the main influences of aggressive behaviour in sport.
- Teachers, coaches and performers must develop an understanding of the causes of aggressive behaviour in order to employ effective strategies to controlling its occurrence.
- The responsibility for eliminating aggressive behaviour should be shared between the player, teammates/peer group, coaches, officials, spectators, the media and even sponsors.

Revise as you go

1. What is the difference between an aggressive and an assertive act?
2. Outline the Instinct theory of aggression.
3. Explain how an act of catharsis may influence aggression.
4. The Frustration-Aggression hypothesis suggests frustration will always lead to aggression - true or false?
5. Outline two criticisms of the Frustration-Aggression hypothesis.
6. How does the Aggressive Cue theory differ from the Frustration-Aggression hypothesis?
7. Explain the Social Learning theory of aggression.
8. Give three practical examples of possible causes of aggression during a game.
9. Suggest three strategies a coach may use to limit the aggressive acts committed by a player.
10. Outline how officials can limit aggressive acts.

CHAPTER 11

Confidence

LEARNING OBJECTIVES:

By the end of this chapter you should be able to:

- explain the term 'self-efficacy'
- discuss the factors which contribute to the development of self-efficacy
- suggest strategies to develop high levels of self-efficacy
- explain the terms 'social facilitation' and 'social inhibition'
- outline the different groups which affect performers
- discuss the relationship between social facilitation, arousal levels and performance
- explain the term 'evaluation apprehension'
- outline Baron's Distraction–Conflict Theory
- discuss the implications of 'home field advantage'
- suggest strategies to develop self-confidence and minimise the adverse effects of social facilitation.

Introduction

All performers are more likely to produce better performances if they have belief in their own abilities to complete the task. Think about your own experiences; if you have high levels of self-confidence have you achieved a better result?

There are numerous examples in sport where victory has gone to the individual or team that possess the most belief in their own abilities. Individual levels of confidence can alter during the course of the event, with dramatic consequences. How often has one incident during the game changed the motivation and arousal levels of the performers, both positively and negatively?

The role of the coach is not only to develop the physical skills of an individual but to ensure the performer approaches the event believing that he or she can perform successfully. The importance of self-confidence is highlighted by Gould et al:

'the most consistent difference between elite and less successful athletes is that elite athletes possess greater self-confidence.'

The potential performance of an athlete can be greatly enhanced if he or she has a high level of self-confidence in his or her own abilities. Similarly, if the performer enters a competitive environment with doubts concerning his or her ability, he or she is more likely to experience increased levels of arousal and possible anxiety.

Self-confidence and self-efficacy

Bandura (1977) proposed the concept of **self-efficacy**. He suggested the self-confidence level of an individual varies depending on the situation and it could actually alter from moment to moment.

There are numerous examples within sport of one unsuccessful attempt leading to a loss of confidence and a rapid decline in performance. There are also examples of one successful action boosting a person's confidence levels, allowing the performer to believe in him or herself and produce outstanding results. For example, a batsman in a cricket match may have never reached the milestone of scoring 100 runs and repeatedly loses his wicket after scoring between 80 and 90 runs. Each time this occurs the batsman may become anxious and lose confidence. However, after scoring his first century, his level of confidence when placed in a similar situation may be higher and he may have a greater belief in his ability to repeat the feat.

Similarly, a young player may perform well in training but when faced with the prospect of competing in front of a large audience in a major event for the first time may feel less confident.

KEY TERMS

Self-efficacy:
the degree of self-confidence experienced by a performer when placed in a specific situation. The perception or self-belief in your own ability to cope with the demands of the situation

EXAM TIP:

Develop knowledge of how to improve the self-efficacy of a performer and use specific examples to highlight your understanding.

TASK 11.01

Reflect on your own experiences and consider situations in which you have felt very confident and not so confident. You may find if you experienced high self-efficacy your motivation levels and your task perseverance were higher. Discuss these specific situations with a partner.

The concept of self-efficacy does not only apply to individuals: it is of equal importance to teams. Consider how many teams appear to play to a higher level and with more consistency if they have high levels of self-confidence.

Cup-winning teams will often quote a high level of self-confidence as a major influence and contributory factor in their success. Managers and coaches frequently make reference to the time taken to adjust to the demands of playing in a new environment or type of competition, and for the team to develop their self-confidence. When victory is achieved, it is often used to motivate the team by highlighting the fact that they have done it once, so therefore they should be able to repeat the performance.

APPLY IT!

During the build-up to the 2003 Rugby World Cup Finals, the England team had recorded victories over all their major competitors. This raised their level of self-efficacy and contributed to their positive attitude and approach to the competition. They believed in their own abilities and approached each game knowing they had the potential to defeat their opponents.

The individual performer's level of self-efficacy can affect the:

- **choice of activity** – high levels will ensure the athlete participates
- **amount of effort applied** – high levels will ensure the athlete is highly motivated and applies him or herself fully
- **level of persistence** – high levels will ensure the athlete works hard and maintains his or her effort and commitment.

TASK 11.02

1. List six different sports in which you have participated.
2. Rank order them (1 being the highest) according to your personal level of self-efficacy.
3. Give reasons why you have a higher level of self-efficacy in the first two compared to the last two.
4. For your top-ranked activity, list three specific situations in which you have high levels of self-efficacy and explain why this is the case.

Development of self-efficacy

Bandura suggested that four key factors contribute to the development of self-efficacy, as illustrated in Figure 11.01. These factors are seen to be influential:

- **Past experiences/past performance accomplishments** – a performer who has experienced success and enjoyment is more likely to develop high levels of confidence. For example, a cricket batsman who has developed a particular shot in training and scored runs regularly using the skill in a game will gain confidence and continue to use it when appropriate.
- **Vicarious experiences (modelling)** – a performer who has watched others achieving the task will feel that he or she is able to do so as well, especially if the model is of similar ability. For example, the cricketer watching one of his peer group successfully playing the shot is more likely to think that he too can achieve success.

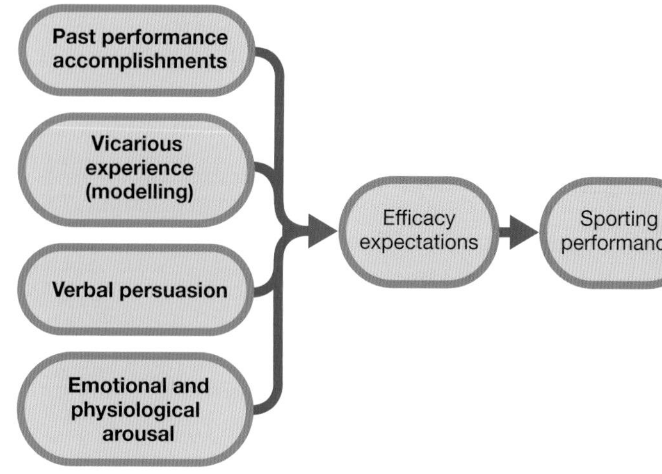

Fig 11.01 Bandura's model of self-efficacy development

EXAM TIP:

Learn the sections of Bandura's development of self-efficacy model and apply each to practical examples.

APPLY IT!

It is often mentioned at events such as the Olympics that the confidence of the team may increase as well as that of the performer if they produce one excellent result. This was the case in Beijing when Rebecca Adlington ended British women's 48-year wait for a swimming gold medal. This report highlights the importance of self-efficacy to performers.

The power of self-belief

The 19-year-old was a surprise winner of the 400m freestyle and has the 800m freestyle and 4x200m relay to come. Karen Pickering, former 100m freestyle world champion, believes Adlington can go on to claim all three. She said: *'Rebecca has her best event, the 800m, to come and the relay team will be buzzing with confidence now.'*

'The 800m is a different event and I don't know what is going to happen, but this British swimming team is amazing and I think there will be more medals this week.'

Adlington went on to shatter the 800 metres freestyle World Record, which was the only world record that had survived from the twentieth century. Team GB had aimed to win three swimming medals and went on to win a total of six, breaking one World, six European and 25 British records in the process.

Fig 11.02 Rebecca Adlington – World and Olympic record holder for 800m freestyle

- **Verbal persuasion** – a performer who receives encouragement about his or her abilities and actions, especially from significant others, will feel more confident about his or her actions or attempts. For example, the coach saying to the batsman 'well done, that was a great shot', or 'try to play the shot, but don't worry if it doesn't work this time'.
- **Emotional arousal** – a performer who is encouraged to perceive his or her physiological and psychological arousal before participation in a positive manner is more likely to develop high self-efficacy. For example, an increased heart rate, respiratory rate and cognitive anxiety should be viewed positively, in terms of being ready to compete, rather than being ill-prepared. For example, the batsman should be encouraged to remember occasions when he has been successful and to view any increases in arousal levels as an opportunity to improve his selective attention and anticipatory skills.

Developing high levels of self-efficacy

The coach has to consider each of the four components above and attempt to ensure that all are encouraged in a positive manner. Possibly the most influential factor is past performance accomplishments. Consequently success, no matter how small, is a key priority in the development of a performer.

Outlined below are a number of strategies to help develop positive expectations:

- experience early success
- observe demonstrations by competent others of similar ability
- set realistic but challenging goals
- set performance goals rather than outcome goals
- offer verbal encouragement and positive feedback
- develop effective stress management techniques
- use mental rehearsal
- avoid social comparison with others and limit the effects of social facilitation
- use attributions correctly by attributing failure to controllable, unstable factors.

A coach can employ different strategies to avoid this condition and boost self-efficacy, including:

- all the strategies outlined to improve self-efficacy
- one-to-one attention
- attribution re-training (see page 189)
- highlight performance goals
- use correct attributions, i.e. attribute failure to external factors.

Research has shown that the most effective methods to use are the final three in the above list. Even though the individual may achieve some success if the task is simplified, ultimately he or she must still believe that he or she is in control of the situation and must attribute reasons for that achievement to his or her own abilities.

TASK 11.03

In pairs, discuss how you could raise the level of self-efficacy of the following performers. Support your answers with practical examples.

- a gymnast entering a competition for the first time
- a basketball player taking free-throws
- a team playing in a cup final
- a group of novice swimmers

APPLY IT!

In the 2004 Athens Olympics, cyclist Victoria Pendleton was overcome by anxiety and effectively froze when competing. She underperformed and left Athens with her confidence crushed. It was a different situation in the 2008 Beijing Olympics. She had to wait until the last day for her event – the sprint – but she won the gold medal comfortably.

Fig 11.03 Victoria Pendleton worked hard to develop her self-confidence which contributed to her winning the Olympic Sprint Gold Medal in Beijing

Boosting self-confidence

With 'compassionate ruthlessness' – mentoring and supporting with total honesty – her coaches Peters and Brailsford developed a team around her to work on all the steps or 'foundation stones' they had identified that might contribute to gold medal success. In the case of Pendleton, Peters worked hard to remove the fear that can undermine confidence and lead to impulsive decisions. As he says:

'They learn what part of their brain is giving them completely negative thoughts and they switch over, and that's a skill.'

It took Victoria Pendleton a year to master the skill, to be able to 'switch over' her focus and be able to shut out the negative distractions. Another key phrase that illustrates this is 'logic not emotion'. In the build-up to the Olympics she had competed in several major events and performed well, which boosted her self-confidence, resulting in a high level state of sport confidence when she arrived in her quest to win the elusive gold medal.

Social facilitation

As we have discussed, the margin between success and failure at elite level is often very small. The nature of modern day sport means the actions of players are closely monitored by large crowds at the event, commentators and often a huge number of spectators via numerous media avenues. As you will know from your own experiences, arousal levels often increase when being observed. The ability of the performer to cope with the pressure of competing in front of an audience is another contributory factor to his or her overall effectiveness.

KEY TERMS

Social facilitation:
the influence of the presence of others on performance, which has a positive effect

Social inhibition:
negative influence on performance caused by the presence of others during performance

Consider how often a performer becomes over-aroused because of the crowd and his or her performance deteriorates. However, a performer can also be motivated by people observing his or her performance, and this allows the performer to produce a level of skill execution that he or she may not have thought possible. The concept of **social facilitation** attempts to explain why this happens. When participating in physical activity, the presence of other people who may not be directly watching may affect arousal levels. For example, there may be other competitors or other performers practising or even competing in the immediate area. All of these people may influence your arousal levels and affect performance.

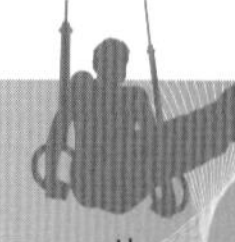

EXAM TIP:

Make sure you understand the relationship between the Drive Theory and social facilitation. Do not get confused and think that as arousal increases so does performance – it depends on the experience of the performer.

Zajonc's model

Robert Zajonc (1965) suggested that:

'...the influence of the presence of others on performance may be positive or negative ...'.

If the presence of others, either spectators or other athletes, has a positive effect on performance, it is classed as **social facilitation**. If it has a negative effect it is known as **social inhibition**.

Zajonc's theory is closely related to the Drive Theory of arousal. He suggested that as the level of arousal increases due to the presence of others, the dominant habit is more likely to occur. If this is the case we would expect the performance of an experienced player to improve and that of a novice to decrease if they were being observed.

Figure 11.04 outlines the relationship between the different groups and the effect on performance. As you can see, the 'others' are subdivided into four categories:

1. **audience** – those watching either as spectators at the event or at home via the different forms of media, including television, the radio or the internet
2. **co-actors** – those performing the same task but not in direct competition, e.g. another player on a badminton court
3. **competitive co-actors** – those in direct competition with the performer, e.g. another badminton player in a game
4. **social reinforcers** – those with a direct influence, e.g. a coach.

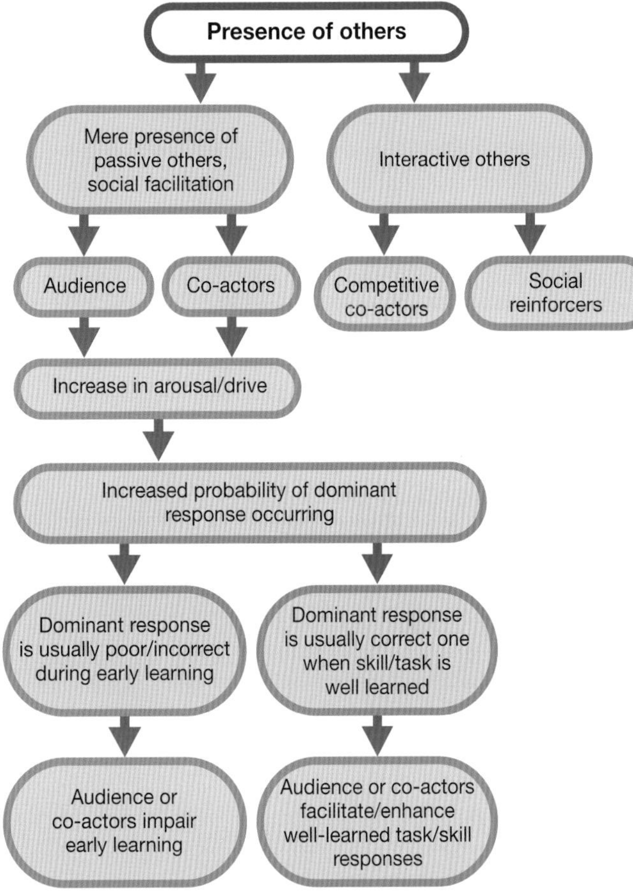

Fig 11.04 The effect of an audience will vary depending on the level of experience

Within a sporting context, the 'passive others' are the important factors for us to consider. For example, the performance of an experienced badminton player when competing in front of an audience will improve as arousal levels increase. However, an inexperienced player is more likely to become over-aroused, causing him to execute his skills poorly as they are not yet well developed.

Other research suggests that the learning of complex skills can be hindered if an audience is present, and the execution of fine skills may also be adversely affected. However, if the skill is simple or gross in nature, co-actors may actually help to improve the final performance.

STRETCH AND CHALLENGE

1. Observe a sporting event of your choice. Identify each of the 'others' as proposed by Zajonc and explain how they influence the performance of an individual performer.
2. Consider an event in which you have participated and explain how the presence of others affected your performance.
3. With reference to Drive Theory, explain how your arousal levels influence your performance.
4. Explain the strategies which could have been used to improve your performance.

APPLY IT!

There are numerous examples of the influence of the crowd on the quality of performance. One event over recent years has possibly demonstrated this effect consistently: the Wimbledon Tennis Championships. The Centre Court crowd and those on 'Henman Hill' watching on the large screen have played their part in supporting British players and affecting the final outcome of their matches. One such match was that between Andy Murray and the Frenchman Richard Gasquet in 2008.

The power of the Centre Court crowd

When a British player is involved in a match at Wimbledon now the crowd doesn't simply buy a ticket but involves itself in face painting, flag-ruffling, sighing and cheering and performing the Mexican wave. It almost becomes one of the competitors – face to face on court with the opposition. With a Wimbledon crowd behind them no competitor has anything to fear, especially if they are British.

We get a sense of the crowd's prominence when listening to Murray and his opponent immediately after their match.

'The crowd were awesome,' Murray said. *'The whole tie-break and the fourth and fifth sets, once I got ahead they got behind me more than they ever have before ... It almost takes your mind off your physical state when you've got so many people behind you.'*

Gasquet had appeared visibly shaken by the commotion from the seats. Towards the end, he even took to appealing to the umpire, his only friend out there and afterwards he said,

'The crowd was for him. It was natural. But it helped Andy a lot, for sure. He played with the crowd ... I hope to play against him in Roland Garros (in France). I won't be alone then.'

Fig 11.05 The Centre Court crowd got behind Andy Murray

EXAM TIP:

Give clear explanations and examples of the different types of 'others' as suggested in Zajonc's model. Be aware of strategies to reduce the effects of social facilitations if performance is deteriorating because of the presence of others.

Evaluation apprehension

One weakness of the social facilitation theory is that not all performers are affected by the presence of others as suggested. Cottrell's work (1968) developed this initial proposal and stated that others only had an effect on arousal levels if the performer felt that his or her actions were actually being evaluated. This is known as **evaluation apprehension**. If this were the case there would be an increase in anxiety levels and a corresponding decline in performance. For example, a badminton player may be highly capable in the training environment and execute skills successfully. However, when placed in a competitive match with other people watching, she may worry about what the spectators, coaches or selectors think about her performance. This results in deterioration in the performer's skill levels. If the observers were of perceived higher status or more knowledgeable, their presence may be even more threatening.

KEY TERMS

Evaluation apprehension:
a sense of anxiety experienced by a performer, caused by the feeling that he or she is being judged by those in the audience

Trait anxiety:
the general tendency of an individual to view situations as threatening

Information processing:
the process of gathering data, processing the relevant stimuli to form a decision and transferring the details to the muscular system

Proximity effect:
the influence of a crowd is more marked when it is close to the play, rather than its size being the key factor

EXAM TIP:

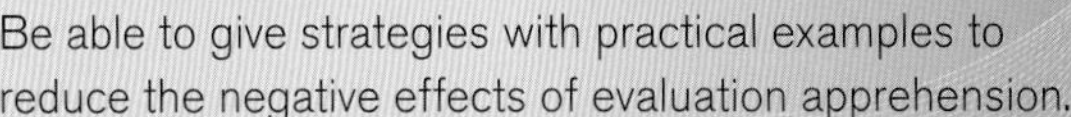

Be able to give strategies with practical examples to reduce the negative effects of evaluation apprehension.

Factors affecting social facilitation

Many factors may account for the differing effects on individual arousal levels, including:

- **trait anxiety** levels (see Chapter 8)
- personality of the performer (extrovert, introvert, stable or neurotic)
- previous experience (success or failure and current expectations)
- age and gender (younger performers may find it more difficult to be exposed to large crowds)
- knowledge of the watching crowd
- status of the observers
- nature of the audience (noise levels, hostile in nature, supportive, etc)
- proximity of the audience
- size of the audience and their surroundings – for example, a small crowd in a large stadium will have less influence than a small crowd in a small stadium.

Baron's Distraction-Conflict theory

Baron (1986) proposed that athletes must focus their attention on the demands of the task in hand, and anything which may distract them will hinder their performance. Think back to your studies of information processing and the suggestion that we can only process a limited amount of information at any time. When discussing the concept of social facilitation, the audience creates this effect. If the task is simple or well-learned, the effect of the audience on it will be less than that exerted on a complex or new skill. The implication for a performer has to be that he or she directs his or her attention to the task and attempts to ignore the distraction created by the crowd.

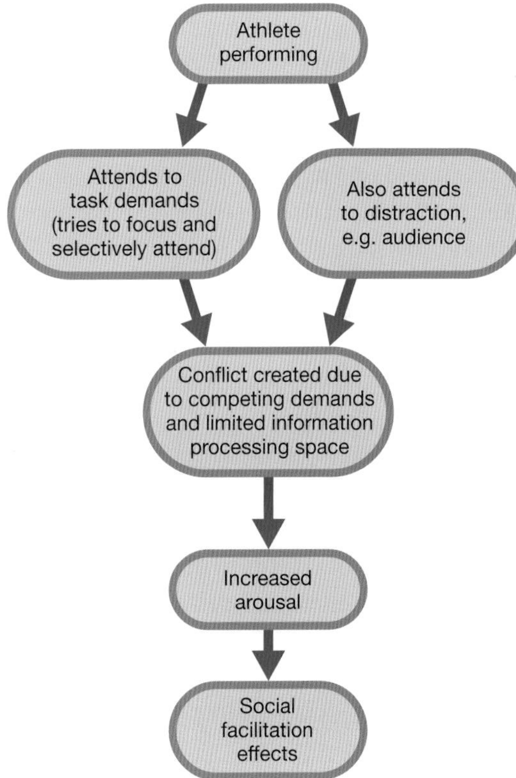

Fig 11.06 Baron's Distraction–Conflict theory

Home and away: advantages and disadvantages

We generally assume that a team playing at their home venue will have an advantage over their opponents. This may be due to a number of factors including:

- a larger number of home supporters
- familiarity of the surroundings
- a lack of travel required prior to the game.

Recent history has provided us with many examples of the home team performing well, especially at national level, and winning World Cup events even when they have not started out as favourites. For example, France won the football World Cup in 1998 and South Africa the rugby World Cup in 1999.

Historically, more medals are won at major championships, such as the Olympics, by the host nation when compared to their results before or after. However, this is not always the case and the performer must be aware of potential difficulties that may occur and impinge on his or her performance.

Key research concerning the 'home and away' advantage has found that:

- In the USA, more home matches are won than away matches.
- During the early rounds of competition, home advantage is helpful.
- Home advantage was mainly due to audience support.
- More fouls are committed by the away team.
- The proximity of crowds to the playing area and resulting noise increase has been seen as a factor.
- Olympic hosts tend to win more medals than in games before or after.
- Home teams tend to play in a more attacking style within the rules (functionally aggressive behaviour).
- As competitions progress, playing at home may hinder performance due to the increased expectations of the home supporters. This also applies to a team who are defending champions.
- If the crowd is close to the play, the opposition may find this more intimidating rather than the actual size of the crowd. This was proposed by Schwartz (1977) and is known as the proximity effect.
- The more important the game the greater the negative effect on the home team.
- Supportive spectators can create expectations of success.
- Potential increases in home players' self-consciousness.
- Higher personal expectations cause home players to think too much rather than just playing automatically, causing 'championship choke'.
- Coaches are now much more aware of these problems and try not to create too much pressure.

Strategies for combating social inhibition

It is important that the coach and the athlete work together to minimise the adverse effect of social facilitation. Outlined below are some of the strategies which can be used to help control arousal levels and prepare the performer for a competitive situation:

- develop the use of mental rehearsal
- train in front of others and gradually increase the numbers
- improve selective attention and cut out the effect of the audience
- reduce the importance of the event
- avoid social comparison with others
- encourage teammates to be supportive
- increase **self-efficacy** (see page 177)
- teach/coach in a non-evaluative environment initially
- use stress management and relaxation techniques
- use **attributions** correctly (see page 186)
- ensure skills are over-learned to encourage the dominant habit to occur as the levels of arousal increase.

ATHLETE PROFILE

During the past few years Claire Vigrass has developed her levels of self-efficacy, so that now she feels she has the ability to either win or at least reach the final stages of major Real Tennis tournaments. Several factors have contributed to this including consistent performances in high quality competitions and training against male players (**past experiences**); watching the performances of other players and learning from their play (**vicarious experiences**); encouragement from her coach, parents and sister, who is also her doubles partner (**verbal persuasion**); and finally the knowledge that she is now able to control her arousal levels more effectively and the fact that her fitness levels have improved dramatically after following a structured training programme (**emotional and physiological arousal**). Claire now has enough confidence to turn professional following her 'A' level studies and play in various tournaments around the world.

One of the major factors in her development has been the exposure to playing in front of larger crowds in different environments and learning to cope with new situations (**social facilitation**). While occasionally she has become over-aroused and suffered from social inhibition, where she has performed poorly, for most of the time Claire has coped well with the pressure and expectations placed on her. In the 2008 National League Final, hosted in Paris, she lost the first game 1–6, but with the support and encouragement of the crowd recovered her composure, eventually winning the match 1–6, 6–3, 6–4.

Fig 11.07 Claire has developed her confidence and is able to play well under pressure

ExamCafé

Relax, refresh, result!

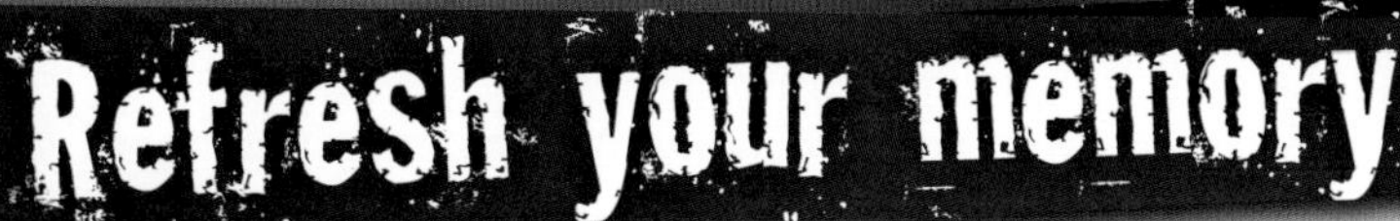

Revision checklist

Make sure you know the following:

Self-efficacy

- Self-efficacy is the level of self-confidence in specific situations which has been linked to motivation and can affect choice, effort and persistence.
- Self-efficacy is developed through past experiences, vicarious experiences, emotional arousal and verbal persuasion.
- Past experiences and performance success are seen as the most important factors in contributing to a performer's expectations of self efficacy.

Social facilitation

- Social facilitation is the arousal effects that the presence of others, either audience or co-actors, have on the individual's level of performance.
- The presence of others will increase the probability that the dominant response occurs by increasing levels of arousal – as suggested by the Drive Theory. For novices or those with poorly learned skills the dominant response will generally result in a poor performance, while for experts or those performing well-learned tasks the effect of an audience will generally be to improve the quality of the performance level.
- Cottrell argued that the effects of social facilitation were enhanced by evaluation apprehension.
- A supportive audience can give home teams an advantage. However, they can also potentially have a negative effect through high expectations.

Revise as you go

1. Why is it important to develop a performer's self-efficacy?
2. How does self-efficacy differ from self-confidence?
3. Name the four main factors which contribute to an individual's level of self-efficacy.
4. Why are performance accomplishments important to develop self-efficacy?
5. Explain the term 'vicarious experiences'.
6. Suggest two methods to develop self-efficacy.
7. What different effects might social facilitation have on novice and experienced performers and why?
8. The effect of social facilitation is caused by others. Name the four categories of 'others'.
9. Explain the difference between a 'co-actor' and a 'competitive co-actor'.
10. Suggest three strategies a coach may employ to reduce the effects of social facilitation and improve performance.
11. How does evaluation apprehension differ to social facilitation?
12. How can the nature of the crowd influence evaluation apprehension?
13. Explain Baron's Distraction–Conflict theory.
14. What is the proximity effect?
15. Suggest two strategies to reduce the effects of evaluation apprehension.

CHAPTER 12

Attribution theory

LEARNING OBJECTIVES:

By the end of this chapter you should be able to:

- *explain the term 'attribution'*
- *the implications for the correct use of attributions*
- *discuss different types of attribution with specific reference to Weiner's model*
- *explain the term 'self-serving bias'*
- *outline the importance of attribution retraining*
- *outline the concept of learned helplessness*
- *suggest strategies to avoid learned helplessness.*

Introduction

Whenever we play sport, we will analyse and evaluate our performance after the event. The reasons we give for our performance may influence our levels of motivation and future behaviour patterns. For example, if we feel the game was lost because of bad luck rather than our own lack of ability, motivation levels are likely to be higher and future participation is more likely. The manner in which a coach evaluates a performance and then provides feedback is vital if the individual is to adopt an approach behaviour in the future.

KEY TERMS

Attribution:
the perceived reasons for the success or failure of an event or pattern of behaviour

The perceived reasons we give for our performance, both success and failure, are known as attributions. The correct use of **attributions** is a crucial factor in maintaining a performer's:

- level of performance
- satisfaction of performance
- task persistence
- future expectations.

Attribution process

The attribution process is outlined below and explains the stages we go through when evaluating our performance.

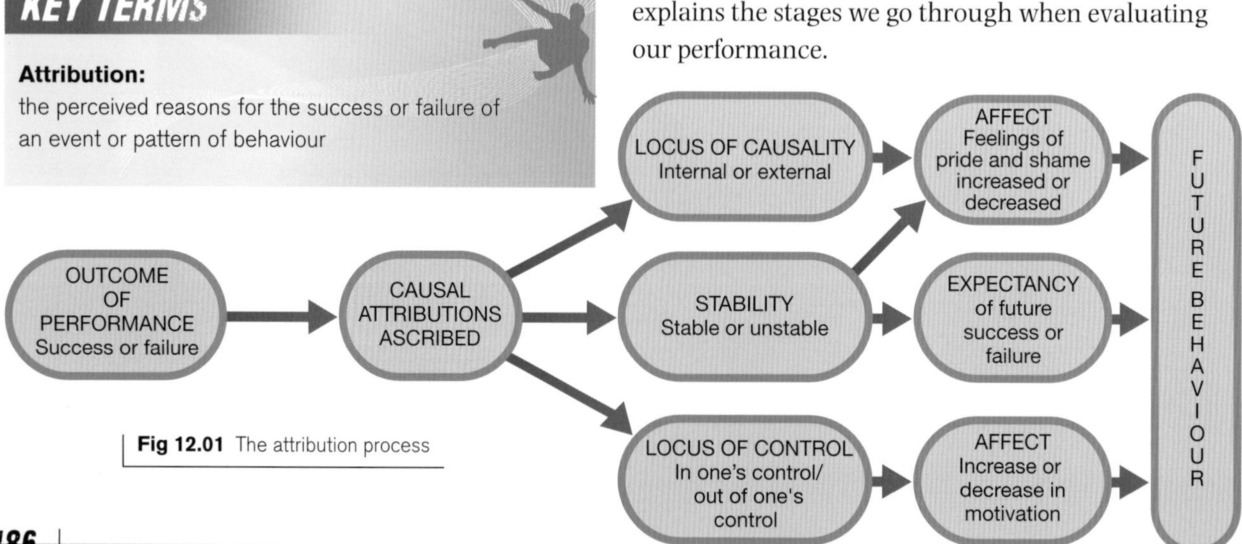

Fig 12.01 The attribution process

Fig 12.02 Using the correct attributions after an event is vital to maintain self-efficacy and motivation

Weiner's Attribution theory

Weiner's Attribution theory (1974) proposed that causal attributions (the factors affecting the result) tend to fall into four areas:

- ability
- luck
- effort
- task difficulty.

He suggested this **locus of causality** could be sub-divided into two broad categories:

1. **internal causes** – factors within our control, such as ability and effort
2. **external causes** – factors outside our control, such as task difficulty and luck.

KEY TERMS

Attribution theory:
this theory suggests that the perceived reasons given by a performer or coach after an event to explain the outcome can affect future levels of motivation

Locus of causality:
the cause of the final outcome is pinpointed as being due to internal or external factors, i.e. those within or beyond the performer's control

Locus of stability:
identifies attributing factors which may have influenced the final result, and which may or may not change in nature over a short period of time

Locus of control:
identifies attributing factors based on the level of control the performer is able to exert on the final outcome

Self-serving bias:
the tendency of a performer to attribute his or her success to internal factors, such as effort and ability, while failure is attributed to external influences, for example, luck and task difficulty

As seen in Figure 12.03 the second dimension in the model refers to the locus of stability. The relates to the changeable nature of the factor being discussed. For example, the ability of the performer would not change markedly from one week to the next, whereas

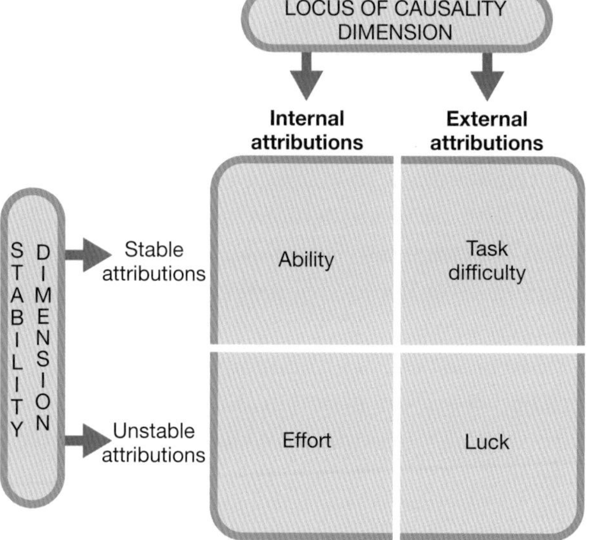

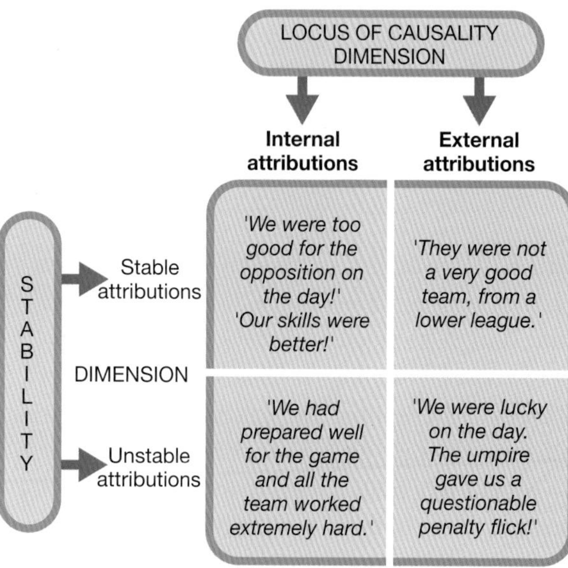

Fig 12.03 Weiner's two-dimensional Attribution model

his or her level of effort may well change dramatically depending on the situation. The stability dimension, therefore, is also sub-divided into:

- **stable factors** – such as the level of individual ability, skill, coaching experience and the nature of the opposition
- **unstable factors** – such as the individual level of motivation and effort, arousal levels, refereeing decisions, quality of teamwork, imposed tactics, injury, form and pure luck.

Weiner's later work (1986) included a third dimension, the **locus of control**. This is also sub-divided into:

- **personal control** – areas of performance over which an individual can take control, e.g. effort, concentration or commitment to training. Based on Weiner's original model, effort is the only factor which can be classed as controllable.
- **external control** – areas of performance over which an individual has little control, e.g. the referee, tactics used by the coach or the quality of the opposition.

EXAM TIP:

1. Be able to draw or interpret Weiner's model and make sure it is labelled correctly with appropriate examples.
2. Be able to explain the attributions you would give to individuals or teams following a variety of results. Give practical examples and justify your reasons for each.
3. To maintain a performer's motivation you can attribute loss or failure to any factors other than internal stable factors.

Attribution was seen to have an influential effect on the performer's level of pride or shame after the event. If he or she felt that success was due to internal factors such as ability or effort rather than external factors, the performer's level of pride increased along with his or her motivation.

Similarly, if failure was attributed to internal factors, this resulted in a sense of shame and a corresponding decrease in motivation.

Controllability also affects moral judgement and reaction to other people. A coach will often base his or her judgements on controllable factors. For example, praise is given to someone who has tried hard, even if the result was not as good as it could have been. However, the coach will be much more critical of a performance which is poor due to laziness or poor concentration.

TASK 12.01

Discuss with a partner two sporting events in which you have recently participated: one in which you were victorious and the other in which you experienced defeat.

1. List the reasons for the eventual outcome.
2. Draw Weiner's two-dimensional model and place each of the named reasons into the different categories.
3. Discuss your findings with your partner.

Effective use of attributions and self-serving bias

To use attributions effectively the coach must know how the performer is likely to react. This may depend on his or her personality, level of experience and current level of motivation. Generally, success is attributed to internal factors. This allows the performer to gain feelings of satisfaction, increasing his or her motivation and task persistence. However, failure should never be attributed to internal factors. In these situations the coach must use either external or unstable factors. This allows the athlete to believe changes can be made to improve his or her performance and it therefore protects his or her self-esteem. The use of attributions in this way is known as **self-serving bias**. This allows the individual to maintain his or her level of motivation and increase task persistence.

The correct use of attributions is important to develop self-esteem, maintain motivation and avoid learned helplessness (discussed later in this chapter in detail).

APPLY IT!

The use of attributions can be seen regularly after sporting events. Consider the statements below and observe how the respective managers use attributions to maintain the motivation level of their team. The following reasons for success and failure were given by two football managers during a post-match interview:

Victorious manager (away team):

- *'The striker took the goal well, despite the goalkeeper trying to put him off and hoping for the offside decision.'*
- *'We came away from home and won against the odds.'*
- *'The team worked hard and concentrated for the whole match.'*
- *'We learned from the previous match, which we lost 3–1, and adjusted the tactics, which worked well.'*

Defeated manager (home team):

- *'The referee didn't award a penalty in the first half.'*
- *'The referee didn't play enough stoppage time.'*
- *'Rugby matches played on the ground previously have ruined the surface and affected our style of play.'*
- *'Strikers had a bad day and missed chances they normally would have scored.'*

TASK 12.02

Read a selection of newspaper reports or watch post-match interviews with several performers, coaches or managers after a sporting contest has taken place. Identify the reasons they give for their success or failure. Attempt to classify them using Weiner's model and assess the impact their comments may have on the individuals or teams involved. There are current video-clips of post match interviews available on the BBC Sport website: www.bbc.co.uk/sport.

APPLY IT!

A talented runner may not believe that she has the ability to succeed, but if the coach emphasises a slight variation in her technique this will produce considerable improvement. This information may be sufficient to ensure that the runner will persevere with the task.

Attribution retraining

Attribution retraining involves the coach or teacher developing and changing an individual's perception of failure, allowing him or her to deal with it effectively and improve future performances. Figure 12.04 outlines how attribution retraining may occur. By altering the performer's perception of their apparent lack of ability, their emotional response changes from one of 'I won't be able to develop and be successful' to 'maybe I can improve if I do this differently, or set more realistic targets'.

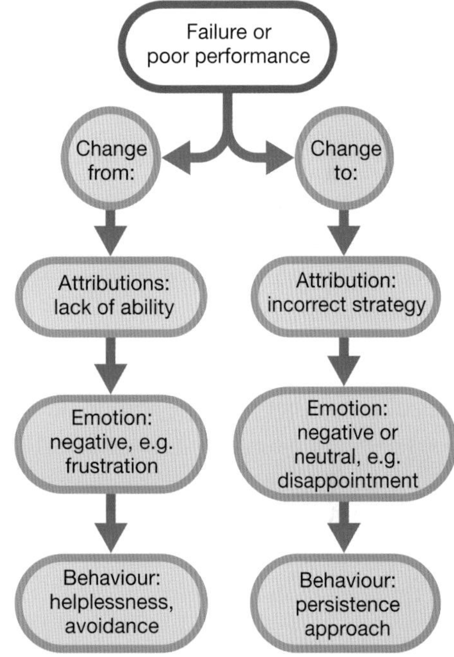

Fig 12.04 The process of attribution retraining

KEY TERMS

Attribution retraining:
the process by which a performer is taught to attribute failure to changeable, unstable factors rather than internal, stable factors, i.e. lack of ability

Learned helplessness:
feelings experienced by an individual when he or she believes that failure is inevitable because of negative past experiences

Learned helplessness

As you can see, the development of a high level of self-efficacy is an important factor in the psychological preparation of an athlete. If the confidence level of the performer lowers this can lead to self-doubt and the performer may question his or her ability to complete the task, which in turn may lead to anxiety.

Dweck (1975) proposed the concept of **learned helplessness**, in which performers attribute failure to internal, stable factors such as ability. Consequently they feel that when faced with particular situations they are unlikely to be successful and failure is the only viable outcome.

Learned helplessness is defined as:

Dweck (1975):
'An acquired state or condition related to the performer's perception that he or she does not have any control over the situational demands being placed on him or her and that failure is therefore inevitable.'

Many reasons may contribute to this acquired psychological state other than inappropriate attributions, including negative feedback, criticism and a lack of success. Also the factors contributing to self-efficacy as discussed in the previous chapter also have a direct bearing on the likelihood of performer thinking in this manner.

EXAM TIP:

Be able to explain the difference between specific and general learned helplessness, and the causes and methods for avoid or elimination.

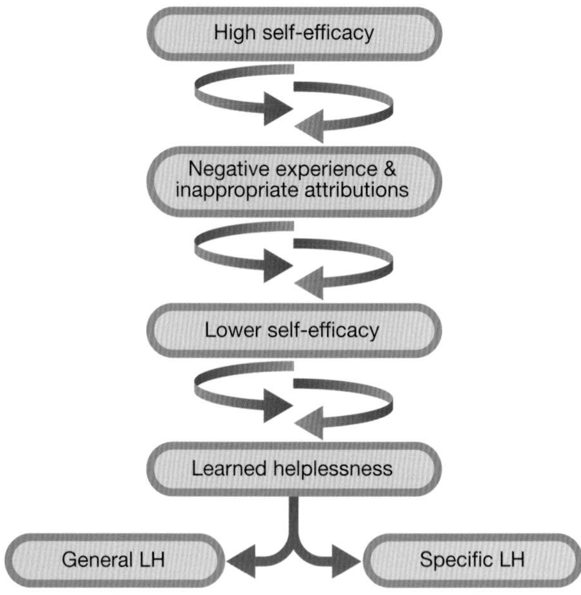

Fig 12.05 Performers may lose self-efficacy and develop learned helplessness

Learned helplessness can be sub-divided into two types:

1. **General/global learned helplessness** – this suggests that the performer will think failure is inevitable in all sports or types of sport. For example, an individual may feel that she is unable to be successful in all water-based sporting activities because she has had previous negative experiences whilst swimming.
2. **Specific learned helplessness** – this suggests that the performer will not necessarily be concerned about all water-based activities but certain sports. For example, when canoeing she may have capsized several times and been unable to control her movement. As a result the performer lacks confidence and feels unable to attempt canoeing again for fear of failure.

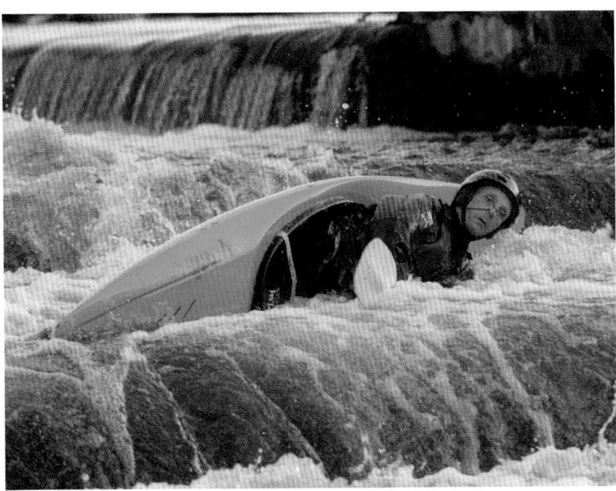

Fig 12.06 A canoeist may have capsized several times and feel unable to attempt canoeing again for fear of failure

STRETCH AND CHALLENGE

With a partner discuss how you could ensure that learned helplessness does not occur in the following situations:

- children learning to complete a gymnastic vault
- school netball team who have lost last three games
- year 7 class learning to throw a discuss
- group of adults attending a fitness gym to improve their health
- swimmer entering their first competition
- a team playing in a cup final.

Strategies to avoid the development of learned helplessness

A coach can employ several strategies to avoid this condition and boost self-efficacy, including:

- all the strategies outlined to improve self-efficacy (see page 177)
- one-to-one attention
- mental rehearsal
- try to set performance goals rather than outcome goals
- avoid social comparisons with other performers
- attribution retraining
- highlight performance goals
- use correct attributions, i.e. attribute failure to external factors.

Research has shown the most effective methods to use are the final three in the above list. Even though the individual may achieve some success if the task is simplified, ultimately he or she must still believe that he or she is in control of the situation and must attribute reasons for that achievement to his or her own abilities.

ATHLETE PROFILE

After each Real Tennis tournament Claire Vigrass evaluates her performance with her coach, Ricardo Smith. Her coach is very aware that she is still classed as a junior, even though her performances in the senior ranks have been highly impressive and as a result feels it is important for her to develop her self-esteem and maintain her high levels of motivation. When Claire won the 2008 US Ladies Open, her performance was credited to her skilful play, good decision making and focused approach. These are all internal factors which meant she felt she would be able to repeat her performance in the future. However, when she lost in the 2008 British Open Final, the attributions were different. While her coach told her she played well and maintained her level of concentration, the main reasons given for her loss were the fact she had played the current World Number 1 (**task difficulty**) and some of the umpire's decisions had been marginal (**luck**). Both these situations show clearly the concept of self-serving bias, aimed at maintaining Claire's level of motivation and belief that she can either repeat the performances or make changes in the future to win matches.

ExamCafé

Relax, refresh, result!

Refresh your memory

Revision checklist

Make sure you know the following:

Attributions and learned helplessness

- ▷ Attributions are the reasons performers give to explain success or failure (causal attributions).
- ▷ Attributions have been found to be very influential on the performer's expectations of future success or failure, level of emotional reactions and future achievement motivation.
- ▷ Weiner's attribution model originally identified two dimensions: locus of causality (internal or external factors); stability (stable or unstable).
- ▷ Weiner later added a third dimension of locus of control. This referred to the level of performer's control the performer was able to exert on the various factors.
- ▷ Self-serving bias is the tendency of a performer to attribute success to internal factors and failure to external factors.
- ▷ Attribution retraining involves performers changing their perspective; being taught to attribute failure to changeable, unstable factors rather than internal, stable factors.
- ▷ Attribution retraining when used effectively, can help performers reduce feelings of being 'doomed to failure' before they even attempt a task.
- ▷ A performer who continually focuses on outcome goals and attributes failure to perceived low ability (internal stable factor), or success to external unstable factors (luck), all of which are out of their control, is likely to experience learned helplessness.
- ▷ Learned helplessness is the perceived feelings of an individual when they feel failure is inevitable because of negative past experiences.
- ▷ Learned helplessness can be general or specific.

Revise as you go

1. What is an 'attribution'?
2. What is the 'attribution process' and how does it affect future behaviour?
3. Why is it important to use attributions correctly?
4. Outline Weiner's locus of causal attributions and give an example of each.
5. Outline Weiner's locus of stability attributions and give an example of each.
6. Explain the locus of control and suggest why it is important in terms of a performer's level of self-confidence.
7. Attributing failure to unstable factors minimises negative feelings – true or false?
8. Failure should be attributed to internal stable factors – true or false?
9. Explain the term 'self-serving bias'.
10. What is attribution re training?
11. Explain the term 'learned helplessness'.
12. What is the difference between general and specific learned helplessness.
13. Suggest two reasons why learned helplessness may occur
14. Outline two strategies to reduce the effects of learned helplessness.
15. How might the inappropriate use of attributions contribute to learned helplessness?

CHAPTER 13

Group success

LEARNING OBJECTIVES:

By the end of this chapter you should be able to:

- *explain the definition of a group and describe its characteristics*
- *outline the stages of group formation*
- *discuss the importance of cohesion within a group*
- *explain Carron's antecedents and their impact on group cohesion*
- *differentiate between task and social cohesion*
- *explain Steiner's model of group productivity and identify reasons for poor group performance such as faulty processes*
- *suggest strategies to eliminate faulty processes*
- *explain the terms 'Ringelmann effect' and 'social loafing'*
- *describe strategies to overcome social loafing.*

Introduction

Within all sports, individuals have to work together if success is to be achieved. The partnerships that have to be developed differ in nature depending on the sport, the number of people involved, the expected individual roles and the outcome expectation. The task of bringing together a collection of performers and moulding them into an effective team is a key priority in many sports. Consider how highly valued a good manager or coach can be and the consequences for them when it comes to winning and losing. There are numerous examples in sport where the most talented group of players has lost to a more co-ordinated team. Within this chapter we will look at how to maximise the effectiveness of each player and develop a cohesive team.

What is a group?

At first the term 'group' may appear straightforward but some clear distinctions must be made between a 'group' and a 'crowd'. The definition below may help to clarify the difference:

McGrath (1984):
'Groups are those social aggregates that involve mutual awareness and the potential for interaction.'

Fig 13.01 A group is different from a crowd

Carron (1982) suggested that groups have the following unique characteristics:

- two or more people interacting
- all the individuals have a common or shared goal
- they all share a collective identity
- there are structured forms of communication.

As the process of working together develops, the roles and norms of individuals within the team may alter. This is commonly known as **group dynamics** and it is important to recognise that change is inevitable and must be managed effectively if the group is to be successful.

Fig 13.02 A team working together

KEY TERMS

Group dynamics:
the process in which a group is constantly developing and changing when interaction takes place

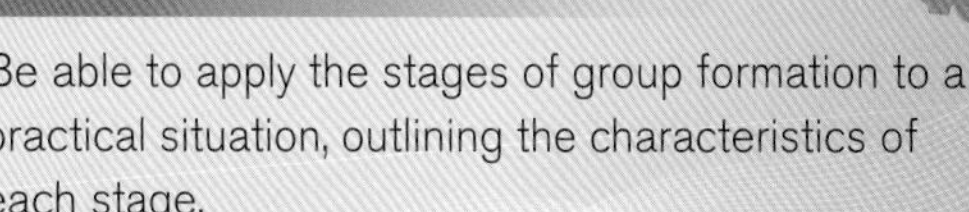

EXAM TIP:

Be able to apply the stages of group formation to a practical situation, outlining the characteristics of each stage.

Stages of group formation

The task of developing a team is not easy. There are many factors which may hinder the process, including differing abilities amongst the players, motivation, personality and attitude, in addition to the possible restriction of preparation time, coaching knowledge and effective leadership.

Tuckman (1965) suggested that there are four key stages which all groups must go through as part of their development:

1. **Forming**, which involves the development of relationships within the group as individuals get to know each other. This often entails a player assessing where he or she may fit into the group structure based on others' strengths and weaknesses. It also provides a player with an opportunity to find out if he or she feels that he or she actually belongs within the group.
2. **Storming**, which often involves some form of conflict within the group as individuals attempt to establish their position, status and role within the group structure. It may involve confrontation with the leader until different roles are established.
3. **Norming**, once the structure has been established the group gains stability and starts to become cohesive. Players start to co-operate and work towards their common goal, accepting the agreed norms of the group.
4. **Performing**. The final stage involves all the players working together towards their common goal. Each individual accepts his or her role and supports other group members accordingly.

The time to complete the process of group formation can vary enormously depending on the complexity of the task, the attitude and the ability of the players, and the time available. Consider the task faced by an international manager/coach who has the most talented players to work with. Often his or her job may be more difficult than that of a club manager because of:

- limited preparation time
- players who are more familiar with other strategies and tactics
- higher levels of expectation.

Remember that once the final stage is reached there will be times when the whole process is repeated. This may occur due to an evaluation of the group's performance which leads to changes being introduced. Alternatively, a new player may join the team bringing different skills and abilities.

TASK 13.01

Devise and complete a task as a group with one person acting as an observer. The task must involve between four and eight students. For example, make up a game using specific pieces of equipment, construct a basic gymnastic routine or devise a group balance.

After completing the task discuss the effectiveness of the group and attempt to identify Tuckman's four stages of progression.

Cohesion

The term **'cohesion'** refers to the dynamic process and tendency of a group of individuals to stay together whilst combining their efforts in order to achieve their goal. If a group is to be successful there has to be an element of cohesion; very few teams win if the players do not cooperate with each other. It has been suggested that cohesion develops as a direct result of success, while others feel cohesion is a prerequisite. However, it is generally assumed that the more cohesive a group, the better the chance of victory.

Different forms of cohesion may be needed depending on the activity. For example, a netball team relies on players doing different things, such as fulfilling specific positional requirements (co-interacting), whilst rowers rely on everyone completing the same action (co-acting).

KEY TERMS

Cohesion:
the extent to which a group works together to achieve a common goal

Task cohesion:
the interaction of group members and their effectiveness in working together to achieve a common goal

Social cohesion:
the interaction of individuals and how well they relate to each other

Several factors (antecedents) may contribute to the cohesiveness of a group. Carron (1982) suggested that these include:

- **Environmental/situational factors** – for example, the size of the group, the time available, training facilities, etc. The larger the size of the group the more interactions and potential coordination problems there will be between individuals.
- **Member characteristics** – including ability, motivation, affiliation to the group, similarity of opinions and status, satisfaction of other team members, etc.
- **Leadership style** – the involvement of the individuals in decision-making and expectations of the group.
- **Team elements** – for example, the desire of the whole team for success and, the nature of shared experiences either victorious or in defeat. Generally, the more success the group experiences, the higher the cohesiveness.

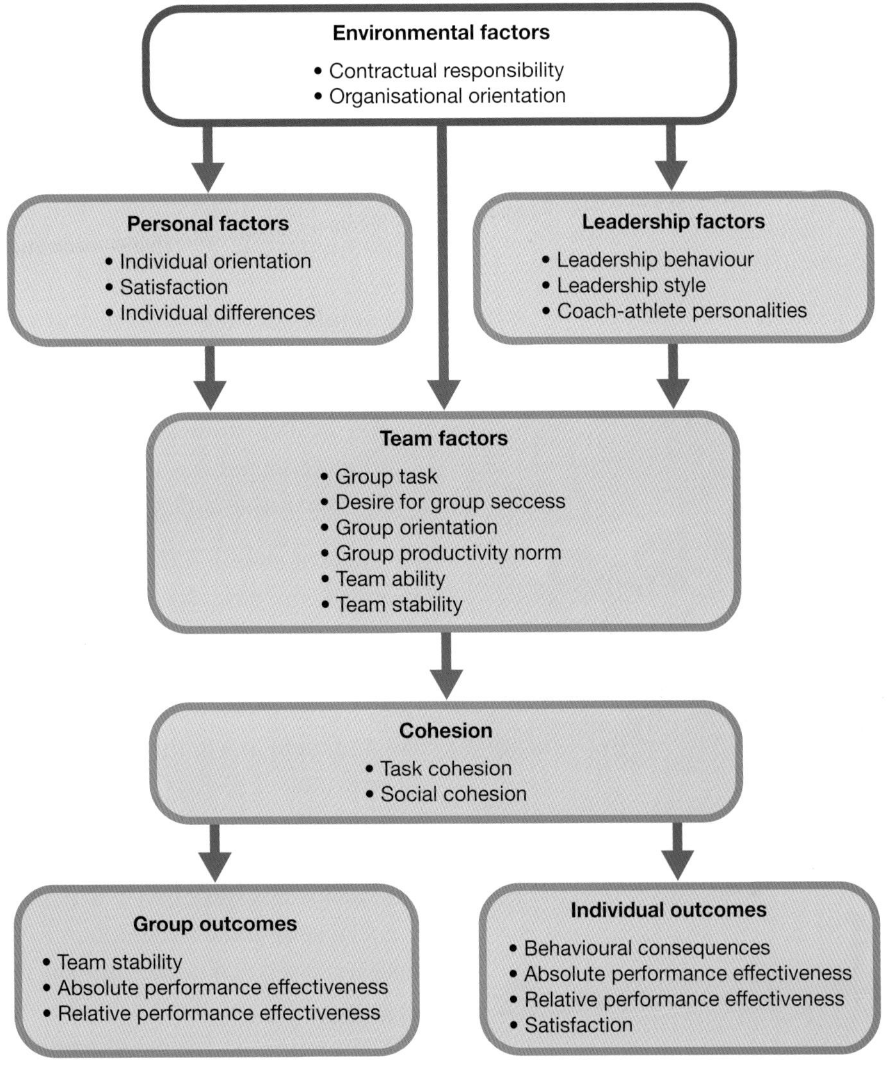

Fig 13.03 Carron's model

Other factors that may also affect the cohesiveness of a group include:

- **Nature of the sport** – interactive sports such as basketball and hockey rely heavily on cohesion, whereas in co-active sports (such as athletics and gymnastics) cohesion is not so important.
- **Stability of the group** – the longer the group is together with minimal changes, the greater the chance of cohesion.
- **External threats** – those who threaten the group may actually help to eliminate internal sub-groups and force the team to work together. For example, criticism from the media may encourage greater cohesiveness and a show of group loyalty.

APPLY IT!

At the 2008 Beijing Olympics there were many examples of excellent group cohesion within Team GB's successful medal haul. Three examples include the Men's Cycling Team Pursuit, the Women's Yngling Sailing and the Men's Coxless Four. All showed the ability to work together under extreme competitive pressure and execute the skills and tactics they had practised during countless hours of training.

Fig 13.04 The gold medal-winning GB Men's Cycling Team Pursuit in the 2008 Beijing Olympics

TASK 13.02

Visit the BBC Sport and/or UK Sport website to discover how any or all of the team, mentioned above achieved their gold medals. Attempt to identify common characteristics that allowed them to be so successful and compare your findings to Carron's model.

Group cohesion can be sub-divided into two categories:

1. **Task cohesion** – this refers to the interaction of individuals and how well they work together to achieve their common goal. For example, each player understands and fulfils his or her positional role effectively, allowing everyone else to do the same.
2. **Social cohesion** – this refers to the interaction of individuals and how well they relate to each other, the level of support offered and the degree of trust. For example, the players enjoy each other's company and may socialise away from the sporting situation.

Each type of cohesion may help to develop an effective team, but it is generally agreed that task cohesion is vital for success and has greater importance than social cohesion. For example, a rugby team may be well drilled and highly skilled, allowing them to win the majority of their games, but may include groups of players that do not socialise with each other. A rival team may socialise very well but lack a coordinated approach to their game and as a result rarely win a match.

Social cohesion often develops as task cohesion improves, but it can undermine the effectiveness of the group. For example, a reluctance to question tactics or strategies for fear of conflict may disrupt the natural development of the group. Also, cliques may form and lead to problems of cooperation. If something like this happens, it is the role of the coach or captain to recognise it and to implement strategies to tackle such issues. This ensures that the task cohesiveness of the group is not jeopardised.

Strategies to develop an effective group and cohesion

As we can see, developing a cohesive team is vital for success and strategies which can be employed to achieve this include:

- practice and training drills
- an explanation of roles and expectations within the group
- the setting of specific targets – individually and as a group
- giving individual players responsibility
- developing social cohesion away from the training or competitive situation
- creating a group identity (e.g. via clothing or a motto)
- encouraging peer support (using constructive advice rather than negative criticism)
- creating an open environment for discussion
- avoiding social cliques
- minimising the difference in status between players
- attempting to maintain stability and avoiding unnecessary changes
- identifying **social loafers** (see page 200).

EXAM TIP:

Understand and explain strategies to improve the cohesion of a group with practical examples.

Steiner's model of group productivity

The skill of the coach or manager is evident when he or she is able to mould a collection of individuals into an effective cohesive unit. However, this is not always an easy task even with a group of highly skilled performers. Steiner (1972) suggested that **group productivity** could be measured using the following equation:

Actual productivity = Potential productivity – Losses due to faulty processes

Where:

- **Actual productivity** is the performance of the group at a given time.
- **Potential productivity** is the quality and quantity of the group's resources relevant to the task. This is dependent upon skill level, the ability of the opponents, task difficulty and the expected outcome. For example, the manager of a national team is able to select the best players and in theory should have the best team. But there are numerous instances where players have underperformed or not been able to apply the strategies correctly. As a result they have not achieved their optimum performance level. It may be the case that in order to achieve the most coordinated approach the best player may have to be dropped from the team as others may contribute more to the overall team performance.
- **Faulty processes** are any factors which interfere with the group reaching its full potential. These are sub-divided into:
  - **Coordination losses** – caused by factors such as a lack of teamwork, poor execution of tactics, ineffective communication or misunderstanding of positional role.
  - **Motivational losses** – caused by factors such as a player losing concentration, under- or over-arousal, loss of motivation due to feelings of not being noticed or valued, low self-confidence, reliance on other players or avoidance behaviour if the task is perceived as too difficult.

KEY TERMS

Group productivity:
the effectiveness of a group when completing a task

Ringelmann effect:
the performance of an individual may decrease as the groups size increases

Social loafer:
individual who attempts to 'hide' when placed in a group situation and does not perform to his or her potential

Ringelmann effect

As the group size increases there is an increased likelihood of co-ordination problems occurring and the performance of an individual decreasing. This is known as the **Ringelmann effect**. Ringelmann's research was completed nearly 100 years ago and was originally based on the amount of force exerted during a tug-of-war pull. The force exerted by a team of eight was not eight times as much as a solo pull. This is caused by a mixture of factors including a lack of coordination and a loss of motivation caused by being within a group.

EXAM TIP:

1. Give examples of faulty processes that may occur within a team and suggest strategies to eradicate or minimise them.
2. Be able to explain why social loafing and the Ringelmann effect might happen and the implications they have on group productivity.

Social loafing

Another factor which may cause a faulty process to occur is that of social loafing. This can be seen when a performer attempts to hide when placed in a group situation, often 'coasting' through the game and not performing to his or her potential. The performer may feel that his or her contribution to the team is not being recognised, evaluated or valued. He or she may also simply be relying on others to cover his or her lack of effort.

Strategies to minimise the effects of social loafing

If a player is loafing he or she is obviously being detrimental to the team performance and strategies to overcome the problem should be implemented immediately. Such methods may include:

- giving the player specific responsibility
- giving feedback; evaluating the performance; praising and highlighting an individual's contribution
- using video analysis
- setting challenging but realistic targets
- introducing situations where it is difficult for social loafing to occur (e.g. playing small-sided games)
- developing social cohesion and peer support
- varying practice to maintain motivation
- developing higher levels of fitness to avoid hiding to take a break
- highlighting the individual's role within the team and his or her responsibility to other players.

STRETCH AND CHALLENGE

Select a successful team and analyse its performance in terms of:

1. effectiveness of task cohesion
2. effectiveness of social cohesion
3. examples of poor cohesion and faulty processes
4. explanation of how cohesion was restored
5. strategies used to reduce social loafing.

APPLY IT!

There are many examples in sport which highlight how managers and coaches attempt to create a sense of group identity and develop both task and social cohesion. Many are sport-related but often social cohesion is developed as well as task cohesion.

Cohesion

Every four years a rugby team is selected to represent the four home nations of England, Wales, Scotland and Ireland and they combine to form the Great Britain & Ireland British Lions. The coaches of the squad have to very quickly create a sense of unity amongst the players and a common identity. Each tour management team will utilise different methods to reach the same end result: a cohesive team. Activities have included outdoor pursuits and problem solving type activities and African drum workshops. One activity involved the creation of the 'Lions' Laws', which was a self-imposed code of conduct which the players discussed and agreed upon. The agreed 'Laws' established their expectations of behaviour both on and off the field of play. These activities are in addition to the hours spent training and discussing tactics to ensure all players know their personal role within the team structure. The former British Lion player Scott Gibbs made the following comment about the cohesion within the squad:

Fig 13.05 Pre-tour training

'There was never anyone who felt alienated in any way. That's a true strength of a squad, that inward support from everybody. That was there in abundance and that was why it was so successful on the field and off the field. We made a lot of friendships and there was never one clique. We had a lot of honesty and I think that was key. There are rules which you all need to adhere to. The fact that this was done in an open forum created a certain list of criteria, which included honesty, desire, ability and conscientiousness and all those kinds of words that pulled people together and created a strong bond in the team and the squad.'

ExamCafé

Relax, refresh, result!

Refresh your memory

Revision checklist

Make sure you know the following:

Group success

- ▷ A group in sport has a collective identity and a common goal and objectives. It involves communication between the group members, interpersonal attraction as well as person and task interdependence.
- ▷ Group dynamics refers to the process through which a group is constantly developing and changing when interaction takes place.
- ▷ Effective groups are formed in four stages: forming, storming, norming and performing.
- ▷ Teachers and coaches attempt to improve the performance of groups by bringing together the best individuals.

Cohesion

- ▷ Cohesion is the extent to which a group work together to achieve a common goal.
- ▷ Cohesion is a dynamic process whereby the members of the team are motivated to stay together as a group.
- ▷ Cohesion can take the form of task cohesion or social cohesion.
- ▷ Groups are usually motivated to remain together for either task and/or social orientated reasons.
- ▷ The precise effects and results of cohesion are debatable but it generally agreed that success is more likely to result if teams are cohesive.
- ▷ The actual productivity of a group = potential productivity – losses due to faulty group processes.
- ▷ Faulty processes are used caused by coordination losses and motivational losses.
- ▷ Collecting the best individuals to play does not always mean they will make the best team.

- The Ringelmann effect and social loafing have been used to explain the effects that may occur as the size of the group increases leading to a decline in motivation.
- Social loafing often occurs when within a player loses their sense of identity and individuality, creating a feeling of being under-valued.
- Social loafing can be reduced by increasing personal responsibility, setting personal goals and providing individual feedback on performance.

Revise as you go

1. Outline Tuckman's four stages of group formation.
2. How does a group differ from a crowd?
3. Explain the terms 'social cohesion' and 'task cohesion'.
4. Explain Carron's antecedents and suggest how they may determine the cohesiveness of a group.
5. Outline three methods a coach may employ to improve group cohesion.
6. What does 'actual productivity' mean?
7. Name two common faulty processes that may reduce group productivity.
8. Suggest why the Ringelmann effect may occur.
9. Why might a group member lapse into social loafing?
10. Suggest three methods a coach may use to reduce faulty processes and eliminate social loafing.

CHAPTER 14

Leadership

LEARNING OBJECTIVES:

By the end of this chapter you should be able to:

- explain the term 'leadership'
- outline the qualities of a good leader
- explain the different types of leader, including autocratic, democratic and laissez faire
- discuss the effectiveness of different types of leadership styles and highlight situations where they are most effective
- explain the difference between emergent and prescribed leaders
- outline and evaluate Fiedler's Contingency model of leadership
- outline and evaluate Chelladurai's Multi-dimensional model of leadership.

Introduction

From your studies of group dynamics it should be obvious that, in order for a collection of individuals to be successful, clear guidance and leadership is required. Consider the importance in the modern world of sport of the coach, manager and captain. Often they are praised for their qualities and contribution to success but they are also the first to be singled out for criticism if the team fail to reach their potential. From your own experiences of watching sport, you will be able to highlight some effective leaders.

EXAM TIP:

1. Be able to outline the characteristics of a good leader.
2. Questions may focus on evaluation of the theories of leadership.

Definitions and qualities of an effective leader

The definitions below explain the process of leadership:

Moorhead and Griffin (1998):
'The use of non-coercive influence to direct and coordinate the activities of group members to meet a goal.'

Barrow (1977):
'The behavioural process of influencing individuals and groups towards set goals.'

Therefore, leaders play a vital role not only in coordinating the interaction between players but in inspiring them, maintaining their motivation levels, setting realistic targets and eliminating faulty processes immediately.

TASK 14.01

Identify someone whom you consider to be a good leader. List the qualities that make him or her effective in the role and explain why you think he or she is a good leader.

The best player does not always make the best leader and specific qualities are needed to complete this role effectively. Outlined below are some of the characteristics which contribute to effective leadership:

- good communication skills
- interpersonal skills
- empathy with individuals
- approachable
- perceptual skills
- highly knowledgeable
- vision
- effective decision-making
- inspirational
- determined
- confident
- organised.

Fig 14.01 As captain, Martin Johnson led the England rugby team to World Cup success. He has now retired from playing but has been appointed England manager, where his leadership skills will be tested in a different way

Theories of leadership – nature versus nurture?

As with other aspects we have studied, the psychological debate of 'nature versus nurture' is again relevant. Are leaders born or are they developed through the process of socialisation? Two contrasting theories are outlined below.

Great Man Theory

This was proposed by Carlyle in the early twentieth century. He suggested that leaders inherit specific personality traits which enable them to be effective. According to this trait theory (which Carlyle only applied to men), leaders possess intelligence, self-confidence, assertion, good looks and a dominating personality. If this theory were correct, an individual would be an effective leader irrespective of the situation. While there may be some similarities between leaders from different backgrounds, there is no conclusive evidence to support this theory. Consequently the trait approach has little credence today as there are many other factors of more relevance, such as how leaders emerge, the situation and the nature of the group being led.

Social Learning theory

Social Learning theory outlines an alternative approach to the development of leaders. This suggests that all behaviour patterns are learnt due to environmental influences. For example, a player may observe his captain dealing with a difficult situation, such as maintaining discipline of the team during the final stages of an important match. In the future the player may be faced with a similar scenario and copy the captain's actions. It is a vicarious experience. A criticism of this theory is that it makes no allowance for any aspect of the trait approach and natural personality characteristics.

Interactionist theory

The **interactionist approach** combines both the trait theory and the influences of the environment. As a result it takes into account the need for differing behaviour patterns or leadership styles depending on the situation, the characteristics of the group and the required outcome.

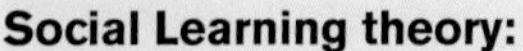

KEY TERMS

Social Learning theory:
this proposes we learn by observing others and then copying their actions. This theory has been covered in detail in several sections of your course already and you should be familiar with the different phases suggested by Bandura

Interactionist theory:
this theory proposes that leadership is formed due to a combination of innate traits and interaction with the environment

EXAM TIP:

Be able to suggest which form of leadership style is best suited to a specific situation and explain what the advantages and disadvantages may be for using a particular style.

Leadership styles and their effectiveness

The term 'leadership style' refers to the manner in which a leader decides to interact with the group. This may depend on the situation and the nature of the group. If the most appropriate style is adopted the group are more likely to be successful in their task. Lewin (1939) researched the effect that different styles of leadership would have on similar tasks with similar groups. The three styles and their effects are outlined below.

Authoritarian or autocratic leader

This leader dictates to the group what actions to take, with very little or no input from the members in terms of decision making. This type of leader is generally not concerned with interpersonal relationships within the group and is task-orientated, with the primary focus being to complete the goal as soon as possible. The group works hard when this leader is present, but can become aggressive and independent when left alone.

This style of leadership is most effective when:

- the situation involves team sports or there are a large number of performers
- decisions have to be made quickly
- there is limited time to complete the task
- there are clear and specific goals
- the task is complex or dangerous.

Democratic leader

This leader encourages the group to discuss ideas and become involved in the decision-making process. However, he or she will make the final decision and oversee the completion of the task. This style of leadership is generally more informal and relaxed within the group. When left alone the group continues to work and cooperate to complete the set task.

This style of leadership is most effective when:

- the situation involves individual sports or individual coaching situations
- the performers are more experienced
- there are friendly relationships with the group
- there are limited facilities are available.
- decisions don't have to be made quickly.

Laissez-faire leader

This leader tends to leave the group to their own devices, allowing them to make their own decisions and offering them little help with the decision-making process. He or she generally adopts a passive role and as a result the task is less likely to be completed. If the group is left alone they usually become aggressive towards each other, do little work and give up easily.

While there are three different approaches, it is not suggested that a leader should choose one style and adhere to it. A leader should actually assess the situation and required outcome, then use this information to tailor his or her behaviour towards the group in the most appropriate way.

Preferred leadership styles

Research has suggested that at different times the leader should alter the leadership style adopted. Specific models of leadership will be discussed in detail later in the chapter. Below are some suggestions for different groups and their preferred style. Remember leadership is not an exact science and the styles listed below are only generalisations.

Task-orientated/ autocratic approach	Relationship-orientated/ democratic
• Larger groups or teams	• Smaller groups or individuals
• Older players	• Younger players
• Male performers	• Female performers
• Novices or weaker players	• Experienced or highly skilled players

Table 14.01 Extreme leadership styles

Selection of leaders

An individual may become the leader of a group in two ways:

- **Prescribed leader** – an individual is appointed to lead the group by a higher authority from an external group. For example, often the captain of a national team is announced by the manager or the governing body.
- **Emergent leader** – an individual becomes a leader based on support from within the team. Emergent leaders are often nominated and elected based on ability, interpersonal skills and expertise. For example, many local club teams appoint their captain annually at their Annual General Meeting based on nominations and votes.

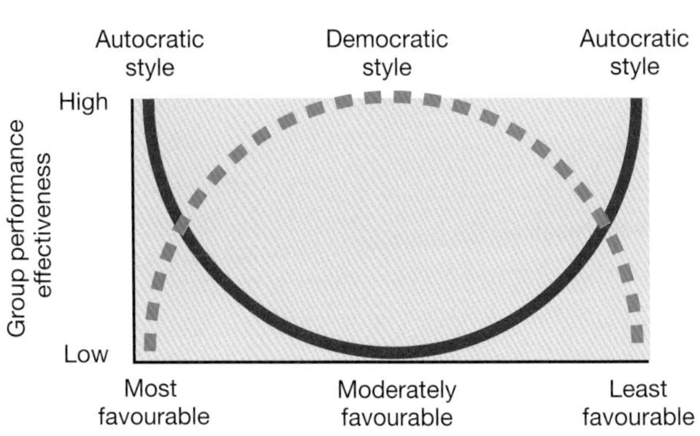

Fig 14.02 Fiedler's Contingency model of leadership

Fiedler's Contingency model

Fiedler's Contingency model suggests the effectiveness of a leader is dependent on (contingent on) a combination of personality traits and the situation. Fiedler (1967) identified two types of leadership styles:

1. **Task-centred/task-orientated leader**, who concentrates on efficiency, setting goals and completing the task as quickly as possible. This leader would adopt an autocratic approach. Such an approach would be desirable when:
   - the situation is potentially dangerous
   - time is limited
   - there are large group numbers
   - quick decisions are required.
2. **Relationship-centred/person-orientated leader**, who concentrates on developing interpersonal relationships within the group. This leader would adopt a democratic approach. This approach would be useful when:
   - time is not such a crucial factor
   - consultation is required
   - personal support may help develop interpersonal relationships within the team.

Favourable situation	Moderately favourable situation	Unfavourable situation
Good leader/student relationship	Friendly leader/student relationship	Poor relationship with the group/hostile
Leader highly respected by group	Group prefers to consult with leader prior to decision	Leader's position is weak
Group of high ability	Reasonable ability level	Group of low ability
High motivation levels within group	Moderate motivation levels	Low motivation levels/poor discipline
Good support networks, e.g. parents, community etc	Some support offered	Weak support networks, e.g. lack of community support
Task is simple or unambiguous	Task has no definite task-orientated outcome	Task is complex with no clear structure

Table 14.02 Task-centred versus relationship-centred styles of leadership

The effectiveness of each style depends on the favourableness of the situation, which is dependent on:

- the relationship between the leader and the group
- the leader's position of power and authority
- the task structure.

Fiedler proposed that the:

- task-orientated style would be effective in very favourable or unfavourable conditions
- person-orientated style would be better employed in moderately favourable conditions.

APPLY IT!

The situation would be favourable if the coach of a team had the clear objective of winning the league, had good facilities and well-motivated players. In comparison, the situation would be unfavourable if a local team had a poor relationship with their coach, poor facilities and no clear objectives for the group. For both of these scenarios a task-orientated style could be used. A third rival team with a moderately favourable situation might have a reasonable relationship with their coach, limited facilities and a mid-table position in the league. In this instance a person-orientated style may be the most appropriate to develop task and social cohesion in preparation for next season.

Chelladurai's Multi-dimensional model

Chelladurai's Multi-dimensional model (1980) suggests that before a leadership style can be chosen, three characteristics or antecedents must be considered:

1. **Situational characteristics**, including factors such as the task difficulty, the nature of the opposition, the group size, the nature of the activity and the time available.
2. **Leader characteristics**, including factors such as personality, experience, skill level and preferred leadership style.
3. **Group members' characteristics**, including factors such as ability, motivation, age, gender and personality.

EXAM TIP:

For effective leadership to take place, a leader should be able to adopt any one of the three leadership styles.

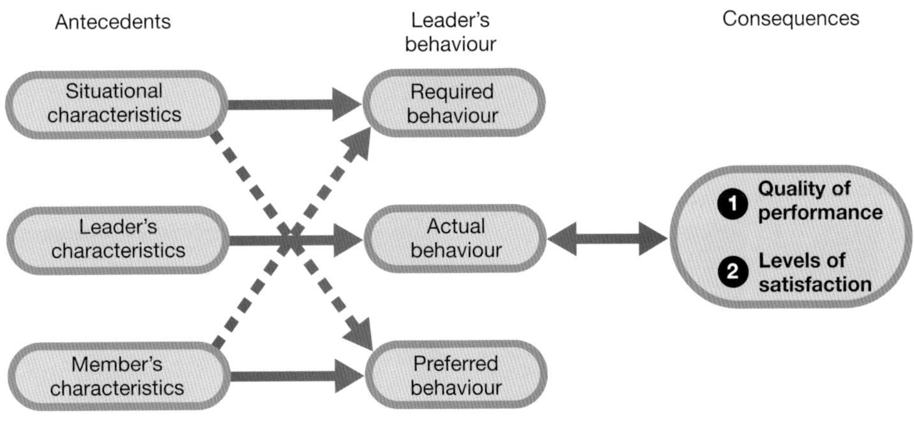

Fig 14.03 Chelladurai's Multi-dimensional model of leadership

When these have been assessed the next stage involves consideration of the three types of leader behaviour:

1. **Required behaviour** – depending on the situation and task, e.g. the coach may need to give instructions quickly during a timeout as time is limited.
2. **Actual behaviour** – the leader's action in a situation, e.g. the coach issues directions in an effective, clear manner. This is often determined by the experience of the coach.
3. **Preferred behaviour** – what the group want depending on their skill and goals, e.g. a team which is goal-orientated will want clear instructions, but a team which merely plays for recreational reasons may simply want a rest and not necessarily want to be given detailed tactical ploys.

The more closely related the three types of leader behaviour are to the situation, the greater the chance of the group members' satisfaction. This in turn should lead to a more positive outcome.

APPLY IT!

A local youth club asks the secondary schools in the area to advertise a new basketball initiative that is starting aimed at introducing beginners to the game and play friendly games within the club. The first sessions involve the leaders/coaches developing the basic skills and fundamental knowledge of the game with the focus on fun and enjoyment. As a result many of the children return and tell their friends, who also start attending.

However, after several weeks it becomes clear that there is a group of 6–8 players who are much better than the rest, having played for various school teams. The leaders of the group start to focus their attention more towards them and games are played specifically to raise their skill levels even further, while the remainder of the group are increasingly left on their own to practise their skills. Several matches are also arranged against other youth clubs instead of the practice sessions. During the next few weeks many of the players in the 'not as good' category fail to turn up to the sessions as they have become demotivated because the leaders are not helping them and have changed the focus and original aim of the basketball initiative. The 'team' players still attend as they are motivated to play and develop their skill.

STRETCH AND CHALLENGE

Copy Chelladurai's multi-dimensional model of leadership and complete it applying each of the following scenarios. How might the chosen leadership style differ to ensure group satisfaction?

- The instructor of a group of novice climbers attempting an abseil for the first time.
- The captain of an international team.

Fig 14.04a and **Fig 14.04b** Different styles of leadership

TASK 14.02

Consider the situation outlined above and discuss the following points. Using Chelladurai's Model as a basis for your discussions consider the following questions:

1. Were the leaders correct in their actions?
2. Explain why some of the players left the group.
3. Explain why some of the players remained in the group.
4. How could the leaders have approached the situation differently?

EXAM TIP:

Remember the multi-dimensional model of leadership relates specifically to sporting situations. Effective leaders adapt their style depending on various factors. Make sure you are able to explain each of the components of the model and support your answer with sporting examples

ExamCafé

Relax, refresh, result!

Refresh your memory

Revision checklist

Make sure you know the following:

- Leadership is any behaviour that enables a group to attain its goals.
- All effective leaders tend to possess similar qualities.
- Leaders can be autocratic (make all the decisions), democratic (consult the group before making a decision) or laissez faire (make no decisions at all).
- Leaders can be emergent (come from within the group and be elected) or prescribed (appointed by someone outside of the group).
- Fiedler suggested effective leaders learn to be both task orientated and person orientated according to their own characteristics and the demands of the situation, together with the demands and expectations of the group. The leadership style depends on the favourableness of the situation.
- Chelladurai's multi-dimensional model is specific to sporting situations and states that optimum performance and enhanced satisfaction are more likely to occur when a leader's required, preferred and actual behaviours are consistent.
- Leaders have to be flexible in their approach and adapt their style.

Revise as you go

1. What is a leader?
2. List five qualities required to be an effective leader.
3. List the characteristics of an autocratic leader.
4. Explain how a democratic leader would interact with the group.
5. Outline the difference between a prescribed leader and an emergent leader.
6. List the three factors Chelladurai suggest need to be considered when adopting a particular leadership style.
7. How do the terms 'actual behaviour' and 'preferred behaviour' of the leader differ?
8. Explain the term 'favourableness' and describe how it affects the style of leadership.
9. What characteristics might a group possess that would makethe democratic leadership style most suitable?
10. When might an autocratic style of leadership be most appropriate to use?

Get the result!

Examination question

During competitive events performers may suffer from anxiety.

Explain how high levels of anxiety may effect the performance of an individual and suggest strategies that could be used to reduce any negative effects of over-arousal. (14 marks)

Examiner says

For this section of the paper you will need to answer one 14 mark question and two 7 mark questions.

Model answer

Student answer

There are several different types of anxiety that might affect the performer. Anxiety is a negative form of stress which can have a bad effect on the performance. One type of anxiety is cognitive anxiety [1]. This means that the performer will have negative thoughts and worry about doing badly or not being able to be successful. Another type is called somatic anxiety [4] and this affects the physical reactions of the body. This might cause increased heart rate, sweating and feeling sick.

There are different theories which link arousal and anxiety. For example the Inverted U Theory says that if we become over-aroused this will cause anxiety and our performance will get worse [5].

To help control anxiety there are lots of different strategies that could be used. These include breathing control [2] and centring [6]. Another method is progressive muscle relaxation [1], which means the muscle groups are tensed up then relaxed and you gradually work through the whole body. Meditation or hypnosis [11] can also be used. Other methods are positive self-talk [10], where you turn all your thoughts into positive ones, and imagery [4], where you imagine yourself completing the task successfully.

Another good strategy is goal setting [8], where you set goals using the SMARTER principle [9]. A coach might set performance goals rather than outcome goals, as this would be less pressure for the performer.

Examiner says

In the first paragraph points 1 and 4 on the mark scheme are credited.

Examiner says

This is a well presented answer and scores 11/14 for content.

Mark scheme

Band range	Band descriptors
11–14	• Addresses all aspects of the question, demonstrating a wide range of depth and knowledge • Expresses arguments clearly and concisely • Good use of examples to support answer • Few errors in spelling, punctuation and grammar, and correct use of technical language
7–10	• Addresses most aspects of the question while demonstrating a clear level of depth and knowledge • Attempts to express arguments clearly and concisely • Uses examples to support answer • Few errors in their spelling, punctuation and grammar, demonstrates use of technical language although sometimes inaccurately
3–6	• Addresses some aspect of the question but lacks sufficient depth and knowledge • Limited attempt to develop any arguments or discussions, normally vague or irrelevant • Attempts to use examples although not always relevant • Errors in spelling, punctuation and grammar and limited use of technical language
0–2	• Addresses the question with limited success • Little or no use of examples • Major errors in spelling, punctuation and grammar, with no use of technical language

(a) **Effects of anxiety on performance**

1. Cognitive anxiety, psychological side, e.g. nerves, worry, apprehension
2. Has a negative linear relationship with performance
3. Increase in levels of cognitive anxiety = decrease in overall performance
4. Somatic anxiety is the physiological aspect, e.g. sweaty palms, high HR
5. Has an Inverted U Theory relationship, optimal level for best performance

Strategies

1. Progressive muscle relaxation
2. Breathing techniques
3. Thought stopping
4. Visualisation/imagery
5. Mental rehearsal
6. Centring
7. Attention focussing/ cue utilisation
8. Use of goal-setting
9. Using SMART/SMARTER principles
10. Positive self-talk
11. Hypnosis

UNIT 3

Optimising performance and evaluating contemporary issues within sport

Section C: Evaluating contemporary influences

CHAPTER 15

Factors affecting the nature and development of elite performance

LEARNING OBJECTIVES:

By the end of this chapter you should be able to describe:

- *the characteristics of World Games*
- *the impact of World Games on the individual, the country and the government*
- *the stages of Sport England's sport development continuum and the factors influencing progression from one level to another*
- *the social and cultural factors required to support progression from participation to performance and excellence*
- *the role and structure of the world class performance pathway*
- *the role and purpose of the following external organisations in providing support and progression to performers moving from grass roots to elite level (including initial talent identification programmes, provision of facilities, resources and coaching):*
  1. *UK Sport*
  2. *national institutes of excellence – English Institute of Sport/equivalent home countries*
  3. *National Governing Bodies*
  4. *Sport England/Wales/Scotland/Northern Ireland*
  5. *Sportscoach UK*
  6. *British Olympic Association*
  7. *National Lottery*
  8. *Sports Aid.*

Introduction

This chapter examines the characteristics of elite sport and incorporates how various organisations provide support for athletes to perform in high status competitions such as World Games.

For the purposes of this specification we are going to:

- make a detailed study of the Olympic Games and Paralympics
- consider the nature of amateur and professional World Championships
- consider who controls these games.

The characteristics of World Games

Once an athlete reaches the highest standards of performance in his or her sport, he or she may have the opportunity to represent his or her country in the most prestigious sports competitions in the world. This is the pinnacle of the athlete's career. Numerous championships could classify as a World Game.

EXAM TIP:

World Games can be used as a base when answering questions to cover issues such as inequality, amateurism and professionalism, commercial sponsorship etc.

Characteristics of World Games
International competition/elite level
Multi-sport, e.g. Olympics or single sport, e.g. football
Global/spectator events
Media/satellite
Commercialisation – TV rights/sponsorship/corporate/ endorsements
Selection/trials – only the best/athlete preparation
Nationalism/patriotism
Political issues/boycotts/terrorism/propaganda
Officials/volunteers
Rewards/trophies
Benefits to host city/reasons to bid?
Amateur or professional
Deviancy – cheating/drugs/gamesmanship
Positive values – striving/effort/sportsmanship/bring countries together
Administration/bureaucracy, e.g. IOC
Symbols, e.g. five interconnecting rings for the Olympic Games
Meeting of cultures/multi-cultural sport events
Able-bodied/disabled – paralympic
Top facilities
Individual/team events

Table 15.01 Summary of the primary characteristics of World Games

TASK 15.01

Using Table 15.01 list the differences between an amateur World Game such as netball and a professional competition such as the football World Cup.

The impact of World Games

In order to appreciate the impact of a World Games on the individual, the country and the government it will be useful to use the London Olympic Games 2012 as a case study.

London Olympic Games 2012

On 6 July 2005 the International Olympic Committee announced that London was to host the 2012 Olympic and Paralympic Games. The Games will bring more than 28 days of sporting activity in the summer of 2012.

The London 2012 Games will provide a lasting legacy for future generations. It is hoped that the Games will help London's long-term plans for:

- economic growth
- social regeneration

Growth and regeneration

- The Olympic Park will be created by restoring large tracts of land in east London, with new green spaces and revived wetlands.
- An Olympic Village will be built and will provide 3,600 new homes after the Games have finished.
- The Games will create opportunities for businesses, bringing thousands of new jobs in sectors ranging from construction, hospitality, media and environmental services.
- The new sporting facilities to be constructed, including swimming pools, a velodrome and hockey facilities, will be available for community use following the Games.
- The games would inspire a new generation to greater sporting activity and achievement, and help to foster a healthy and active nation.
- Though the Games will be held in London other areas will also benefit, e.g. Weymouth for sailing events.

What will the Games cost?

The Mayor and the Government have agreed a public funding package of up to £2.375 billion to help meet the costs of staging the Olympic games in London in 2012. The first £2.050 billion of the funding package will be met from up to £1.5 billion from the lottery and up to £550 million from London Council Tax, which would cost the average London household (Band D) £20 a year or 38p a week.

The Mayor's vision is for London to become an exemplary sustainable world city, based on:

- strong and diverse economic growth
- social inclusivity to allow all Londoners to share in London's future success, and
- fundamental improvements in environmental management and use of resources.

KEY TERM

Sustainable development: development that is about ensuring a better quality of life for everyone, now and for generations to come. A widely used international definition is 'development which meets the needs of the present without compromising the ability of future generations to meet their own needs' (source: The Bruntland Report, 1987).

Travel

London will be a connected and convenient host city for the Olympic and Paralympic Games, with:

- 80 per cent of athletes staying within 20 minutes of their events
- five airports, including Heathrow – the best-connected airport in the world
- 10 railway lines carrying 240,000 people every hour to the Olympic Park
- 240 km of dedicated Olympic lanes in London.

Massive improvements to the transport system are planned, making it more efficient and reliable over the forthcoming years.

Health

It is hoped that the presence of the world's top athletes will inspire the population of the UK to become more active and increase their own aspirations.

The Games will provide more resources to make getting healthy in London easier as some of the sporting facilities built for the Olympic Games and Paralympic Games will be kept after the Games for use by both professional sportsmen and women and the wider community – including the Olympic Stadium, the Aquatics Centre, the Velopark, the Hockey Centre and the Indoor Sport Centre.

These facilities will provide much-needed opportunities for competitive and recreational sport for Londoners, especially those in growing communities across the Thames Gateway area of east London. They will also improve London's chance of hosting international sporting events in the future.

APPLY IT!

The Mayor has launched the *Kids Swim Free* scheme which allows children to use public swimming pools in the school holidays. Chairman of London 2012, Sebastian Coe, said that the scheme could uncover Olympians of the future.

Security issues

Some people are worried that hosting the Olympic Games could make London a target for terrorism. London is well prepared for an emergency and the prospect of such a high-profile sports event will fuel more work and resources to make the city even more secure, now, during the Games and long after.

The UK – and London especially – has unparalleled experience and expertise in pro-active multi-agency policing. The Metropolitan Police Service (MPS) is one of the largest police forces in the world and has earned an international reputation for excellence in policing and securing major public events. The MPS was involved in the seven-nation Olympic Security Advisory Group for the 2004 Olympic and Paralympic Games in Athens, so has expert knowledge of what is required to make London secure and welcoming.

APPLY IT!

Seeking a legacy for Essex

The Action Plan developed is divided into two main sections:

- Cross cutting themes
- Action areas.

Cross cutting themes	Action areas
• Young people • Equity/inclusion • Sustainability • Friendships and cooperation • Inspiration/aspiration • Entrepreneurship and innovation • Image of Essex	• Supporting volunteers • Preparation and training camps • Increasing physical activity and sports • Participation levels • Cycling development • Improving sports performance • Culture and festivals • Tourism • Ports of entry, transport and logistics • Winning 2012 Games-related and other public sector supply contracts • Business displacement • Learning and development • Weald Country Park • Thames Gateway South Essex

Table 15.02 The Essex Action Plan

Bidding to become a host city

The selection of the host city is important as the success of the Games can often be dependent on the site chosen. Each candidate city must demonstrate to the International Olympic Committee (IOC) that its bid to stage the world's greatest multi-disciplinary event has the support of its people and its political authorities.

Why should countries and cities bid for an event that will cost their citizens huge amounts of money? Reasons include:

- international recognition
- economic investment in infrastructure, tourism and attractive conference venues
- other cities in the successful country can gain through training camps
- the 'feel good' factor for a country
- the boost to participation figures that in turn will improve the health of the population

TASK 15.02

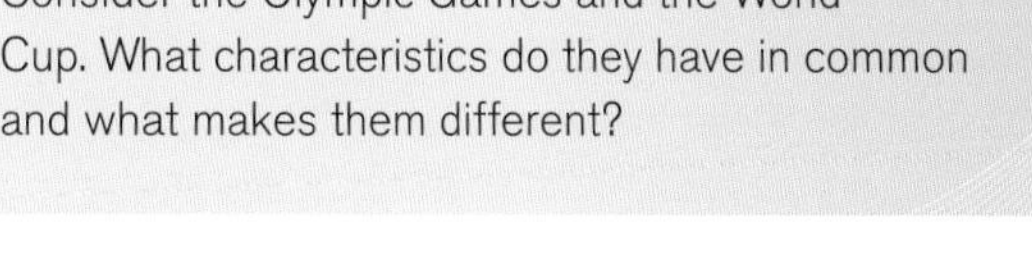

Consider the Olympic Games and the World Cup. What characteristics do they have in common and what makes them different?

- social integration and inclusion
- employment benefits
- a legacy of facilities that can be used by the community once the Games are over.

Factors required to support progression

What are the social and cultural factors required to support progression from participation to performance and excellence? In order to explore the optimisation of performance to achieve elite status we must first understand what we mean by an elite performer.

What is meant by elite sport?

Elite sport refers to performers who have reached a level of excellence according to national and international standards. For our purposes excellence will mean the superior, elite athletes at both amateur and professional level, able bodied as well as disabled, who reach the pinnacle of performance in their sport.

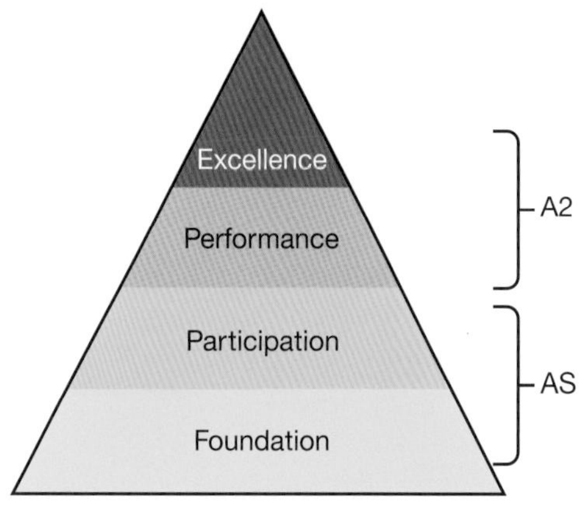

Fig 15.01 Sport participation pyramid

TASK 15.03

Outline your progress in a particular sport. Consider the factors that influenced your initial participation and those that were significant in how far you have progressed in that sport.

KEY TERMS

Elite sport:
the most talented sportsmen and women. Only a few can reach this standard of performance yet require a substantial level of funding and resources

Participation pyramid:
a model to show the development of an athlete from beginner to elite level

Grass roots sports:
sports that take place in the community at a local level

The wider the base of sport participation the more likely it is that more athletes will reach the apex. Thus, if we encourage more people to compete at the foundation and participation levels, then more elite athletes are likely to emerge (see Fig. 15.01).

However, a country should not rely on individuals to succeed purely as a result of individual initiative and circumstances, but as a result of a national policy to spot and develop talent. A truly effective national sport policy will produce champions in selected sports on a regular basis.

Elite athletes in the modern day sport world require substantial funding and support. It is therefore vital that organisations with a remit to achieve excellence in sport do their job. There is a need for all the relevant organisations to liaise and coordinate their efforts.

Why achieve excellence?

Before we go any further let us first discuss the purpose of trying to achieve excellence in the field of sport, both for the individual and society. Table 15.02 identifies some of the benefits sport can provide for both individuals and their society.

However, not all aspects of pursuing excellence in sport are positive. Consider some of the less attractive effects:

- It is only an exclusive minority who can ever reach this level of performance and yet they require substantial funding and resources which could otherwise be directed towards the foundation and participation levels.
- The moral values of sport, such as sportsmanship, have to some extent been lost as the rewards for winning have increased and the stakes become higher. Acts of deviancy, such as doping and violence, have increased.
- Over-specialisation and excessive training lead to physical and psychological damage.

Individual	Society
• Sport represents a challenge	• Sporting success can boost national pride and morale
• As a society we encourage excellence academically, e.g. in the arts	• Helps to reduce anti-social behaviour
• Sport can provide an alternative employment pathway	• Sport is big business
• It provides individuals with self-esteem and the ability to act as a role model for others	• Sport is considered a healthy pursuit which if pursued by the mass of the population will in turn reduce spending by the NHS
	• Elite sport can help boost **grass roots sport**
	• People are still curious to discover the limits of human potential

Table 15.03 Some of the benefits of sport

However, the UK is committed to developing sporting excellence as it prepares to host the Olympic Games in 2012. Never have so many questions been asked of the organisations involved in developing sporting talent.

What qualities are required for elite performance?

The first step is to discover the talent. What qualities would be needed in a performer to attract the attention of a talent scout? A performer can be considered according to his or her physical and psychological attributes.

REMEMBER!

A national government will be very interested in the perceived benefits of elite sport to its country.

Physical qualities	Psychological qualities
• natural ability • high level of fitness and health • high pain threshold • possibly preferred body type for a particular sport	• high level of competitiveness • willingness to train • commitment and sacrifice • mental toughness

Table 15.04 Qualities required for elite performance

Testing for talent

Certain physical and psychological parameters can be tested. Examples of the former would be foot speed and power potential, whilst the latter is more concerned with a performer's ability to withstand very competitive environments and could be tested via mental skills questionnaires.

Sport-specific organisations have to identify the essential characteristics of and events within their sport. They need to establish norm values, which are often adapted from accepted models based on measurements of elite performances at Olympics and World Games. The precise timing and **identification screening** is difficult to determine but there will usually be two to three phases starting in early childhood at approximately 3–8 years, then a secondary phase between 9 and 17 years where the athlete has already undergone some sport-specific training, and finally a more complex and sophisticated phase with the high calibre athletes. These phases will vary depending on the sport and the system. The information gathered is then compared to the sport specific profiles created by the sport.

The problems with this approach are:

- It does not take into account an individual's desire to win, ambition and drive – these factors may in fact be more important than the VO_2max of an individual.
- Whilst some hereditary factors can't be changed, such as height and length of limbs, others can, e.g. weight and strength through education and training.
- The **socio-economic status** and facilities available to the individual can affect the type of sport that he or she can viably participate in. For example, a child might be identified as being physically suitable for a particular sport but her family may not be able to afford for her to take up the sport.

KEY TERMS

Identification screening:
a system for the initial selection of people based on their potential to develop into an elite athlete

Socio-economic status:
the status of a person involving both economic and social factors

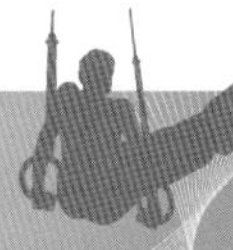

EXAM TIP:

You need to develop an understanding of the factors that determine whether an athlete will reach an elite level in his or her sport.

Social factors: The most effective talent identification programmes will be tied to the school programme as it allows wide participation, regardless of socio-economic status and the use of specialist teachers helps to alleviate the costs.

However, social factors can be just as influential in determining which sport an individual will initially begin to participate in with progression to elite levels.

Social influences: There are a number of social influences that can affect a child's participation in a particular sport:

- tradition
- ideals
- popularity of sport
- parental influence/ pressure
- teacher's speciality
- accessible facilities.

Talent identification and development programmes

Talent identification and **development** programmes need to consider:

- physiology
- **anthropometry**, e.g. height in basketball
- psychology
- hereditary factors
- sociological factors.

KEY TERMS

Talent identification:
a process by which children are encouraged to participate in the sports at which they are most likely to succeed, based on testing certain parameters. These parameters are designed to predict performance capacity, taking into account the child's current level of fitness and maturity (Peltola 1992)

Anthropometry:
the scientific measurement of the human body

Talent development:
the progression of a talented individual within a coordinated sport structure

We have already mentioned the connection that exists between the participation level and the excellence level on the participation pyramid. That is, the larger the base of participation the more likely it is that a greater number of athletes will filter towards the apex. Therefore it is important that the base of talent identification is widened. One of the best methods is to centre the search in schools as this is the best way of reaching a maximum number of children. Also, the sports themselves need to become more democratic by reducing the incidents of discrimination, be it racial, sexual or class-based. One sign of how skewed British sport is can be demonstrated by the fact that 60 per cent of Olympic medals at the Sydney Olympics were won by athletes who had been educated at private schools, despite only 7 per cent of the population being educated privately.

Systematic talent identification programmes

Traditionally most countries have waited for athletes to identify themselves as a result of success in competition, but this may not be good enough for modern sport. Some countries have developed scientific methods to identify talented individuals and to help individuals choose the sport most suited to their abilities. This then becomes a **systematic policy** of talent identification and it is not new. It has operated in countries from the **Eastern bloc** and China since the 1960s and 1970s.

KEY TERMS

Systematic policy:
a policy that has been developed methodically in an organised, coherent manner

Eastern bloc:
the Soviet Union (USSR) and the countries it controlled in central and eastern Europe. This included East Germany (GDR)

Advantages	Disadvantages
It helps to accelerate an individual's progress to an elite level	Large numbers of young people need to be tested to produce valid results
It helps an individual to select a sport to which he or she is most suited	An expert coach's 'eye' can still be the best guide
It helps a coach to concentrate training methods on the most suitable athletes	It requires substantial funding
It allows a country to get the best from its resources (it can select the sport it is best suited to developing, e.g. Switzerland and skiing, and Kenya with running	It can be difficult to reliably predict future development from a young age
	Talented children generally exhibit all-round ability so it is difficult to direct them at a specific sport early on
	Specialism before the age of 13 years can be considered dangerous both physically and psychologically

Table 15.05 The advantages and disadvantages of a systematic programme

During the 1972 Olympics quite a few medallists were scientifically selected by the GDR system. The system's features included:

- a high level of organisation and structure
- a compulsory programme of PE in schools
- the early identification of sport talent
- a club system for talented individuals in separate sports
- the ruthless elimination of those who did not 'measure up'
- a scientific approach to elite performance training
- long-range objectives
- selected schools which had to support talent scouting competition separated into age groups
- substantial financial and material support
- 2000 training centres, 70,000 young people and 10,000 full-time coaches.

In its preparation for the 2008 Olympic Games Beijing adopted similar features to that of the GDR system.

Characteristics of elite sport development systems

Oakley and Green (2003) suggest that talent identification and development programmes should have the following characteristics to be effective:

- clear delineation (clearly defined roles) and understanding of the agencies involved, and effective communication between them to maintain the system
- simplicity of administration through sporting and political boundaries
- talent identification monitoring systems
- provision of sports services to create a culture of excellence in which all members of the team (athletes, coaches, scientists and managers) can interact
- well structured competitive programmes with ongoing international exposure
- well developed facilities with priority for elite athletes
- targeting of resources on focus sports
- comprehensive planning for each sport's needs
- recognition that excellence costs in terms of capital and revenue expenditure
- lifestyle support during and post elite performance phase of an athlete's career.

How does this compare to the system in the UK? What is the track record of the UK in developing sporting excellence?

Traditionally, the UK has lacked a co-ordinated, strategic plan to develop talent. This process began to take shape in the 1980s with a national organisation responsible for coaching being established, now known as Sports Coach UK. The key to achieving a nationally co-ordinated plan is for all the agencies involved to work together, integrating the support services of sport science, sport medicine, coaching, lifestyle coaching and technology.

Traditionally in the UK, school sport has been the base of the competitive organised structure. Does it still provide this base since the decline in school sport in the 1980s? If not, how can an elite sport policy at junior level be implemented?

This is not such a problem in Germany and the Netherlands, where clubs have always provided this base. Other European countries have adopted a **centralised** strategic approach to elite sport at an earlier stage than the UK, one example being France.

Turning to gender, the gap between male and female performances has narrowed in Italy, France and the Netherlands,. Therefore they show more overall improvements as an overall team. In the UK the performance gap between men and women has widened (except in sailing and equestrianism).

Countries with successful systems produce winners in the same events year on year. In medal terms we need a strategy of converting bronze and silver medals to GOLD!

KEY TERMS

Centralised:
to draw under central control. State legislation coordinates and supports policies

EXAM TIP:

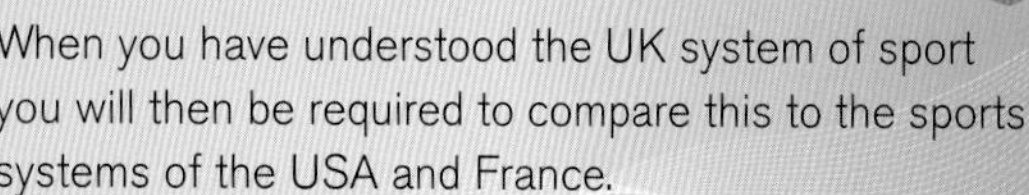

When you have understood the UK system of sport you will then be required to compare this to the sports systems of the USA and France.

TASK 15.04

Read through Oakley and Green's characteristics of elite sport development systems and extract key points to answer the following questions:

1 What should an effective talent identification and development programme contain?
2 If you were in charge of your sport, what measures would you take to ensure the effective development of elite athletes?

Role of external organisations

There are a number of external organisations that have a role in providing support and progression to performers moving from grass roots to elite level (including initial talent identification programmes, provision of facilities, resources and coaching). These are described here.

UK Sport

The primary aim of UK Sport (founded in 1997) is the development of Britain's elite athletes together with a countrywide policy for the prevention and testing of doping and it is responsible for attracting and running major sporting events. It is funded jointly via the government and lottery cash worth £30 million a year. The money is used to either support elite athletes directly or fund the back-up services they need such as medical care.

Anatomy of a world class athlete: A useful way of looking at the requirements of developing world class athletes is the UK Sport's Anatomy of an athlete:

- **Talent identification** – includes Sporting Giants; Girls4Gold; Pitch to Podium
- **Performance lifestyle** – deals with life as an athlete; work/life balance; financial and time management; media handling

- **Coaching** – preparation; peaking; liaison with sports scientists
- **Research and innovation** – £1.5million per year – equipment; facilities; training science; coaching tools; medical management
- **Sports science and medicine** – injury prevention; rehabilitation; finite edge over competitors; physiotherapy; sports medicine; physiology; soft tissue therapy; strength and conditioning; performance analysis; biomechanics; psychology and nutrition
- **Programme** – World Class Performance Programme provides funding for coaching, travelling, access to best training facilities; access to private medical scheme.

EXAM TIP:

For the purposes of PHED 3, UK Sport is more relevant than Sport England for the development of elite sport.

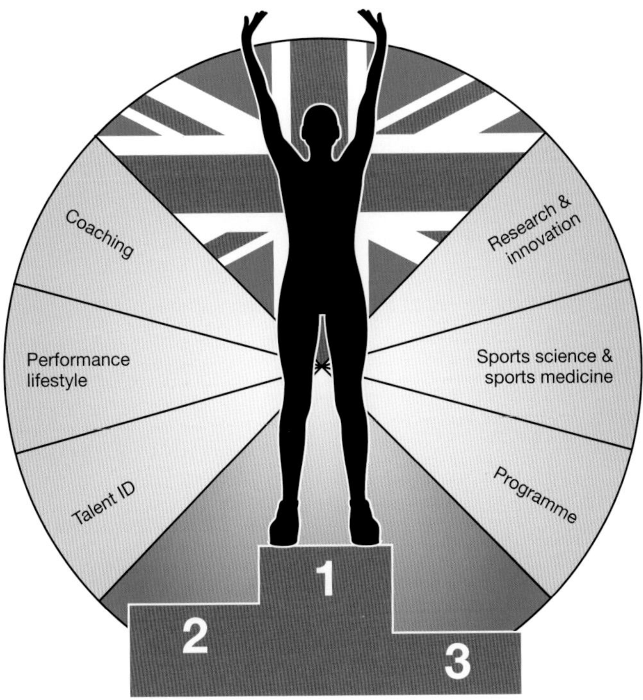

Fig 15.02 Anatomy of a world class athlete

UK Sport has a remit to:

- encourage and develop higher standards of sporting excellence in the UK
- identify sporting policies that should have a UK-wide application
- identify areas of unnecessary bureaucracy (overly rigid or complex procedures)
- develop and deliver appropriate grant programmes in conjunction with the governing bodies and home county sport councils
- oversee policy on sport science, sports medicine, drug control, coaching and other areas where there is a need for a consistent UK-wide policy
- coordinate policy for attracting major international events to the UK
- represent the UK internationally and increase the influence of the UK at an international level.

APPLY IT!

Girls4Gold

Phase One testing for the Girls4Gold Talent Identification Programme came to an end in 2008 as over 300 Olympic hopefuls rose to the challenge in Loughborough in the hope that they may discover they have the potential for 2012 medal success in the sports of cycling, rowing, canoeing, windsurfing, modern pentathlon or bob skeleton.

Hot off the heels of their success in Beijing, Dave Brailsford, the Performance Director of British Cycling, alongside his team of elite coaches came to cast their eyes over the applicants, to see whether there were any budding Rebecca Romeros or Victoria Pendletons in the making.

Girls4Gold is a joint initiative between UK Sport, the English Institute of Sport (EIS) in partnership with the six targeted Olympic sports. Following the launch of the initiative, led by Olympians Victoria Pendleton and Shelley Rudman in June, over 900 17 to 25-year-old women had applied to the initiative by the end of the same month. However, following the huge interest in Girls4Gold as a result of the success of Team GB in Beijing, the application deadline was extended, attracting a further 400 applications.

The World Class Performance Pathway
This will operate at three key levels:

- **World Class Podium** – this programme will support sports with realistic medal capabilities at the next Olympic/Paralympic Games (i.e. a maximum of four years away from the podium).
- **World Class Development** – this programme is designed to support the stage of the pathway immediately beneath the podium. It will comprise of sports that have demonstrated they have realistic medal winning capabilities for 2012.
- **World Class Talent** – this programme is designed to support the identification and confirmation of athletes who have the potential to progress through the World Class Pathway with the help of targeted investment. Olympic athletes will be a maximum of eight years away from the podium, but it could be much less for paralympic athletes.

There are issues with the World Class Performance Pathway, at the time of writing, for instance:

- There is roughly a £60m gap between what is needed to deliver medals in 2012 and what is on the table.
- Of the £600m assigned to the sports, over half is coming from the Lottery. The government has promised £220m.
- Finally, it has always been assumed that the 'private sector' will chip in £100m to complete the picture, but this has been lowered first to £80m (due to the Lottery increase) and then to £60m.
- In the present financial climate almost every company will scrutinise anything that means spending money that isn't vital. Small commercial enterprises are unlikely to raise the full £60m.
- The London organisers (LOCOG) have already sold large rights to Adidas, Lloyds and BP amongst others.
- The individuals and their sports are already selling themselves to the hilt.
- Rowing, sailing, cycling, swimming and athletics already have commercial tie-ins that preclude another layer of sponsorship, and the Hoys and Adlingtons of the team are for once earning decent money.
- Badminton, hockey, shooting, archery spent a grand total of over £25m between them and came home from Beijing without a medal.

KEY TERMS

World Class Performance Pathway:
from 1 April 2006, UK Sport assumed full responsibility for all Olympic and Paralympic performance-related sport in England, from the identification of talent all the way through to performing at the top level

APPLY IT!

Some 1500 of the nation's leading athletes at the Podium and Development levels alone benefit from an annual investment of £100m (comprising both National Lottery and Government Exchequer funds), with many more involved at the Talent level. The Programme works by ensuring that athletes get the support – delivered through their sport's national governing body – that they need at every stage of their development.

APPLY IT!

World Class Events

Through our National Lottery funded World Class Events Programme UK Sport are investing some £20 million into UK hosted events between 2006 and 2012, and have identified 28 World Championships and 27 European Championships that we will be investigating bidding for and staging over the next few years. Indeed, in 2008, UK Sport is supporting 17 events, including a record six World Championships.

UK Sport has four key directorates through which it carries out these tasks:

1. performance development (advises governing bodies and allocates funding)
2. UK Sports Institute (central services based in London with regional network centres)
3. international relations and major events (the UK needs to be in a strong position given the benefits that accrue from major sporting events)
4. ethics and anti-doping (coordination of an effective testing programme and coach education).

Significant changes to the sporting system took effect from 1 April 2006. UK Sport assumed full responsibility for all Olympic and Paralympic performance-related support in England and the UK, from the identification of talent all the way through to performing at the top level.
Source: www.uksport.gov.uk/

APPLY IT!

Talented Athlete Scholarship Scheme (TASS)

The scheme fast tracks young sporting talent, the potential medal winners of the future, and is specifically designed to cater for the special needs of athletes within the education system, aiming to reduce the drop out of athletes caused by academic and financial pressures.

Organisations such as the EIS, Sport England, SportsAid, UK Sport, University College Sport and the National Governing Bodies are all involved in this scheme.

The transfer of the World Class Potential programme in England, together with responsibility for the direction of the Talented Athlete Scholarship Scheme (TASS), TASS 2012 Scholarships and the English Institute of Sport, integrates the funding and management of high performance sport and provides for the first time, a one-stop-shop for governing bodies and athletes. UK Sport can now have a meaningful impact on decisions across the pathway and ensure that resources are targeted where they are most required.

In taking on this new responsibility, and remaining focused on a 'no compromise' approach, UK Sport has redefined the terms under which funding and support will be provided. It will operate on three key levels under the umbrella of the World Class Performance Pathway (see page 226).

Combined with the announcement in the April 2006 budget that much higher amounts of funding would be made available for high performance sport through to 2012, UK Sport now has the best possible environment to effect change, deliver its ambitions and make a real difference to athlete support in this country. UK Sport is able to start to work towards the 'ultimate goal' – fourth place in the 2012 Olympic medal table, and first in the Paralympic medal table.
Source: www.uksport.gov.uk/

National institutes of excellence

United Kingdom Sports Institute

The aim of the United Kingdom Sports Institute is to provide elite British sportspeople with the practical and professional support needed to compete on the world stage. Each Home Country has its own institute.

The English Institute of Sport (EIS) is a nationwide network of world class support services, designed to foster the talents of elite athletes in the UK. Services are offered from nine regional multi-sport hub sites and an evolving network of satellite centres.

High performance training venues are the platform for success. Led by Steve Cram, the former World mile record holder and Olympic medallist, it is a dynamic, pro-active organisation dedicated to realising the potential of the modern competitor.

The strategy and ethos of the EIS is set by its national team. The services are delivered by a co-ordinated network of regional teams which feature complementary skills and experience.

The range of services supplied by the EIS includes:

- the primary services of sports science and sports medicine
- support including applied physiology, biomechanics, medical consultation, medical screening, nutritional advice, performance analysis, psychology, **podiatry**, strength and conditioning coaching, sports massage and sports vision
- the Performance Lifestyle programme which provides supplementary career and education advice.

The quality of the delivery is assured by the close relationship the EIS is developing with national governing bodies, performance directors, coaches and the athletes themselves. Almost 2000 competitors are currently in the EIS system.

Funded by the Sport England Lottery fund, the EIS operates under the directorship of Wilma Shakespear, a pivotal figure in the development of the Australian Institute System embodied in the EIS ethos – 'making the best better'.

Source: www.eis2win.co.uk

TASK 15.05

The EIS is based on a regional rather than a 'one centre' approach. Discuss the advantages and disadvantages of this approach.

sports council wales
cyngor chwaraeon cymru

The Welsh Institute of Sport is located within Cardiff City Centre parkland. Since opening in 1972, the Welsh Institute of Sport's remit is to provide facilities to help develop excellence in Welsh sport extends to providing excellence in facility management.

The role of the Institute has been gradually changing since its inception with a greater emphasis being placed upon the provision of services for the top echelon of sports men and women throughout Wales.

The Institute has a long history of co-operation with other partner organisations with a view to producing the best quality services available in the most efficient and effective manner possible. This is highlighted by the provision of office facilities for both National Governing Body Coaches and the Federation of Disability Sport Wales. These contacts have helped the Institute stay firmly in tune with its end user whether it be an Olympic athlete or a casual squash player and has led to a level of customer care not often seen in a sports centre of this size.

Source: www.welsh-institute-sport.co.uk/

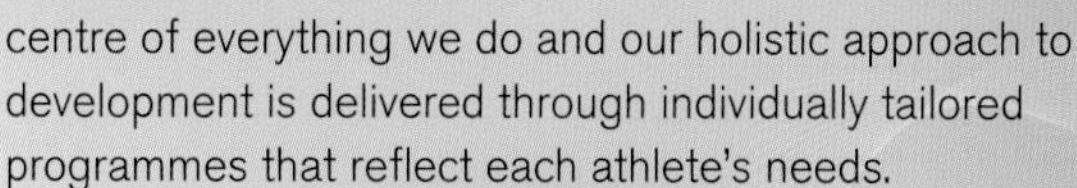

The Scottish Institute of Sport is nurturing Scotland's sporting talent to deliver world class performances. Athletes are at the centre of everything we do and our holistic approach to development is delivered through individually tailored programmes that reflect each athlete's needs.

A hub of expert support service providers work together to manage and deliver cutting edge programmes in coaching, technical support, sports medicine, sports science, strength and conditioning, and career and lifestyle guidance.

CREATING WINNERS

Since 1998, Institute-supported athletes have achieved 11 World Champions, 2 Olympic Gold medals, 4 Olympic Silver medals, and many more.

IDENTIFYING TALENT

A pilot initiative used the T-CUP technique to get our coaches and athletes thinking like winners.

Source: www.sisport.com/sisport/

TASK 15.06

What are the similarities and differences between the aims of the different Home Country Sports councils

National Governing Bodies

There are approximately 300 governing bodies in the UK. Many are run by unpaid volunteers, though depending on the size of the organisation this has in many cases become the responsibility of paid administrators. They are largely autonomous from government and are represented by the Central Council for Physical Recreation (CCPR) to Sport England.

National governing bodies are responsible for overseeing their own sport in the country. There is no set pro forma for governing bodies: some are large, some are wealthy whilst others are not. However, there are some common aims, including to:

- establish rules and regulations in accordance with the International Sport Federation (ISF)
- organise competitions
- develop coaching awards and leadership schemes
- select teams for country or UK at international events
- liaise with relevant organisations such as the CCPR, Sport England, local clubs, British Olympic Association and International Sport Federations.

Challenges for governing bodies

- New sports are attracting participants and providing competition for the older, more established sports.
- The decline in school sport has led to governing bodies having to consider how best to develop talent.
- There has been a blurring in definition of amateur and professional sport.
- The need to compete internationally with countries who have developed systematic forms of training has made the governing bodies develop the coaching and structuring of competitions and devote more money to the training of their elite sportspeople.
- Funding has become a key issue. National governing bodies receive money from their member clubs but elite sport requires huge sums of money. For this the governing bodies have had to market themselves in the modern world, especially in trying to attract television coverage which in turn brings in sponsorship deals.
- Lottery funding often brings with it certain requirements such as meeting government targets of participation and developing talent.
- NGBs must produce **whole sport plans (WSPs)**.

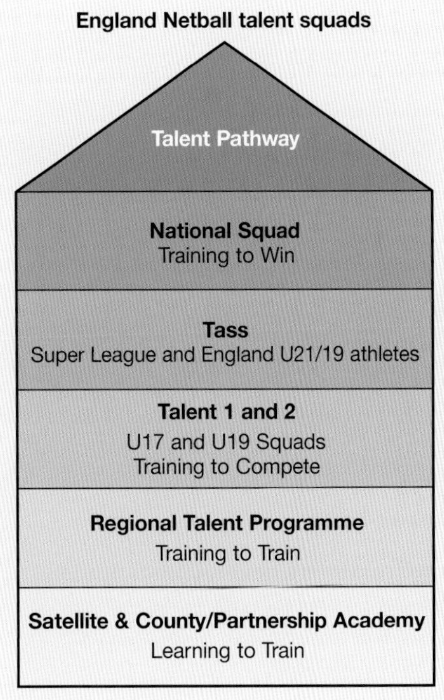

Fig 15.03 Performance athlete development model

What are whole sport plans (WSPs)?

- A whole sport plan (WSP) is a plan for the whole of a sport from grass roots right through to the elite level, that identifies how it will achieve its vision and how it will contribute to Sport England's 'start, stay and succeed' objectives.
- WSPs are Sport England's new way of directing funding and resources to NGBs.
- WSPs will identify the help and resources NGBs need to deliver their whole sport plans, for example, via partners such as county sports partnerships and programmes (e.g. the Physical Education and School Sport and Club Links Strategy (**PESSCLS**). They will give us the opportunity to measure how the NGBs are delivering their sports.

What will WSPs achieve?

- In short, 'grow, sustain, excel' (Sport England's objectives).
- The WSPs will allow Sport England to give focused investments to NGBs against the resources they need to achieve their objectives.
- Measurable results will give us an indication of how well NGBs are performing and whether Sport England is getting value for money from our investment.
- Whole sport plans will help create more links with regions and partners in all aspects of sport, benefiting us all through shared best practice.

KEY TERMS

Performance athlete development model:
a ten-year development programme based on the achievement of standards rather than an age-related framework

Whole sport plan (WSP):
a WSP is a plan for the whole of a sport from grass roots right through to the elite level, that identifies how it will achieve is vision and how it will contribute to Sport England's 'start, stay and succeed' objectives

PESSCLS:
a major government policy to improve the links between schools and local sports clubs

APPLY IT!

Development Plan for Gymnastics in England 2005–2009

Strategic objectives for English Gymnastics are:

- Increase NGB-led participation in gymnastics by 12 per cent by 2009
- Increase suitable qualified coaches from 31,000 to 45,000
- Increase the number of volunteers and officials
- Increase the number of affiliated and accredited clubs, providing requisite support
- Ensure child protection policies are in place and implemented
- Raise the level of performance range of opportunities in each discipline of gymnastics
- Improve the profile and marketing of gymnastics at country, regional and local level.

Sport England/Wales/Scotland/Northern Ireland

Sport England is the government agency responsible for developing a world-class community sports system. It is involved in the World Class programme, academies and institutes with sport college status.

Grow, Sustain, Excel: Sport England Strategy 2008–2011

The strategy commits Sport England to deliver on a series of demanding targets by 2012/13:

- one million more people doing more sport
- a 25 per cent reduction in the number of 16 year olds who drop out of five key sports
- improved talent development systems in at least 25 sports
- a measurable increase in people's satisfaction with their experience of sport – the first time the organisation has set such a qualitative measure
- a major contribution to the delivery of the five hour sports offer for children and young people.

Sport England is working closely with the national governing bodies of sport to deliver the new strategy, and will also build strong partnerships with local authorities.

Sport England will also reduce bureaucracy by combining its multiple funding strategies into a single pot of funding for governing bodies.

Source: www.sportengland.org

sports council wales
cyngor chwaraeon cymru

The Sports Council for Wales is the national organisation responsible for developing and promoting sport and active lifestyles. It is the main adviser on sporting matters to the Welsh Assembly Government and is responsible for distributing funds from the National Lottery to sport in Wales.

The Council fully subscribes to the Welsh Assembly Government's vision for a physically active and sporting nation, as outlined in its strategy document 'Climbing Higher'. Its main focus is to increase the frequency of participation by persuading those who are currently sedentary to become more active and to encourage people, young and old, to develop a portfolio of activities through which to achieve healthy levels of activity.

The themes of the Council's work are:

- active young people
- active communities – developing people and places
- developing performance and excellence

Source: www.sports-council-wales.org

TASK 15.07

Research into the success or otherwise of the Development Plan for Gymnastics.

Sport Scotland is the national agency for sport in Scotland. Their mission is to encourage everyone in Scotland to discover and develop their own sporting experience, helping to increase participation and improve performances in Scottish sport.

They operate three National Centres: Glenmore Lodge, Inverclyde and Cumbrae. The centres provide quality, affordable, residential and sporting facilities and services for the development of people in sport.

They also act as the parent company of the Scottish Institute of Sport (SIS) (see page 226) which prepares Scotland's best athletes to perform on the world stage by providing performance planning expertise and individually tailored programmes for Scottish Governing Bodies and athletes.

Vision

We passionately believe in the benefits of sport, from the enjoyment and sense of achievement that participation brings, to the shared pride that national success generates.

We are committed to the development of safe sport for all people in Scotland.

Three principles underpin all of our work:

- Developing a sporting infrastructure
- Creating effective sporting pathways
- Embedding ethics and equity throughout sport.

Source: www.sportscotland.org.uk

Sport Northern Ireland is a lead facilitator in the development of sport and will work with partners to:

- increase and sustain committed participation, especially amongst young people
- raise the standards of sporting excellence and promote the good reputation and efficient administration of sport

Sport NI's aims will be achieved by developing the competencies of its staff who are dedicated to optimising the use of its resources.

Its main partners include:

- district councils
- education and library boards
- governing bodies of sport
- government departments and statutory agencies
- voluntary clubs and organisations
- the education sector
- the commercial sector.

Sport NI is also responsible for distributing Lottery Sports Fund awards.

Sport NI is part of a broad Sport network and has a close relationship with its equivalent organisations in England, Scotland and Wales, as well as the UK Sports Council, which has responsibility for UK-wide sport.

Source: www.sportni.net

Sportscoach UK

Sportscoach UK provides a range of educational and advisory services for all coaches, and works alongside the award schemes of the individual governing bodies. It runs the 16 national coaching centres which are primarily based in institutions of higher education. The aims of the organisation are to:

- lead and develop the national standards of coaching
- work with organisations such as local authorities, national governing bodies, the British Olympic Association and higher education to improve the standards and professional development of coaches
- provide high quality education programmes, products and services such as coaching literature, videos, seminars and worksheets, factsheets and databases.

It also runs **Coachwise Ltd**, Sports Coach UK's wholly-owned trading company.

What should a high quality coach education programme contain? This includes:

- sport-specific knowledge (techniques/strategies)
- performance-related knowledge (fitness/ nutrition/mental preparation)
- ethics and philosophy (codes of practice)
- management/vocational skills (planning/ time/money)
- teaching/coaching methodology (communication skills)
- practical coaching experience.

The **UK Coaching Framework** was officially launched in 2008, and highlights how SportsCoach UK plans to work in close partnership with the Governing Bodies of Sport and each of the Home Country Sports Councils to enhance the quality of coaches at all levels. It aims to achieve its goals over three main phases:

- 2005–2008 (three years from start date)
- 2009–2012 (seven years from start date) and
- 2013–2016 (11 years from start date).

The objectives are to:

- help coaches play a key role in increasing sport participation
- improve sport performances
- build a career structure for coaches.

The **UK Coaching Certificate** is an initiative to endorse coach education programmes, across sports within the UK, against agreed criteria including:

- endorsement of the coaching qualification a coach will take
- development of appropriate resources to deliver effective and high quality coach education programmes

- quality assured administration and management structure of coach education provision provided by sports
- quality assured training provision of coach education programmes

British Olympic Association

The **British Olympic Association (BOA)** is a National Olympic Committee (NOC). The International Olympic Committee requires each country to have its own Olympic committee. The BOA is one of 205 NOCs currently recognised by the International Olympic Committee (IOC).

The BOA provides the pivot around which Team GB revolves prior to, and during, the Olympic Games. Working with the Olympic Governing Bodies, the BOA selects Team GB from the best sportsmen and women who will go on to compete in the 28 summer and 7 winter Olympic sports at the greatest sporting competition in the world.

The BOA now includes as its members the 35 National Governing Bodies of each Olympic sport.

The British Olympic Association is free from government control and traditionally receives no money from the government. Its aims are to:

- encourage interest in the Olympic Games
- foster the ideals of the Olympic movement
- organise and coordinate British participation in terms of travel and equipment of competitors and officials
- assist the governing bodies of sport in preparation of their competitions
- advise on public relations with the press
- provide a forum for consultation among governing bodies
- organise an Olympic day in the UK
- raise funds through the British Olympic appeal, mainly from private sources, business sponsors and the general public
- advise on training, nutrition and sports psychology for Olympic coaches
- provide medical and careers advice for athletes
- sponsor medical research into fitness and athletic injuries.

The British Olympic Association runs various programmes and facilities to meet the needs of Team GB athletes throughout the four-year Olympic cycle.

- **Olympic Medical Institute** – ensures that Team GB athletes have access to the best, sports-specific medical advice, whenever they need it.
- **Olympic Training Centre** – provides a world class training and preparation facility for the dedicated use of British high performance athletes, coaches and support staff from across the sporting spectrum. Situated in the picturesque alpine village of Lofer, Austria.
- **Olympic and Paralympic Employment Network (OPEN)** – assists athletes in their quest to establish career-path employment alongside their sporting ambitions.
- **Performance Lifestyle** – programme designed to help athletes balance all other aspects of their life with their sport.
- **Olympic Passport Scheme** – allows elite athletes access to national and local sports centres at reduced costs and provides a range of other beneficial services.
- **Athlete Medical Scheme** – provides comprehensive medical cover to over 1,500 nominated and potential Team GB members, ensuring the athletes have access to the best sports-specific medical advice when it is needed.
- **Planning for Success Workshops** – gives Olympic athletes the opportunity to benefit from the advice and experience of seasoned Olympians to help with goal setting and time management throughout the Olympic cycle.
- **BritishOlympians.com** – a network of Team GB athletes available for commercial appearances including after dinner and motivational speaking.
- **British Olympic Foundation** – is the charitable arm of the BOA, committed to inspiring through sport and education.
- **Arena DMC** – is a Cyprus-based Sports Training Service Company, the officially appointed Ground Handling Operator in Cyprus for the British Olympic Association & Team GB since November 2002.

- **Coral Beach Hotel and Resort, Paphos, Cyprus** – the British Olympic Association's official warm weather training facility in Europe, was used as a holding camp for Team GB prior to the Athens 2004 Olympic Games.

REMEMBER!

The aim is to finish 4th in the overall medal table in 2012.

The British Olympic Association belongs to the International Olympic Committee (IOC). It is the umbrella organisation of the Olympic movement whose primary responsibility is the regular staging of the summer and winter games. The role of the executive board is to:

- observe the Olympic charter
- administer the IOC
- attend to all internal affairs of the organisation
- manage the finances
- inform the session of any rule changes or bye-laws.

Hotlinks
Find out more about the International Olympic Committee at www.olympic.org.

REMEMBER!

The BOA is unusual in receiving no direct government funding. This has its advantages and disadvantages.

The National Lottery

The National Lottery Sports fund has earmarked £20.5 million a year for UK Sport to administer to our top UK medal hopes through the World Class Performance Programme and to help attract and stage major sporting events in the UK.

World Class Performance Programme (WCPP) athletes originate from all corners of Great Britain. The breakdown of the Olympic and Paralympic squads indicates that over the four-year period they have remained broadly static in terms of country representation.

The tables show that around 30 per cent of athletes on the WCPP are athletes with a disability of some kind. This is a proud reflection of the world class success of Paralympians and the priority given to funding Paralympic sport by UK Sport.

OLYMPIC	2001 (%)	2002 (%)	2003 (%)	2004 (%)	2005 (%)	Avg. (%)
England	351 (89.5)	363 (87.5)	347 (88.5)	322 (88.2)	280 (87.2)	333 (88.3)
NI	2 (0.5)	3 (0.7)	1 (0.3)	1 (0.3)	1 (0.3)	2 (0.5)
Scotland	24 (6.1)	31 (7.5)	29 (7.4)	25 (6.8)	23 (7.2)	26 (6.9)
Wales	15 (3.8)	18 (4.3)	15 (3.8)	17 (4.7)	17 (5.3)	16 (4.2)
	392	415	392	365	321	377

PARALYMPIC	2001(%)	2002 (%)	2003 (%)	2004 (%)	2005 (%)	Avg. (%)
England	162 (79.8)	146 (81.1)	138 (80.7)	118 (80.3)	102 (76.1)	133 (79.6)
NI	0 (0.0)	0 (0.0)	0 (0.0)	0 (0.0)	0 (0.0)	0 (0)
Scotland	23 (11.3)	20 (11.1)	17 (9.9)	14 (9.5)	14 (10.4)	18 (10.8)
Wales	18 (8.9)	14 (7.8)	16 (9.4)	15 (10.2)	18 (13.4)	16 (9.6)
	203	180	171	147	134	167

Table 15.06 Athletes on the World Class Performance Programme

Category	Female	per cent	Male	per cent	Total
Olympic	126	43.8	162	56.3	288
Paralympic	40	32	85	68	125
Non-Olympic	–		6	100	6
Total	166	39.6	253	60.4	419

Table 15.07 Male and female athletes on the World Class Performance Programme, 2005

In terms of gender, some 40 per cent of the athletes on the WCPP are female, an indication of the contribution made by sportswomen to sport in the UK. The figures, as at May 2005 when 419 athletes were on the programme, are shown in Table 15.06.

The WCPP makes a positive effort to support world class events in all four home countries, and encourages applications from under-represented groups that meet the criteria.

'I wouldn't be where I am today – I wouldn't have achieved a World Championship gold medal or an Olympic silver medal. There's no chance that I would achieved these goals because it's simply not possible at this level without the support I've received through Lottery funding.' (Chris Hoy went on to win the gold medal in the Cycling 1km time trial in Athens in 2004and won three gold medals in the keirin, individual sprint and team sprint in Beijing in 2008.)

Advantages	Disadvantages
• UK medal winners have increased • Feel good factor for the country • Visible role models for the youth • Health benefits • Social benefits – social inclusion; enhance international reputation of UK • Success helps generate private sector investment • Helps us stage world class events which keep the UK in a more controlling position in world sport • Legacy of facilities, equipment and development initiatives • Increased participation and volunteering • Economic impact – Direct: measurable increased spend in the local community – Indirect: increased tourism, subsequent investment • A 'no compromise' approach means only athletes with realistic hopes will be funded	• Money could be spent on education and health • Tax payers' money mean athletes and organisations should be accountable • Major events tend to be in specific areas so the whole country does not benefit equally • People feel they will not be good enough so don't participate

Table 15.08 Advantages and disadvantages of Lottery Funding

The planned investment in World Class Performance and World Class Operations (a programme underpinning the WCPP) for 2005–09 showing a total investment of £97.8 million, which compares favourably with the period 2001–05 when the total WCPP investment was £92 million.

APPLY IT!

Over the whole of the UK since 1997, Lottery commitments of £13.9 million have been made to staging some 100 major events under the WCPP with total staging costs amounting to £55.5 million.

Economic impact

These include an economic impact of £3.16 million from the 2003 World Indoor Athletic Championships in Birmingham, on which Lottery investment was over £1.1 million; and an economic impact of £1.67 million from the 2003 World Cup Triathlon in Manchester on a Lottery investment of £40,000.

STRETCH AND CHALLENGE

What impact does a World Games, such as the Olympic Games, have on an elite athlete and the host country?

Sports Aid

Sports Aid was established to enable top amateur athletes (at both junior and senior level) to train with similar privileges enjoyed by state sponsored athletes abroad. It is a self-financing organisation, similar to the British Olympic Association, which draws funds from commercial, industrial and private sponsors and fund raising projects. Outstanding competitors usually receive the money. They receive grants according to their personal needs, the costs of their preparation, training and competition, and are usually recommended by their governing body. Since 1976 over £5 million has been given to more than 5,000 competitors. Grants are awarded through Sport Aid's charitable trust to talented athletes who are in education, on a low income or have disabilities.

Sports Aid has three main objectives:

1. To further the education of young people through the medium of sport.
2. To encourage those with a social or physical disadvantage to improve their lives through sport.
3. To enable those living in poverty to take advantage of the opportunities offered by sport.

A typical grant is £500 a year. To qualify, athletes would be between 12 and 18 years old, in genuine financial need and a member of a national squad.

HOT LINKS

Find out more about Sports Aid at www.sportsaid.org.uk

ATHLETE PROFILE

Rochelle Plumb is a member of the European Ladies Senior Horseball Team. She has reached the higher levels of her sport and can therefore be classed as an elite performer. She has represented Britain at the Junior and Ladies European Cup. The World Pato-Horseball Championship is something she still aspires to. It is being considered as a potential Olympic sport. In 2008 the Ladies Team gained the Silver Medal in the European Championships held at Ponte de Lima.

Pato-Horseball is a mixture of rugby, polo and basketball played on horseback. A ball is handled and points are scored by shooting it through a high net (approximately 1.5 m by 1.5m). It is one of the ten disciplines officially recognised by the International Equestrian Federation. It has gained a high profile and its success has spread across Europe and overseas.

Over the last 17 years, the British Horseball Association has gone from strength to strength, hosting an open championships competition, an annual league of senior and junior matches, regional, riding school and university competitions, as well as local friendly training, games, camps and social events.

Rochelle is studying Human Biology at Loughborough University and is having to manage her time effectively in order to train and compete. Rochelle's choice of university was very much based on the fact that she could continue with her horseball training. The university is considering the possibility of raising a horseball team.

Fig 15.04 The British Horseball Association is a member body of the British Equestrian Federation and the Federation of International Horseball

ExamCafé

Relax, refresh, result!

Refresh your memory

Revision checklist

Make sure you know the following:

- World Games are the pinnacles of sporting achievement and as such are the focal point for commercial marketing and sponsorship, vehicles for political propaganda and individual ambition.
- Sport policy in the UK is characterised by a high degree of inconsistency and includes many organisations which are involved in creating and carrying out policies.
- Sport organisations need to continue to evolve to meet the needs of the modern athlete in the modern sport world.
- The broader the base of the sport participation pyramid the greater the talent pool to draw upon in order to maximise the chances of sporting excellence.
- The political and economic investment in elite sport needs to be coherent and have staying power.
- The National Sport Institutes of the four home countries, though different, share similar characteristics as Centres of Excellence such as high levels of facilities, coaching and support services.
- There has been a steady expansion in the internationalisation of sport, and this has brought challenges for the national governing bodies (NGB) to adjust their rules and take note of the international sporting calendar.
- The pattern of funding for sport in the UK is dominated by sponsorship. Government grants (local and central) and funds from the governing bodies and private individuals make the next share. Relatively small but important market niches are funded by SportsAid and BOA.
- People from ethnic minorities, low socio-economic groups and women face more barriers in their struggle to reach elite levels in sport than those from the dominant groups.

Revise as you go

1. Give six characteristics of the Olympic Games as an example of a World Game.
2. Give three reasons why a city would bid to host the Olympic Games and three examples of how participating in a World Game can have on an impact on an athlete.
3. Explain the stages of the World Class Performance Pathway
4. Draw the sport participation pyramid and briefly explain each stage.
5. What reasons can the government have for investing in elite sport?
6. What personal factors can determine the level to which an athlete may succeed in a sport?
7. Define the term 'talent identification'.
8. What characteristics should an effective talent identification and development programme contain?
9. What particular challenges does the UK face in developing effective talent identification programmes?
10. Using examples of some policies describe the main aims of the following organisations in relation to elite sport:
    - UK Sport
    - Sport England
    - Sports Coach UK
    - national governing bodies.
11. What might the advantages and disadvantages be of the British Olympic Association receiving no government funding?
12. How are elite athletes funded in the UK?

CHAPTER 16

The legacy of 'rational recreation'

and its relevance in the modern-day sports world

LEARNING OBJECTIVES:

By the end of this chapter you should be able to describe:

- *the social cultural factors influencing the development of rational recreation from pre-industrial times to the current day*
- *the development of rational recreation as a result of changing socio-cultural factors through the Industrial Revolution, urbanisation, the emergence of the middle classes, improved communications, the church, public provision and the changing nature of working conditions for the masses and how this has influenced the current day sporting arena*
- *the development and spread of rational recreation within society and globally due to the influence of ex-public school boys, formation of national governing bodies and the emergence of mass spectator sport and how this can be still seen in the current day sporting arena*
- *the historical view of the amateur and professional when compared with the current viewpoint*
- *the contract to compete and its relevance to modern-day elite sport*
- *the concepts of gamesmanship and sportsmanship and the Olympic ideal*
- *whether the Olympic ideal still has a place in modern-day sport.*

Introduction

Before we can understand how sports have developed, we first have to appreciate that sport is not a separate entity but an integral part of society. For the purposes of this specification, you will need to understand three basic phases in British society:

- pre-industrial society
- industrialisation
- post-industrial/advanced technological society.

Developments in sport tend to mirror the developments in society, e.g. as society began to become 'civilised', so, too, did many of the sporting recreations of the time. This was reflected in the development of rules, skills and etiquette for many games.

We will look at some of the major social changes during the Victorian era and into the twentieth century and then, most importantly, demonstrate the effect these changes had on the development of sport and recreational activities.

Sport and leisure were no exceptions to the forward momentum and the **civilising of society**. It was no coincidence that modern sport began in Britain, the first industrialised country in the world. Modern sport developed in an atmosphere where certain social and economic conditions occurred:

- **industrialisation**
- effective communications
- **urbanisation**
- affluent society
- a population with sufficient leisure time and surplus disposable income.

EXAM TIP:

1. Although pre-industrial Britain is not directly examined, you need to have a reasonable understanding of this period in history in order to appreciate the significant developments in sport and in society.
2. The focus of this specification is not 'dates and dust' but an understanding of how changes in society affected sport and recreational activities.
3. You need to understand how recreational pastimes reflect the lifestyles of a population and that they are subject to change as society develops.

Socio-cultural factors influencing the development of rational recreation

Pre-industrial Britain (pre-1750)

The majority of the population lived in rural areas and worked on the land. The upper classes were the wealthy landowners who held political power.

KEY TERMS

Industrialisation:
process in the 18th and 19th centuries when Britain moved from being a predominantly agricultural country to one where the economy was dominated by manufacturing

Civilising of society:
the evolution of human manners, in particular the practising of self-restraint in social situations. Code of behaviour and etiquette became the norm. Sports became less violent in their nature

Urbanisation:
the process whereby the mass of the population changes its lifestyle from living in villages and rural areas to living in towns and cities

Popular recreation:
recreational pursuits that were current before the Industrial Revolution. These activities were characterised by being played occasionally by the lower classes, having few rules, relying on physical force rather than skill and with limited structure

The working classes had little free time and their lives were harsh, but they had a strong sense of community that would be lost with the onset of industrialisation. Due to this lack of free time, their recreations only took place occasionally and mostly on religious holidays and festivals. As they did not participate regularly in recreational activities, many of the activities did not develop structurally but retained their traditional nature over hundreds of years. The term given to this type of recreation was 'popular recreation', e.g. mob football. The agricultural workers were also uneducated, as schooling was not to become compulsory until 1870, whereas the upper classes had been educated in their elite public schools for centuries.

Characteristics of **popular recreation**, e.g. mob football:

- being occasional due to little free time
- having only a few simple unwritten rules
- the activity being participation-based rather than spectator-based
- physical force rather than skill
- many injuries/violent
- lower-class involvement
- local rather than regional or national events
- limited structure, equipment and facilities.

The Victorian era (1839–1901)

Queen Victoria reigned from 1839 to 1901 and this era witnessed a major transition in society. The image of Victorian Britain is that of a country of immense contrasts between rich and poor people, but it is also seen as a period when the nation was prosperous and stable. For our purposes, we need to have some understanding of life in Victorian times and into the twentieth century. In particular, we need to discover how these changing social and economic conditions affected leisure and the development of sport.

The Industrial Revolution (c.1750–1850) was in full swing during Victoria's reign and most people's lives had undergone dramatic changes, most notably the move from the countryside to the towns (urbanisation) with cramped living and working conditions.

The resulting change in working patterns from agriculture and cottage industries to working in factories posed problems for employers and employees unused to such regulated activities. In the middle of the nineteenth century, Britain was seen as 'the workshop of the world'.

Britain was the first European country to undergo an industrial revolution with the growth of factory production replacing craft workshops, and its economy expanded. By the middle of the nineteenth century, Britain was the world's leading industrial power. Britain was the most highly specialised country in manufacturing: in 1901, less than 10 per cent of its labour force worked in agriculture, and it was also the most urbanised country. By 1851, half the population lived in towns or cities, and by 1901 this had risen to three-quarters. The upsurge in the population was a visible sign of economic growth.

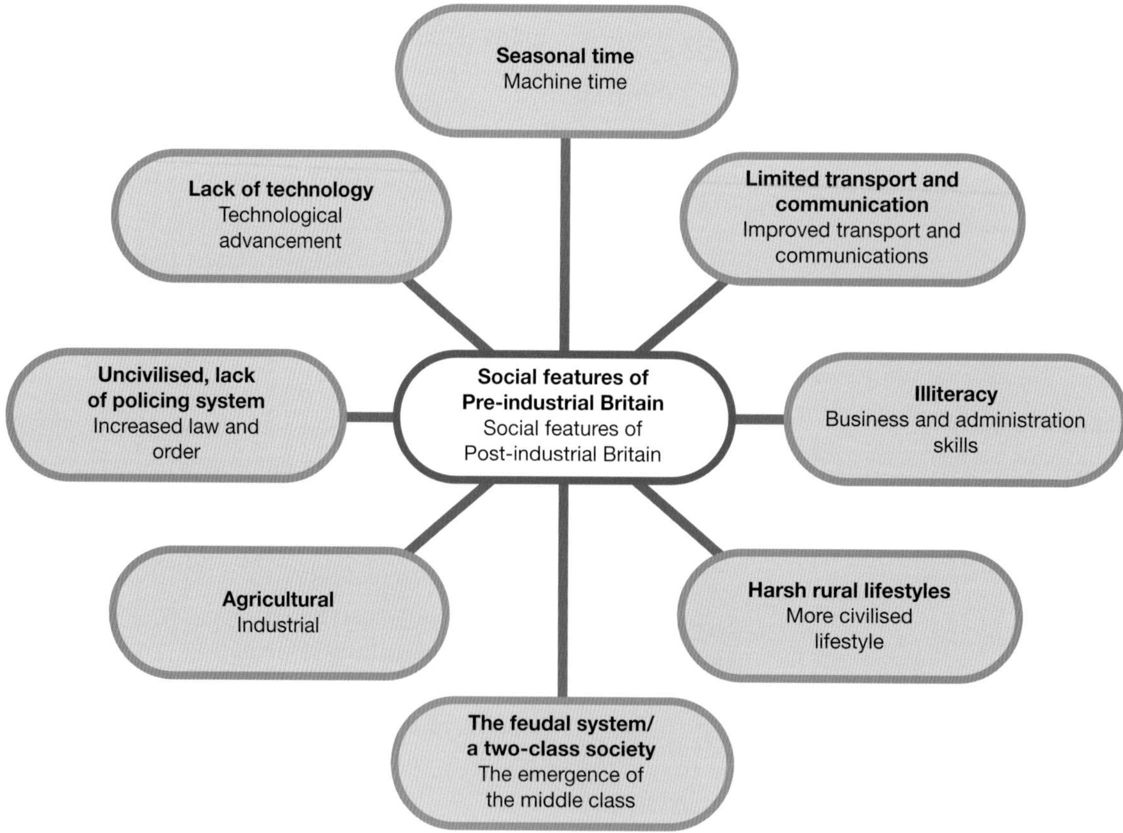

Fig 16.01 Pre- and post-industrial factors that influenced sport

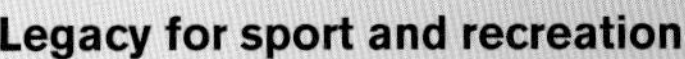

From the start of the Industrial Revolution until 1901, the population almost trebled to 37 million.

Working conditions needed to be addressed as industrialisation initially restricted the recreational opportunities of the working classes. The new urban population was a cause of some concern, particularly the hours that women and small children worked in the textile and coal industries. The working week was twelve hours a day, six days a week, and on the seventh day the working class were expected to attend church, so there was little time for rest and leisure. The term 'machine age' was coined and with it came a mixture of anticipation and anxiety. The material prosperity that was accumulating did so at a cost to the environment and people's lives. Issues such as urban squalor, spoiled landscapes and dislocated communities would have to be tackled.

Improvements began to be made. Numerous factory reforms were introduced (e.g. the Reform and Factory Act 1832, the Ten Hours Act 1847 and the Factory Act 1878) to try and combat this problem.

The drive towards new model trade unions was an attempt to provide some security for members. The working classes began to benefit from some more free time with the advent of the Saturday half-day, early closing for shop workers on Wednesdays and, from 1870, the granting of bank holidays under Lubbock's Act. The concept of the bank holiday was a significant step forward in the provision of nationally recognised leisure time for all and particularly for those without the industrial muscle to insist on it. Wages began to increase, and the working classes had some disposable income.

Scientific and industrial invention thrived during the Victorian era. This was demonstrated in 1851 when Queen Victoria opened the Great Exhibition in the Crystal Palace, which was a testament to modern architectural design in iron and glass. Edison invented the first electric light bulb and improved numerous other inventions such as the telegraph, telephone and motion picture projector.

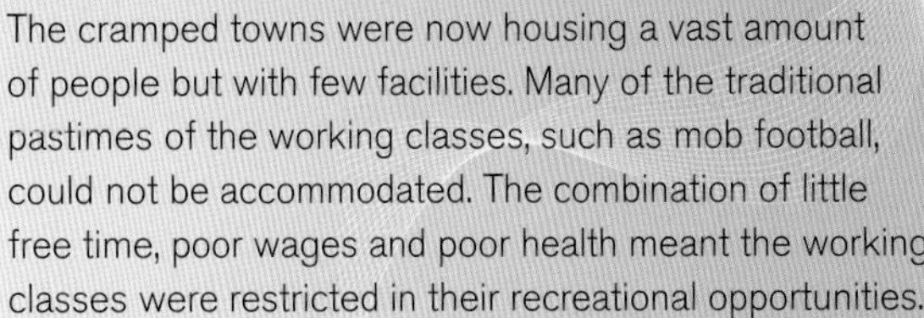

REMEMBER!

Legacy for sport and recreation

The cramped towns were now housing a vast amount of people but with few facilities. Many of the traditional pastimes of the working classes, such as mob football, could not be accommodated. The combination of little free time, poor wages and poor health meant the working classes were restricted in their recreational opportunities.

As conditions improved, the working classes were able to participate in more activities, and spectator sports and facilities began to develop. More disposable income meant they had more money to spend on leisure. On the first ever August bank holiday, people set out on excursions to the seaside, by train, steamer and on foot, on an unprecedented scale. The roads were packed with cyclists, and the town and city parks were full. Within twenty years, the bank holiday saw 500,000 people leave London for the coast and country.

Scientific inventions were not confined to industry. Sports, such as rugby football, lawn tennis, basketball and volleyball, were being invented. Sports equipment was being developed, such as the new lawn tennis kits, and the change in golf clubs and golf balls began to price working-class people out of a sport that had initially belonged to them. New technology such as the steam press enabled the working classes to purchase cheap newspapers and interest in sport and leisure boomed. The invention of the bicycle added to the options of transport, particularly cheaper modes of transport, but also became an accepted leisure pursuit for ladies, for whom less restrictive, more practical clothing was designed, as in the article of clothing the 'bloomers'. Commercialisation of leisure was well under way by the latter quarter of the nineteenth century.

Most people and goods were transported on the rivers and canals and that is the reason why many early towns were built close to waterways. Many aquatic activities, such as rowing and swimming, began as functional activities needed by those societies and later developed into sports, developing rules of competition. Then came hard roads with the gentry 'horse and carriage' and these were later developed to accommodate the boom in cycling. The railway was the significant development in transport for the Victorian era, enabling goods, people and ideas to be transported nationally and internationally.

REMEMBER!

Legacy for sport and recreation

The railways encouraged the popularity of the excursion, such as day trips to the seaside. Work holidays also added to the establishment of the seaside resorts, with whole communities travelling together, re-creating the community spirit of pre-industrial Britain. Blackpool was developed for the workers in the Yorkshire textile industry, and postcards, ice cream, fish and chips, and so on all helped to redefine leisure as it evolved in the Victorian era. Outdoor and adventurous activities, such as rambling, fishing, cycling and mountaineering, were all given a boost as the railways allowed access to more isolated parts of the country, with return possible in a day. Football fixtures were arranged further afield and spectators were increasingly able to travel with their team, leading to the 'home and away' tradition.

The old popular recreations were giving way to **rational recreation**. Popular recreations were finding it hard to survive in this newly civilised and increasingly moral environment. The cramped living conditions resulted in a severe lack of space, making it impossible for popular recreations like mob football to survive. The middle and upper classes required disciplined and productive workers, and were also keen to suppress excessive behaviour amongst the working classes. This was exemplified by their popular recreations such as cock fighting and mob games. Crowds of working-class people involved in riotous behaviour were considered a threat to the authorities, properties and productivity. It was deemed necessary to control leisure, as society was suffering political unrest in the form of a discontented workforce and appalling problems of public health.

Characteristics of rational recreation:

- regular participation
- complex written rules
- highly structured in nature
- being spectator-based as well as participation-based
- the need to use refined skills rather than force
- being a middle- to upper-class development
- being regionally and nationally based
- the use of sophisticated equipment and facilities.

Social reform during this period gathered momentum. The era was renowned for its attention to high morals and proper conduct, inspired by Queen Victoria and her husband, Prince Albert. The importance placed on civic conscience and social responsibility led to major developments in improving the lot of the poor. **Philanthropists**, or social reformers, emerged as influential voices. Working and living conditions of the poor were addressed, and recreational facilities, such as parks and baths, began to be provided for the working classes.

REMEMBER!

Legacy for sport and recreation

Civic responsibility announced itself in the establishment of town parks by middle-class local government, council members or individual philanthropists. Reasons for the provision of parks were to improve the health of the population, to discourage crime, to attract people away from alcohol, to encourage workers to participate in rational and rule-governed behaviour and to demonstrate a sense of social justice. Working men's clubs, institutes, Friendly Societies and libraries were also established in order to further the education of the working classes.

The influence of industrial patronage regarding leisure was not widespread, but some individual projects would be considered revolutionary even today. The Cadbury company in Birmingham was pro-active in improving the conditions of work and general living standards for their workers. They were the first company in England to use the half-day Saturday, and they built Bourneville Village, still in evidence today, with medical care, schools, a swimming pool and recreation grounds. They were keen on improving the fitness and health of their workers and, cynically, one might assume that they merely wanted to improve the productivity of their workforce. However, as Quakers, they also had a genuine concern for improving the lot of the poor.

Education became an issue. The need for an educated population who could work effectively under the new 'modern' production systems resulted in the introduction of compulsory state education from 1870. Up to this point, education had been the privilege of the upper classes in their elitist public schools.

EXAM TIP:

Blood sports were merely a part of a violent and cruel society. The emergence of the middle classes, with their civilising and moral impact, led to many of these activities being banned. Interestingly, the present-day debate about fox hunting continues.

KEY TERMS

Rational recreation:
the middle classes changed the recreations of the working classes, giving them rules and codes of conduct

Middle class:
the term was used from around the mid-18th century to describe those people who were below the aristocracy in rank but above the workers

Philanthropists:
people who carry out charitable or benevolent actions

REMEMBER!

Legacy for sport and recreation

The upper (and later the middle) classes developed many sports, particularly team games, via their public schools, and stressed the physical and moral benefits to be gained from participating in sport. This was a return to the Renaissance belief that the 'whole man' should be one who is intellectually, physically and spiritually developed.

The working classes in the state schools were not deemed worthy of recreational activities until much later in the twentieth century. They were to experience a tedious form of drill in an attempt to keep them disciplined, obedient, prepared for military life and healthy.

Education became an issue. The need for an educated population who could work effectively under the new 'modern' production systems resulted in the introduction of compulsory state education from 1870. Up to this point, education had been the privilege of the upper classes in their elitist public schools.

The **British Empire** had expanded and was now so big that 'the sun never set on it'. The empire provided resources of raw materials for industry and markets for manufactured items. Britain exported its goods and its customs, government and religion, as well as its sporting recreations, to the rest of the world via soldiers, administrators, missionaries and so on. Overseas trade grew in importance with the expansion in manufacturing. America, or the 'New World' as it was known, was the big new destination for British goods. In 1800, nearly 60 per cent of Britain's exports crossed the Atlantic.

REMEMBER!

Legacy for sport and recreation

The British Empire also imported and exported sports. Polo was imported from India and cricket exported to the West Indies. The people involved in these sporting and cultural exchanges were soldiers, teachers, doctors, missionaries, engineers, clergy and so on.

The churches had expanded into the new urban areas to try to ensure that the working classes, now removed from their traditional lifestyles under the village priest and local landowner, would still be guided by religion. The church was disapproving of traditional popular recreations, such as mob football, as they were disorganised and lacked any moral learning. However, as numbers of parishioners gradually began to decline, the Church was to actively use rational sport to encourage attendance and instil moral codes of behaviour. In particular, they needed to attract the working classes away from the pubs. This was known as the **temperance movement**.

KEY TERMS

British Empire:
British imperialists spread their forms of government, religion and culture, including sports, to those countries that they colonised

Temperance movement:
a movement practising restraint or moderation, especially abstinence from alcoholic drink

REMEMBER!

Legacy for sport and recreation

Now that many sports had been 'rationalised', the Church could support them as they had been civilised and could be used to instil a sense of morality in the working classes. They encouraged youth movements such as the Boys' Brigade, the Scouts and Sunday school teams. Everton and Aston Villa both started out as church teams. The churches also provided facilities such as church halls for recreation. In Birmingham, approximately a quarter of football clubs were directly connected to religious organisations between 1870 and 1885.

Muscular Christianity was an evangelical movement led by Charles Kingsley, who believed in the combination of the Christian and chivalric ideals of manliness. He believed healthy bodies were needed alongside healthy minds to serve God. However, sport was only valued for what it could achieve in moral terms.

In addition, humanitarian and religious organisations, such as the Young Men's Christian Association (YMCA), reflected the Victorian concern for the poor and needy of the period. Its aims were to develop high standards of Christian character through group activities and improve the spiritual, social and recreational life of young people. Again, this organisation sought to use sport to achieve its aims. Through this organisation came the invention of basketball and volleyball in America.

Youth movements, such as the Boys' Brigade, the Church Lads' Brigade and the Scouts, all emerged as part of this need by the **middle classes** to 'control' the behaviour of the working classes in a period of potential social unrest. These youth organisations shared some basic similarities. They provided recreational activities for working-class youths who needed a leisure outlet, and they provided religious, moral and militaristic values, deemed important by the social elite. The militaristic element was very strong at this time as there was always the threat of war.

The **Boer War** was fought in South Africa between 1899 and 1902, resulting in the acquisition of the Transvaal and the Orange Free State by the British Empire. Massive losses were suffered by the British troops, and this was blamed on the unfitness, lack of discipline and general poor health of the working classes.

REMEMBER!

Legacy for sport and recreation

Military drill was to provide a basis for the early experiences of school physical activity for the working classes. It was intended to raise the general health and fitness of the working classes, instil discipline and obedience, teach weapon familiarity and prepare them for the military. Even after the military content was removed (1904), drill-style school exercise was to remain for a couple more decades.

'Social class' was also a term that was being redefined during this era. Pre-industrial Britain was generally split into two main classes – upper and lower. The middle classes emerged as a result of the Industrial Revolution.

The middle classes emerged when entrepreneurs realised the potential to make a lot of money. Having made great fortunes through trade, the middle classes then converted this into political power in the Reform Act 1832. They were able to ensure that political decisions reflected their interests rather than the interests of the upper classes alone. They were striving to create a society based on merit and personal achievement rather than one based on privileged birth. They emphasised competition, thrift, prudence and self-reliance as necessary qualities for social advancement. Through education reform, schemes of civic improvement and the growth of the market, the Victorian middle classes were also influential in improving the lot of the working classes. The increasing scale of industry and overseas trade fuelled the need for banks, insurance companies, shipping and railways. The expansion of local government and increasing powers of government provided the strata of professions such as lawyers, civil servants, teachers, and doctors. The age was ripe for the domination of society by the middle classes.

The middle classes were also the most religious of the social classes and became the new moral voice of society. A good example of the combination of political power and morality could be seen in the banning of cruel blood sports (e.g. the Cruelty to Animals Act 1840), previously enjoyed by both the upper and lower classes.

REMEMBER!

Legacy for sport and recreation

The upper classes had enjoyed rational recreations, such as real tennis, for many centuries. Their recreations were characterised by having early organisational features, such as rules, and sophisticated facilities and equipment. However, the upper classes were also similar to the working classes in that they enjoyed the combination of alcohol, gambling and cruel blood sports. The upper classes often acted as patrons towards sporting events and individual performers. Today we would call them sponsors. An example would be the Duke of Cumberland acting as a patron to a working-class fighter. The fighter would fight for the name of his patron and the patron could gain financially out of a successful arrangement.

The newly emerging middle classes, who wanted to emulate the lifestyle of the upper classes, tried to dissociate themselves from the rowdy pursuits of the lower classes. The religious and moralising middle classes were, however, suspicious of the decadence that was associated with leisure by the upper classes and wanted to formulate activities of their own that would also serve some social function and thus be of some purpose to society. Through leisure, the middle classes wanted to stabilise and transform society by the adoption of rational recreations. Sports like cricket, football and rugby began to be organised with national competitions such as the FA Cup. New sports were invented such as lawn tennis (Figure 16.02), acting as a substitute for real tennis, and the bicycle (the urban substitute for the horse) became a familiar sight in Britain.

With the growth of railways, people began to travel more and day trips became affordable. The administration of sport became largely the responsibility of the middle classes who used their organisation skills to establish clubs and governing bodies. Governing bodies were needed as sports became more popular, so an organisation to oversee the running of each sport was important. With their accumulated wealth, they were able to buy land, build facilities and establish what are now considered very British traditions such as the Wimbledon Lawn Tennis and Croquet Club.

The working classes had lost their old recreational pursuits with the advent of industrialisation. Early working and living conditions in the urban areas were poor, with long hours, little free time and low wages. They were to be introduced to the rational forms of recreation by the middle classes, who imposed their own value systems on the working classes, such as teamwork, respect for rules and fair play. The rise in spectator sports, particularly football, was no coincidence with so many people in a small area needing regular and exciting entertainment.

Fig 16.02 Lawn tennis was played by the middle classes in Victorian times

EXAM TIP:

Governing bodies, even today, tend to be controlled by the upper/middle classes, whose values may seem to belong to a past age.

Social class	Characteristics and legacy for sport and recreation
Upper class	• Also called the aristocracy/nobility/gentry • Had ample leisure time, opportunities and choice – often termed the 'leisured class' • Role in life was to be landowners, owners, employers, officers, diplomats – that is, the leaders in society • Enjoyed cruel blood sports and the gambling and alcohol associated with leisure • Enjoyed traditional recreational activities such as field sports, cricket, real tennis • Many of these activities would have been rational in nature • Education – attended the elite public schools and were influential in developing team games for character-building qualities • Established the amateur code, which had a monetary and social class distinction. Amateurs should not be paid for participation in sport and many sports such as rowing also dictated which social classes could take part
Middle class	• Emerged as a result of the Industrial Revolution; also called the 'nouveau riche' (new rich) • Wanted to copy the lifestyle of the upper classes and disassociate themselves from the lower classes, e.g. lawn tennis was a substitute for real tennis, the bicycle an urban substitute for the horse • Became the moral force in society with many reforms in working conditions and the banning of cruel blood sports • Became the administrators of governing bodies, and agents and promoters of sport
Lower class	• Also called the 'working class' • Industrial Revolution caused a major change in living and working conditions: urbanisation, regimented factory work • Enjoyed popular recreations such as mob football and cock fighting until banned by the middle and upper classes • Tended to become the professionals in sport as they needed to earn money from sport in order to make a living • Women from this group of people had the least recreational opportunities of all

Table 16.01 Characteristics of the Victorian class system

TASK 16.01

1. Outline the negative and positive social factors that affected the recreational opportunities of the working classes in the nineteenth century.
2. Why did the control of sport pass from the upper classes to the middle classes in the nineteenth century?

Industrialisation was to provide new ways of defining male and female roles. In particular, the sense of separating male and female social roles emerged (it is important to remember, though, that these roles were also dependent on the social class these women belonged to). The female role was idealised by Queen Victoria herself as representing femininity, which was centred on the family, motherhood and respectability. She was called the 'mother of the nation'.

In the late industrial era, the female role was cast in the private sphere and the male role to the public sphere of business, commerce and politics. However, the middle-class female was also expected to work for the service of others, displaying innate moral goodness. Many women took on the role of philanthropists, actively visiting those less well off than themselves such as widows, orphans and the sick. It was from this type of work that the first feminists began to demand more rights for women. This was to take on a political mission, starting with better education and employment conditions for middle-class ladies, better wages and working conditions for working-class women, and culminating in the vote for women in the early part of the twentieth century (1917).

TASK 16.02

Why would working-class women experience less recreation than their male counterparts?

REMEMBER!

Legacy for sport and recreation

As female liberation emerged, the physical activities enjoyed by women began to be more active. Therefore the tight corsets and heavy materials that women had been required to wear began to change in favour of less restrictive clothing.

Working-class women had the least opportunities of all the social classes. They were expected to work and adopt the domestic role, so any form of leisure time was severely restricted. They were poor, with little political power, and their education was very limited.

Middle- and upper-class ladies did experience more freedom of movement than the working-class woman. The middle- and upper-class lady was gradually encouraged to demand more physical forms of recreation. Activities such as croquet were ousted by lawn tennis. Fashions began to change as more physical movement became acceptable. The girls' public schools began to copy the boys' schools in academic and sporting terms. Games like hockey, netball (a derivative of basketball from America) and tennis were acceptable activities as they adhered to dress codes, had rules and could be played in the privacy of a school, club or garden.

Amateurism and professionalism

Two crucial sporting cultures were to collide in the nineteenth-century British sporting scene. They were the codes of amateurism and professionalism.

Amateurism was the dominant force in Britain, as it was the code established by the gentry in their public schools. The early amateurs were drawn from the elite social classes, hence the term 'gentleman amateur' – that is, one who is from the gentry or upper classes and who does not earn money from the sport. Amateurism was also concerned with the manner in which the sport was played. Winning alone was not considered important but how you performed was seen as being of equal importance. You were expected to play fairly and with respect for your opponents. Many believe that this value, still promoted in British sport today, has held us back when it comes to being hungry for success at major sporting events. It is in direct contrast to the American belief that 'winning is the most important and only thing!'

Professional sport is a much older concept than amateurism and can be traced as far back as the gladiators of Ancient Rome. Like professional footballers today, these gladiators were also paid for their performances, trained seriously and provided entertainment to the masses (see page 256).

However, in Britain, the concept of professional sport became tainted with social class snobbery. The working classes needed to be paid to play sport, as they could not afford to take time off work without pay. In 1894, the Rugby Football Union and the Northern Union split due to the refusal of the sports authorities to allow northern players enough leisure time to compete on the same basis as players in the south. The issue of **'broken-time payments'** was to eventually lead to the professionalisation of sports such as football and rugby.

The current viewpoint of these concepts is covered further in this chapter (see pages 254–259).

KEY TERMS

Amateurism:
based on the ideal that participation in sport should be for the love of it rather than for monetary gain

Professional sport:
a sporting activity that is engaged in for financial gain or as a means of livelihood

Broken-time payments:
payments made to compensate working-class players for loss of earnings while playing sports such as soccer and rugby football

EXAM TIP:

For this specification, you will not be examined directly on amateurism and professionalism. However, it is useful to understand these concepts as they are integral to the development of many sports and reflect the social class distinctions of the era.

Professional sport is linked to the idea that winning is the most important thing. The upper classes in British society felt that ethical and moral values were lost if winning was the 'only thing'.

TASK 16.03

What are the similarities between a gladiator in Ancient Rome and a professional footballer today?

Twentieth-century Britain

The Edwardian era corresponds with the relatively short reign of King Edward VII (1901–10). However, the 'Edwardian style' broadly encompasses the years up to World War I (1914). The era was termed the 'gilded age' as the effects of industrialisation were beginning to benefit many people's lives. Many might say that the ocean liner the *Titanic* epitomised the lavish excesses being enjoyed at the time.

The Edwardian era continued the advancements made in scientific and technological progress. Material novelties epitomised this new age, such as the telegraph, telephone, typewriters, elevators and so on. The era also ushered in the first mass-produced motor car and many gadgets were invented for the home.

The new forms of sport depended on consumer goods and services such as the new leisure industries. Ordinary people realised that what had previously been the privilege of the few was now within their reach, with the growing assumption that they also had a right to leisure. Much of this depended on the availability of spare cash and the ability of the masses to pay for their pleasure.

Sport became ever more organised with bureaucracies, finances, performers, officials and spectators all becoming part of the public's imagination through the many publications devoted to sport. What began as local and regional events became national and then international affairs controlled by international committees such as FIFA which was formed in Paris in 1904.

Social consequences of World War I (1914–18) for sport and recreation

Women began to change their perceptions of themselves and the outside world as they took on many of the men's jobs during World War I, and also enjoyed the escape of the dance halls and cinema, which was to give them a glimpse of even more possibilities for their own lives. Women had contributed to the war effort both in factories and on the land. There was some relaxation of their domestic and social roles, and they emerged more independent and confident. However, working-class women were still much more restricted than men and middle-class women.

The establishment of the Women's League of Health and Beauty demonstrated the changes during this era, especially the increase in physical activity for women in society and the growing knowledge about the therapeutic effects of exercise. Established in 1930, the League was based on a system of exercises structured and graded to suit different needs and abilities and taught by highly trained instructors. The exercises were based on remedial health exercises and after-work classes were put on for mill workers, office and shop employees. A feature of the organisation was public displays of large groups of women performing movement to music.

Anti-militarism was demonstrated in various ways. There was a mood to build a new country and a determination not to see a repeat of conflict on such a global scale again. The country returned to its lavish living amongst the upper and middle classes, and the recreations of the working classes continued to increase in variety and amount.

Changing views of children were reflected in the Syllabuses of Physical Training in the state schools. They were taking more account of children's ages and stages of development, with lessons becoming more informal than the previous drill style of teaching. More fun and play activities were being introduced with a more interactive teaching style.

Entertainment

The cinema was to take over from the church and the pub as meeting the needs of ordinary people – it was cheap, entertaining, sociable and educational. Broadcasting via the wireless dominated almost every home, and the peak audience went into the millions and also caused a growth in home-based entertainment. The development of the motor car trade gave many people a chance to escape to new environments under their own steam as well as on coach trips, which could collect people on their street corners and give a sense of community at the same time. Travel firms catering for low-income groups thrived at this time. In the 1930s, some 7 million people went to Blackpool, and the seaside resorts were becoming even more popular. This trend in holidaymaking was also made popular by the private agreements between firms and workers for 'holidays with pay', which would be covered by legislation by 1938. So a major shift in social thinking had occurred. Before World War I, it became recognised that all workers had the right to a holiday – by the late 1930s, it was recognised through legislation that everyone had a right to 'holidays with pay'. Outdoor recreational activities, as an opportunity to enjoy the countryside and fresh air, became a national pastime, also made popular by the success of the Scout movement and similar organisations. Organisations increased to cope with the growing numbers of walkers, cyclists, climbers and campers. Football continued to thrive even in the worst hit depression areas of Britain and many players were drawn from these areas.

EXAM TIP:

Sport was becoming more organised, commercialised, defined by social class and of national importance.

Commercialisation

The greatest change in the 1950s (following World War II) was the unprecedented consumer power throughout all levels of society. The increase in wages, the proliferation of domestic hardware and the opportunities for hire purchase led to the time when 'people had never had it so good'. The television set was to further transform the leisure interests of a nation. It was to provide a relatively cheap source of entertainment, education and leisure. It was also blamed for a decline in church attendance, cinemas and even attendance at football matches. Major sporting events, such as the Olympic Games and World Cup soccer, could be watched by hundreds of millions. Individual sports were becoming more popular than they had been, such as golf and tennis, and many sports were becoming multi-million pound businesses, (motorcyclists and racing drivers included), the majority of the money coming from advertising, sponsorship and TV coverage rather than gate receipts as in the past.

The growth in municipal facilities allowed more people to participate purely for the enjoyment factor and many people were prepared to spend vast amounts of money for their children to experience more expensive sports. Although commercialisation of sport is often criticised, it has also provided a more varied cultural diet for the mass of the population. The need to win has pervaded all sports, particularly at the highest levels, as the prize for success became so lucrative. The fortunes of cricket reflect these changes. The organisers accepted the need for a change in attitude in favour of the new commercial interests – the traditional three-day and five-day matches are giving way to shorter, more exciting contests with financial backing coming from commercial organisations such as the big banks.

Table 16.02 summarises the major points of each era.

TASK 16.04A

Read the account of the history of football on pages 253–254 and pay particular attention to the developments occurring in society, then attempt Task 16.04b.

EXAM TIP:

You will be learning much more than the history of football – you will also gain an insight into Victorian and twentieth-century society.

Table 16.02 Summary of factors influencing the development of rational recreation

Early nineteenth century (c. 1800–30)	Late nineteenth century (c. 1870–1900)	Early twentieth century (c. 1900–30)	Mid-twentieth century (c. 1930–60)	Late twentieth century to present day (1960 onwards)
• Rural • Agricultural • Population live in countryside • Two social classes: upper and lower/working • Education for upper class only in public/private schools • Sport mainly in form of 'popular' recreation: limited rules and organisation, e.g. mob football	• Industrialisation • Factory work/poor conditions (72 hour week/low pay) • Emergence of middle class through ability to make money through trade • Education for working classes • State school education began in 1870 • Sport became rationalised via public schools: developed rules and structure • Amateur code strictly defined for upper and middle classes (do not get paid for sport and winning not as important as how to play) • Professional: working-class people needed to earn • Strict divide between the two classes	• Increase in technology • Communications • Improving work conditions (less hours of work/more pay) • Trade unions/Labour Party • World War I (1914–18) • More international competition • England dominating world in sport • Professional sport increasing	• Commercialisation • World War II (1939–45) • 1930s was economic depression • Lessening division between amateur/professional • 'Open' competitions • Professional sport took over from amateur sport • England losing dominance • Other countries catching up and taking winning more seriously	• Globalisation • More people spectating than participating • Media/satellite • Professional sport has more status than amateur sport

APPLY IT!

The history of football

It is a useful exercise to trace the history of certain sports and understand the influence that changes in society had on their development. Football is a classic example of a traditional working-class popular recreation being transformed into a rational, rule-bound, disciplined activity, believed to possess the qualities that would bring society together in a common aim.

Popular or mob version

The game that flourished in the British Isles from the eighth to the nineteenth centuries had a considerable variety of local and regional versions, which were subsequently to form the present-day sports of association football and rugby football. At this stage of the game's development, the term 'popular recreation' is used to suggest they were initially disorganised, violent, more spontaneous and usually played by an indefinite number of players. Frequently, the games took the form of a heated contest between whole village communities or townships – through streets, village squares, across fields, hedges, fences and streams. Kicking was allowed, as in fact was almost everything else.

It is certain that in many cases pagan customs, especially fertility rites, played a major role. These games were played only occasionally, such as holy days, as these were the times when the lower classes enjoyed some free time.

Shrovetide football, as it was called, belonged in the 'mob football' category, where the number of players was unlimited and the rules were fairly vague (e.g. according to an ancient handbook from Workington in England, any means could be employed to get the ball to its target with the exception of murder and manslaughter!). The repeated unsuccessful intervention of the authorities shows how powerless they were to restrict it in spite of their condemnation and threats of severe punishment.

Reasons why the authorities disapproved

- With the spread of Puritanism, 'frivolous' amusements (and sport happened to be classified as such) constituted a violation of peace on the Sabbath. Football remained a taboo on the Sabbath for some time.
- Resentment of football was mainly for practical reasons. The game was regarded as a public disturbance that resulted in damage to property, e.g. in Manchester in 1608, football was banned because so many windows had been smashed.
- An industrialised society required a disciplined workforce who was punctual and fit for work. The excesses of mob football resulted in many injuries and time off work.

Rationalisation of football

The game remained essentially rough, violent and disorganised. A change did not come about until the beginning of the nineteenth century when a game previously played by lower-class 'village boys' was taken into the public schools by the sons of the gentry. In this new environment of unlimited and unsupervised free time, it was possible to make innovations and refinements to the game. This can be referred to as the technical development of games, where the skills, tactics, facilities and general organisation of the game developed.

Fig 16.03a Mob football

Fig 16.03b A Premiership game

continued

continued

Each school developed its own adaptation and, at times, these varied considerably. At this point in time, the public schools could only play inter-house competitions, as all schools did not recognise the same rules. Inter-school matches could not take place until **codification** had occurred via the universities.

All these early styles were given a great boost when it was recognised in educational circles that football could actually be educationally beneficial. The Clarendon Commission, a government report on public schools in the 1860s, formally recognised the educational value of team games. What is more, it was accepted that it also constituted a useful distraction from less desirable occupations such as heavy drinking and gambling.

A new attitude began to permeate the game, eventually leading to a **'games cult'** in public schools. This materialised when it was observed how well the team game served to encourage such fine character building qualities as loyalty, selflessness, cooperation, subordination and deference to the team spirit. Games became an integral part of the school curriculum. A more organised form of football matched the concept of athleticism (physical endeavour with moral integrity), a movement developed in public schools, and Muscular Christianity (healthy bodies and minds to serve God), a movement developed in society. As sports became rationalised, developing Sunday school teams and church youth movements became acceptable, particularly as a tool in making the Church appear attractive to the young. The moral benefits that could be gained from observing 'rule-governed' activities were stressed rather than 'sport for sport's sake'.

The governing body for football – the Football Association – was born on 26 October 1863. Only eight years after its foundation, the Football Association already had 50 member clubs. The first football competition in the world was started in the same year – the FA Cup, which preceded the League Championship by seventeen years.

The rational game of football was introduced to the working classes via the churches, schools and workplace. In the industrial heartlands, football was to be reclaimed by the working classes and was to be called 'the game of the people'. They began to make broken-time payments, leading to the eventual professionalising of the game. The southern amateurs were to eventually be eclipsed by the northern professionals. Similarly to today, whenever a sport becomes professional, training methods and the importance given to winning lead to rapidly improving standards of performance.

International matches were being staged in Great Britain before football had hardly been heard of in Europe. The first was played in 1872 and was contested by England and Scotland.

This sudden boom of organised football, accompanied by staggering crowds of spectators, brought with it certain problems with which other countries were not confronted until much later on. It was professionalism. This practice grew rapidly and the Football Association found itself obliged to legalise professionalism as early as 1885.

The spread of football outside Great Britain, mainly due to the British influence abroad, started slowly, but it soon gathered momentum and the game spread rapidly to all parts of the world. This international football community grew steadily, although it sometimes met with obstacles and setbacks. In 1912, 21 national associations were already affiliated to the Fédération Internationale de Football Association (FIFA). By 1925, the number had increased to 36. In 1930, the year of the first World Cup, it was 41; in 1938, 51, and in 1950, after the interval caused by World War II, the number had reached 73. At the time of writing, FIFA has 208 members in every part of the world.

The maximum wage was abolished in 1961 after George Eastham challenged Newcastle United's right to refuse him a transfer in a court of law. The 'retain and transfer' system had previously existed unchallenged and now a player had the right to decide his own destiny. It was time for market forces to rule.

KEY TERMS

Codification:
the systematic organisation of laws or rules into one recognised system or code

Games cult:
intense interest and devotion to the pursuit of team games by boys within their public school

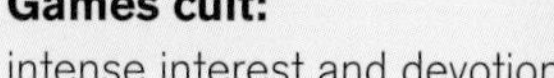

TASK 16.04B

1. Suggest three characteristics of mob football.
2. What social and economic changes led to the rationalisation of football?
3. How did the public schools contribute to the technical development of games?
4. What values did the public schools bring to the game of football?
5. Why was the Football Association formed in 1863?

Contract to compete

Whenever we walk onto a football pitch, a netball court, participate in a swimming competition or any other type of competitive sport, we have entered into an unwritten **mutual agreement** with our opponents.

What is the nature of such a **contract to compete**? It is an unwritten agreement whereby opponents have mutually agreed to:

- abide by the written and unwritten rules of the sport
- always give 100 per cent effort
- allow opponents to demonstrate their skill
- accept and understand the need for codes of behaviour such as sportsmanship (see below) and etiquette, e.g., shaking hands before the start of a football match.

Sometimes such a contract may be broken, when:

- these rules are not followed
- others are denied the equal opportunity to participate (e.g. when other players are using drugs to enhance their performance).

EXAM TIP:

1. Do not confuse 'contract to compete' with the professional sportsman's contract.
2. Examination questions will often require you to provide a discussion about the terms 'gamesmanship' and 'sportsmanship' and whether they are relevant today.

KEY TERMS

Mutual agreement:
where opponents agree to abide by the written rules of the sport

Contract to compete:
an unwritten mutual agreement to abide by the written and unwritten rules of the sport

Etiquette:
the conventional rules of behaviour embodied within a sporting situation

Sportsmanship:
qualities encouraged in sport such as fairness and especially the observance of the unwritten rules or 'spirit of the game'

Fair play:
equitable conduct; just or equal conditions operate for all involved in the sporting contest

Sportsmanship and gamesmanship

Sportsmanship is synonymous with **fair play**. It is a quality displayed by a person or team such as fairness, generosity, observance of the written and unwritten rules, and knowing how to lose gracefully and honourably. These qualities have been highly regarded by British society. An example might be kicking the ball out of play if someone is injured. However, there is evidence that sportsmanship is in decline (see Table 16.03).

Evidence that sportsmanship has declined	How can we encourage sportsmanship?
• Increasing number of sports-related prosecutions (e.g. aggression, doping) • More emphasis on winning • Monetary rewards (wages, sponsorship deals, endorsements) make the risk worth it • Spectator behaviour encourages performers to show aggression • The media hype up events and rivalries	• Fair play schemes and campaigns • Positive role models • Better quality officials and use of technology • Development of positive values early on in childhood • Punishment for negative behaviour • Encouraging codes of conduct for players, spectators and clubs

Table 16.03 The decline in sportsmanship and possible solutions

Gamesmanship is not the breaking of the rules but bending the rules in order to gain an advantage. An example would be tying your shoelaces before your opponent is about to serve. Technically the written rules have not been broken but it is an unethical, tactical ploy to put the opponent off.

KEY TERMS

Gamesmanship:
bending the rules of the game to gain an advantage

Amateurism:
based on the ideal that participation in sport should be for the love of it rather than for monetary gain

APPLY IT!

Gail Emms talks about gamesmanship in badminton: *'People don't understand all the psychology that goes on. When we're facing each other across the net, my job is to make sure the other girl doesn't get one over on me. A lot of it's about momentum. When one pair is on a roll, the other is doing all it can to stop you. So you change the shuttle a lot, you wipe imaginary sweat from the court. All that sort of thing. It happens in tennis even more.'*

Amateurism, athleticism, Olympism and professionalism

Four sport ethics have dominated the British sporting scene. These are:

1. amateurism
2. athleticism
3. Olympism (see pages 262–264)
4. professionalism (see pages 256–259)

Amateurism

Amateurism is a concept which evolved in nineteenth-century England amongst the upper classes, who became known as 'gentleman amateurs'. It was an ideal based upon participating in sport for the love of it rather than for monetary gain, and the participation was deemed more important than the winning. It encompassed the belief in fair play or sportsmanship and abiding by the spirit as well as the rules of the game. The 'all rounder' was highly regarded by the amateurs who believed that he celebrated god-given abilities. Amateurism originally had a social class distinction as it excluded the lower classes, not least because the gentleman amateurs did not wish to be beaten by their social inferiors. The 'manual labour clause' in rowing was a good example of this. The clause stated that no one could compete if 'they were a mechanic, artisan or labourer'.

Many amateur performers struggled in the twentieth century with commercial pressures and offers of monetary rewards. This led to a situation where some athletes were receiving 'under the table' payments leading to the term **shamateur**. Trust funds were established to try and counter this situation. A trust fund was set up by the governing body of the sport that would hold money received from advertising and so on until the athlete retired from the sport.

KEY TERMS

Shamateur:
a term describing amateur performers who receive payments secretly

Athleticism:
physical endeavour with moral integrity

Fig 16.04 Gentleman amateurs playing cricket

Over the last 100 years many changes have occurred. One of the significant changes that occurred at the end of the twentieth century was the Rugby Football Union, the bastion of amateurism, turning professional in 1996. Today the pure ideal of amateurism is difficult to adhere to, and amateurs can now officially receive financial aid from sponsorship, trust funds and organisations such as Sports Aid and the National Lottery. Even the Olympic Games now accept professional performers from sports such as tennis and basketball. Over 150 years, amateur sport has been squeezed by professional sport and become less influential.

Athleticism

Athleticism can be defined as physical endeavour with moral integrity. It became a cult in the latter part of the nineteenth century, with its foundations in the English public schools. These schools took seriously their role of producing gentlemen with qualities of honour, integrity, courage and leadership. Athleticism could only be developed by instilling a strong moral code and was considered to nurture:

- moral qualities such as working as part of a team and conforming with authority
- physical qualities, such as the value and enjoyment of a healthy lifestyle, the correction of the temptation to over-study and the ability to learn to cope with winning and losing in a competitive society
- spiritual links of godliness and manliness (which has been called Muscular Christianity).

TASK 16.05

Give specific examples from a sport of your choice to explain how the contract to compete can be broken.

TASK 16.06

1. To what extent are the values of amateurism, athleticism and olympism still relevant in modern day sport? Consider the discussion points in Table 16.04 and whether they best serve the modern day approach towards sport.
2. Write down some of the common characteristics encompassed in the terms amateurism, athleticism and olympism. To what extent may these characteristics hinder the progression of a performer in the modern day sports world?

Still relevant in modern sport	Less relevant in modern sport
• We still culturally encourage respect for rules and others. • Physical Education in schools stresses the moral values as much as the physical benefits. • The Olympics are still the biggest competition in the world and they are based on amateurism and ethics (athletes take the Olympic oath). • Fair Play Awards have been given more significance in recent years at the highest level. • Athletes are considered role models for children. • Sport and society would be dysfunctional without any values. • Doping is illegal therefore we must still retain some ethical values. • Traditional values allow everyone to take part at their own level as it is about doing your best.	• Traditional values can hinder hunger for success because the end product/winning is not seen as serious. • Sport in other countries (such as the USA) is based on different principles, i.e. the **Lombardian ethic** that winning isn't the most important thing, it's the only thing (win at all costs). • These values belong to a past culture of 'gentlemanly sport' – the social values of the upper classes. Nowadays all classes compete. • Commercialisation (there are now huge monetary rewards for success) stresses the need to be good at sport. • Professional sport is more dominant than amateur sport at the highest levels. • Professional sports are creeping into the Olympics. • Increasing legislation and prosecutions in sport-related incidents suggests that these values are losing their stronghold.

Table 16.04 The values of amateurism, athleticism and Olympism

The concepts of amateurism, athleticism and olympism have formed the traditional British approach towards sport. However, it is possible that these values may not be the best preparation for developing elite athletes with the hunger to win in the modern day sports world. The dominant sport ethic in the USA, the Lombardian ethic, commonly accepted as the 'win at all costs' ethic, sharply contrasts with the more gentlemanly British mentality. The American ethic emphasises the competitive, achievement-orientated, reward-based type of sport behaviour, i.e. the end justifies the means, encompassed in the phrase 'nice guys finish last.' This ethic is more closely connected to professional sport.

The relationship between amateurism and professionalism

Professional sport is a concept that can be traced back as far as ancient Rome and is therefore a much earlier concept than amateurism, which emerged in the nineteenth century in England. Earning money from sport has been an avenue of upward social mobility for centuries, starting with the Roman gladiators and continuing to the present day sport stars such as David Beckham and Rafael Nadal.

Ancient Rome and industrial England in the nineteenth century shared similar social characteristics, such as the mass of a population living closely together with leisure time to fill and a disposable income to spend on entertainment. However, by the nineteenth century the dominant sport ethic in England was amateurism rather than professionalism.

Professional sport was very much in evidence in England prior to the nineteenth century in a variety of sports. Examples were pedestrianism (an early form of race walking), prize fighting (including early forms of boxing and self defence) and athletics. By the nineteenth century the middle and upper classes favoured the amateur code whilst the professional performers or athletes were always from the lower classes, as they did not have the luxury to participate in sport for the love of it. If they wished to pursue a sporting activity seriously they needed to earn money from it. Because of this they found themselves excluded from many events by the gentleman amateurs who treated professional sport with disdain, believing it lacked the moral codes they held so dear. Hence, amateurism and professionalism became part of a strict social class divide in the nineteenth century and early twentieth century, particularly in England. In the structure of professional sport, the following generalisation of roles could be made:

- lower class: **performer**
- middle class: agents, promoters and managers
- upper class: **patrons**.

In professional sport the performer was (and still is) paid by results, hence training and specialising in their 'trade' was important.

Sports have undergone major changes in their amateur/professional status. Rugby football is a useful case study.

KEY TERMS

Performer:
someone who takes part in sport or other activity

TASK 16.07

Consider some of the quotes on page 257 and answer the following question:

What are the advantages and disadvantages, suggested by the players, of Rugby Union turning professional?

'We're better players now, without a shadow of a doubt. I played in the amateur era and you just couldn't dedicate as much time to it.'

'The game has moved on so far now you need to dedicate every day of the week to rugby.'

'I don't think there's quite the risk of player burnout that some people fear. With professionalism it means that when you're not playing or training, you're relaxing and your recovery time is good.'

'We've got great fitness coaches and great advisers who know if you're burning out; in fact many people just say "burnout" because they're tired.'

'The game has developed immensely. The physical nature is now so unrelenting and unsympathetic almost to the point that it's ridiculous.'

'England has so far avoided doping controversies suffered by other countries but players could be tempted in the future if pressures are not eased.'

'In the amateur ethos the pitches were poor, the standard of rugby was consequently poor. It was slow and not a good spectacle.'

'There are issues with regard to the politics of the game and how it is run, specifically in England where you have the club versus country debate. The issue is for guys playing international rugby who then come back to club rugby without any break.'

'From a personal point of view there are more games being put on the list and I think that's a money-making scheme.'

Fig 16.05 The advantages and disadvantages of turning professional

Professionalism at a price

In the twentieth and twenty-first centuries, many sports have become professional and amateurism has become constrained and squeezed. Note that you can be an amateur and compete for your country in some sports, such as in judo. However, where a sport has both amateur and professional performers, the professional performers tend to be regarded as being of a higher standard.

Many professional performers have a high status in their sport and if the sport receives a high level of **media** coverage they become household names. As professional performers they are paid by results and therefore success in their sport is crucial. This places heavy expectations on them, from themselves, coaches, spectators, the media and so on. The pressure to perform consistently and at a high level can cause the 'win at all costs' ethic to be adhered to, overriding the more traditional British values associated with sport. Therefore, deviant behaviour in the form of aggression, cheating and even doping can be considered necessary in order to win. (Deviant behaviour will be covered in detail in Chapter 17.)

Sponsorship and **endorsements** are very good earners for sportsmen and women and a charismatic, high profile performer is more likely to attract lucrative sponsorship deals. However, sponsors bring with them their own pressures, particularly expecting the performer to make regular appearances. Sponsors might even encourage a player to play when injured.

KEY TERMS

Patron:
a person who sponsors any kind of athlete or artist from their private funds

Media:
forms of mass communication to the general public, comprising newspapers, radio, television, internet and all forms of advertising

Sponsorship:
the provision of funds or other forms of support to an individual or event for a commercial return

Endorsements:
athletes display companies' names on their equipment, clothing and vehicles. The athletes are contracted to publicly declare their approval of a product or service

Fig 16.06 Professional players are not necessarily better than amateur performers, but they are paid for playing their sport

EXAM TIP:

Do not assume professional sport means a high level of skill and amateur sport means a low level of skill. However, where the two codes exist in the sport, e.g. football, the professional players are likely to compete at a higher standard.

Take note that professional or amateur is not about the level the player competes at but the administration of the sport – i.e. does it pay its players?

Amateurism 19th century	Professionalism 19th century
• a concept which evolved in nineteenth century England amongst the upper classes • the term 'gentleman amateur' emerged • based upon participating in sport for the love of it rather than for monetary gain • participation was deemed more important than the winning • encompassed the belief in fair play or sportsmanship and abiding by the spirit as well as the rules of the game • the 'all rounder' was highly regarded by the amateurs believing one was celebrating god-given abilities • amateurism originally had a social class distinction as it excluded the lower class from participating in many activities	• earning money from sport has been an avenue of upward social mobility for centuries • traditionally the working classes were associated with professionalism as they were the ones who needed to earn their livelihood from sport • the importance of the monetary reward ensured professionals would specialise in an activity and train seriously • professional competitors were often excluded by the middle-class amateurs from competing in the same competitions

Table 16.05 The historical view of the amateur and professional when compared with the present day

Amateurism present day	Professionalism present day
• many amateur performers struggled in the twentieth century with commercial pressures and offers of monetary rewards • over 150 years amateur sport has been squeezed by professional sport and become less influential • one of the significant changes that occurred at the end of the twentieth century was the Rugby Football Union, the bastion of amateurism, turning professional in 1996. Today the pure ideal of amateurism is difficult to adhere to and amateurs can now officially receive financial aid from sponsorship, trust funds and organisations such as Sport Aid and the National Lottery • even the Olympic Games, initially based on the amateur concept, now accept professional performers from sports such as tennis and basketball	• during the 20th century professional sport increased its status at the expense of amateurism • sports in the modern world need to be able to survive commercially • money enables a national governing body to promote the game, finance coaching, competitions and so on • many professional performers have a high status in their sport and if the sport receives a high level of media coverage their faces become household names. Sponsorship and endorsements are very good earners for sport performers and a charismatic, high profile performer is more likely to attract lucrative sponsorship deals • as professional performers they are paid by results and therefore success in their sport is crucial • this places heavy expectations on them, from themselves, coaches, spectators, media and so on • professionals can be owned/contracted/hired and fired/transferred/sold and high standards of performance are crucial • they are considered part of the entertainment industry and because they are in the public eye they suffer from a lack of privacy

Table 16.05 continued

APPLY IT!

Possible examination questions, linking the topics of amateurism and professionalism from the nineteenth century to the present day, are shown below with suggested answers.

Q: Why is the professional sport performer highly regarded in modern day society?

A:

- Professional sports tend to get more media coverage, giving the sport a high profile.
- The athletes become well-known, household names. They are seen as **role models**, often achieving celebrity status.
- Modern societies respect winners and high earners as most are based on a meritocratic system.
- Professional sport tends to follow the Lombardian ethic – winning isn't the most important thing, it's the only thing.
- Professional sport is often considered to be more entertaining and exciting with high standards of performance.
- Professional sport allows upward social mobility with some performers achieving the dream of 'rags to riches'.

Q: Why did the amateur performer have a higher status than the professional performer in the nineteenth century?

A:

- Amateurs were from the middle and upper classes – the most powerful groups in society.
- Professionals were from the working classes who often worked for the patron (upper class).
- Amateurs applied moral values to sport which distinguished them from the lower class professionals.
- The amateurs had the power to exclude the working classes, e.g. manual labour clause in rowing and the existence of closed competitions, where amateurs and professionals were not allowed to compete together.

TASK 16.08

Research sports that have retained their amateur status. Some examples might be judo or swimming. Consider the advantages and disadvantages of this situation for these sports.

KEY TERMS

Role model:
an individual admired for his or her skill, values or attitudes. Role models can influence young people's behaviour

Olympism – the Olympic Ideal

Baron Pierre de Coubertin visited England in the nineteenth century and was so impressed with the moral values the English public schools attached to sport that he established the modern Olympic Games, in 1896, along similar principles.

KEY TERMS

Olympism:
a concept balancing the mind and body which encourages effort, educational values and ethical behaviour

He had become increasingly concerned about the poor health and lack of patriotism within his own country. He believed the English approach towards sport would help to combat these problems as well as furthering international understanding. The Olympic Games have gone from strength to strength and today are the largest and most prestigious of the World Games.

Facts about the Olympic Games:

1. The symbol of the Games is five interconnecting rings representing the five continents: Europe, Asia, Oceania, Africa and the Americas.
2. The motto is *Citius, Altius, Fortius* – meaning 'swifter, higher, stronger'.

Fig 16.07 The opening ceremony of the Olympic Games in Beijing, 2008

3. The following message appears on every scoreboard – 'the most important thing in the Olympic Games is not to win but to take part, just as the most important thing in life is not the triumph but the struggle. The essential thing is not to have conquered but to have fought well.'

The Olympic Ideal

The six goals of the Olympic movement are incorporated in the term Olympism:

1. personal excellence
2. sport as education
3. cultural exchange
4. mass participation
5. fair play
6. international understanding.

The Olympic oath, taken by an athlete on behalf of all competitors, states:

'In the name of all the competitors I promise that we shall take part in these Olympic Games respecting and abiding by the rules which govern them in the true spirit of sportsmanship.'

Its text was modified at the 2000 Sydney Games and now includes a phrase confirming the will of the athlete to avoid doping. Since 1972, a referee has made the same undertaking on behalf of all the judges and officials.

Let us consider these original ideals and discuss whether they are still relevant today.

1. **Personal excellence** – this competition is the largest in the world and allows athletes from the Olympic sports to show their individual level of excellence. Conversely, athletes from sports not accepted as part of the Olympic programme fight hard to be able to display their levels of excellence. Each year more and more sports become integrated into the Olympic programme. The Games used only to include amateur sports but today the blurring of amateurism has made this more difficult. Consequently sports such as tennis and basketball are also now included. It could be argued that for these sports the Olympics is not their real showcase and their level of performance may be best displayed at tournaments such as Wimbledon or the American championships.

   The controversy of doping also brings into question whether all Olympic records have been won by natural ability or whether it is the excellence of the laboratories that have proven more significant.
2. **Sport as education** – people learn many things from participating in sport, from motor skills to appreciation of movement, to values such as working with other people. The National Olympic Committees (NOC) run Olympic Days involving schools in an effort to boost participation in sport and the popularity of the Games. Through the extensive media coverage we learn about many sports.
3. **Cultural exchange** – as an international competition many different countries and cultures are involved. Athletes travel to many different countries and again through the media the rest of the world often learns about the host cities and the cultures of the competing countries. However, it could also be suggested that the globalisation of sport and particularly the Americanisation of sports are beginning to make traditional sports 'shrink'. Also, sports such as basketball are beginning to have more coverage and influence outside the USA.
4. **Mass participation** – 'Sport for All' is a movement promoting the Olympic ideal that sport is a human right for everyone regardless of race, social class and sex. The Olympic Games is the largest competition in the world and as

such is viewed by millions of people. It is widely recognised that extensive media coverage can boost participation figures at grass roots level. National Olympic Committees are supposed to make it a policy to increase participation overall. One method is the Olympic Day Run – open to men, women and children of all ages. National governing bodies and the IOC are implementing policies to reduce discrimination in their sports and events, and increase participation in groups that have traditionally not been overly associated with the sport.

5. **Fair play** – this value has been very important in the sports world since the nineteenth century when the middle and upper classes in England made it an integral part of participating in sport. Also known as sportsmanship it is the observance not only of the rules but also the spirit of the game. It is the essence of the contract to compete. You need to consider positive factors such as the Fair Play Awards and negative factors such as the increase in prosecutions for sport-related offences, such as aggression and drug-taking. The IOC has taken a stance on drugs in sport by:
   - coordinating their efforts in the prevention of drug-taking
   - sponsoring conferences
   - accrediting laboratories
   - establishing a list of banned substances.
6. **International understanding** – with so many countries coming together and learning about one another's cultures it should be possible for us all to adopt a more understanding and tolerant approach towards our differences. The Olympic Games have rarely been cancelled but they were for World War II. Unfortunately the Games have been affected by wider political situations and are often remembered as much for the political events surrounding them as for the athletic achievements. One of the key reasons for this is that the Games have provided a focus for the country hosting the event. Their political systems are given prominent media coverage and instances have occurred when governments have used this to promote their political message.

Year	Venue	Political situation
1936	Berlin	• Germany used the Games for Nazi propaganda • Hitler's Aryan race theory was discredited when Jesse Owen, a black athlete, won four gold medals
1972	Munich	• Israeli athletes and officials were assassinated by Palestinian terrorists
1980	Moscow	• 52 nations boycotted as a protest against the Soviet invasion of Afghanistan

Table 16.06 Political situations that have affected some Olympics

STRETCH AND CHALLENGE

Describe the structural changes that have occurred in association football from its popular origins to its rational form and explain the social determinants that have been influential.

ATHLETE PROFILE

Horseball is a relatively new sport. Interestingly, it was created in France in the 1970s as an exercise to improve skill and discipline between horse and rider. It made its first appearance in Britain at an exhibition tournament at the Horse of the Year Show in 1990. As it is a relatively new sport, the national and international governing body have had to establish it as a sport in terms of both the technical and ethical issues as well as raising its profile across the world.

The players do not get paid and so it is classed as an amateur sport, but the officials do (although this is a nominal sum in the UK). However, some coaches are paid, especially in France where horseball is very popular. The coaches are often high-level riding instructors who also coach horseball.

Fig 16.08 Horseball started as an exercise to improve skill and discipline between horse and rider

ExamCafé

Relax, refresh, result!

Refresh your memory

Revision checklist

Make sure you know the following:

- ▷ The traditions of recreational and sporting activities go back many centuries.
- ▷ The United Kingdom was the birthplace of modern sport.
- ▷ Sports were rationalised and codified, mostly in the nineteenth century.
- ▷ The social class system was to prove influential in the manner and values that sports developed.
- ▷ The middle classes became the moral force in society and instigated the administration and bureaucracy that was to epitomise modern sport.
- ▷ Amateurism and professionalism developed monetary and social class distinctions.
- ▷ Amateurism used to be the dominant sporting value in nineteenth-century England.
- ▷ Today amateurism has become squeezed by professionalism, having to bow to the commercial pressures of the modern day sports world.
- ▷ The UK originally housed the headquarters of the national and international governing bodies.
- ▷ Many of the sporting ethics established in the nineteenth century remain relevant in the present day sports world.
- ▷ The contract to compete is an unwritten mutual agreement by opponents to abide by the rules, give 100 per cent effort and allow the opposition to demonstrate their skill.
- ▷ Sportsmanship is synonymous with fair play; gamesmanship is the bending of the rules to gain an advantage.
- ▷ The monetary rewards available today have negatively affected performers' ethics leading to an increase in deviant behaviour (see Chapter 17).

Revise as you go

1. Which social class was mostly involved in popular recreation?
2. What kind of football was an example of popular recreation?
3. Why did popular recreation decline?
4. Give three characteristics of rational recreation.
5. Give three reasons to account for the type of leisure the upper classes enjoyed in the nineteenth century.
6. Which social group devised the concept of amateurism in the nineteenth century?
7. Why did professional football become so popular in the nineteenth century?
8. What effect did the middle classes have on sport and recreation in the nineteenth century?
9. The Victorian era was a period of social reform. What were the intentions of the numerous Factory Acts during this time?
10. Which factors caused organised sport to expand rapidly during the period 1901–18?
11. What is meant by the term 'contract to compete'?
12. What would have to happen for the contract to compete to be broken?
13. What is meant by the term 'amateur'?
14. What is meant by the term 'sportsmanship'?
15. How does the Lombardian ethic differ from the code of amateurism?
16. Explain what is meant by gamesmanship and give a sporting example.
17. Why has sportsmanship declined over the last few decades?
18. Discuss whether the Olympic Ideal is still relevant today.
19. What reasons did Coubertin have for reinventing the modern Olympic Games?
20. Describe four symbols of the Olympic Games.

CHAPTER 17

Sport, ethics, deviancy and the law

LEARNING OBJECTIVES:

By the end of this chapter you should be able to describe:

- positive and negative forms of deviance in relation to the player/performer and spectator
- the causes of violence in sport in relation to the player/performer and spectator
- the implications of violence in sport on the player/performer, spectator and the sport
- strategies for preventing violence within sport to the player/performer and spectator
- the reasons behind elite performers using illegal drugs to aid performance
- the implications to the sport and player/performer of drug taking
- strategies for eliminating players/performers taking drugs
- arguments for and against drug taking and testing
- the uses of sports legislation in relation to:
  - performers (e.g. contracts; injury; loss of earnings)
  - officials (e.g. negligence)
  - spectators (e.g. safety; hooliganism)
- the increased number of prosecutions within sport and the reasons for this.

Introduction

In this chapter we shall consider deviant and violent behaviour and also the problems and implications of the use of banned substances in sport. The legislation covering these points will also be looked at.

Deviancy and sport

So far we have focused on the traditional values of amateurism, athleticism and olympism. These values have underpinned British sport and as a nation we have viewed them positively. However, as we know, the sports world is also full of behaviour that goes against these principles and ethics. This type of behaviour can be referred to as **deviant** or **dysfunctional behaviour**.

Deviant behaviour is behaviour which goes against society's general norms and values. This can be criminally deviant, that is, against the law, or morally deviant, whereby no law has been broken but society would generally not consider the behaviour in a positive light. Consider looking after a four-year-old for a day. Much of what you would say would confirm society's values, such as, respect for other people, respect for property and so on, e.g. you might find yourself saying 'Don't hit your little brother, be nice to him' or 'Don't stand on that, you'll break it.'

Dysfunctional behaviour

If we consider the phrase 'against society's norms and values' it is clear that someone or some group in society has imposed their set of ideas on others. This group would be considered the dominant group in society and in the UK could be deemed to be white, male and middle class. This is the group that has the most control and power in terms of distribution of resources and decision making at the highest levels. Therefore groups of people who fall outside these boundaries may well hold opposing views and opinions and have different behaviour patterns, but this would not necessarily mean they were 'wrong'. Thus deviancy is relative and deviants may be victims of a power system that makes the rules.

Athletes become part of a community bonded by a sense of commitment and are often encouraged to behave in ways that would not be accepted in other areas of life. 'On the field' deviant behaviour includes 'violations of norms that occur while preparing or participating in sports events' (Coakley 1993). It can be caused by the pressure of the media, coaches, sponsorship deals and so on. If the athlete's behaviour breaks the rules of the sport it can be dealt with appropriately, but a culture has developed that accepts this type of behaviour and even deems it necessary for the sake of the win.

TASK 17.01

List examples of deviant behaviour in a variety of sports and say why you consider it to be deviant behaviour.

There are two types of deviancy:

1. **Negative deviancy** – in sporting situations this can include violations such as deliberately fouling another player or taking performance enhancing drugs. The main motivation is to win at all costs.
2. **Positive deviancy** – athletes are encouraged to behave in ways that would be unacceptable in other spheres of life. This can be classed as over-conformity to the sport ethic. An example of positive deviancy may be where an athlete is encouraged to over-train or perform when injured; in other aspects of life we would not encourage someone to cause further damage to his or her health.

Positive deviancy is a slightly more difficult aspect of deviant behaviour and might relate to the motivation for that behaviour, e.g. it may be about not letting people down rather than simply wanting to be the best.

KEY TERMS

Deviancy:
behaviour which goes against society's general norms and values

Dysfunctional behaviour:
this occurs when a part of the social structure does not contribute positively to the maintenance of society, resulting in disharmony and conflict

Negative deviancy:
in sporting situations this can include violations such as deliverately fouling another player or taking performance-enhancing drugs. The main motivation is to win at all costs.

Positive deviancy:
athletes are encouraged to behave in ways that would be unacceptable in other spheres of life. This can be classed as over-conformity to the sport ethic. An example of positive deviancy may be where an athlete is encouraged to over-train or perform when injured.

We will now consider the specific issues of:

- aggression and violence
- hooliganism
- doping.

EXAM TIP:

For this specification you will only be directly examined on negative deviancy – aggression and violence, doping, and hooliganism.

Aggression and violence

TASK 17.02

'Serious sport has nothing to do with fair play. It is a mixture of hatred, jealousy, boastfulness and disregard of all rules and sadistic pleasure in witnessing violence. In other words it is war minus the shooting.' (George Orwell, 1936)

In groups, prepare a discussion that both supports and refutes the statement made by George Orwell.

All sport involves some sort of **conflict**, which can be positive or negative – it is the essence of competition. If it is controlled it is functional, but if not it can soon become dysfunctional, i.e. negative to the players, officials, spectators and the very sport itself.

We attempt to control any conflict situations by channelling that **aggression** in a positive way which can act as a catharsis or stress relief. Channelled aggression or **balanced tension** is the ability to utilise all your resources to achieve optimum performance without using unlawful or unethical strategies. Spectators are not able to release their tension in the same way as the performers who are actively exerting themselves. This can cause frustration which may lead to violence.

Conflict appears in many forms:

- within yourself, e.g. striving for a personal best
- against another team or within a team, e.g. between top goal scorers
- against the environment/nature, e.g. the conquest of a mountain
- against a crowd, e.g. players becoming aggressive or abusive towards spectators
- against officials.

Conflict can also be determined by the nature of the activity, for example contact or non-contact sports.

KEY TERMS

Conflict:
change and/or progress made by one group at the expense of another

Aggression:
the intention to harm another human being either verbally or mentally

Balanced tension:
a degree of stress can be productive if it is controlled and channelled

Hooligan:
a disorderly, violent young person usually associated with the game of football

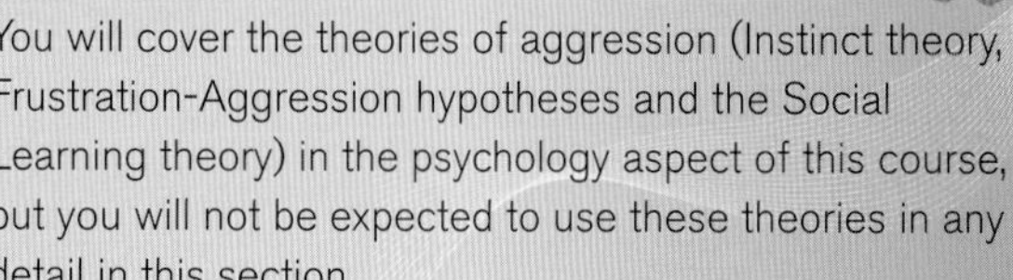

EXAM TIP:

You will cover the theories of aggression (Instinct theory, Frustration-Aggression hypotheses and the Social Learning theory) in the psychology aspect of this course, but you will not be expected to use these theories in any detail in this section.

TASK 17.03

Draw up a list of the causes of aggression in a sport performer.

Spectator violence – football hooliganism

Professional football is by far the most popular spectator sport in Britain. Today it is estimated that between 4 and 5 million people attend a football match in England and Wales every year. This number is smaller than it used to be and there are many complex reasons for this, such as changing leisure patterns. However, many people blame football's relative decline up until the mid-1980s on football hooliganism.

Although football hooliganism only became recognised by the government and the media as a serious problem in the 1960s, hooligan behaviour at football, particularly in England, has a long history. 'Roughs' were regularly reported as causing trouble at matches in the professional game's early years at the end of the nineteenth century, on occasions attacking and stoning referees as well as the visiting players. It was not until the early 1960s, however, that the media coverage of football began once more regularly to report hooliganism at matches. Around this time, too, there was a general 'moral panic' (Cohen, 1973) about the behaviour of young people, sparked by:

- rising juvenile crime rates
- uncertainty about the future
- the emergence of a number of 'threatening' national youth styles, like that of the 'teddy boy'
- racial tensions symbolised by the Notting Hill disturbances of 1958.

It was around this time that football hooliganism in England began to take on a more cohesive and organised appearance.

EXAM TIP:

For the purpose of this specification you will need to understand that there are a variety of causes of hooliganism and be able to discuss the validity of these theories.

Possible causes of hooliganism: The mid-1960s saw alliances being formed between groups of young men drawn largely from working-class housing estates and suburbs. Some sociologists believe this acted as an outlet for defending local masculine reputations and territories, such as streets and terraces.

An English disease?: Football hooliganism is often cited as an 'English' problem, possibly because, as mentioned earlier, England has a long history of football spectator disorders, going back to the early days of the professional sport in England in the nineteenth century. But evidence does not support this. In the early 1960s, the English wanted to pull out of European club competition because of their fears about foreign supporters and players becoming aggressive towards them. However, football hooliganism does appear to be an issue for the national side, although other countries also have serious hooligan incidents.

Theories about hooliganism: Most of the evidence on hooligan offenders suggests that they are:

- in their late teens or their 20s (though some 'leaders' are older)
- mainly in manual or lower clerical occupations or, to a lesser extent, are unemployed or working in the **'grey' economy**, and that they come mainly from working-class backgrounds
- ritualistic and non-violent, i.e. they do not always engage in acts of violence in their behaviour (Marsh et al, 1978)
- not always from working-class backgrounds. Unsurprisingly, London hooligans tend to be more affluent than their northern counterparts, and it is certainly 'stylish' and 'macho' in these football circles to have a distinctive style in terms of dress, for example
- sometimes spontaneous and 'random' in their acts of violence but can also be involved in political conspiracies and the more formal organisation of hooligan assaults. Though reports of the extent to which hooliganism is 'organised' with political influences may be over-dramatised, the English national side does seem to have been something of a focus for the expression of racist sentiments among some young fans, especially in the 1980s.

KEY TERMS

Grey economy:
grey goods are not illegal: they are sold outside normal distribution channels that have no relationship with the producer of the goods

However, sociologists at Leicester University (Dunning et al 1988) criticised Marsh et al (1978), not for arguing that terrace behaviour was ritualistic or rule-governed, but rather for understating the amount of 'real' violence which occurred at matches. They suggest that hooliganism is a particular form of aggressive **masculinity**, especially in lower class communities. In these 'rough' neighbourhoods young males are socialised (at home, at work, in peer group gangs, etc.) into standards that value and reward publicly assertive and openly aggressive and violent expressions of masculinity. Young men are expected to be able to 'look after themselves'.

KEY TERMS

Masculinity:
possessing qualities or characteristics considered typical or appropriate to a man. Example characteristics might be dominant, strong, forceful

Fig 17.01 Football hooligans

Some fights are even pre-arranged, by telephone, away from matches, especially there are limited opportunities for fighting in and around stadia because of police surveillance techniques. As well as acquiring a 'manly' status, the camaraderie, loyalty and 'entertainment' value of hooligan involvement is also prized by young men whose opportunities for status and excitement via other channels is relatively limited.

Heavy drinking is often a key element in a 'good day out', and drinking offences figure strongly in national football arrest statistics in England. However, drinking occurs in many other sports, e.g. rugby, but does not seem to result in hooliganism.

The sociologist Ian Taylor (1987) argues that the class fraction identified by the Leicester research (1988) as the main production ground for hooliganism cannot account for the rise of the high-spending and fashionable soccer 'casual' who was at the heart of English hooliganism in Europe in the 1990s. 'Casuals' use their conspicuous consumption of expensive and stylish clothing as another means of competing with their hooligan rivals. Taylor favours the 'masculinity' theory rather than class as being the key to the current hooligan problem.

More recently, Robson's important and detailed work on Millwall fans, *'No-One Likes Us, We Don't Care'* (2000) suggests that the practices of hooliganism – and racism – among some of the club's fans should also be interpreted as a form of resistance; fans are objecting to the intrusion of more middle-class sensibilities into the sport and local culture. Many working-class fans have been isolated by high ticket prices and corporate hospitality.

Armstrong (1994, 1997) asserts that gang members of *'The Blades'* at Sheffield United come from a range of locations and backgrounds. Armstrong claims they are involved in hooliganism primarily because it provides 'social drama' and the opportunity to 'belong', achieve 'honour' and inflict shame on opponents. For him, hooligan groups are, in fact, very diverse in their make up – they can include fans drawn from across classes and anti-racists. They show few signs of organisation and they mainly enjoy confrontation rather than violence.

Finn (1994) sees hooliganism as an example of the search for a 'flow' or peak' experience; an intense, emotional experience not usually encountered in everyday life. Flow experiences allow for an open expression of shared, collective emotionality. Hooligans, like other fans, seek peak or flow experiences through their involvement in football; unlike other fans, however, they reject the vicarious role of a football supporter in favour of a more active and rewarding role as a direct participant in spectator confrontations. Kerr (1994) also believes that hooliganism, like other sorts of affective crimes (crimes which are motivated by emotional arousal, such as joy-riding), reflects the search for high levels of emotional arousal through risk-taking against a general background of long periods of boredom.

A summary of hooligan theories

It is clear that:

- risk and excitement are central to the hooligan phenomenon
- it is largely young men who are involved
- heavy drinking and violence seem to be linked though at least some of those young men regularly involved in hooliganism seem to be aggressive in certain circumstances with or without drink
- hooligans can be drawn from a wide variety of backgrounds with differing motivations
- racism is an issue in certain situations, particularly at a national event
- incidents of violence or poor refereeing on the field can trigger hooligan disturbances but, once again, it is difficult to argue that such incidents are a deep cause of hooliganism. After all, some hooligan incidents occur hours before a match has even kicked off! Also, there are many more violent sports than football which have not had the same problems of hooliganism
- when newspapers report on football, they use the sort of language which seems more appropriate to the world of war than that of sport (Hall, 1978). This probably helps to heighten rivalries between opposing fan groups, as do the 'predictions' newspapers sometimes make that 'trouble' is likely to occur between rival fans or that the police and local residents are preparing for an 'invasion' of visiting fans or are being placed on 'red alert'. This sort of reporting has been identified by fans themselves as being dangerous, both in terms of its identification of miscreants and also in its alleged distortions and prejudices.

Controlling hooliganism

Most Premier League matches these days require between 25 and 100 police officers to control crowds and limit hooligan outbreaks, but 'high risk' matches demand more.

The police have now established a complex intelligence network for exchanging information about 'troublesome' fans, under the auspices of the National Criminal Intelligence Services (NCIS) Football Intelligence Unit. The use of Football Trust-funded closed circuit TV (CCTV) equipment by the police in and around grounds has also contributed to limiting problems in these areas and to the successful prosecution of offenders. In fact, it is now an offence to trespass onto the pitch or its surrounds, following the Football Offences Act of 1991, and anyone who does so is likely to be traced from CCTV coverage of their activities.

Recent legislation has helped the police deal with hooliganism, though some of it is also controversial:

- The Public Disorder Act of 1986 allowed courts to make exclusion orders banning fans from grounds.
- The Football Spectators Act of 1989 allowed courts to impose restriction orders on convicted fans to prevent them attending matches abroad involving England or Wales.
- The Football Offences Act (1991) created three new offences of disorderly behaviour:
  1. Throwing missiles towards the pitch or spectators.
  2. Taking part in indecent or racialist chanting.
  3. Going on the pitch or its surrounds without lawful authority.

Over the past 20 years or so, clubs have been forced by circumstances, by legislation or both, to spend a considerable amount of money on trying to make their grounds more hooligan proof. Linked with these anti-hooligan and modernising measures is the issue of spectator safety. The post-war years have seen a number of spectator disasters, one example being the FA Cup semi-final at Hillsborough in Sheffield in 1989, where 96 Liverpool supporters were crushed to death in a section of terracing surrounded by high perimeter fencing. Since major football grounds in Britain became modernised, unfenced and all-seated in the early 1990s following Hillsborough, they do seem to have become safer and less violent venues than those of even five years ago. As the size of football crowds has continued to rise in England, and as perimeter fences have given way to surveillance cameras and new catch-all offences for hooliganism, so match arrests and the size of police commitments at English football have steadily declined.

In addition to these changes, many clubs have also introduced family enclosures as a means of encouraging parents to attend matches with their children in safety. Clubs have traditionally provided rather poor facilities for female fans and for youngsters. A national Community Programme in Professional Football run jointly by the PFA, the FA, the Premier League and the Football League, is now in operation at almost all of the 92 professional clubs. This scheme aims to increase local community involvement in clubs and promote better behaviour among young spectators.

Recent government legislation also provides for:

- restrictions on the carriage and consumption of alcohol at football
- the banning from matches of previous football offenders
- the making of racist abuse and missile throwing offences
- the making of trespass onto the playing area illegal.

Part Two of the Football Spectators Act (1989) was designed to be used to prevent hooligan offenders from travelling abroad to watch international matches.

Despite these problems the game is currently enjoying a boom in its:

- attendance
- finances (at least at the top)
- ability to attract major foreign players
- image.

EXAM TIP:

Be prepared to outline strategies that the clubs, communities and security forces can use to prevent or reduce the incidence of hooliganism.

Its new commercialised and highly marketed format may be leaving behind sections of the game's 'traditional' audience, including, perhaps, some hooligan fans. The following are all helping to regulate and control attendance at matches:

- high ticket prices
- the loss of terracing has made grounds safer and less violent
- the sometimes oppressive management and stewarding of the football audience
- the extensive merchandising of top English clubs
- the changing (more 'feminised') atmosphere at football clubs in England
- the increasing number of season ticket holders at English clubs.

'Traditional' young male fans – 'lads' – may well be bored by, or excluded from, the 'new' football in England. One view is that some of them are now rather more interested in new dance/drugs cultures than in the 'passionless' and more 'middle-class' sport the English game is allegedly becoming (Gilman, 1994). Some people might put this change in the game down to the Americanisation of sport which is happening globally. English football clubs have imported intrusive ideas for promoting the sport from the USA:

- blaring music
- cheerleaders
- animal mascots
- licensed products from key rings to children's clothes.

Aggression, violence and hooliganism – a summary

Possible causes	Consequences	Solutions or remedies
• Nature of the sport, e.g. football is linked with aggression whilst gymnastics is not • History of an event, e.g. a derby involves intense local rivalry • Observed violence (if players or spectators see a violent act it can often incite a violent response) • Nature of stadium, e.g. all seater • Referee's decisions • Monetary rewards • Peer pressure • Excitement/adrenalin rush • Political groups • Loyalty/patriotism • Importance of event • Media hype • Alcohol • Frustration	• Loss of sponsors • Poor image for attracting new talent • Loss of spectators • Banning of supporters • Loss of points/elimination from competitions • Negative role models • Incites trouble within a wider population	• Crowd segregation with family zones • Limit attendance • Fair-play charters • Punishment more severe, e.g. fines/prosecutions • Develop positive role models – shame negative role models • Develop club/community links/ education programmes • Tighter security/CCTV, etc. • Control alcohol availability • Responsible media reporting • Improve facilities

Table 17.01 Violence in sport

Doping – use of performance-enhancing drugs

The issue of doping in sport goes back to Ancient Greece and Rome where athletes resorted to taking drugs to either mask pain or to enhance performance. For the purposes of this specification you only need to focus on the present day. Any method used to enhance performance is called an **ergogenic aid** and includes the use of technology for improving the effectiveness of equipment. In this case we are only concerned with performance-enhancing drugs.

Table 17.02 outlines the types of doping agents that are banned by the World Anti-Doping Agency (WADA).

Drugs which are banned during competition	Substances banned during and outside the competitive season	Prohibited methods	Classes banned in specific sports
• **Stimulants** • Narcotics • Cannabinoids • Glucocorticoids	• Anabolic agents, e.g. steroids • Hormones and related substances, e.g. peptide hormones • Beta-2 agonists • Anti-oestrogenic agents • **Diuretics** and other masking agents	• Enhancement of oxygen transfer, e.g. EPO (**erythopoietin**). The synthetic version has become the cheat's way of using the drug. • Pharmacological, chemical and physical manipulation, e.g. **anabolic steroids** • Gene doping	• Alcohol • **Beta blockers**

Table 17.02 Drugs banned by WADA

Table 17.03 highlights various types of drugs, their side effects and their use in specific sports.

Types of drugs	Reasons for use	Side-effects	Sport
Anabolic steroids – artificially produced male hormones	• Promote muscle growth • Ability to train harder with less fatigue • Repair body after stress • Increased aggression	• Females develop male features • Liver/heart damage	• Athletics • Swimming • Power/explosive events
Narcotic analgesics – 'pain killers'	• Reduce pain • Mask injury	• Highly addictive • Respiratory problems • Nausea	• All sports
Stimulants – stimulate body both mentally and physically	• Reduce tiredness • Increase alertness • Increase endurance	• Rise in blood pressure/ temperature • Addiction • Death	• Cycling • Boxing
Beta blockers	• Steady nerves • Stop trembling	• Lowers blood pressure • Slows heart rate • Tiredness	• Shooting • Archery • Snooker
Diuretics – remove fluid from body	• Lose weight quickly	• Dehydration • Dizziness • Faintness	• Jockeys • Boxers
Peptide hormones – naturally occurring, e.g. EPO	• Build and mend muscle • Increase oxygen transport	• Muscle wasting • EPO increases red cells in blood	• Similar to steroids
Blood doping – injection of blood to increase number of blood cells	• Body has more energy to work	• Allergic reactions • AIDS/hepatitis • Blood clots	• Running • Cycling • Marathons • Skiing

Table 17.03 Different drugs, their uses and side-effects in sport

KEY TERMS

Ergogenic aids:
refers to any substance that improves performance

Doping agents:
a term used to denote any illegal drug such as cannabis or narcotics which will help improve an athlete's performance

World Anti-Doping Agency (WADA):
partnership of governments and sport in the attempt to standardise anti-doping programmes

Stimulants:
substances such as amphetamines used to stimulate physiological activity; they improve endurance and mental alertness

Diuretics:
drugs used to reduce the weight of athletes in sports such as gymnastics

Erythopoietin (EPO):
a naturally occurring hormone produced by the kidneys that stimulates red cell production

Anabolic steroids:
artificially produced male hormones which help to repair the body after periods of stress

Beta blockers:
drugs used by athletes to steady nerves in sports such as archery

Blood doping:
the removal and reinfusion of a person's blood to improve the aerobic capacity by increasing the number of red blood cells

Table 17.04 highlights some discussion points including:

- why performers take anabolic steroids
- the harmful side-effects
- why the ban on drugs is not lifted
- strategies to prevent performers taking drugs.

Why performers take anabolic steroids	Why performers shouldn't take drugs – the harmful side-effects	Why not lift the ban on drugs?	Strategies to prevent doping
• To train harder • Build muscle for explosive events • Fear of 'not making it' • Rewards are worth the risk • To be entertaining • Pressure from coaches, media and self • Drugs easily accessible • Increased aggression	• Health risks and death • Consequences if caught, e.g. shame/ban • Not fair/immoral (The International Olympic Committee's stance against drugs is based on their code of fair play and competition whilst protecting the health of the athlete) • Negative role model for children • Loss of earnings and sponsorship • It encourages more athletes to take drugs who would not otherwise do so	• Technologically advanced countries have an advantage in terms of coaching, scientifically-based equipment, etc • If properly monitored it is not a health risk. Many drugs are naturally occurring • Drugs may be used for normal medical care • People should be free to choose • Athletes don't ask to be role models • The money on testing could be invested elsewhere • Many of the banned substances on the WADA list are not illegal – they are available over the counter • In many cases testing has proved unsound, jeopardising athletes' careers	• Random and out-of-season testing • Better coordination between organisations • Education programmes for coaches and athletes • Stricter punishments and life bans • More money into testing programme • Unified governing body policies • Better technology for testing • Use of both positive and negative role models

Table 17.04 Discussion points on drug-taking in sport

EXAM TIP:

1. Be prepared to provide arguments and counter-arguments about the role drugs play in modern-day sport.
2. You will not be required to know the in-depth physiological effects of drugs

Drugs and the International Olympic Committee (IOC)

The IOC was forced to take action in the 1960s following the death of a cyclist who overdosed on amphetamines in the Rome Olympics and after scandals at the Tokyo Games in 1964. Consequently the IOC formed the Medical Commission in 1966. In 1981 it clarified its aim to:

- accredit laboratories around the world
- introduce the standardisation of sanctions

- lead an education drive against doping in sport
- encourage and sponsor research into sport science to show other viable alternatives to doping.

WADA was given this responsibility in 2002. If a substance fulfils any of the following criteria it is placed on the prohibited list:

- it has the potential to be performance enhancing
- it represents a risk to the athlete's health
- it violates the spirit of sport.

APPLY IT!

UK Sports director of worldwide impact and standards – this is a new post which includes responsibility for major events, international relations and drug-free sport.

Testing for banned substances

Should Britain's drug testing be placed in the hands of an independent authority? Many would say this is unarguable. While the same organisation that funds elite athletes also tests them for drug abuse, a conflict of interest exists. It has been suggested it is like allowing a fox to guard the hen house! People tend to believe that where there are no vested interests, there are no cover-ups.

The World Anti-Doping Code helps evaluate practice and procedure: more out-of-competition testing, target testing, whistle-blowing, fairness and independence in the hearing processes and international cooperation.

The new rule is that three missed tests constitute a doping violation. One might be because a 'life situation' occurred, e.g. a family incident, two might be a genuine mistake, three – unlikely to be viable. A hearing will then be held. USADA publish the missed tests of US athletes. Will this be done in the UK? One problem is that the higher profile athletes can afford very expensive lawyers. Legal challenges are expensive.

There would be little public support for the public funding of drug-convicted athletes, once they have served their penalty. The issue also affects coaches. The World Class Performance Programme allocates public money to athletes to help pay for their coaching. Those coaches include Darren Campbell's mentor, Linford Christie, who received a two-year ban in 1999 for testing positive for the steroid nandrolone. The policy is that drug-convicted athletes are banned for life from public funding but even this could face legal challenges.

How much trust do we place in international sports federations to conduct their own testing? Many international federations prefer to conduct testing themselves, a system open to suspicion.

The WADA investigation said that there were seven cases in tennis where exonerations were granted on what are now clearly unsustainable grounds. Trust is sabotaged where international federations are suspected of cover-ups.

Can we test for human growth hormone? These tests will allegedly only capture athletes taking HGH within 24 hours of competition.

UK Sport believes it is important to teach athletes values and ethics that enable them to resist temptation. UK Sport's drug-free campaign will focus on schoolchildren as young as seven. The education budget has been tripled to £200,000. But while the properly indoctrinated seven-year-olds are growing up, there might be a few drug cheats yet slipping through.

Pros and cons of drug testing

Why across-the-board drug testing would be good

- A uniform code of testing ensures the rules would be consistent from sport to sport and country to country. No sport or athlete could gain an advantage.

- Random tests are much more efficient than restricted testing periods, which give offenders the opportunity to flush drugs from their bodies and to time their periodic cycles of use.
- Professional athletes who belong to a union would not face lower standards created in the give-and-take of collective bargaining. Professional leagues would not be able to bargain away higher standards in return for financial concessions.
- The costs could be shared across sports and countries.

Why across-the-board drug testing wouldn't work

- Drug testing is inconsistent, and false positives are prevalent. A career could be damaged by a faulty test.
- What is classified as 'performance-enhancing' in one sport might not provide an advantage in another. One-size-fits-all testing does not take the actual effects of the substance on an athlete's performance into consideration.
- Professional athletes have a right to bargain over every aspect of their careers.
- The considerable financial cost may not produce a valuable result.

TASK 17.04

Can you add to these pros and cons of drug testing?

EXAM TIP:

You will not need to know the testing procedures but you will need to provide arguments for and against drug testing in sport.

KEY TERMS

Tetrahydrogestrinone (often referred to as THG or 'The Clear'):
is an anabolic steroid. It has affinity to the androgen receptor and the progesterone receptor, but not to the oestrogen receptor. The drug has been considered a designer drug

Sanctions:
the penalty laid down in a law for contravention of its provision. The IOC has a list of prohibited substances which athletes must not violate

Sport law:
the application of legal principles to all levels of competition of amateur and professional sport and to physical activity

APPLY IT!

Paying the price

Dwain Chambers is an English sprinter. His primary event is the 100 metres sprint but he also regularly runs in the 60 metres, 200 metres and 4×100 metres relay. His personal best of 9.97 seconds in the 100m is the second fastest time recorded by a British sprinter. By 2001, he had become the top British sprinter, breaking the 10 second barrier twice at the World Championships in Edmonton, Canada.

However, in October 2003, he tested positive for the banned steroid THG in a drugs test. Chambers received a two-year athletics ban, and a lifetime Olympic ban. He had all of his racing accomplishments since 2002 annulled, wiping out his European record.

Chambers returned to the track and field circuit in June 2006, and won gold with his teammates in the 4×100 m at the 2006 European Championships. After a break, Chambers returned to sprinting, winning a silver medal in the 60m at the 2008 IAAF World Indoor Championships. He has filed unsuccessful appeals against his Olympic ban.

Sport and the law

The deviant acts of violence, hooliganism and doping are against society's norms and values and are therefore likely to be considered to be against the law.

Sport law is:

'The application of legal principles to all levels of competition of amateur and professional sport and to physical activity.'
(Lewison/Christenson, Encyclopaedia of World Sport, 1996)

Sport was traditionally considered to be separate from the law and they were rarely linked. However, the number of deviant acts within sport appears to have increased, or it may be that incidents have been more widely reported by the media. Thus, the authorities have been forced to make sport as accountable as other social activities. Should incidents such as assaults be viewed separately to a similar instance outside the sport setting?

The needs of various groups should be considered:

Performers:

- Performers have accepted and understood the activities they participate in by abiding by the rules of the activity. However, should an opponent act outside the rules of the activity, e.g. violently, the performer could legitimately claim assault. The number of prosecutions has risen. Duncan Ferguson (1995) was the first professional soccer player to be imprisoned for an on-the-field assault.
- Performers are employees like anyone else and as such can be said to have the same employment rights as any other workers. Jean Marc Bosman, a Belgian footballer, forced the authorities to address the issue of players' rights to play the game in any European country. The European Court of Justice recognised in this case that there was no reason why professional sports players should not enjoy the benefits of the single market and in particular the free movement of workers, resulting in the abolution of transfer fees and opening national competitions to players throughout Europe.
- Performers seek success, sometimes unethically by the use of banned substances. Should they be banned? For how long?

Referees have been prosecuted for allowing situations to occur which have caused permanent damage to a performer. The implications for referees, many of whom are voluntary and amateur, are considerable.

Supporters' behaviour has also caused a considerable amount of concern in legal circles. Hooliganism in the 1970s and 1980s brought into question the ability of football clubs to regulate the behaviour of their supporters. Various pieces of legislation have emerged such as:

- Football Offences Act of 1991
- The Public Disorder Act of 1986
- Football Spectators Act of 1989.

Participants have a right to expect that facilities and equipment are properly maintained in order that their health and safety is ensured. This applies to recreational performers as well as elite performers.

Cases where sport meets the law

Such cases can include:

- negligence and sport (e.g. if a sport centre was deemed negligent in its maintenance of sport equipment for the public)
- criminal assault/manslaughter on the sports field
- the issue of whether a performer has consented to some extent to a certain level of violence (when does an opponent step over the line from what would be considered reasonable behaviour?)
- risk management and risk assessment in the sport workplace

- event management, risk and insurance
- statutory regulation, health and safety in sport
- employment relations and rights in sport
- European law (the case of Jean Marc Bosman and its implications for sport transfers)
- intellectual property and advertising
- marketing and sponsorship rights
- law of contract
- environmental law and sporting activities
- adventure tourism, risk, lawful sports and insurance issues
- doping in sport – principles, rules, cases
- disability rights – principles and cases
- gender and sexual discrimination, harassment in sport
- child protection in sport
- race relations and race discrimination in sport
- sport and leisure disasters and the law.

STRETCH AND CHALLENGE

Discuss the suggestion that sport performers should be allowed to use drugs to enhance their performance.

ATHLETE PROFILE

The British Horseball Association is a member of the British Equestrian Federation and abides by their high standards and expectations. There are rules to protect riders, horses and officials. There are two referees at each match, one on horseback who rides amongst the players, and one on a raised platform (called 'the chair'). They can communicate with each other and discuss incidents during play. Referees are able to yellow card and red card (send off) players, just as they are in football, for bad conduct, repeated offences, and bad language! There is also a system of awarding free passes and free shots at goal. Some players will try dirty play but it is not appreciated by the audience and the referees are quick to award fouls. Referees qualify by undertaking a special course for officiating horseball matches in which they are taught how to defuse difficult situations.

At the beginning of more important games, players are introduced to the crowds and for international matches the relevant national anthems are played. Afterwards, it is expected of the players that they shake hands.

Fig 17.02 Of course, there are the usual grumbles about referees decisions but, on the whole, they are respected and the rules are obeyed

ExamCafé

Relax, refresh, result!

Refresh your memory

Revision checklist

Make sure you know the following:

- Many of the sporting ethics established in the nineteenth century remain relevant in the present day sports world.
- The monetary rewards available today have negatively affected performer's ethics leading to an increase in deviant behaviour.
- Deviant behaviour goes against society's norms and values – can be positive or negative.
- Society has begun to demand that sports performers be more accountable for their behaviour, both inside and outside the sporting arena. Sport Law is the application of legal principles to all levels of sporting activity.
- The media and large commercial companies have begun to exert significant control over the national governing bodies.
- The serious nature of high level sport and the extensive material rewards available have increased the number of deviant acts – that is, performers seem to be more prepared to commit violent and unethical acts in order to gain the rewards.
- The law has become increasingly involved with sport and the number of prosecutions has risen.
- Sports performers take drugs for physical, psychological and social reasons.
- Many theories have been developed to account for the continuing problem of football hooliganism. Be prepared to discuss these.

Revise as you go

1. Give four factors at a football match that can cause hooligan behaviour.
2. How can sporting situations encourage aggression?
3. What elements within a football match can lead to spectator violence?
4. Name three prevention and control measures that have been implemented to try and combat hooliganism.
5. Early theories of hooliganism concentrated on social class. What other theories have been developed to try and explain hooliganism?
6. Hooliganism is said to be a form of deviant behaviour. What is meant by deviant behaviour?
7. What social issues can encourage a performer to take drugs?
8. What are the problems associated with a performer taking drugs?
9. What are anabolic steroids and why do athletes take them?
10. What is meant by blood doping?
11. What are stimulants and why would sport performers use them?
12. Why should athletes not take drugs?
13. What strategies can organisations implement in order to reduce/stop doping in sport?
14. Why has the number of sport prosecutions increased in the last decade?
15. Provide one argument for and one argument against drug testing.

CHAPTER 18

Factors that have influenced the commercialisation of modern-day sport

LEARNING OBJECTIVES:

By the end of this chapter you should be able to describe:

- *the advantages and disadvantages to the performer, coach, official, spectator, sport and World Games of the following factors:*
  - *commercialisation*
  - *sponsorship*
  - *media*
  - *technology.*

Introduction

Modern-day sport is influenced by four main factors: commercialisation, sponsorship, the media and technology. These factors all have one common link: money.

Commercialisation

Commercialisation has brought about profound changes in the structure of many sports, with media companies often able to call the shots.

The emergence of commercialism

Initial commercial developments occurred in the nineteenth century as spectator sports emerged. It is no coincidence that commercial sports first appeared in England – the first country to develop industrialisation and communication networks.

Allied with this was the emergence of a mass of the population with increasing free time and disposable income in need of excitement and entertainment. People's entertainment value was exploited by individuals who saw the opportunity to organise regular sporting events. Promoters and agents emerged and **commercialism** became an integral part of sport. Since then:

- Sport has become a global product advertised and marketed across the world.
- The vast profit potential of sport in the television age was first recognised in the 1980s, attracting entrepreneurs.
- The important issues were media rights, sponsorship deals and merchandising.
- The huge sums paid for TV and other media rights have turned sport into a global business.

- Sports clothing and equipment industries form another important part of the global sport complex, such as Nike and Adidas.
- The Olympics have come to rely heavily on the money from exclusive rights deals negotiated with top sponsors.
- Building brand awareness through sport has become an important part of modern marketing.
- Top-level soccer has changed out of all recognition over the last 20 years, as huge amounts of money have flowed into those clubs able to capitalise on global media interest.
- The richest clubs buy the best players they can afford – a system that has opened a wide gap between the top ranking clubs and those without financial backing.
- The old **turnstile** system of **cash receipts** – attractive to money launderers but a nightmare for club auditors as the system could be abused by the people manning the turnstile – has given way to sophisticated electronic systems, which enable supporters to buy merchandise as well as tickets.
- Organising bodies such as the National Basketball Association, National Football League and National Hockey League behave like multinational companies, spreading their influence and products around the globe through aggressive marketing and well-directed media campaigns.
- The success of US-style business practices has jolted even traditional sports such as rugby and cricket.
- The betting industry has long been bound up with sports such as horse racing, boxing and football. In the UK horse racing accounts for 70 per cent of revenue for the top three bookmakers, yet less then a tenth of the UK population are regular race followers.
- New technology could transform the gambling industry in the future, broadening the range of sports betting (e.g. online betting) and making it a more regular part of daily life.
- The increasing concentration of money and power in a limited number of giant sporting **conglomerates**, especially those which combine media clout with club ownership or merchandising interests, has caused increased unease. In 1998 BSkyB tried to buy control over Manchester United but the bid was blocked by the UK **Monopolies and Mergers Commission (MMC)**. The MMC ruled that the takeover could damage the quality of British football by reinforcing 'the trend towards greater inequality of wealth between clubs, weakening the smaller ones'.
- Millionaires have rescued many sports clubs, but patronage by rich individuals has largely been replaced by corporate sponsorship.
- Many athletes do not have much control over their own careers.

Golf and tennis are among the few major sports which have a relatively democratic form of government; the players decide very much how things should be run and make their own decisions about when and where they will play and which sponsorship deals to take.

KEY TERMS

Commercialism:
an emphasis on the principles of commerce with a focus on profit

Turnstile:
a mechanical gate or barrier with metal arms that are turned to admit one person at a time

Cash receipts:
a written acknowledgement of receipt of money

Conglomerate:
a corporation made up of several companies running different businesses

Monopolies and Mergers Commission (MMC):
independent public body that regulates the growth of major industries in the UK. The MMC was replaced in 1999 by the Competition Commission

Advantages of commercialism in sport:	Disadvantages of commercialism in sport:
• provides capital for sport leading to improved resources/ facilities/coaching • leads to more events • provides role models (which can encourage increased participation in sport) • allows athletes to earn an income/train full-time • raises the profile of sport itself	• encourages deviant behaviour as success becomes crucial • encourages more people to spectate rather than participate • tends to support already popular sports and so the gap widens between other sports • favours male over female/elite over grass roots/able bodied over disabled • leads to a squeeze on amateur sport, e.g. rugby union turning professional • can reward certain types of play/behaviour to suit marketing objectives – for example, rewarding a cricketer if he hits the ball towards an advertising hoarding

Table 18.01 Advantages and disadvantages of commercialism in sport

The characteristics of commercial sport

Commercial sport has close links with:

- professional sport
- sponsorship/business
- entertainment (sport becomes a spectacle or display for spectators)
- gate receipts/an affluent population
- contracts (athletes/clubs/businesses/stock market/merchandise/TV rights)
- athletes as commodities/endorsements/an asset to the company
- the media
- winning and success.

Professional performers

Professional performers:

- receive their income from participating in sport
- are paid by achieving successful results
- must specialise in a sport, which requires serious training
- can be owned, contracted, transferred and sold
- need to deliver high standards of performance on a regular basis
- are entertainers who become household names
- are public commodities and as such suffer from a lack of privacy.

APPLY IT!

Rising star Michelle Wie

Golfing phenomenon Michelle Wie has been adopted by publicists and marketing experts. Though an undoubted talent she has not yet won any major tournaments, however, the media hype, lucrative endorsements and the press conferences have ensured she already has a significant public profile.

She has finished in the top ten in a few major women's tournaments and performed respectably in some men's events. When she played in the John Deere Classic (July 2005), takings for the tournament rose by 40 per cent and television ratings increased by more than 50 per cent. In response some television networks changed their schedules in order to guarantee Wie's tee times. Perhaps the fact that Wie has not played in so many tournaments is a clever marketing ploy; it removes the chances of too many defeats which might spoil the attraction of 'unknown potential'.

So why is so much attention paid to her by the media and commercial companies?

She looks good – tall, slim, elegant and dresses in eye-catching outfits. She captures the perfect image for the

continued

continued

future of golf, both in terms of attracting females and young people to the game as well as promoting the game for people other than middle-aged, white members of exclusive clubs. Michelle Wie is also hugely competitive with no fears about breaking into the men's game. She has not made any secret of the fact that she is ambitious especially in 'taking on the men'. The sporting battle between the sexes is still an attractive prospect to many people. The men's tours are realising, and cashing in on, the publicity opportunities of such challenges. When Wie turned professional, it coincided with The Royal and Ancient announcement that women would be eligible to qualify for the 2006 Open. Nike and Sony have already signed her to contracts adding up to $10 million. She has become a major corporate enterprise.

How might this affect a young golfer?
Secondly, she will face the ever higher expectations, attention and subsequent pressure. She already has an entourage who follow her round on tour including image consultants, marketers, psychologists, coaches and so on. How much control will she be able to maintain in her life? Will the hype and exploitation ultimately ruin her? What is good for selling merchandise may not be the best recipe for a young developing player.

Sponsorship

Sponsorship and **endorsements** are very good earners for sport performers and a charismatic, high profile performer is more likely to attract lucrative sponsorship deals. However, sponsors bring with them their own pressures, particularly expecting the performer to make regular appearances. Sponsors might even encourage a player to play when injured.

Which sportsmen appeal to sponsors?

The sportsmen who are at the top of their sport and who appeal to the most spectators and fans are the most attractive to companies looking to increase their sales by advertising in sport.

- Tiger Woods is the world's highest-paid sportsman, earning $87 million in just 12 months. He has what it takes to be marketable: he is articulate, good looking, clean-cut and scandal-free.
  As the face of Nike Golf, Woods has helped create a brand with $600 million in annual revenue. Woods should become the first sportsman to cross the $1 billion threshold by 2010.
- David Beckham has earned over $33 million from sponsorship deals and now plays his soccer in America.

Fig 18.01 Most of David Beckham's income is derived from sponsors such as Gillette

Women's sports do not attract the same level of media coverage or sponsorship. A recent report by the Women's Sport and Fitness Foundation [WSFF],

'Backing a winner: Unlocking the Potential in Women's Sport', offered a stark range of statistics. For example over a three-day period in March 2008, (covering all the daily national newspapers found) that 'just 2 per cent of articles and 1 per cent of images in the sports pages are devoted to female athletes and women's sports – just 1.4 per cent of sports photography featured women'. This was in stark contrast to the coverage of footballers' wives, models and politicians' wives. In the same period Sky devoted only three of its 72 hours of sports programming to women's sport. Of 10 sport Internet sites analysed, only 5 of 367 links went to articles on women's sport; there were no female sport images on the front pages on any of those sites.

One sport where women do have a chance to match men in terms of endorsement deals is tennis. After winning Wimbledon in 2004 Maria Sharapova earned more than $18 million in one year, making her the world's best-compensated female athlete.

Fig 18.02 Winning a Grand Slam can lead to huge amounts of earnings and sponsorship, as was the case for Maria Sharapova

Advantages to a company of sponsoring a sport	Disadvantages of sponsorship to sport
• Adds value to the brand proposition • Brand stands out from the rest of the competition which is often similar in quality, content, price • Association with excellence at the highest level of sport • Personalises and localises its image by sponsoring grass roots sport; establishes community relations • Hospitality to do business with clients • Employee relations – company pride and loyalty, attract and retain staff	• Uneven development across sports especially male versus female; elite versus grass roots • Media attractive sports tend to gain higher media coverage and therefore sponsorship • Can sometimes make sports change their format e.g. one day cricket/limited overs • Sponsors can withdraw when their objectives are not being achieved • Some products may not be in keeping with the image of sport e.g. tobacco

Table 18.02 Advantages and disadvantages of sponsoring sport

KEY TERMS

Media:
forms of mass communication to the general public, comprising newspapers, radio, television, internet and all forms of advertising

Sponsorship:
the provision of funds or other forms of support to an individual or event for a commercial return

Endorsements:
where athletes display companies' names on their equipment, clothing and vehicles. The athletes are contracted to publicly declare their approval of a product or service

TASK 18.01

Discuss whether an athlete should consider the nature of a sponsor's product. For example, an athlete may be offered a contract from a tobacco company. Suggested discussion points are given in Table 18.03.

Yes	No
• as a role model they have a social responsibility/ consideration of human rights • product should suit nature of sport e.g. healthy/reflect equal opportunities • could bring criticism upon themselves and the sport	• they never asked to be a role model • unlikely that other forms of financial support would be available • financial needs override ethical objectives • other companies may withdraw financial support

Table 18.03 Should athletes consider the nature of a sponsor's product?

APPLY IT!

Stanford Super Series

The brainchild of Sir Allen Stanford, the Stanford Super Series was the result of a five-year agreement between Stanford 20/20, the England and Wales Cricket Board and the West Indies Cricket Board. The first of the five planned annual events comprised six 20/20 matches which were played at the Stanford Cricket Ground in Antigua from 25 October, 2008, and culminated with the final 20/20 for 20 match on 1 November, 2008.

Teams which participated in the Stanford Super Series were:

1. Stanford Superstars – a team selected from the best of the best of the regional Stanford 20/20 Tournaments
2. England – the ECB selected national team
3. Trinidad and Tobago – the reigning regional Stanford 20/20 Tournament Champions
4. Middlesex – the reigning English County Twenty20 Champions.

The series featured a Legends Beach Cricket day, four main warm-up matches, the Domestic Champions match with a total purse of US$400,000, and the Stanford 20/20 for 20 match that represented the richest team prize for a single sporting match – US$20,000,000.

How Stanford's $20m was split:

- the ECB and WICB each received $3.5m
- the 11 winning players received $1m each
- the four remaining members of the winning squad shared $1m
- the winning back-room staff members shared $1m
- the ECB and WICB each received $3.5m.

Former England captain Graham Gooch believes that test cricket could become a thing of the past, with players focused on earning huge sums from a series of revolving Twenty20 tournaments.

Who actually controls sport?

When sport became more organised and structured in the nineteenth century, sports were controlled by their own governing bodies which were established for this purpose. In the UK this was very much in the hands of the middle and upper classes who favoured the amateur code. This code did not welcome the commercial side of sport.

In the late twentieth century a shift in power occurred and the traditional governing bodies have had to change their approach towards the relationship between sport and money. In order to compete in the modern-day sport world many of these traditional governing bodies have had to embrace the commercial world for what it can offer their sport.

Though sport enjoys mass participation, the power over rule-making, merchandising and media rights still lies with a small number of individuals and companies. Sports such as football, cricket and rugby are controlled by either a monopolistic ruling body or a small group of individuals or companies. Although unions have developed considerable power over the years, they act more as a blocking mechanism than an active participant in running the sport.

Ruling bodies are now losing ground to large efficient companies like News International, owned by Rupert Murdoch. He is seen as one of the most powerful men in world sport and is in control of the Fox, Sky and Star TV networks, giving him great power in broadcasting. Murdoch's companies have been expanding through the Internet, which is seen as the future of sports coverage for fans.

FIFA decides where the World Cup is to be staged – the biggest commercial decision in world football. The shortcomings of the system came to an angry public attention when Germany were named as host for the 2006 competition, beating the widely anticipated winner, South Africa, by a single vote.

The development of the Olympics as a major global event came during the IOC presidency of Juan Antonio Samaranch (1980–2001). His autocratic style led to much criticism, but he was a shrewd leader and guided the event into the new world of media domination.

The performer and barriers to excellence

Equal opportunities in sport and physical education were addressed in your studies at AS level. Clearly not all individuals are as equal as each other. Political rights do not always translate into equal opportunities.

You need to be able to appreciate how sponsorship and the media, technology and World Games impact on athletes from different social categories such as athletes with a disability, those from an ethnic minority and/or low socio-economic background and female athletes.

Discrimination can be overt or covert. The former can take the form of less tournament earnings and membership clauses to sports clubs (consider the early playing experiences of Tiger Woods who was unwelcome in some golf clubs in the USA). The latter can include attitudes and prejudices, usually based on negative stereotypes.

EXAM TIP:

You may not be asked a direct question on equal opportunities but be prepared to give extra depth in your answers by referring to athletes from different social categories.

EXAM TIP:

It is very important that you observe ethical principles when discussing equal opportunity issues. The response required is a balanced judgement of the issue.

KEY TERMS

Dominant group:
the group in society that controls the major social institutions

Hegemonic group:
one group that has leadership over other groups

Discrimination:
to make a distinction; to give unfair treatment especially because of prejudice

Stereotypes:
a standardised image or concept shared by all members of a social group

Ethnic groups as a barrier to excellence

In the UK, national governing bodies were established by white middle-class males and this tendency still exists today. This means control, decision making and reflection of cultural values are not in the hands of people from ethnic minority groups, low socio-economic groups, people with a disability and females.

KEY TERMS

Racism:
a set of beliefs or ideas based on the assumption that the world's population can be divided into different human biological groups designated 'races'

EXAM TIP:

Race is the physical characteristic of an individual, while ethnicity is the belonging to a particular group, e.g. religion, lifestyle, etc.

Factors affecting opportunities for athletes from ethnic minority backgrounds

- Discrimination in the form of racism
- Decision making in the UK predominantly in the hands of white middle class
- **Channelling** into certain sports, e.g. athletics, and away from others, e.g. tennis and swimming, due to either monetary or social factors. Channelling may have been a significant factor – perhaps by not being channelled into tennis clubs, black people were unlikely to succeed in great numbers. Tiger Woods may have destroyed a myth that black people couldn't play golf
- Stereotyping such athletes as suitable for some sports and not others
- The traditional route for many athletes from ethnic minority backgrounds has also been from a low socio-economic group meaning some sports were cheaper and therefore more accessible
  - Athletic contests where winning is determined by objective measurements, rather than by the judges' opinions could have been favoured by athletes from an ethnic minority being viewed as providing a fairer outcome

KEY TERMS

Channelling:
people from certain groups in society can be channelled into particular sports for which they are considered to have the appropriate physical and psychological qualities

White flight:
this refers to white players being disinclined to participate in a sport believing they have no hope of succeeding. Can be seen in basketball and sprinting.

Gender:
the biological aspect of a person, either male or female

Masculinity:
possessing qualities or characteristics considered typical or appropriate to a man. Examples might be dominant, strong, forceful

Socialisation:
the learning of cultural norms and values

- Success of one sports performer, e.g. Tiger Woods in golf, can provide a sense of social acceptance and consequently provide role models for children from similar backgrounds
- Some countries target certain sports which they perceive they will be able to dominate. Examples may be poorer countries concentrating on running due to the less sophisticated facilities that are needed in comparison with other sports
- Even following success in high level sport fewer athletes from these backgrounds make a future career in management positions.

Factors affecting sporting opportunities for female athletes

In the UK, women have historically experienced **gender** inequality. Sport evolved along the male and **masculinity** concepts of competition, achievement, aggression and dominance, which led to poorer opportunities for women and resulted in lower participation rates. Positive female sporting images portrayed by the media have tended to be similar to other Western cultures – activities which require grace, have little physical contact and so a lower level of aggression.

- Women and men learn their expected role through **socialisation**, which simply means the learning of cultural values. Males and females are socialised into being masculine or feminine respectively.
- Sport was always seen as a male preserve. Males developed and controlled most of the modern day sports. Men as the dominant group in society denied or limited opportunities for women in the types and amounts of sports they could participate in.
- The role of women in the West was stereotypically seen as the domestic role. The types of sporting activities women were encouraged to do tended to promote the more feminine aspects of women such as non-contact sports and improving the appearance, i.e. toning muscles (aerobics) rather than building them (weightlifting).

- Women have been denied opportunities on the medical belief that sport would damage their fertility
- Women have historically attracted far less media coverage and consequently sponsorship deals
- World Games still limits the number of events for women compared to those available for men.

In the present day, opportunities for women have increased, though are still less than for men, in terms of:

- more females participating in sport
- a greater variety of sporting activities available
- more clubs, facilities and competitions
- more media coverage leading to more role models
- more women in positions of responsibility in sports organisations, such as national governing bodies.

Sexism

Sexism, like racism, is a set of beliefs or ideas about the purported inferiority of some members of the population, in this case women. The inferiority is thought to be based on biological differences between the sexes: women are naturally equipped for specific types of activities and roles and these don't usually include ones which carry prestige and influence.

KEY TERMS

Sexism:
The belief that one sex is inferior to the other, a belief that is most often directed at women. Traditionally women have been denied the same legal, political, economic and social rights enjoyed by men.

The media and the body as a social construct

The notion that the body might be of sociological interest has become popular since the 1980s. This can relate to society's 'ideal' shape for men and women. This belief holds the view that people see themselves and others by the way their society views them. In the Western world a thin body shape for women is likely to offer high status and may be achieved using methods such as dieting and surgery. The media are heavily responsible for the extent to which ideas like these become social norms.

The media also gives much less coverage to women's sports while favouring sports and athletes that match the concept of **femininity**. Women's team games are not given much coverage even though team games form the basis of many physical education programmes in schools. Individual activities such as tennis, and recently golf, are beginning to attract more media coverage. With media coverage comes more sponsorship deals – so less media coverage has significant consequences for women's sport.

APPLY IT!

Women's soccer in the USA
The success of the American women's soccer team (who won the 1999 World Cup which was virtually ignored by the UK) highlights some interesting issues. Since their victory, members of the team have become household names and it was believed they had won a victory in the battle for sexual equality. The final was played before a crowd of 90,000, the largest audience for a women's sporting event anywhere. Big league sponsors contributed and Nike, Adidas and Budweiser beer (traditionally male products) ran adverts featuring the team.

KEY TERMS

Femininity:
possessing qualities or characteristics considered typical or appropriate to a woman. Examples might be graceful, dainty, gentle

Male hegemony:
the dominance of males over females

EXAM TIP:

Remember – women, ethnic minority groups and low socio-economic groups will participate in less sport for similar reasons and the strategies to improve opportunities will also be similar.

Evidence	Reasons	Action required
• Inequalities in sport • Unequal provision of facilities • Less sport for women • Fewer female coaches/ administrators • Restricted club access • Participation rates less than men at all levels	• Domestic role • Social stereotyping • Concept of femininity • Physical vulnerability to perform some sports – the 'medical case'. • Sport matches the concept of masculinity • Males traditionally control sport – **male hegemony** • Less media coverage • Less role models • Less funding/tournament earnings • Discrimination	• Equal provision at all levels from physical education to high level competitive sport • More facilities • Social acceptance of all sports • Better links between schools/clubs • Widen women's horizons • Increase media coverage of female sport • Increase training of coaches/ administrators • Legislation at government level, e.g. **Sex Discrimination Act** /Title IX

Table 18.04 Unequal sporting opportunities for women and attempts to counter them

Social class as a barrier to excellence

Society can be divided into social classes defined on the basis of wealth, income, occupation and hereditary factors. The upper and middle classes or dominant group tended to occupy the highest positions of wealth, status and power. It is increasingly difficult to differentiate between the middle and working classes but generally the distinction is still based on the type of work done (manual or non-manual work).

- Historically in the UK, the middle and upper classes have always had more leisure time and disposable income – opportunities necessary to participate in sport regularly.
- The middle and upper classes have controlled sports, particularly the administration of what were considered working-class sports, such as football and boxing. They have ruled the governing bodies, and been the agents and promoters.
- In the UK, in the late nineteenth and early twentieth centuries, professional players tended to come from the lower classes (as they needed to earn money from sport) while the middle and upper classes tended to be the amateurs (participating in sport for the love of it rather than for monetary gain).
- The working classes had to wait for the provision of facilities and a right to recreation.
- This has led to a difference, even today, in the participation rates of people from lower socio-economic groups and to some extent in the achievement in gold medals in particular sports. This can be attributed to a number of factors:
  a) the cost of facilities and training
  b) the dominant middle-class culture which operates in many sports institutions, such as sports clubs, having different value systems such as rules of behaviour, dress codes and so on
  c) the lack of leadership roles in coaching and administerial positions in sports institutions
  d) lower self-esteem
  e) fewer children from lower socio-economic groups attend private schools (especially in the UK) and most of the medal winners from the UK were educated at private rather than state schools.

The media

The media includes newspapers, radio and television broadcasting, and the Internet, by which information is conveyed to the general public.

Newspapers

1. The tabloids, such as the *Sun* or the *Mirror*, tend to have a large section devoted to sport, but focus on particular types of sport – mainly those with broad appeal and male-dominated, e.g. football.
2. The broadsheets such as the *Guardian* or the *Daily Telegraph* tend to cover and analyse sport in more depth; they offer slightly more variety of sport, but still tend to focus mainly on male-dominated sport.

Radio

Radio started to report live events in the 1920s, and enabled people to listen to commentaries on football matches, and eventually tennis, cricket and rugby.

Television

Television has the advantage of being able to broadcast instantaneous sporting action to a large audience comparatively cheaply. Because the relatively low cost of sports broadcasting compares favourably with drama and light entertainment, and because of the high ratings gained, it is not surprising that sport features so heavily on television schedules, particularly at weekends.

The relationship between sports and the media has become symbiotic. Media commentators claimed that BSkyB (part of News International) would lose 60 per cent of its subscribers if its Premier League rights were to be lost. A bidding war saw Premier League rights for 2001–04 sold for over $500m a year, with BSkyB yet again outbidding its rivals.

Television has helped to bring lesser-known or rarely-watched sports to the foreground; it has helped participants to reach superstar status, and consequently raised the performers' earnings. This has sometimes put athletes under great pressure to make more performance appearances than is good for them, physically or mentally.

However, television reporting can also over-dramatise problems within the sports world. Also, deals made between sporting bodies and the media can favour certain sports, such as the alliance between Adidas and FIFA.

The Internet

The Internet carries various information resources and services, such as electronic mail, online chat, file transfer and file sharing, online gaming, and the Inter-linked hypertext documents and other resources of the World Wide Web. The influence of the Internet on sport has been phenomenal.

TASK 18.02

As a group draw up a list of the ways in which sport and the Internet are linked.

The effect of the media on sport

Some sports have changed to make them more suited to media coverage. Television coverage can also influence positively or negatively the participation rates in a sport. Over the last 50 years, terrestrial television coverage in the UK expanded. The new channels need to seek out new markets, and when Channel 4 arrived in the early 1980s, it boosted the viewing and participating figures for volleyball and table tennis, and gave significant coverage of kabbadi, which is played mainly in India though there are moves to make it a world-wide game. The advent of satellite channels in recent years has allowed even more sport coverage on TV.

- Rights to Soccer's World Cup (2002–06) were sold for $2 billion, shared between Kirch/Taurus and Sporis/ISL.
- Volleyball became a regular sports feature between 1980 and 1984 – the number of affiliated players rose by 70 per cent.
- Conversely, when table tennis no longer received television coverage, the number of participating players dropped by a third. The governing bodies in both cases were convinced that the changed rates of participation were not coincidences. If women's sports received more coverage, would we see the rise in female participants that so many organisations are trying hard to achieve?

Sports commentators

The media reports on what actually happens and as such is objective; yet as readers, viewers or listeners, we must take into account the values and beliefs of those who commentate on the events. The commentators are the mediators who describe and analyse the action for the viewer at home. They can become celebrities in their own right and are sometimes associated with just one sport; e.g. Murray Walker (motor racing), John Motson (football), the late Dan Maskell (tennis at Wimbledon), Harry Carpenter (boxing). The style of presentation has become closely related to the culture of the mass audience. Events are hyped up, where the commentators discuss the likely outcome of an event for hours before, advising viewers on how to interpret the situation.

Media coverage and social values

- Television coverage concentrates on the conduct of the participants and spectators, and is generally sympathetic to officials. Different sports receive different emphasis of coverage; e.g. tennis players who behave badly are often described as 'brats' which has a very middle-class tone, whereas in soccer, the language used might be 'thugs', possibly showing more intolerance of working-class behaviour.
- Gender inequalities in sport can be reflected by the media. Men figure more as participants and media sport professionals, whereas women tend to comment on women's sports, if at all. There have been recent challenges to this position, e.g. Sue Barker, Gabby Logan and Claire Balding. Non-contact sports for women are given more positive media coverage, such as tennis, gymnastics and track athletes. The massive inequality in coverage tends to reaffirm the stereotype that sport is for men, and women have little to comment on.
- The media can help generate a sense of nationalism, particularly since the development of international coverage of events where the symbols of nationalism are displayed for all to see – rituals, flags, ceremonies, parades, uniforms and anthems – making them highly emotive events.
- In the UK, sportspeople from ethnic minorities can become potent role models for young people, and their representation can promote equality of opportunity. However, the media can also promote the stereotype that black people can excel in sport and physical activity but not in other areas of life. Similarly to women, people from ethnic minorities are not prominent in the controlling positions of power in the media, like commentators and directors, writers, producers, photographers, etc.

The media is often cited as having a huge influence on spectators and it is not surprising that this can have positive and negative effects. The media conveys a number of different sport themes:

- **Success themes** – qualities shown are competitive, aggressive, domination of others, obedience to authority. Should success also be portrayed as empathy, support, cooperation and equality? Elite sport tends to be shown at the cost of grass roots sport.
- **Masculinity and femininity themes** – male sport is shown more than female sport though the latter has increased. Female sport tends to be shown as a 'special feature' whereas male sport tends to be shown more regularly. Women's sports magazines tend to concentrate on those sports which emphasise the 'feminine shape'.

The Olympic Games does represent some equality for female participants. At Athens in 2004 women represented 40.7 per cent of all the athletes taking part in 45 per cent of the events. There are still fewer events available to women, but there has been a steady expansion.

The Beijing Olympics saw the visible success of our female participants such as Nicole Cooke (cycling) and Rebecca Adlington (swimming). With increased media coverage comes new role models, leading to greater participation and the image of successful women as a result of strength, determination and ability.

Fig 18.03 Team GB's women were very successful at the Beijing Olympics in 2008

The impact of the media on participation

Focus on elite sport may:

- increase participation in a sport but if success does not come quickly the new participants can easily lose interest
- have the effect of making spectators feel their efforts are not as valued as those of the high level performers. This can lead to spectatorism having a negative impact on participation
- introduce and educate people about new sports
- increase the number of inactive spectators leading to higher levels of obesity.

How does the media and commercialisation affect sport?

Some sports have changed as a result of commercial and media interest. For example:

- Rules have been introduced to speed up the action to prevent spectator boredom.
- Changes have been made in scoring to create more excitement.
- Breaks are provided in play so sponsors can advertise their products.
- The format of competitions has changed such as Twenty20 cricket.
- The competitive season has been extended.
- Athletes can be put under pressure to perform even when injured.
- Business administrators now have more control of sport.
- The fourth official has been introduced to help with decisions.
- More media coverage can increase participation in a sport. Therefore less coverage of female sport can affect participation, figures and funding.
- The readers, listeners and viewers of sport are heavily influenced by the values and beliefs of those who commentate on the events, influencing their interpretation of different situations.
- The media can hype up events which can be detrimental in some circumstances.
- Interactive technology enables individual viewers to make individual choices, such as following their favourite player.
- The increase in technology has led to a more personal experience for the viewer – cameras can be fitted in a racing car, under water and in a goal.
- Action replays and freeze frames allow more detailed analysis to take place.
- Certain prestigious sport events are ring-fenced, particularly international events. Sometimes these are only available to the more exclusive satellite or cable subscription channels and not to the ordinary viewer on terrestrial TV.

TASK 18.03

1. What are the characteristics of commercial sport?
2. What qualities would a company look for when deciding who to sponsor?
3. Why might gymnastics attract less media coverage than football?
4. Discuss how the financial rewards available may affect the ethics of an athlete

TASK 18.04

In the nineteenth century the control of a sport was largely down to the NGB. Suggest how this may have changed.

EXAM TIP:

Some possible questions and suggested answers

Q: How can a professional performer be considered a commercial object?

A:

- He or she signs a contract just as a person signs a business contract.
- He or she can be 'hired and fired' by the owner or manager.
- The performer is used to advertise and endorse a company's product, bringing a financial return to a company.
- His or her image is exploited to achieve company goals. Therefore the performer needs to market and sell him or herself.
- By achieving successful results consistently the performer is financially rewarded, which is important as this is his or her income.

Q: What are the pressures of being a role model?

A:

- There is an invasion of privacy by the media. The media are as interested in the private lives of athletes as much as their sporting prowess.
- Their behaviour is considered to influence the behaviour of young people and therefore they need to maintain a good, clean image.
- As they need to perform consistently and regularly this often leads to over-training and even performing when injured.
- Physical and psychological stress can be the result of a highly competitive environment.

Impact of the media, sponsorship and commercialisation on World Games

Olympic marketing

Juan Antonio Samaranch, IOC President from 1980–2001:

'Marketing has become an increasingly important issue for all of us within the Olympic movement. The revenues derived from television, sponsorship and general fundraising help to provide the movement with its financial independence. However, in developing these programmes we must always remember that it is sport that must control its destiny not commercial interests. Every act of support for the Olympic movement promotes peace, friendship and solidarity throughout the world.' (2004)

Funds today are raised from the sale of TV rights, sponsorship, licensing, ticket sales, coins and stamps. The IOC retains 7–10 per cent of the revenues with the remainder going to the Organising Committees, the International Sport Federations (ISF) and National Olympic Committees. Included in these are the International Paralympic Committee and Paralympic Organising Committee.

Successful marketing ensures:

- the financial stability of the Games
- continuity of marketing across each Olympic Games
- equitable revenue distribution between all the committees and support for emerging nations
- free air transmission across the whole world
- the safeguarding of Olympic ideals against unnecessary commercialisation
- the support of marketing partners to promote Olympism and Olympic ideals
- a reduction in dependence on US television rights which could make the games vulnerable
- TV rights continue to account for just less than 45 per cent of Olympic revenue.

Sponsorship

Sponsors enjoy exclusive rights in their respective business areas. Though they pay heavily for this they also recognise the potential of the global marketplace and the impact of the Olympic Games. All 200 National Olympic Committees now receive funding via the sponsorship programme – known as TOP (The Olympic Programme).

The Olympics, together with the Wimbledon Tennis Championships, remain the only major sporting events that do not have stadium advertising.

The future of the Olympic Games

- Commerce (business) needs to be balanced by philanthropy.
- The traditions of the Games must be upheld, continuing its theatrical impact as a pageant.
- Every effort must be made to reduce discrimination and enable the potential best athletes to participate.
- The size of the Games needs to be controlled.
- Cultural differences must be recognised.
- The belief in the philosophy of Olympism must be emphasised – that there is joy, and educational and ethical value in sporting effort.

The Paralympic Games

The Paralympics are for athletes with physical and sensorial disabilities. Paralympic means 'parallel' to the Olympic Games. The Paralympic Games are about ability, athletic endeavour and elite performance. Many countries have national research and training centres to provide the optimal environment, facilities and equipment for athletes with disabilities to train for their specific sports.

TASK 18.05

What would be the advantages and disadvantages of integrating the Paralympic and Olympic Games? Consider the viewpoints of the athletes and the organisers.

Technology

Technological influences

The human body seems to be able to reach higher and higher levels of performance – what is helping athletes improve so dramatically? Technology is undoubtedly the major influence whether it is in the equipment and facilities or sports science which helps coaching and training methods. An athlete's performance is now measured in minute detail, such as timing in the 100m, and technology such as Hawk-Eye can help officials in their decisions.

Equipment

New materials have contributed to amazing advances in sports – lycra in running suits, super-light strong metals in bikes and tennis racquets, high-tech shoes, the use of fibreglass in cricket bats, etc. Millions are spent every year in developing better equipment for sportsmen and women. Some improvements are made for safety reasons. Better mats had to be developed in the 1950s as pole-vaulters cleared greater heights. These improved mats were used in the high jump as well, contributing to a change in the style of jumping, where athletes could safely jump head-first – the Fosbury flop technique used today.

Computers, advances in nutrition, weight-training machines, new playing surfaces, and many more technological advances have been influential in the development of sport.

There can be a conflict between manufacturer and governing body, e.g. Callaway Golf who had its most successful golf club banned as it hit the ball too far, with the governing body reasoning that it did not want to change the courses or the nature of the game, and subsequently regulating against such equipment.

Regulations or adaptations of regulations come to preserve the character of the game. The manufacturer wants to sell more and gain brand prestige through innovation. Another example was the International Tennis Federation (ITF).

After the ball size was changed to slow down play at Wimbledon, and the manufacturer paid a substantial figure for this, it gained criticism from ex-player and commentator John McEnroe and the manufacturer was later told by the ITF that the ball was being phased out.

APPLY IT!

Aqualab is Speedo's global research and development facility. The team work to push the boundaries of sports science and technological innovation to create leading edge swimwear, equipment and apparel. Aqualab works with experts from diverse industries including aerospace, engineering and medicine as well as leaders in sports science, fabric technology and garment construction. Innovations such as Fastskin are rigorously trialled and tested with athletes. Michael Phelps beat his own 200m Fly world record wearing Fastskin.

Assistance for officials

Cameras have assisted umpires and referees in making tough decisions. The photo-finish was first used for track events at the 1932 Olympics. This eliminated any doubt as to the winners in crucially close events.

Kevin Roberts Editorial Director, *SportBusiness International* at Sport and Technology: The Conference 2007, commented that *'technology is available, technology is used in sports to reinforce or disprove the views of the human officials, however without referees or umpires, there is no sport.'*

Stuart Cummings (RFL) believes technology has had a positive influence on the game. The sport has been viewed as one of the 'pioneers' in applying technology. Cummings outlined that in 1996, the video referee was introduced, the first invasion game to do this. The move brought about scepticism from people who thought it would highlight errors, but as Cummings comments: *'During my time as a referee, refereeing at an international level, I always enjoyed the game better from my point of view when the video referee was in place. I always felt confident in my own decisions and that the video screen would prove me right. Technology is great to have and it's important that we are seen to have the right outcomes.'*

Cummings then referred to the four-way open microphone system (two touch judges, one on-field referee and one video referee) which can have problems, citing an instance in Cardiff in 2008, where the video referee came and gave a call in live play, but it generally works well, e.g. for offside judgements which has cleaned up an area of the pitch for the referee.

'I don't personally see it as conflicting, I see the referee using technology to enhance his decision making.'

Instant replay, introduced in the 1980s, has also affected how sports are played – when decisions get tough, it acts as an impartial referee.

Does cricket need technology for one of the most complex decisions that takes place, the LBW (leg before wicket)? Cricket embraces technology and the governing body has spent much money trying to find the best technology to use, especially at the highest level.

It is generally believed that certain conditions concerning technology should be adopted:

1. The game is played and officiated by humans, therefore technology should not take away any of the theatre of the game.
2. Technology must not change the way the game is played. For example, if Hawk-Eye was introduced, five day test matches would become three days.
3. Technology needs to have a high percentage of accuracy (98–99 per cent).

Four international trials have been carried out to date:

- in 2002 in the Champions Trophy in Sri Lanka (umpire able to consult with television officials)
- in 2004 in England with a stump microphone and umpires with an ear piece
- in 2005 in the Super Series in Australia where the umpire could consult the television officials regarding any decision, and
- a trial in England in 2008 that allowed players the opportunity to appeal a decision.

The summary from the trials was that, in some aspects, the sport is not ready to embrace the technology, technical problems were evident, e.g. time delays and, the most interesting from the recent trial is that players did not actually want this technology (being able to appeal).

For line decisions, technology is excellent providing there are enough cameras, for thin edges it is not available, for clean catches it does not help and for LBW decisions, while some aspect is based on fact, the prediction is an opinion and 'technology does not help informing opinions'.

Interestingly, a lot of decisions are not as simple as 'yes' or 'no'. They are often open to interpretation, and technology used in football, as determined by IFAB, only allows for use for goal line technology, as you have to be 100 per cent accurate. Bland cited the example of Hawk-Eye in football, which has recently been tested (at Reading FC) and was proved to be very accurate, boasting shots at 300 frames per second, three cameras around the goal and a three-second decision turnaround.

Cameras associated with computer software such as ProZone, track players and referees, not interfering with the decision-making because the information is fed back post-match. Bland pointed out 'that it is based on training and developing excellence.'

Technology used in professional football is 'minimal' with communications systems being used, however the fourth official cannot give a decision, they are responsible for monitoring the technical area (International Football Association Broad regulation).

Technology for engaging audiences

The crowd at Wimbledon embraced Hawk-Eye suggesting this is a good example of adding to the fans' experience. Similarly, the yellow first and 10 line in American Football, the K-Zone which charts/plots pitches in Baseball, and PVI's 360 degree camera array (Spincam – composed of 100 cameras) to break down play are all features to enhance the spectator experience. Also up and coming is player tracking using virtual/visual recognition, which in the US is a players' association issue.

Sponsorship

New technologies have created a proliferation of means to reach, and interact with, an audience. This creates the potential for a new approach to sponsorship rights, carving up sponsorship opportunities into distinct, platform based rights or selling bundles of rights in a comprehensive sponsorship package.

The traditional objectives for sports sponsorship continue to hold true: for sponsors, to enhance brand profile, equity and value; and for rights holders, to generate revenue. However, the traditional model of event sponsorship contracts, including priority rights to acquire broadcast sponsorship and commercial airtime around television coverage of an event may not be the best way to achieve these objectives in the future. Why is this so?

The technology and consumption trends described above are having two key impacts on the traditional sports sponsorship model.

1. The fragmentation of media – people are spending more time online, watching clips on mobiles and choosing any of a hundred TV channels. This means the traditional 'interruption' model of TV advertising is being undermined. The fragmentation also offers faster and easier global dissemination.
2. With fragmentation comes the need to engage with people. Successful marketing campaigns illustrate this trend – they engage with users to enhance their experience, rather than just bombard them with branding and hope it sinks in.

These trends are arguably making sponsorship an increasingly more attractive and valuable marketing medium and we are already witnessing the interesting consequences for sports sponsorship contracts.

Chips and the London Marathon

The Flora London Marathon is the largest annual fundraising event in the world. It is also the most high-tech race in the history of the event, with each of the 35,000 runners having their own personal 'microchip timers'.

As part of the pre-race registration procedure, each runner receives an electronic identification chip. This small silicon chip, with its passive transponder, is attached to the runner's shoelaces and emits a signal each time the runner passes over the 'reader mats' strategically placed at 5km intervals.

The chips give an accurate time and position on the progress of all entrants and the marathon's official results are based on the elapsed time of each runner between crossing the mats at the start and finish lines. The signals emitted by the chip are managed by an integrated computerised system designed and developed over the last seven years by Marathon IT, the London marathon's independent information technology services provider.

The processed data including analytical graphics is also used to feed BBC TV Sport for immediate on-screen display to millions of viewers worldwide. The same information is routed to the marathon's command post and press centre where the information is disseminated to the world's sports media.

APPLY IT!

Football

Technological innovations are being used to:

- improve coaching methods
- monitor player performance
- collate match analysis and statistical data
- produce interactive broadcasting methods
- introduce HD to enhance viewers experience
- enhance gaming and interactive betting
- distribute content via broadband, WIFI and 3G
- improve perimeter advertising through LED screening.

What do the fans think?

The Orange Technology in Football Survey, carried out by the Football Fans Census, spoke to 3,072 soccer fans on the subject of technology between 15 and 22 March 2006. The survey was conducted online and supporters of 215 teams were represented, including all clubs in the Premiership, Football League and Scottish Premier League. Thirty-nine per cent of respondents were season ticket holders. The survey respondents were predominantly male (85 per cent) with females making up 15 per cent of the sample – reflecting the male bias among soccer supporters in the UK and globally.

With England's famous 1966 FIFA World Cup triumph famously decided by a crucial goal line decision that is still being debated 40 years on, the Orange survey has revealed that over three-quarters of soccer fans would like to see more technology brought into the game to avoid issues like these in the future. Sir Geoff Hurst's second goal in that World Cup Final was allowed to stand even though it was unclear whether the whole of the ball had crossed the line.

Survey results revealed that 82 per cent of soccer fans felt that new technology, such as goal line cameras, TV match officials and smart officials, would considerably improve their enjoyment of the game. With inconclusive goal line decisions still prevalent in the game today, including the recent controversy in last season's Champions League semi-final between Chelsea and Liverpool, 57 per cent of fans surveyed were adamant that goal line technology was the most important technological advancement that was needed in soccer.

Chelsea and England player Frank Lampard commented: *'Obviously everyone remembers the famous Sir Geoff Hurst goal from 1966, which luckily went in our favour and helped us win the World Cup! But of course it's still no easier today to work out if a ball has crossed the line, as was shown in our game against Liverpool last year in the Champions League.'*

APPLY IT!

Tracking football

Lampard believes that the introduction of electronic animated tracking device Hawk-Eye in cricket and tennis has been successfully introduced and it doesn't seem to have stopped the flow of matches in these sports. *'Obviously technological advancements may not be so easy in football but it could possibly help to stop the current debates that take place whenever a disputed goal is scored or a player is unfairly sent off,'* said Lampard.

He added: *'Of course in football, decisions go for you and against you, but I can understand why the fans want to see the technology changed. Every football player wants to win a game fair and square and sometimes things happen so quickly in matches that it's impossible for the referee or assistant referee to see what has happened.'*

It's on the subject of gaining conclusive evidence about whether the ball has crossed the line that fans are unanimous – 73 per cent of respondents embrace the idea of goal line cameras that can send picture messages straight to a mobile device with the referee to resolve goal disputes. The same number would also like to see the introduction of footballs with intelligent chips that can tell a referee within seconds whether the goal should stand.

Fans are also positive about following some of the technological advancements brought into rugby in recent years. Indeed, 68 per cent would welcome soccer adopting the TV match officials that are used successfully in Six Nations Rugby, while 64 per cent admitted that referees' comments being heard by the viewer or listener is something that would improve their enjoyment of soccer.

Darrell McLennan Fordyce, head of sports and games at Orange commented: *'Technology in football is now a huge national debate, and the results from this survey show that fans want it to have a more prominent role in deciding disputed decisions. Orange is a keen supporter of any technological advancements that help to enhance the great game.'*

According to the survey results, 30 per cent of soccer fans were interested in having access to player performance data (such as which players are doing the most running, passing etc during a match) on their mobile phone. The appetite for this data is strongly influenced by age, teenagers – the demographic most familiar with mobile technology are positive overall to the idea, other age groups are negative overall, increasingly so as they get older.

Radio Frequency Identification

The 2006 FIFA World Cup saw the large-scale use of RFID technology in tickets for the first time, with all 2.9m tickets being embedded with an RFID tag.

World Cup organisers expected the use of RFID to provide greater security at entry gates and deter the counterfeiting of tickets, which have plagued past events. The technology offered a high degree of security, and organisers said it would not contain personal data, only a number that identified each ticket holder.

However, ticket purchasers had to submit various personal details on the ticket registration forms, which then appeared on the ticket, and the RFID tag had the potential to make the ticket holder visible to tracking devices beyond the turnstile. The level of data being captured and potential for tracking people raised concerns in some quarters that this is a step towards a 'big brother' society or football ID card scheme.

Overall however, 59 per cent of fans felt that this was a step forward in improving security and ticketing arrangements more than it raised concerns about personal liberty. However, for a sizeable minority (41 per cent) the concerns the technology raises about personal liberty were significant.

APPLY IT!

Hawk-Eye

Hawk-Eye's principal application has been to enhance television production by using tracking data to resolve controversial decisions, help explain the game and get the viewer closer to the action. Since 2003, Hawk-Eye has been used at almost all major cricket and tennis events worldwide and was tested at the Australian Tennis Open in January 2006.

Technology and the athlete

How has technology impacted on the athlete?

Oscar Pistorius agreed to work with athletics authorities to try to discover if his artificial legs give him an unfair advantage. The Paralympic champion, 20, had both legs amputated below the knee as a child and runs on carbon fibre blades.

The test showed that running with prosthetic blades leads to less vertical motion combined with less mechanical work for lifting the body. As well as this, the energy loss in the blade is significantly lower than in the human ankle joints in sprinting at maximum speed. It was estimated that he would have a 30 per cent mechanical advantage over an able bodied runner. He won the appeal to overturn the judgment denying him the opportunity to run in the Beijing Olympics but failed to make the South African team.

Sport analysis

The use of video-taping in training has helped athlete's improve greatly. Being able to watch themselves perform, athletes now know exactly what they're doing right and wrong. Watching their own performance improve can also boost their motivation to carry on working harder.

Motion capture is ideal for a wide range of sports applications in research, rehabilitation, physical education and practice. Physical limitations and movement optimisation are of great interest to athletes, coaches, researchers and doctors. Motion capture allows us to learn more about injury mechanisms and prevention. It can also be used to improve a player's technique for better results in various sports applications.

STRETCH AND CHALLENGE

Outline the advantages and disadvantages of technology to:

- the performer
- the sport
- the spectator.

APPLY IT!

Sports Technology as a Career

(Subject Outline at a British University)

The Sports Technology programme is intended for students wishing to pursue a career in the sports related industry with an emphasis on technology involving the design and development of sports equipment and products and technological developments in the improvement and measurement of sporting performance. The programme recognises the growth in the sports industries and the need for technologists to support the development of new equipment and products and to improve existing products and methods of measuring performance. Golf Operations within the programme reflects the sophisticated nature of golf as a sport, and provides students with the skills and abilities to operate in a commercial sporting environment. They may be interested in managing golf operations, and/or enhancing golf performance using technology to maximise the potential of amateurs and professionals alike.

The University has its own sports centre and a recently built extensive sports arena nearby. A new sports biomechanics laboratory has been recently opened. Facilities include hi-tech 3D motion analysis systems and force platform equipment, and all students have practical experience of using this equipment.

ATHLETE PROFILE

The media coverage of horseball varies. In the UK, television coverage occurs where the strongest horseball teams are based, such as London, Nottingham, Bristol, Newcastle, and the Forest of Dean.

Rochelle has had a slot on the local TV station after the 6:00 pm news and has been featured on local radio several times.

The *Horse and Country* TV channel covered a horseball event at Stoneleigh in 2008 while the *Horse* magazine coverage is much more widespread. Many teams get their results and photos published in the local press.

In France, where the sport is very popular, the television coverage is extensive and big crowds attend the matches.

Fig 18.04 During the World Cup in Portugal (2008) matches were televised live, and reports were given during news bulletins

ExamCafé

Relax, refresh, result!

Refresh your memory

Revision checklist

Make sure you know the following:

- ▷ The basic structure of sports has remained the same but commercialisation has been influential.
- ▷ Mass audiences sometimes demand drama and excitement rather than aesthetic appreciation.
- ▷ Control of sport needs to be balanced between the owners and athletes.
- ▷ Amateur sports are becoming pressurised by the need to generate more money.
- ▷ Sport, sponsorship and the media are all interdependent on each other for their success and popularity.
- ▷ The media can transform sport into a crucial part of people's lives. Without coverage, sport would have a much lower profile.

Technology occurs in the form of:

- ▷ equipment and clothing developments in order to improve athletes' performance
- ▷ assistance for officials' decisions
- ▷ wider accessibility for fans in the manner in which they receive sport entertainment.

The modern Olympic Games:

- ▷ began in the 19th century in order to bring nations together and for athletes to take part in fair competition
- ▷ have become the world's biggest and most prestigious sport competition
- ▷ reflect many of society's problems such as political turmoil and the commercialisation of sport.

London 2012 Games are hoped to bring:

- ▷ economic growth
- ▷ regeneration of poor areas
- ▷ increased participation amongst the general population.

Revise as you go

1. What are the characteristics of commercial sport?
2. What qualities make an athlete attractive to potential sponsors?
3. What are the advantages and disadvantages of sponsorship to the performer?
4. How can female athletes be at a disadvantage in terms of attracting sponsorship deals?
5. How can the media reinforce discrimination in sport?
6. How can the media act as an educator about sport?
7. How can successful marketing help the future of the Olympic Games?
8. List six ways in which technology has affected a variety of sports.
9. List four ways in which spectators can benefit from the application of technology in sport.
10. What benefits do sponsors of the Olympic Games gain?

Get the result!

Examination question

Advancements in technology have improved sport beyond all recognition.

Evaluate the impact of technology on the performer, coach and spectator in the modern-day sporting arena and discuss whether these advancements have improved sport. (14 marks)

Examiner says

For this section of the paper you will need to answer one 14 mark question and two 7 mark questions.

Model answer

Student answer

Technology has always played an important role in the changing nature of sport, but recently advancements have seen many more changes. Some of these have been good and some bad.

For the performers technology has helped them improve their performance by allowing them to train more effectively. For example there are more testing methods [5], different ways to analyse techniques, like video and biomechanical analysis [11]. There have also been developments in training methods [14] and diets because people now know the effect it has on the body in more detail [1]. Lots of people now use things to help them recover from training and injury [3] like ice baths and oxygen chambers [4]. Also the equipment has improved [7] and more testing is done to ensure the best performances, for example tennis rackets are always being updated with new materials to make the balls travel faster.

Examiner says

No marks awarded for the first paragraph as this is merely a repetition of the question.

Examiner says

In the second paragraph points 5, 11, 14, 1, 3, 4 and 7 on the mark scheme are credited.

Model answer

The coach has also used technology to help them. Like the performer they now have better vouching information [bod 13], testing systems and ways to analyse performance [repeat 11]. Lots of coaches use videos of performance to look at their opponents strengths and weaknesses to plan their tactics [repeat 11].

The spectator has also been affected by changes in technology. Now people can watch sport from all around the world virtually at any time of day or night[16]. Also there is now interactive technologies, for example you can listen to the referee talking to the players or choose which angle you watch the game from [15]. The commentators use technology to help explain what has happened to help you understand more about the game and what has happened [17].

Examiner says

In paragraph three point 13 is awarded a 'bod' mark – this is the 'benefit of the doubt' given by the examiner – it is considered close enough to the mark scheme. It is worth noting that the next time the mark is tenuous it wouldn't be awarded. There are two repeats of point 11, which has already been awarded in the second paragraph, so no mark here.

Examiner says

In the fourth paragraph points 16, 15 and 17 are awarded.

Examiner says

This makes a total of 11/14 for content and 3 marks for written communication.

Mark scheme

This is a breakdown of what the examiner would expect to see in the answer. It shows you how you can pick up marks.

(a) **Performer**

1. Increased knowledge of diet, e.g. carbo-loading
2. Supplementation, e.g. creatine, sports energy drink
3. Faster rehabilitation
4. Due to O_2 tents, hypobaric chambers, ice baths
5. Improved testing to provide continuous feedback on effectiveness of training programmes
6. Advancements in stress management techniques to control arousal

7. Tailor-made equipment ensures everything is designed to performers preferences
8. Facilities that recreate climates/environments, no need to travel/time out of country
9. Instant feedback on performance through HR monitors/smart shirts
10. Advancements in clothing enable performers to continue at higher intensity

Coach

11. Video analysis of matches to highlight tactical/strategic issues
12. Technique analysis can be done instantaneously with use of software such as Dartfish or ProZone
13. More detailed information to provide a more focussed training programme
14. New training techniques to improve performance, e.g. SAQ

Spectator

15. Improved home experience through increased number of cameras
16. Wider range of sports more accessible through advancements in media
17. Development of technology such as Hawk-Eye have increased the interactive feel

(b) (i) Sub max 4 marks

1. Over-strong desire to win/over arousal/pressure
2. May be encouraged/asked to do so by coach/team mates/pressure from sponsors/crowds
3. Players loses control due to action of opponents/referee decisions/retaliates/frustration
4. Player lacks moral/ethical restraints on personal behaviour
5. Financial rewards
6. Importance of game/cup final/equivalent.

(ii) Sub max 4 marks

1. Opposition player fouls/protection from violence
2. Off field of play, contracts with employers/administration of wages/assets/Bosman ruling
3. Sponsorship deals/commercial deals
4. Protection from media intrusion into private life
5. Protection from hooligans during and after games
6. Maintenance of restricted areas during training/competitions
7. Protection from racism/equal opportunities. (7 marks)

(c) **Yes** Sub max 4 marks

1. Battle against drugs is expensive/time-consuming
2. Detection not effective/always behind chemists
3. Difficult to define drug as compared to aid/supplement
4. Sacrifices performer makes to achieve success is personal
5. High performance leads to more spectators/sponsors/money
6. Level playing field for all

No Sub max 4 marks

7. Side effects are dangerous/health risks

8. Young tempted to use drugs/ role model effect
9. Coaches/peer pressure may force performers to use drugs
10. Sport about using natural talent
11. Drug use outside this concept
12. Cheating/unethical
13. Costly
14. Only the richer countries will be able to afford the technology, therefore uneven playing field (7 marks)

Examination question

An individual must have a range of personal qualities and receive some external support to enable them to reach an elite level of performance.

Within the United Kingdom, what support or structures exist to help an individual develop to an elite level? Give examples to illustrate your answer. (7 marks)

Model answer

The structures that exist to help an individual to develop into an elite performer are:

Out of school clubs. These clubs develop the skills that are taught in school.

Satellite academies [11] – are for clubs to set up for the most gifted in their sport [12] to develop their game even more, e.g. football academies run by premiership football clubs.

Talent Identification [10] – this is where scouts observe young players and see if they have the potential to become an elite player. These are run by the governing body or scouts in each area of the country [9].

Specialist facilities [6] – elite performers need good facilities to train and develop their skills. These are provided by the English Institute of Sport [5] and other centres of excellence.

Examiner says

This is a well structured answer, with clear sections for each point made. There is good use of relevant examples as requested. The organisations are correctly named and linked to the support they provide.

A common mistake in this type of answer would be to merely list a number of organisations, which would not be credited.

Mark scheme

There are 7 marks for 7 of the following (maximum of 4 per section): Maximum of 4 if support/structures only. Maximum of 2 if naming organisations only.

Each example must be linked to a specific structure/support. There are no marks for just naming an organisation. It must be qualified.

Examples	Structures and support
1. NGB/Sport England/World Class programme/SportsAid/gifted & talented/aim higher/Sponsorships/ Scholarships	2. Financial support
3. set performance targets/ performance development plans	4. Support linked to success/world ranking
5. English Institute of Sport/ Sportscoach UK/UKSI/NGBs/ SportEngland/centres of excellence/academies/UK Sport	6. Network of elite or high quality coaching/facilities
7. English Institute of Sport/Centres of Excellence/NGB/ Higher Education	8. Sports science/technology/ nutrition/medicine/physiotherapy
9. NGB/World Class Programme run by UK Sport/EIS regional scouts	10. Talent Identification Programme
11. Academies/centres of excellence/ specialist schools/ colleges/county squads international development groups	12. Graded levels of competition/ Training elite groups

UNIT 4

Optimising practical performance in a competitive situation

Practical coursework

CHAPTER 19

Practical coursework

LEARNING OBJECTIVES:

By the end of this chapter you should be able to:

- *understand the requirements of the chosen role i.e performer, coach/leader or official*
- *know how to prepare for assessment*
- *complete an analysis of your personal performance and compare it to that of an elite performer*
- *explain the causes of indentified weaknesses and demonstrate how to use theoretical knowledge to improve your practical performance.*

Introduction

The aim of the practical coursework component is to build on the core skills developed in the first year of the course and to apply them in a competitive situation or similar performance conditions. For example, the term 'competitive situation' is not really applicable to some outdoor and adventurous activities, such as climbing, but assessment should be completed in the natural environment. Similarly those students choosing 'dance' as their activity will be expected to perform in front of an audience.

Just as you have refined and developed your skills during various Physical Education National Curriculum lessons and GCSE Physical Education lessons, the same is expected at A-level. As a result you will now be assessed in only one activity and in one role. Therefore you must chose which of the roles, i.e. performer, offical or coach/leader you feel most confident in fulfilling. You may actually receive higher marks as a coach than as a performer or vice versa. Check with your member of staff and see what they think. Just because you prefer one role doesn't actually mean it's your strongest one!

The focus of the second year is to assess not only your physical, coaching and officiating skills as well as the application of strategies and tactics, but to bring together all the various theoretical components allowing the optimisation of performance. The task you face is to use your knowledge and understanding of the theoretical aspects of the course to identify weaknesses in your or others' performance and their possible causes. You then need to use this knowledge to eradicate the faults.

The first key piece of advice is to obtain a copy of the relevant specification criteria as soon as possible. You can get this either from your teacher or download it from the AQA website at www.aqa.org.uk.

Practical performance and preparation for assessment

Much of the advice offered in this section is similar to that given for AS level. However, it is worth refreshing your memory to remind yourself how to access the marks. Table 19.01 outlines the examination board requirements for the A2 course. The skills developed in the first year will now be assessed in a competitive or relevant performance situation.

This unit is worth a total of 20 per cent of the overall A2 course. The marks are allocated as shown in Table 19.01.

REMEMBER!

Performer – assesses their own performance
Coach/leader – assesses another performer
Official/referee – assesses their own performance

Section A – Optimising practical performance in a competitive situation Maximum 60 marks
For the Category 1 activities which include the majority of the game type activities. • 20 marks for each area of skill application • Game activities are split into the following sections: 1. effectiveness of attacking skills 2. effectiveness of defensive skills 3. effective implementation of strategies and tactics. For the Category 2 Activities which include athletics, weightlifting and swimming the sections are: 1. technical quality of event 1 2. technical quality of event 2 3. application of strategy/tactics. Category 3 activities which include dance, diving, gymnastics trampolining. The three areas are all different and you will need to check the specification for the exact requirements
Section B – Observation, analysis and critical evaluation of performance **Maximum 30 marks**
• 15 marks for identification of the weaknesses of the performer (5 marks for each of the 3 areas named in Section A) • 15 marks for comparison to an elite performer (5 marks for each of the 3 areas named in Section A)
Section C – Application of knowledge and understanding to optimise performance **Maximum 30 marks**
• 15 marks for identification of possible causes of weaknesses of each assessment area highlighted in • 15 marks for identification of corrective practices to allow improvement of performance

Table 19.01 Allocation of marks for the practical coursework component

Category 1		Category 2	Category 3
Association Football	Lacrosse	Athletics	Dance (Contemporary/Creative/Ballet)
Badminton	Mountain Activities	Olympic weightlifting	
Basketball	Netball	Swimming	Diving
Boxing	Rowing and Sculling		Gymnastics
Canoeing/Kayaking (Moving/Inland water)	Rugby Union/League		Trampolining
Climbing	Sailing/Windsurfing/Kitesurfing		
Cricket	Kitesurfing		
Fencing	Skiing/Snowbarding		
Gaelic football	Softball/Baseball/Rounders		
Goalball	Squash		
Golf	Table tennis		
Handball	Tae Kwon Do		
Hockey (Field/Roller/Ice)	Tennis		
Horse Riding	Track/Road cycling/Mountain biking		
Judo	Volleyball		
Karate	Water polo		

Table 19.02 Activities available for assessment

Many students may often neglect the practical coursework element and tend to focus on the theoretical aspects. However, a large percentage of the final marks is allocated to this section – 20 per cent of the final mark allocation for the A-level course. Therefore time should be devoted to developing the skills required from the onset and not left until later when you are close to the final assessment or moderation.

To fully understand the nature of performance and how to facilitate improvement, links should be made with the theoretical components as frequently as possible. Individual strengths and weaknesses should be identified and, as the course progresses, possible causes and corrective measures can be implemented.

The selection of activities must be carefully considered as there may be restrictions. In addition to your own experience, other factors may include:

- the time available to complete extra training or practice at coaching or officiating
- the opportunity for extra-curricular activities
- the accessibility of facilities and resources
- the expertise of teachers and coaches.

The nature of assessment requires the demonstration of relevant named core skills related to a specific activity in a competitive situation or relevant performance situation, e.g. a dance in front of an audience. It may be difficult for some students to fulfil the requirements depending on their choice of activity. For example, many students may offer skiing during the AS course, as they are competent skiers, but they would be unable to offer it at A2 level unless they competed in actual race events. Consequently your activity must be selected carefully to avoid a panic in the later part of the course.

The marking of the practical activities is conducted by continual assessment. This allows for ongoing development of performance and caters for students who may have an 'off day' during a moderator's visit. The assessment will focus on your performance in a competitive situation which includes your demonstration of core skills, strategies and tactics; the application of the psychological and physiological qualities needed within a fully competitive environment or appropriate alternative.

In order to develop your skills in the competitive situation, training sessions are easier with others, not just because it is more sociable but because they can actually help to improve your performance by observing and coaching. If the practice takes place with another student who has limited knowledge of the activity, outline the identified weaknesses of the skills and prepare a sheet of the correct techniques and coaching points required.

However, if time can be spent with a teacher or another student who is experienced or offering coaching as their chosen role, and is able to identify your weaknesses, this may be of greater benefit. Allocated time for development may be available either during lessons or extra-curricular activities.

Further time for development may take place at a local club and the expertise of the coaches there may be utilised. If this is the case it may be advisable to inform them of the specification criteria, so that they are aware of your aims and the specific skills that need to be developed.

When possible video record any practice sessions and analyse your development. Evaluate any progress and restructure your training schedule as required.

To develop the effective application of your skills in a competitive situation, set targets for each game or event and ask someone to evaluate your performance. Do not set too many each time, possibly two or three, but try to concentrate on these and don't get over-concerned with other areas of weakness – they can be targets next time.

When developing skills or working with others don't try to change everything at once or expect a huge improvement in performance overnight. The process may take months or years to complete. Many elite performers strive to make minor modifications to their technique in order to achieve the optimum performance. The aim of the A2 course is not to make you compete, coach or officiate at this level but to be competent performers. Try to remember this when developing your practical performance.

Assessment procedures

The school/college will be assigned an external moderator to ensure the marking criteria are applied correctly by the teachers, when compared to recommended national standards. The moderation may involve:

- one school/college
- a group of schools/colleges
- video evidence.

The moderator may not see all the activities being offered by the school/college due to time restrictions, availability of facilities or numbers involved. However, the assumption must be made that he or she will observe any possible combination of activities and as a consequence you should be fully prepared. This may involve not only the actual practical performance but any analysis of performance requirements. The best way to prepare for the moderation is to start practising, analysing or officiating the core skills as early in the course as possible and give yourself the opportunity to experience as many conditioned situations as you can to develop your skills.

The moderation usually involves both AS and A2 students. Consequently it may be easy to lose focus and concentration. Many students assume the moderator is not watching them because they are at the other end of the sports hall or far side of the playing field. Don't be complacent – he or she may be assessing you at any time!

It also helps to make the effort to dress appropriately and 'look the part'. This will at least give the moderator the impression that some preparation and thought has been given to the assessment rather than simply turning up on the day.

The nature of physical activity inevitably involves mistakes being made during performance; it is almost unavoidable. Even performers at the highest level make errors of judgement or are influenced by the environment, occasion and opponents. If mistakes are made don't worry about them, redirect your attention and concentrate on the task ahead. The moderator will look at the overall performance not just one small part.

If the selected activity is a team game or one that involves other performers don't try to be the centre of attention all the time. The assessment is based on your ability to fulfil a role within a specific position. Marks may be lost because of the inability to implement certain tactics, strategies and systems of play.

Analysis of personal performance

Before any personal development of skill and technique can occur, your own performance must be analysed and evaluated. This can be achieved in a number of ways:

- teacher/coach observing performance and providing feedback
- another student observing performance and providing feedback
- video recording of own performance and personal analysis.

If possible the latter is in many ways the most useful, as you can see the faults (via visual guidance) and develop a better understanding of the exact modifications needed. Video footage is also useful as a means of stopping the action and making specific comparisons to the technical model or someone highly competent, which may be more difficult during live or full speed actions.

Once the actual skill or specific area has been analysed the next stage in the process involves the evaluation of the effectiveness of its application, during competitive situations.

As mentioned previously, for game activities these are split into the following sections:

- effectiveness of attacking skills
- effectiveness of defensive skills
- effective implementation of strategies and tactics

Other activities have alternative categories which are more appropriate, e.g. swimming and athletics may require the comments to be based on two events, and gymnastic events may be based on agilities and twists. Detailed requirements need to be obtained from the specification criteria.

Once this process has been completed a structured development programme should be constructed and followed to eradicate the identified weaknesses in the skills. For example, if as a coach you find it difficult to alter tactics to suit a changing situation, time must be devoted to gaining an understanding of alternatives. Similarly as an official if you find that you have difficulty in refeering set pieces or judging difficult sequences on the trampoline,your practice must focus on these particular araes. Assess your development frequently either via a teacher/coach or by video recording. Don't just assume because practice is taking place an improvement will occur – you may be practising the wrong technique!

REMEMBER!

Remember the 'coaching cycle'.

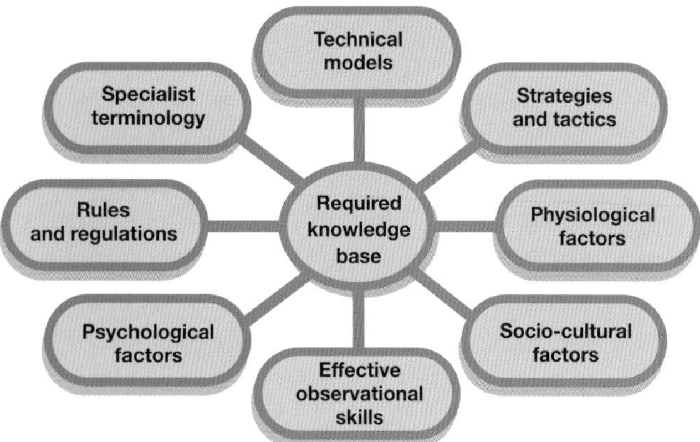

Fig 19.01 The coaching cycle

Refer back to the advice in Chapter 15 of the AS textbook on how to carry out successful observations. The same principles apply.

Requirements of a practical performer – Section A (practical performance)

The assessment of your practical ability now focuses on your effective execution of the core skills and techniques, that you demonstrated at AS level, in a competitive situation or equivalent scenario. Your ability to use a range of skills under pressure in a full game situation, including following the correct rules and regulations will be assessed. You will also be assessed on your ability to use and modify different strategies and tactics depending on the situation.

HOT LINKS

Visit the AQA website, www.aqa.org.uk and print out a copy of the specification criteria for your chosen activity.

Fig 19.02 As a performer you must execute core skills and techniques effectively

The marks will be allocated in three broad areas, each worth 20 marks:

Assessment Area 1	Technical Quality	Aspect 1 (e.g. in games this will include attacking skills, but dance would be performance of the sequence)
Assessment Area 2	Technical Quality	Aspect 2 (e.g. in games this will include defending skills, but dance would be choreography of the sequence)
Assessment Area 3		Application of strategic/tactical awareness (e.g. in games this will include various systems and formations of play suitable for different situations, but dance would be variation and use of space and movement within the overall dance)

Table 19.03 Requirements of a performer

In order to achieve the higher marks you should aim to develop a range of skills which can be completed correctly when faced with a pressured situation and which can be adapted as required.

As part of the mark for each section your physical and psychological capabilities will also be assessed. Therefore you should aim to train to improve your fitness levels to cope with the demands of a full game situation. As part of your analysis of your performance, in addition to simply evaluating your strengths and weaknesses in terms of your skills, be critical of your ability to maintain those standards throughout the competitive event. If you know that stamina and speed are particular weaknesses, aim to develop those areas along with your skill levels.

Similarly your ability to maintain the correct arousal level is equally important. It may be a worthwhile exercise to ask someone to observe your performance in a competitive situation and ask them to evaluate the effectiveness of your concentration levels. Pose the following questions:

- Did I appear to be distracted by the crowd?
- Were there times when I seemed to 'drift' out of the game?
- Did I appear to become over-aroused and loose concentration?
- Did I become aggressive at any time?

While the answers may be subjective, it may prove to be a useful starting point for evaluating your performance. If there were particular psychological areas which caused a decrease in performance, consider methods to eradicate the weakness.

Remember: just as physical skills and fitness need practice, so do new psychological techniques. Don't rely on it being okay on the assessment or moderation day; devote time to improve this aspect of your performance – most top class sports performers do!

Requirements of a leader/coach – Section A (practical performance)

The expectation of a leader/coach at this level is to plan, coordinate and lead an individual, group or team in a competitive situation or equivalent scenario. The skills you developed in the first year of the course, in terms of analysing the various core skills and techniques must now be developed further and applied in a more pressurised situation. You will be expected to evaluate the situation quickly and make the necessary adjustments to improve both the skills of the individuals and make the tactics more effective.

HOT LINKS

Visit the AQA website, www.aqa.org.uk and print out a copy of the specification criteria for your chosen activity.

The marks will be allocated in three broad areas, each worth 20 marks:

Assessment Area 1	Technical Quality	Aspect 1 (e.g. in games this will include coaching attacking skills, but dance would be performance of the sequence)
Assessment Area 2	Technical Quality	Aspect 2 (e.g. in games this will include coaching defending skills, but dance would be choreography of the sequence)
Assessment Area 3		Application of strategic/tactical awareness (e.g. in games this will include coaching various systems and formations of play suitable for different situations, but dance would be variation and use of space and movement within the overall dance)

Table 19.04 Requirements of a leader/coach

Fig 19.03 As a coach or leader you must develop your own coaching style

During the first year of the course you developed the skills of analysing techniques in isolation and conditioned practices. Now you must attempt to get as much practice refining those skills within the context of a full game or performance situation. This may occur at training sessions, extra-curricular matches/performance or in a club situation.

To be an effective coach/leader numerous skills have to be mastered. One of the most important is the ability to communicate your ideas and suggestions to the performers. Whilst you may be highly proficient at evaluating the situation, if your communication skills are poor and you are unable to transfer that information to the performers, they may become confused and frustrated, which may in turn actually lead to a decline in performance. Therefore you should ideally turn theory into practice and revisit the work from the AS course, especially the areas of guidance, feedback, methods of practice, feedback and teaching styles. These areas will provide an excellent basis for you to develop your own coaching style and help you to adapt depending on the situation.

Other aspects of this role that will be assessed include your ability to prepare your performers both physically and psychologically prior to the event. This will require you to implement effective warm-up routines and create an atmosphere where performers can achieve their optimum levels of arousal. Consider methods that allow this to happen, including goal setting, mental rehearsal, stress management techniques and various other methods that will have been studied as part of the Psychology section of the course. Following the competition or performance you should also be able to evaluate the outcome and discuss appropriate strategies to improve future performances, both physically and psychologically. For example, if an individual has obviously lacked the stamina to maintain the skills required throughout the event suggestions should be made on how to improve this aspects of fitness. Similarly if they have become over-aroused and aggressive in a particular situation, suggest how this can be avoided in the future.

The final area in which marks will be awarded assesses your ability to evaluate the performance and make tactical changes as required. If there is no need to change that is fine, don't make chnages for the sake of them. However if there is a need, changes should be decisive and effective. Performers should know what is required of them and you must have the ability to relay those decisions quickly. Don't be too worried if the changes don't have the desired effect; the key thing would be that you realised that after performance and learnt from the experince to help you in the future.

Requirements of an official – Section A (practical performance)

This year as an official you will be expected to officiate your chosen activitiy in a fully competitive situation or equivalent environment, e.g. mountain activities would be assessed as part of a three day expedition with a minimum of two nights camping whereas netball would be a normal match as expected by the national governing body. Therefore you must obtain a copy of the specification criteria as soon as possible to gain a full understanding of what will be required of you.

HOT LINKS

Visit the AQA website, www.aqa.org.uk and print out a copy of the specification criteria for your chosen activity.

The marks will be allocated in three broad areas, each worth 20 marks:

Assessment Area 1	Technical Quality	Aspect 1 (e.g. in games this will include refereeing of attacking skills, but athletics would be officiating one event)
Assessment Area 2	Technical Quality	Aspect 2 (e.g. in games this will include refereeing of defending skills, but athletics would be officiating a different event))
Assessment Area 3		Ability to communicate, justification of decisions, maintenance of accurate scores and implementation of appropriate safety measures to minimise the risk of injury

Table 19.05 Requirements of an official

Fig 19.04 As an official you will be assessed on your ability to apply rules

For both Areas of Assessment 1 and 2 as well as being assessed on your ability to interpret and apply the rules and regulations correctly and consistently, you will be assessed in your physical and pyschological capabilities. Consider the following questions:

- Am I fit enough to officiate the event so that I don't tire and make mistakes?
- Am I able to maintain concentration throughout the event and not get distracted?
- Do I get over-aroused in pressurised situations and make poor decisions as a result?

The answers to these questions may help to target areas for improvement. Just as a performer will be observed and analysed it would be beneficial for you as an official to undergo the same experience. This will help to construct a plan of areas to be developed and improve your officiating skills.

As you can see from the details above the role of the official is slightly different to that of the performer and the coach/leader in terms of how the marks are awarded. While the Areas of Assessment 1 and 2 are similar the third section is quite different. Rather than the emphasis being on strategies and tactics, the assessment will focus on the following areas:

- Ability to communicate with performers and officials – you will be expected to use the correct hand signals to explain your decisions, if needed use a whistle correctly, link with other officials both in terms of decisions made and scoring, as well as verbally expressing your decisions and thoughts.
- Ability to justify the decisions made to maintain fair play – when decisions are made performers, during a game or event, should be able to understand the reasoning behind your judgements. It may be that your interpretation of some of the laws are slightly different to theirs. If this is the case verbally explaining your decisions can help to ensure performers do not become over-aroused and break the 'contract to compete' and maintain acceptable levels of sportsmanship. You should also remember you will be assessed on your ability to show consistency with your decisions throughout the event. If the situation is not in a competitive situation, such as mountain activities, there will not be the opportunity to be assessed in this role as the criteria and situation do not allow for this role.
- Ability to keep accurate records of scoring or incidents involving the performers – obviously some activities will have more demands in this respect than others. However if you do have

to keep score, e.g. during a badminton match, you must be familiar with how an official would complete this at an elite level tournment. If the situation involves complex scoring systems, such as diving, you must spend time practising how to keep the records and how to judge the performer. In addition to the scoring if any incidents involving players require you to take action, e.g. a yellow card, you must know how to record the incident to allow the correct follow-up procedures to take place.

- Implementation of safety procedures – as an official you are responsible for the safety of the performers. This includes the playing area and any equipment that is used during the competition. Therefore you must be aware of the checks you need to carry out before the start of play. For example, dangerous objects on the field of play, the condition of the playing surface, the proximity of any spectators and the equipment worn or used by performers is acceptable and within governing body regulations.

As you can see the role of the official is not merely a simple case of blowing a whistle or judging a movement. The art of officiating, just like performing and coaching, takes a considerable amount of practice. The same advice applies: start officiating as soon as possible, and it must be in the full competitive situation. Refereeing a half-court game or just keeping score during a badminton match is not enough – it must be done properly.

Section B – observation, analysis and critical evaluation

The aim of this section is to assess your ability to identify weaknesses in performance and then make comparisions to an elite performer. The analysis should be based on the three Areas of Assessment, i.e. for games they would be attacking skills, defensive skills and strategies and tactics. However the evaluation is not merely stating the techincal weaknesses of various core skills but how those weaknesses impact on performance and the consequences that follow.

Each of the Areas of Assessment requires four weaknesses. Therefore you will need to highlight twelve weaknesses in total.

The role in which you have chosen to be assessed will determine who will be evaluated. These are listed below:

- Performer – complete an analysis of your own performance
- Leader/coach – complete an analysis of a named performer
- Official – complete an analysis of your own performance

TASK 19.01

Analyse your performance or that of another performer and identify four weaknesses for each of the three Areas of Assessment. Compare the identifed weaknesses to a named elite performer (it does not have to be the same one for each weakness) and explain the impact on their performance.

Fig 19.05 Compare your performance with one of an elite performer, such as Andrew Strauss

Section C – Application of knowledge and understanding to optimise performance

The aim of this section is to assess your knowledge of the theoretical components and your ability to apply that knowledge, allowing you to improve performance. The factors which may be potential causes of weakness can be drawn from any aspect of the specification. If possible this should be the case as it illustrates your appreciation and understanding of the whole specification, not just components within it. Many students tend to limit their answers to the psychological and physiological components and make limited reference to the socio-cultural factors.

The term 'corrective measures' or 'corrective practices' expects a student to make reference to a variety of theoretical information and not simply outline physical drills or practices.

The question could be posed for any skill or aspect of performance:

'In theoretical terms, what factors may have caused my weaknesses, what can I do to improve and how will this help?'

The reasons identified may not actually have contributed to any weaknesses in performance but the process of identifying them must still take place. Try not to use the same possible cause for each skill; identify different factors. A common fault is to repeat the same cause for several skills, e.g., 'lack of practice', or 'not enough flexibility', etc. If you repeat yourself you may not be credited with the marks.

Synthesis of theory and practical

Based on the analysis of performance completed in Section B, each weakness identified should have a possible theoretical cause explained in detail with an appropriate corrective measure. This demonstrates an understanding of the application of the theoretical components and should allow you to appreciate how many factors can actually affect the performance of an individual.

Outlined below are topics which may have affected the development and performance of your chosen activities. The lists are not complete and other factors may be included. If there are other areas which may have influenced your development, explain the reasons why and outline how this knowledge can be used to rectify the situation.

Physiological factors

These might include:

- inefficient use of levers and bones
- lack of specific fitness components
- physiological composition of the individual
- dietary considerations
- inappropriate training methods
- poor application of training principles
- lack of structured training programme
- poor development of appropriate energy systems
- poor rehabilition from injury or lack of preventation.

Psychological factors

These might include:

- plateaus and associated causes
- theories of learning experienced
- types of practice
- methods of teaching
- forms of guidance
- types of motivation
- transfer of learning
- effectiveness of information processing system
- aggression
- attitude
- group dynamics and leadership
- arousal levels
- achievement motivation
- stress, anxiety and poor stress management techniques
- self-efficacy and learned helplessness.

Socio-cultural factors

These might include:

- physical education experiences
- National Curriculum
- experiences of play, sport and physical recreation
- historical factors and traditions
- equal opportunities – gender, race, social class, disability, socio-economic group
- provision of facilities – public, private and voluntary
- National Lottery
- government initiatives
- funding
- role models
- effectiveness of national and local organisations.

As you can see from the list on pages 321-2 there are many theoretical aspects that may be linked to your development; you just have to think about which might have had the greatest impact on you personally.

When completing this section think logically and arrange your notes in an organised manner. This makes revision and discussion more effective and thorough.

An example of this structured procedure is outlined below in Table 19.06, with a possible cause for each of the identified weaknesses taken from a different theoretical area.

Course = A2 • Activity = cricket (batting) • Area of assessment = defending	
Weakness 1	Batting – play too hard at the ball against spin bowlers. I sometimes push forward too hard in defence against slow bowling. I want to get a large stride forward to counteract the spin on the ball, but I sometimes over-emphasise this and lunge forward too quickly at the ball. This often results in the ball popping up close to fielders, giving them a catching opportunity.
Possible cause (psychological factor)	I have low self-efficacy regarding this type of shot. This has been caused by the four elements outlined by Bandura: • past performance accomplishments – lost my wicket playing this shot several times before • vicarious experiences – seen others in my team playing this shot unsuccessfully • verbal persuasion – my coach has told me not to attempt the shot unless I need to • emotional arousal – I become anxious when playing against spin bowlers who bowl on the correct line and length.
Corrective practice	To develop my self-efficacy I could: • past performance accomplishments – practise the shot in training and develop my technique; I could also attempt the shot more regularly in less important games • vicarious experiences – watch how other players approach the shot and learn from their actions • verbal persuasion – my coach can encourage me to boost my confidence and we can discuss how to approach the shot in a positive manner • emotional arousal – develop effective stress management techniques, such as controlled breathing and imagery to employ when batting
Weakness 2	Bowling – length of delivery is very erratic. I regularly bowl balls too full in length or much too short, allowing the batsman to score easy runs. I am only an occasional bowler and I am unaware of the action which I need to produce a consistent length of delivery.

Table 19.06 Exemplar of Section B and C for Assessment Area 1 – Application of Defending Skills

Table 19.06 continued

Possible cause (psychological factor)	A lack of effective practice means I am not aware of the weaknesses in my bowling action. I am still in the associative stage of learning and am unable to detect if the speed of run-up, the angle of release or height of release is the major problem causing the inconsistent length of delivery. Video analysis has illustrated I often release the ball behind my head, creating a large angle of release and consequently a full delivery (too close to the batsman). The height of my release also varies and I need to release the ball further through my action. A lack of effective practice means I am not aware of the weaknesses in my bowling action. I am still in the associative stage of learning and am unable to detect if the speed of run-up, the angle of release or height of release is the major problem causing the inconsistent length of delivery. Video analysis has illustrated I often release the ball behind my head, creating a large angle of release and consequently a full delivery (too close to the batsman). The height of my release also varies and I need to release the ball further through my action.
Corrective practice	Massed practice, concentrating on my point of release, will aid familiarity with speed, angle and height of release. This should be linked with visual and verbal guidance, illustrating the good and bad points, to allow reinforcement to take place. Visual guidance could be completed through the use of video analysis and the placement of cones to highlight the target area. Verbal guidance from my coach could be used to identify when to release the ball or give me specific feedback about my technique.
Weakness 3	Running to stop a ball caused by a lack of speed over a short distance. If the ball is coming close to me I can move quite quickly a few metres either way, but if the ball has passed me I struggle to turn and chase it to the boundary. This causes me to not stop the ball crossing the boundary rope and runs are added to the other team's score.
Possible cause (physiological)	Lack of agility and speed over a short distance. Much of my training is focused on the development of skills required to play cricket rather than the fitness needed to play at a good level. Time with my coach is limited and the skill development is the focus of attention.
Corrective practice	Development of agility and speed by incorporating specific exercises into a structured training programme. Circuit training could involve shuttle runs aimed at turning quickly and sprinting in the other direction, as well as exercises to develop speed and power. These could include bench jumps, step-ups, lunges and alternate leg changes. I could also use plyometrics and speed sessions. The speed training could involve different distances up to 40m as this replicates the game situation.
Weakness 4	Moving backwards into position to catch a ball close to the boundary. I tend to watch the ball for too long in the air before moving to try and catch it. As a result my hands and arms are not the correct position; they are above and behind my head rather than my whole body being behind the ball. On numerous occasions I have partially caught the ball only for it to drop out of my hands. The fact that my body is not behind the ball also means there is little chance for me to gather a rebound opportunity.
Possible cause	Lack of selective attention and poor response time. While I watch the batsman play the shot I don't anticipate what shot he might play. When the shot has been played I am focused on the ball and its flight but don't anticipate quickly enough where it may land. This may also be caused by my lack of concentration if I have been in a particular position for several overs and the ball has not come to me very often.
Corrective practice	To improve my selective attention I could do a number of things. Rather than focus on the batsman hitting the ball I could watch the bowler more closely and try to anticipate where the type of shot based on where the ball has pitched, e.g. if the ball hand landed shot of a length inviting the batsman to play a hook shot, the chances are the ball may come in my direction. I could also use stress management techniques e.g. thought stopping, where before every ball I say a key word to focus my attention on the play at the time and not let e mind wander. Finally, I could discuss the situation with my captain or coach and explain that being in one fielding position for too long causes me to lose concentration. An easy strategy to avoid this would be to alter my position regularly causing me to re-focus and maintain concentration.

Comments on the examples above:

- For each assessment area, i.e. attack, defence, strategies and tactics, there must be four weaknesses, causes and corrections. In other words, you need to discuss twelve factors in total.
- For each weakness there must be a comparison made to a named elite performer. This has not been shown on this example, but once you have highlighted your weakness, explain in terms of the application of those skills why the elite performer is more effective.
- The technical terminology used is specific to the activity of cricket.
- It is possible to use one theoretical area several times. For example, the possible causes for two weaknesses may both be psychologically based.
- No repetitive answers – search the specification and use different reasons, to show the moderator you have an understanding of many areas from both AS and A2 modules.

TASK 19.02

Using the table outlined below, complete the following tasks for the identified weaknesses highlighted in Task 19.01:

- Suggest a possible theoretical cause of each weakness.
- Outline a practical method which could be implemented based on this knowledge.

Repeat the procedure for three other identified weaknesses. Repeat for all aspects of performance which need to be analysed.

Completing the analysis in this way should allow for the development of a logical and structured understanding of each area.

It may be useful to structure your analysis as shown in Table 19.07 below.

	Personal performance	**Elite performer**
Weakness 1	*Selected skill and weakness of application in a competitive situation*	*Explanation of application of same skill and effective outcomes*
Cause of weakness	*Theoretical explanation for weakness*	
Corrective practice	*Theoretical explanation of how to implement corrective strategy (not just an outline of drill/practice)*	
Weakness 2		
Cause of weakness		
Corrective practice		
Weakness 3		
Cause of weakness		
Corrective practice		
Weakness 4		
Cause of weakness		
Corrective practice		

Table 19.07 Exemplar sheet of how Sections B and C may be completed

REMEMBER!

Key points to remember when preparing for the practical coursework

The following points can be applied to any of the different specifications:

- Check the requirements and choose the role carefully.
- Start preparation for the final assessment at the beginning of the course – don't leave it until the last few weeks!
- Learn the correct techniques and rules for the chosen activities.
- Take time to analyse your strengths and weaknesses.
- Set realistic targets for performance development.
- Evaluate your progress regularly and revise your targets.
- Look for the links between the theoretical aspects of the course and personal practical performance.
- Update your notes regularly and use them as a revision resource.
- Enjoy it – the practical aspect of the course is supposed to be fun!

HOT LINKS

These websites will be useful when you research your chosen sport and chosen role in order to complete your coursework:

www.aqa.org.uk
www.activeplaces.com
www.arielnet.com
www.bodybuildingforyou.com
www.brianmac.demond.co.uk
www.news.bbc.co.uk/sportsacademy
www.bbc.co.uk/science/hottopics/obesity
www.netdoctor.co.uk/diseases/facts/osteoporosis
www.pponline.co.uk
www.pz.football.co.uk
www.specialolympics.org
www.sportscoachuk.org
www.sports-fitness-adviser.com
www.sportsscience.org
www.sportstec.com
www.teachpe.com
www.thecoachingcorner.com
www.usatoday.com/sports
www.video.google.com

Index

Bold page numbers indicate a definition of the term. *Italic* numbers indicate an illustration or table.

A

absolute VO_2max **16**
acceleration **82**–3, 86
acetyl-coenzyme-A 5
acetylcholine (ACh) **41**, 42
achievement goal theory 122–3
achievement motivation 119–23, 121, *122*
actin **32**, 33–6, *34*
action/reaction, law of 86–7
active recovery **13**
adaptive responses 25
adenosine triphosphate (ATP) **2**–5, *3*, *4*, 7, *7*, 8
  ATP-PC (alactic) system *19*, 19–20, *20*
  binding of 35
Adlington, Rebecca 176
aerobic energy system
  and recovery 9–14, *9–14*
  glycogen breakdown through 5
  Krebs cycle **6**–7
aerobic metabolism **4**
aerobic training *51*
age, impact on VO_2max 17
aggression **270**, *275*
  and assertion 167–8, *168*
  causes of 169
  channelled 167
  definitions 167–8
  reduction and control of 171
  theories of 169–71
Aggression Cue hypothesis 170
aids to performance. *see* ergogenic aids
Ainslie, Ben 137
air resistance **89**, 90
alactacid debt. *see* fast replenishment stage
all or none law 40
Allport, G.W. 157
altitude training 56–**7**, *57*
amateurism **249**, **256**–7, *257*, 258, *260*, *261*
anabolic steroids **49**, **276**
anaerobic metabolism **4**
anaerobic training *51*
Anatomy of a World Class Athlete 225–6, *226*
angle of release of projectiles 90
angular acceleration **94**
angular displacement **94**
angular distance **94**
angular momentum 95–**6**
angular motion 92–7, *93–7*
angular speed **94**
angular velocity (AV) **94**
anthropometry **222**
anti-militarism 248
anxiety
  as negative form of stress 141
  competitive trait 145
  management techniques 147–53
  somatic or cognitive **130**, 142, *143*
  state 144
  trait 144
  types of *143*, 143–5, *145*
approach behaviour 121, **122**, 123
Aronson, E. 156
arousal **170**
  attentional narrowing *135*, **135**
  definition 128–**9**
  theories of 129–33, *129–33*
  zone of optimal functioning (ZOF) **134**–5
assertive behaviour **167**
assessment
  preparation for 314, 325
  procedures 315
athletes
  and technology 302–3
  use of aerobic energy system 8–9
  use of ATP-PC (alactic) system 19–20, *20*
  use of lactic acid (lactate anaerobic) system 21
athleticism **256**, *257*, 257–8
Atkinson, J.W. 120
ATP-PC (alactic) system *19*, 19–20, *20*
attentional control 148–50
attentional narrowing *135*, **135**
attentional wastage **135**
attitude object **157**
attitudes
  changing 161–3
  components of *157*, 157–8
  definitions 156–7
  formation of 158–9
  measurement of 159–61
  positive/negative 157
  Triadic Model *157*, 157–8
attributions 123, **124**
  process *186*
  retraining *189*, **189**
  use of and self-serving bias 188
  Weiner's theory *187*, 187–8
authoritarian leaders 206
autonomic nervous system (ANS) 142, **143**
autonomous phase of learning 130
avoidance behaviour 121, **122**
away matches 182

B

balanced forces 87
balanced tension **270**
Bandura, A. 170, 174, 176
Baron, R.A. 167
Baron, R.S. 181
Barrow, J.C. 204
Berkowitz, L. 170
beta blockers **49**, 50, **276**
beta(ß)-oxidation 7
biofeedback 146, 150–1
biomechanics
  angular motion 92–7, *93–7*
  force 87–9
  linear motion 80–5, *82*, *84*, *85*
  projectile motion 90–2, *91*, *92*
  see also Newton's Laws of Motion
blood doping **276**
blood lactate accumulation *22*, 22–4, *24*
body composition, impact on VO_2max 17
body temperature 13, 65–7, *66*
Bowers, K.S. 116
breathing control 150
British Empire **243**
British Olympic Association 233–4
broken-time payments 249
buffering **25**
Bull, H. 167

C

caffeine **47**, 48
carbohydrate window 13
cardiovascular drift 67
Carron, A.V. 195, 196

cash receipts **285**
catastrophe theory 132–3, *133*, **134**
Cattell, R. 116
centring 150
channelled aggression **167**
channelling **301**
Chelladurai's Multi-dimensional model 208–10, *209*
churches 245, 246
circuit training *52*
civilising of society **241**
class system 246–7, *248*, 293
coaching 230–1
cognitive anxiety 143, *143*
cognitive dissonance 162–3
cognitive responses 141, **142**
commentators 293
commercialisation 251, 284–7, *286*, 293–8
competition period 61–2
Competitive Sport Anxiety Inventory (CSAI-2) 146–7
conduction 66
confidence. *see* self-confidence
conflict **270**
conglomerates **285**
continuous training *51*
contract to compete **255**
contraction of muscles 39–42, *41*
control over sport 287–8
convection 66
core temperature **65**
cori cycle 12, **13**
coupled reaction 19, **20**
coursework. *see* practical coursework
creatine kinase 19, **20**
creatine supplementation 19, 20, **47**
Csikszentmihalyi, M. 136
cue **170**
cue arousal theory 170
cue-utilisation theory **135**

D

dehydration 48
delayed onset of muscle soreness (DOMS) 76–**7**
democratic leaders 206
detraining effect **57**
deviancy
  defined 268–9
  doping *275*, 275–9, *276*, *277*
  hooliganism **270**–74, *275*, 280
  positive/negative **269**

direct gas analysis 15–**16**, *16*
discrimination **159**, **290**
displacement **81**–2, *82*
dissonance **162**
distance **81**–2, *82*
distorted parabola 90
distraction-conflict theory 181, *181*
diuretics **276**
Dollard, J. 169
dominant group **290**
dominant habit or response **129**–30
DOMS (delayed onset of muscle soreness) 75–7
doping *275*, *275–7*, *276*, *277*
Drive Theory **129**–30
drugs. see doping
Dweck, C.S. 190
dysfunctional behaviour. *see* deviancy

E

eccentric contractions 54, 55, 76, **77**
eccentric force 92, **93**
elastic energy 54, 55
electrolyte balance 48
electron transport system **6**, *7*
elite sport and performers
  benefits of pursuing excellence 222
  definition 219, **222**
  identification screening **221**–3
  organisations providing support 225–36
  personality traits 110–11, 116
  support for 220
  talent testing and identification **221**–2
endomysium **32**
endorsements 259, **260**, *287*, 287–9, **288**, *288*, *289*
endothermic reaction 19, **20**
energy
  aerobic system 5–19
  anaerobic systems *19–24*, 19–25
  ATP-PC (alactic) system *19*, 19–20, *20*
  defined **2**–3
  lactic acid (lactate anaerobic) system 20–5, *21–4*
  sources of in the body 3–5
English Institute of Sport (EIS) 228
entertainment 251
epimysium **32**
equal opportunities 290–93
equipment 298–9

ergogenic aids **47**
  caffeine **47**, 48
  creatine supplementation **47**
  herbal remedies 48
  illegal substances 49–50, *275*, *275–7*, *276*, *277*
  protein supplements 47
  water and electrolyte balance 48
erythopoietin (EPO) **276**
ethnic minorities 290–301
etiquette **255**
eustress 141
evaluation apprehension 180–**1**
evaporation 67
excess post-exercise oxygen consumption (EPOC) **10**–14, *11–14*
excitatory postsynaptic potential (EPSP) **41**–2
exercise
  intensity and lactic acid accumulation 24
  thermoregulation during 65–7, *66*
exothermic reactions 3, **4**
extrovert-introvert dimension of personality 112, *113*
Eysenck, H. 111, 112–16

F

fair play **255**
Fartlek training 51
fasciculi **32**
fast oxidative glycolytic fibres (FOG) 36, *37*
fast replenishment stage *11*, **11**
fast twitch glycolytic fibres (FTG) 36, *37*
fast twitch muscle fibre (type 1) 36–**7**, *37*, *38*
fatty acids **4**, 7, 8
femininity **292**
Fiedler's Contingency model 207–208, *208*
flow experience 136, *136*
fluid intake 48
football
  history of 253–4
  hooliganism **270**–74, *275*, 280
  use of technology in 301–2
force *87*, 87–9
free body diagrams 89, *89*
friction 88–**9**
frustration-aggression hypothesis 169–70, *170*

G

games cult **255**
gamesmanship **255**, 256
gender 17, **290**, 295
General Adaptation Syndrome (GAS) *142*, 142–3
general conditioning stage 61
genetics, impact on VO_2max 17
Gill, D.L. 167
Girls4Gold 226
glycogen 4, 5, 9
glycogen loading **57**–8, *58*
glycolsis 20
goal setting 151–3
goals, achievement 122–3
Golgi tendon organs (GTO) 55, **56**
Gould, D. 128, 174
governing bodies 229–300, 289
grass roots sports **220**
Great Man Theory 205
grey economy **271**
Griffin, R.W. 204
Gross, J.J. 111
groups
- cohesion of **196**–9, *197*, 201
- definition 194–5
- dynamics **195**
- productivity of **199**
- Ringelmann effect 200
- social loafing 200
- stages in formation of 195–6

H

heart, during recovery from exercise 12
heat loss from the body 66–7
hegemonic group **290**
herbal remedies 48
Hollander, E.P. 111–12, *112*
Holmes, Kelly 161
home matches 182
homeostasis 143
hooliganism **270**–74, *275*, 280
horizontal forces 88–9
human growth hormone (HGH) **49**–50
humidity 67
hydration 48
hyperbaric chambers 74–**5**
hyperplasia **43**
hyponatremia 48
hypothalamus **65**
hypoxic tents **75**

I

ice baths **75**
Iceberg Profile 118–**19**, *119*
identification screening **221**
illegal substances 49–50, *275*, 275–9, *276*, *277*
imagery 147–8
impulse 84–5, *85*
industrialisation **241**, 242–5
inequalities 290–93
inertia **81**, 85–6
information processing **181**
injuries in sport
- intrinsic and extrinsic factors 72, *72*
- management of 73, *73*
- prevention 73, *73*
- rehabilitation 74–5

innervation of skeletal muscle 40
instinct theory 169
institutes of excellence *227–8*
instrumental aggression **167**
intelligence-psychoticism dimension of personality 116
interactionist theories 116–17, **206**
introvert-extrovert dimension of personality 112
inverted-U theory **130**, *131*, 131–2

K

Krance, V. 128
Krebs cycle **6**–7

L

lactacid debt. *see* slow replenishment stage
lactate dehydrogenase (LDH) 5, 20
lactic acid 12, 23
lactic acid (lactate anaerobic) system 20–5, *21–4*
laissez-faire leaders 206–7
law of conservation of angular momentum 96
law of conservation of momentum 84
law of inertia 85
law, sports **279**, 280–1
Laws of Motion, Newton's. *see* Newton's Laws of Motion
leadership and leaders
- characteristics of 205
- Chelladurai's Multi-dimensional model 208–10, *209*
- definitions 204
- selection of leaders 207
- styles 206–10, *207*
- theories of 205–6

learned helplessness 123, **124**, *190*, 190–1
Lewin, K. 117
lifestyle, impact on VO_2max 17
Likert Scale 160
linear motion 80–5, *82*, *84*, *85*
locus of causality **187**
locus of control **187**, 188
locus of stability **187**
London Marathon 300–1
London Olympic Games 2012 217–19
lungs, during recovery from exercise 12

M

macrocycles 60, *60*, 61–2, *62*, *63*
male hegemony **292**
masculinity **271**, **291**
mass **81**
maximal oxygen consumption (VO_2max) 14–18, *15*, *16*, **16**, *22*, 22–3
McClelland, D.C. 120
McGrath, J.E. 140, 141, 194
measurement of personality 118
media **260**, **288**, 292, 293–8
mesocycles 60, *60*, 63
microchips 300–1
microcycles 60, *60*, 63–4
middle classes **245**, 246
mitochondria 5, **6**, *6*
mole **6**, *7*
moment of inertia (MI) 95, **96**
moments of force 93
momentum 83–4
Monopolies and Mergers Commission (MMC) **285**
mood states 118–19
Moorhead, G. 204
motion. *see* movement
Motion, Laws of. *see* Newton's Laws of Motion
motivation, achievement 119–22
motor neurons 40
motor unit 40, *41*, 42, 43
movement
- angular motion 92–7, 93–7
- force 87–9
- linear motion 80–5, *82*, *84*, *85*
- projectile motion 90–2, *91*, *92*
- *see also* Newton's Laws of Motion

multiple unit summation 42

muscle belly **32**, 40
muscle contraction 39–42, *41*
  sliding filament theory of 33–6, *34*, *35*
muscle fibre 40, *41*
  and lactic acid accumulation 24
  types of 36, *37*, *38*
muscle glycogen, replenishment of 12–13, *13*
muscle hypertrophy **43**
muscles
  relaxation 151
  variation in strength of response 42, *42*
mutual agreement **255**
myofibrils 33, *33*
myosin **32**, 33–6, *34*
myosin cross bridge **36**

N

n.Ach **120**
n.Af **120**
nature **111**
negative deviancy **269**
net force **87**
neuro-muscular system **43**
neurotic-stable dimension of personality 113, *113*
newspapers 295
Newton's Laws of Motion
  First 84, 85–6, 94
  Second 86, 94
  Third *86*, 86–7, 94
nurture **111**

O

observation of stress levels 145
officials, technological assistance for 299–300
Olympics 262–4, 297–8
  British Olympic Association 233–4
  host cities 219
  London 2012 217–19, *219*
onset of blood lactate accumulation (OBLA) *22*, 22–4, **23**
Osgood's Semantic Differential Scale 160
outcome goals 123, 152
oxygen deficit **10**
oxygen tents **75**

P

parabolic flight 90, *90*, 91
Paralympic Games 298
participation pyramid 219, **220**
patrons **260**
peak flow experience 136, *136*
peaking **62**
Pendleton, Victoria 144, 178
performance aids. *see* ergogenic aids
performance athlete development model *229*, **230**
performance goals 152
perimysium **32**
periodisation *60*, 60–5, *62*, *63*, *64*
person-centred leadership 207–8, *208*
personality
  achievement goal theory 122–3
  achievement motivation, theory of 119–22, *121*, *122*
  and elite performers 110–11, 116
  and sporting performance 119
  definitions 111
  extrovert-introvert dimension 112–13, *113*
  interactionist theories 116–17
  measurement of 118
  mood states 118–19
  psychoticism-intelligence dimension 116
  sceptical/credulous approach **119**
  stable-neurotic dimension 113, *113*
  structure of 111–12, *112*
  trait theories 112–16, *113*
persuasive communication 161–2
PESSCLS (Physical Education and School Sport and Club Links Strategy) **230**
philanthropists 244, **245**
phosphocreatine **4**, 19
phosphofructokinase (PFK) 20
Physical Education and School sport and Club Links Strategy (PESSCLS) **230**
physiology, impact on VO_2max 17
plyometrics training *53*, 54, *54*, **55**
PNF(proprioceptive neuromuscular facilitation) *53*, 55, **56**, *56*
popular recreation **241**
positive deviancy **269**
power stroke *34*, 35
practical coursework
  activities available *313*
  analysis of performance 315–16
  application of knowledge and understanding 321
  assessment procedures 315
  exam board requirements *315*
  leader/coach requirements 317–18
  observation, analysis and evaluation 319
  officials, requirements of 318–20
  performance requirements 316–17
  preparation for assessment 314, 325
  synthesis of theory and practical 321–24, *322–3*, *324*
pre-season training 61
prejudice **159**
preparation period 61
prevention of injuries 73, *73*
principles of training *58–9*
process-orientated goals 152
professionalism **249**, 258–9, *260*, *261*, 286
progressive muscle relaxation 151
projectile motion *90*, 90–2, *91*, *92*
proprioceptive neuromuscular facilitation (PNF) *53*, 55, **56**, *56*
protein supplements 47
proteins 4
proximity effect **181**
psychoticism-intelligence dimension of personality 116
pyruvate dehydrogenase 5

Q

questionnaires
  attitude measurement 159–61
  stress measurement 146–7

R

racism **290**
Radcliffe, Paula 77
radiation 66
radio 294
radio frequency identification (RFID) 302
ratchet mechanism 36
rational recreation, development of
  amateurism and professionalism **249**
  characteristics 244
  commercialisation 251
  Edwardian era 250
  entertainment, growth in 251
  popular recreation 241
  pre-industrial Britain 241
  summary *252*
  Victorian Britain 242–8
  World War I, consequences of 250
reaction force *87*, 88, *88*

recombinant erythropoietin (Rh EPO) **49**
recovery **9**
active **13**
aerobic energy system 9–14, *9–14*
rest **13**
recreation. see rational recreation, development of
rehabilitation for injury 74–5
relationship-centred leadership 207–8, 208
relative VO_2max **16**
relaxation 151
resistance training 43
respiratory exchange ratio (RER) **18**–19, 24
respiratory system, during recovery from exercise 12
rest recovery **13**
resynthesis of ATP 7, *7*, 8
reticular activating system (RAS) 112, 128–**9**
Rh EPO (recombinant erythropoietin) **49**
Ringelmann effect 200
rotational movements 93, 94
rugby 259

S

sacroplasmic reticulum **36**
sanctions **279**
SAQ (speed, agility and quickness) training *53*
sarcomeres **32**, 33–4, *34*
sarcoplasm 19, **20**
scalar quantities 80–**1**, 82
Scotland, Sports 231
Scottish Institute of Sport (SIS) 228
self-confidence
and self-efficacy 174
development of self-efficacy *176*, 176–7
distraction-conflict theory 181
evaluation apprehension 180–**1**
home or away 182
influence of 175
loss of 174–5
social facilitation 178–81, *179*
social inhibition **178**, 179, 182
self-efficacy 123, **123**, 174, **175**, *176*, 176–7
self-report questionnaires
attitude measurement 159–61
stress measurement 146–7
self-serving bias **187**, 188
self-talk 150
sexism **292**
Seyle, H. 140, 142
shamateurs **256**
significant other **117**
skeletal muscle
all or none law 40
contraction 39–42, *41*
innervation of 40
motor unit 40, *41*
muscle fibre, types of 36, *37*, *38*
resistance training 43
sliding filament theory of muscle contraction 33–6, *34*, *35*
spatial summation **41**–2
structure of 32–3, *33*
variation in strength of response 42, *42*
sliding filament theory of muscle contraction 33–6, *34*, *35*
slow replenishment stage *11*, **11**, 12–13
slow twitch muscle fibre (type 1) 36–**7**, *37*, *38*
SMARTER principle 152–3
social class 246, *248*, 293
social cohesion **196**, 198
social facilitation **178**–81, 179
social inhibition **178**, 179, 182
social learning theory 170–1, 205, **206**
social loafing 200
social mobility **258**
social reform 244
socialisation **231**
socio-economic status **221**
somatic (definition) **129**
somatic anxiety **130**, 143, *143*
somatic responses 141, **142**
spatial summation **41**–2
speed **82**
speed, agility and quickness (SAQ) training *53*
sponsorship 259, **260**, *287*, 287–9, **288**, *288*, *289*, 300
sport
benefits of 220
control over 289–300
media, impact of 294–5
Sport Competition Anxiety Test (SCAT) 146
Sport England 230–1
Sport Northern Ireland 232
Sports Aid 236
Sports Council for Wales 231
Sports Scotland 231
sports supplements. *see* ergogenic aids
Sportscoach UK 232
sportsmanship **255**
sprint interval training *51*
sprinting 85
stable-neurotic dimension of personality 113, *113*
state anxiety 144
State Trait Anxiety Inventory (STAI) 146
Steiner 199
stereotypes **159**, **290**
stimulants **276**
stress **142**
anxiety as negative form of 141
causes of 142, *142*
definitions 140
General Adaptation Syndrome (GAS) *142*, 142–3
interactionist approach *145*
management techniques 147–53
measurement of levels of 145–7
positive/negative 141
process of 141
types of anxiety *143*, 143–4, *145*
stressors *142*, **142**
stretch reflex 55, **56**
stretching techniques *53*, 55, **56**, *56*
supplements. *see* ergogenic aids
sustainable development **220**
sweating 67
synthesis of theory and practical 321–24, *322–3*, *324*

T

talent testing and identification **221–3**, 226
Talented Athlete Scholarship Scheme (TASS) 227
tapering **62**
task cohesion **196**, 198
task-centred leadership 207, 208, *208*

task-oriented goals 123
teams. *see* groups
technology 298–303
television 294
temperance movements **245**
tendons 32
tetanic contraction 42
tetanus 42
tetrahydrogestrinone (THG) **279**
thermoreceptors **65**
thermoregulation during exercise 65–7, *66*
thought-stopping 148
threshold **22**
Thurston Scale 160
torques 93
training
- altitude 56–**7**, *57*
- and lactic acid accumulation 24
- different types of *51–3*
- double periodisation 64
- impact on VO_2max 17
- periodisation *60*, 60–5, *62*, *63*, *64*
- plyometrics *53*, 54, *54*, **55**
- principles of *58–9*
- proprioceptive neuromuscular facilitation (PNF) *53*, 55, **56**, *56*
- resistance 43
- sessions 64
- use of technology 301

trait anxiety 144, **181**
trait theories of personality 112–16, *113*
traits **111**
transition period 62
Triadic Model *157*, 157–8, **162**
Triandis, H.C. 156
triglycerides 4
tropomyosin 34–**6**
troponin 35, **36**
Tuckman, B. 195
turnstiles **285**

U

UK Sport 225–7
unbalanced forces 87
United Kingdom Sports Institute 227–8
urbanisation **241**, 242

V

vector quantities 80–**1**, 82, 83, 91–2
velocity **82**, 90
vertical forces 88
vicarious experience **170**–1
Victorian Britain 242–8
viscosity **49**
VO_2max 14–18, *15*, *16*, **16**, *22*, 22–3

W

Wales
- Sports Council for 231
- Welsh Institute of Sport (WIS) 228

water 7, 48
wave summation 42
weight **81**, 88
weight training *52*
Weiner's attribution theory *187*, 187–8
white flight **291**
whole sport plans (WSPs) **230**
Wie, M. 286–7
Wing, B. 25
women and gender inequalities 291–92, *293*, 295
World Anti-Doping Agency (WADA) **276**
World Class Performance Pathway 222–**3**, *235*, 235–6, *235*
World Games
- characteristics of 216, *217*
- commercialisation, impact of 297–8
- impact of London Olympic Games 2012 217–19, *219*

Z

Zajonc, R. 179
zone of optimal functioning (ZOF) **134**–5

Nesta and Rob would like to thank Ffion, Ellie, Rees and Cai for their patience during the writing of this book. Also, thanks to Rochelle and Claire for taking the time to share their sporting experiences.

Graham would like to thank his family, friends and colleagues for their patience and support during this project.

The authors and publisher would like to thank the following individuals and organisations for permission to reproduce photographs:
p.6 Jeff Haynes/AFP/Getty Images; **p.11** Lawrence M. Sawyer/Photodisc; **p.15** Photodisc. Photolink; **p.17** Photodisc. Photolink; **p.38 TR** Michael Steele/Getty Images; **p.38** TL Karl Weatherly/Photodisc; **p.47** Toshifumi Kitamura/AFP/Getty Images; **p.56** Doug Pensinger/Getty Images; **p.57** Mark Shearman/Action Plus; **p.62** Photolink/Photodisc; **p.64** Photolink/Photodisc; **p.67** Photolink/Photodisc; **p.72** ©Getty Images/Harry How; **p.74** ©Alamy Images/Frances M. Roberts; **p.75** ©Actionplus/Neil Tingle; **p.76** ©Actionplus/Neil Tingle; **p.80** Jason Reed/Reuters/Corbis; **p.84** ©PA Photos/Rebecca Naden/PA Archive; **p.86** Kazuhiro Nogi/AFP/Getty Images; **p.95 MR** Olga Besnard/Shutterstock; **p.95 BR** Sportsphotographer.eu/Shutterstock; **p.96** Karl Weatherly/Photodisc; **p.110** ©Rex Features **p.117** ©Getty Images/Martin Rose/Bongarts; **p.122** ©Rex Features/Steve Bardens; **p.125** Claire Vigrass/ Graham Thompson; **p.129** ©Photoshot/Xinhua/Liu Dawei; **p.130** ©Reuters/Kai Pfaffenbach; **p.132** ©PA Photos/Mark Baker/AP; **p.137** ©Photoshot/Xinhua/Wang Song; **p.141** Rex Features/Image Source; **p.144** Jamie Squire/Getty; **p.158** ©Getty Images/Mike Hewitt; **p.161** ©Getty Images/Stringer/for Norwich Union; **p.163** ©Rex Features; **p.166** Karl Weatherly/Photodisc; **p.167** ©Getty Images/Bruce Bennett; **p.171** Matthew Fearn/PA Archive/PA Photos; **p.176** ©Rex Features; **p.178** Jamie Squire/Getty; **p.180** ©Rex Features/Steve Bardens; **p.183** Claire Vigrass/ Graham Thompson; **p.187** ©Getty Images/Quinn Rooney; **p.191** ©Alamy Images/Pixel Youth Movement 2; **p.194** ©Getty Images/Quinn Rooney; **p.195** Stephen Munday/Getty Images; **p.198** ©Getty Images/Mike Hewitt **p.201** ©PA Photos/Phil Walter/Empics Sport; **p.205** Paul Seiser/Action Plus; **p.210 L** ©Alamy Images/David Crausby; **p.210 R** Paul Seiser/Action Plus; **p.237** Trevor Plumb; **p.247** Corbis; **p.253 BL** ©Reuters/Ian Hodgson; **p.253 BR** ©Rex Features/Glyn Thomas; **p.256** Bettmann/Corbis; **p.259** ©Alamy Images/Radius Images; **p.260** Kevin Lamarque/Reuters/Corbis; **p.262** ©Corbis/John Mabanglo/EPA; **p.265** Trevor Plumb; **p.272** ©Rex Features/Sipa Press; **p.281** Trevor Plumb; **p.287** ©Rex Features/Gillette; **p.288** ©Rex Features; **p.296** ©Getty Images/Adam Pretty; **p.303** Trevor Plumb; **p.316** Masterfile; **p.318** Jon Feingersh/Photolibrary; **p.319** Adam Burn/Getty; **p.318** Gareth Copley/Pa Photos.

The authors and publisher would like to thank the following for permission to reproduce copyright material:
p.225 UK Sport; **p.228** English Institute of Sport; Welsh Institute of Sport; Scottish Institute of Sport; **p.230** Sport England **p.232** Sport Northern Ireland.

A list of the texts cited in this Student Book is available from the corresponding Teaching Resource Pack.

Every effort has been made to contact copyright holders of material reproduced in this book. Any omissions will be rectified in subsequent printings if notice is given to the publishers.